CW00818790
RAF VALLEY

AERODROMES OF FIGHTER COMMAND THEN AND NOW

Cool grass, misty mornings,
Sunny days, starlit nights,
Alarms and fears, invasion warnings,
Hurris scramble to unseen fights,
And we wait.

Helpless, we watch them fly,
Spanners our ignoble brands,
Helpless, we hear them die,
Wringing our unclean hands,
Whilst we, we sit and wait.

ERIC MARSDEN, B FLIGHT, No. 145 SQUADRON, 1940

AERODROMES OF FIGHTER COMMAND THEN AND NOW

Robin J. Brooks

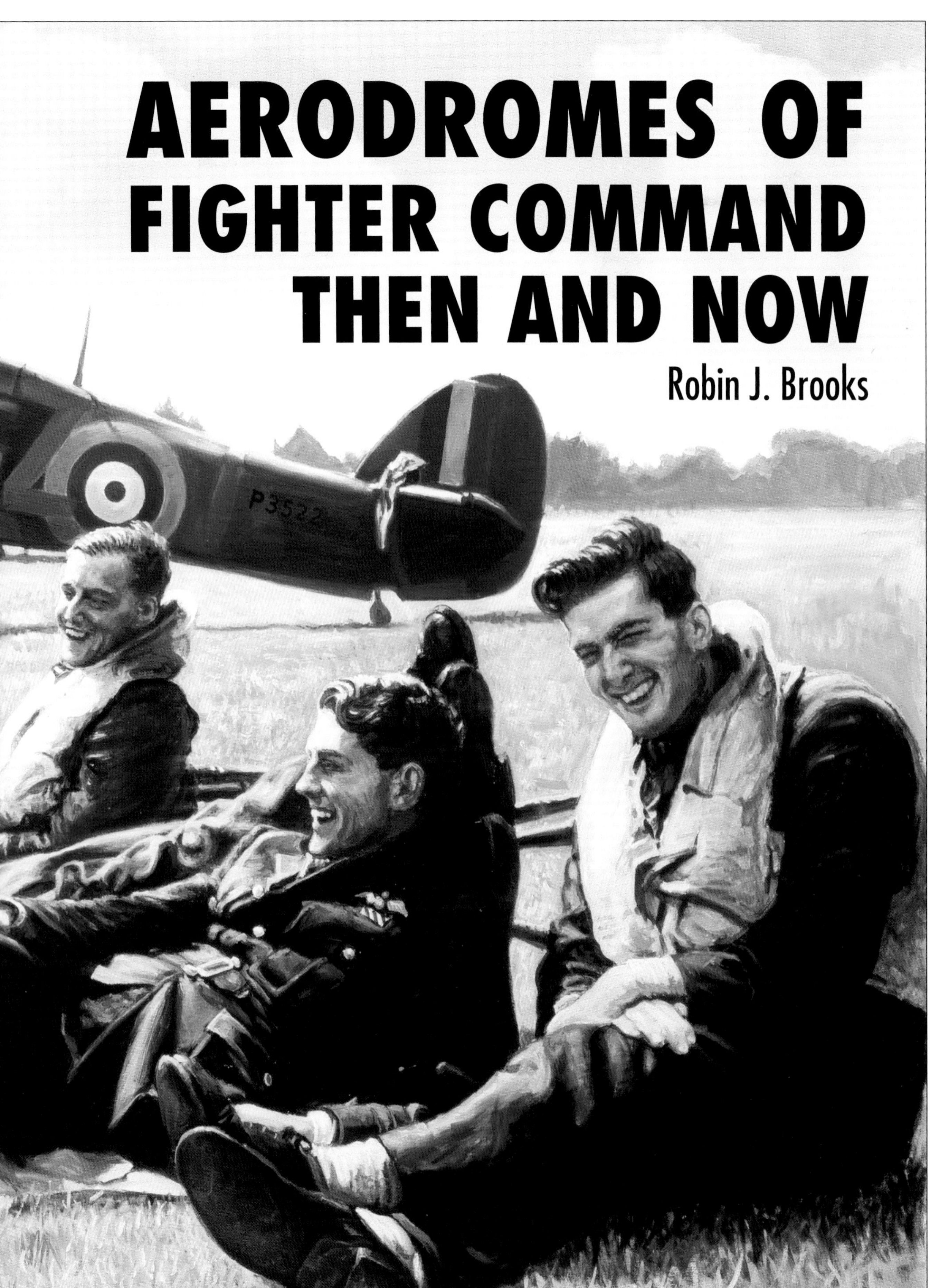

Credits

ISBN: 9 781870 067829

Edited and designed by
Winston Ramsey, Editor-in-Chief

PUBLISHERS
Battle of Britain International Ltd
The Mews, Hobbs Cross House,
Hobbs Cross, Old Harlow, Essex CM17 0NN
Telephone: 01279 41 8833. Fax: 01279 41 9386

PRINTERS
Printed by Ozgraf S. A., Olsztyn, Poland.

FRONT COVER AND FRONTISPIECE
Pilots of No. 32 Squadron at their dispersal at Hawkinge in July 1940. From L-R: P/O R. F. Smythe, P/O K. R. Gillman, P/O J. E. Proctor, F/Lt P. M. Brothers, P/O D. H. Grice, P/O P. M. Gardner and P/O A. F. Eckford. From a painting by George A. Campbell.

REAR COVER
August 8, 1939 — pilots of No. 79 Squadron practice 'scrambling' at Biggin Hill.

Acknowledgements

This book could not have been put together without the very generous help of Aldon Ferguson and Andrew Thomas who trawled through their files to supply many of the wartime photographs. Gail Ramsey also sourced more from official archives. The Editor is also very grateful to Peter Cornwell generously gave us the benefit of his vast experience of the period.

We also extend our grateful thanks to Steve Casely, Chris Cooper, Elaine and Keith Davis for helping with the comparison photography.

We are also indebted to the following individuals for their assistance: Bob Andrews, Simon Andrews, Stephen Ayes, Dick Barton, Denis Bateman, Peter Berry, Keith Braybrooke, Dave Brocklehurst, Sergeant Darren Cole, Ann and Ian Colporth, Keith Cornwell, Michael Daniels, Officer Cadet Sarah Day, Michael Dent, Kevan Dickin, Richard Drew, Rowley Effingham, Carol-Anne Elliott, Glasgow Prestwick Airport, Peter Elliott, RAF Museum, John Evans, Paul Francis, Norman Franks, Chris Goss, David Green, Alan Hale, Geoffrey Hall, Michael Hayes, Ian Herbert, Marjorie Hobby, Squadron Leader Baz Irvine, Paul James, Nissan UK, David List, Officer Cadet Niall Moroney, Lugina Oates, Flight Lieutenant Rod Pitt, Mark Postlethwaite, Rebecca and Evan Preece, Emma Railton, Ivor Ramsden, Chris Ransted, Wilhelm Ratuszynski, Gordon Riley, Andy Saunders Tim Sergeant and Ian Dieffenthaller, City & Country, Martin Sheldrick, Dave Smith, Stephen Smith, Colonel Roy Stanley, James Teagle, Kent Thirley, Hugh Thomas, Winston Thomas, David Thompson, Lawson Tickell, Graham Trant, Robert Truman, Geoff Walkington, Steve Whines, Officer Cadet Danny Yeomans, Tim Zillessen.

WINSTON RAMSEY, EDITOR, 2014

Photographic Credits

A1 Classic Cars: 309 top. **Elaine Aitken:** 196 bottom right. **F. R. Andrew via C. Ashworth:** 96 top. **Essex Wing ATC:** 59 bottom. **Australian War Memorial:** 53 top left and right, bottom left. **Jim Barton:** 199 centre left. **Peter Berry:** 316 bottom left. **C. N. Bishop:** 201 top. **Charles E. Brown:** 158 top and bottom left, 161 top and bottom left, 245 top left. **Roy Calvert/Colin Hanson:** 126 top. **Simon Chamberlain:** 196 centre. **Joe Crawshaw:** 165 centre. ***Daily Mail*:** 192 top, 193 bottom. **Elaine Davis:** 343 bottom. **Ken Delve:** 30 top. **RAF Digby:** 241 both. **English Heritage:** 176 top, 227 bottom, 230 top, 236, 266, 269 bottom, 272 bottom, 275 bottom, 283 top. **John and Julie Evans:** 52 top, 53 bottom right. **Aldon Ferguson:** 44 top and bottom, 45 top and centre, 46 top, 47 top, 62 centre, 111 centre, 264 top and centre, 280 top, 281 top and centre, 282 top and centre. **Reg Findlay:** 41 top left. **Paul Francis:** 224 bottom. **Gerd E. Gerhard:** 244 bottom. **G. S. Gillard:** 227 top left. **Warrant Officer Gillis via P. Arnold/R. Bracken:** 255 top right and centre. **Global Aviation:** 282 bottom. **Geoffrey Hall:** 76 bottom, 141 top, 145 top, 157 bottom, 217 bottom. **J. Harris:** 29 top. **Michael Hayes:** 78 top, 79 top. **John Hewitt:** 166 top. **Imperial War Museum:** 14 top (CH1233), 15 top left (CH1234), 28 (Luft 1093-3), 32 top (Luft 1173-3), 34 (CE16 and CE21), 39 top (AP10678C), 48-49 (CH1640), 59 top left (CH1700), 60 top (CH6934), 70-71 (HU91898), 101 top (CH13356), 102 bottom left (CH18732), 105 top (Luft 1128-3), 124 top (CH7210), centre (HU86321), 127 top (CH7917), 128 top (HU104510), 146 top (CH12733), 159 bottom (HU103463), 162 centre (CH14209), 163 top (MH27952), 165 top left (CH430), 168 (Luft 1139-4), 170 top (CH14643), 190 top (CH5879), 202 top (CH5251), centre (CH13319), 224 top (CH17252), 230 centre (CE106), 232 top (CH15610), bottom (CH15606), 235 top (CH1931), centre (CH1925), 249 top (CH1458), 254 top (CH4391), bottom (Luft 1692-2), 268 top (CH14808), 274 top (CH7291), 296 bottom (E276), 306 top (C822), 308 top (CH6512), 320 top (CH4288), 323 bottom (Luft 1440-4), 328 top (CH11880), 331 bottom (Luft 1242-3), 336-337 (HU93131), 341 top (CH4180), 342 top (CH4179), 343 top (HU90046), 344 (Luft 991-3), 346 top (HU93133). **A. Isbister:** 324 top. **W. Jackman:** 19 **Andrew Long:** 106 top. **Edward Lowdell:** 269 top left. **Manx Aviation and Military Museum:** 36 top left centre, 37 top. **Montrose Air Station Heritage Centre:** 315 top and centre. **A. Moor:** 142 both. **Philip Moore:** 283 bottom. **Arthur Moreton:** 198 centre, 206 top. **Museum of Army Flying:** 55 bottom. **Ron Nendegg via Jim Barton:** 152 all. **Nissan UK:** 333 top. **Pace:** 140 top. **Simon Parry:** 69 top left. **No. 305 Polish Squadron:** page 177 top and bottom. **RAF Museum:** 10 all, 11 top, 27 top, 54 top, 59 centre, 60 bottom, 77 top right, 92 top, 99 top right, 200 top, 271 top, 307 bottom, 310 top, 327 top, 350 bottom. **Ivor Ramsden:** 35 bottom, 36 top and bottom, 37 bottom. **Wilhelm Ratuszynski:** 258 top. **Gordon Riley:** 283 bottom. **Andy Saunders:** 173 top and centre, 202 bottom, 208 top, 209 top. **Shetland Museum:** 324 centre. **Sikorsky Museum:** 194 bottom. **Samuel Sjoberg:** 323 top, 324 bottom. **David J. Smith:** 26 top. **No. 609 Squadron:** 184 top. **Roy Stanley:** 179 bottom, 180 top, 182 bottom, 183 both. **Ed Storey:** 255 top left and centre. **Robin Taylor:** 273 centre left. **James Teagle:** 160 top right **Andrew Thomas:** 30 centre, 33 top, 35 centre, 39 centre, 41 centre, 62 top, 65 top and centre, 104 top, 111 top, bottom left, 231 top and centre, 260 top, 292 top, 304 top and centre, 322 top, 326 bottom left, 330 top, 335 top, 346 centre, 348 top. **Winston Thomas:** 93 bottom. **Stuart Thurtle:** 234 bottom. **Graham Trant:** 291 top. **Robert Truman:** 160 top left, 261 top. **US National Archives:** 86 top and centre, 214 top left and right, bottom. **RAF Valley:** 43 top. **Ian Waller:** 235 bottom. **John Watts:** 124 bottom. **G. Wells via Dave Collyer:** 217 centre. **Andrew Wilson:** 82 centre. **C. Wilson:** 138 top.

Editorial Note

Fortunately, the advent of Google Earth has enabled us to dispense with one very costly aspect of our previous airfield books — the aerial photography — and the Google Earth images in the volume are reproduced under licence.

We have also dispensed with Ordnance Survey maps for two reasons. First, modern technology now enables one to pinpoint locations very easily using Google Maps, Google Earth, Street View, GPS and even mobile phones. Secondly, as many of the airfields were abandoned over 50 years ago, the pattern of the layout no longer shows up on the present-day OS editions but, for those readers who like working with maps, the grid references for all the airfields are given below.

No. 9 GROUP Cranage SJ 730697, High Ercall SJ 608186, Honiley SP 233736, Jurby SC 361983, Squires Gate SD 317311, Ternhill SJ 642308, Valley SH 305758, Woodvale SD 302098.

No. 10 GROUP Angle SM 858019, Beaulieu SU 350008, Boscome Down SU 182398, Charmy Down ST 764700, Chilbolton SU 393385, Church Stanton ST 208154, Colerne ST 803715, Exeter SY 002938, Fairwood Common SS 568912, Filton ST 600804, Harrowbeer SX 513680, Holmesley South SZ 215988, Ibsley SU 153087, Middle Wallop SU 303385, Pembrey SN 401035, Perranporth SW 740528, Portreath SW 672465, Predannack SW 468164, Roborough SX 503605, St Eval SW 875685, St Mary's SV 922104, Warmwell SY 765885.

No. 11 GROUP Biggin Hill TQ 415606, Bradwell Bay TM 005082, Castle Camps TL 633420, Croydon TQ 306635, Debden TL 562351, Detling TQ 812595, Ford SU 995029, Friston TV 555989, Gatwick TQ 270404, Gravesend TQ 675720, Hawkinge TR 211395, Hendon TQ 215905, Heston TQ 118781, Hornchurch TQ 530845, Hunsdon TL 426138, Kenley TQ 328580, Lasham SU 675435, Lympne TR 110355, Manston TR 332599, Martlesham Heath TM 242454, Merston SU 885031, Northolt TQ 098850, North Weald TL 488044, Redhill TQ 298476, Rochford (Southend) TQ 872895, Stapleford Tawney TQ 493970, Tangmere SU 913061, Westhampnett SU 875075, West Malling TQ 680555.

No. 12 GROUP Baginton SP 346748, Church Fenton SE 531378, Colebay Grange TF 005605, Collyweston ST 803715, Coltishall TG 262225, Digby TF 042570, Duxford TL 464558, Fowlmere TL 415446B, Hibaldstow SK 083009, Hutton Cranswick TA 008514, Kingscliffe TL 028978, Kirton-in Lindsey SK 945972, Leconfield TA 030435, Ludham TG 400195, Matlask TG 145340, Wellingore SK 988545, Wittering TF 028025.

No. 13 GROUP Acklington NU 229006, Aldergrove J156789, Ayr (Heathfield) NS 358245, Catterick SE 250968, Drem NT 505810, Dyce NO 879126, Montrose NO 725598, Prestwick NS 365268, Scorton NZ 241005, Sumburgh HU 395105, Turnhouse NT 156734, Usworth NZ 340585, Wick ND 363527.

No. 14 GROUP Castletown ND 215669, Peterhead NK 079473, Skaebrae HY 269207, Skitten ND 373571.

RAF Fighter Command came into being in July 1936 with eleven squadrons and seven airfields. Although initially grass, by the outbreak of war strips of tarmac 800 yards long had been constructed at Biggin Hill, Debden, Hendon, Kenley, Northolt and Tangmere. While the Air Officer Commanding-in-Chief, Air Chief Marshal Sir Hugh Dowding, delegated tactical control to his Groups, the fighters being vectored in the air by their Sectors, he retained strategic control to ensure that Fighter Command operated as a whole. By July 1940, Dowding had 54 squadrons spread over 31 aerodromes covering Groups Nos. 10, 11, 12 and 13, with Nos. 9 and 14 in process of completion (see page 9). We have split the airfields into their Groups although some changed their allegiance, for example Debden began as part of No. 12 Group and Church Fenton No. 13 Group but in August 1940 Debden was transferred to No. 11 and Church Fenton to No. 12. In November 1939, there was also debate as to whether Duxford should be switched to No. 11 Group but in the end it was decided to leave it with No. 12 so that the groups were better balanced. Some airfields only had a fleeting existence in Fighter Command but what will become very evident in the descriptions that follow is that the rotation of squadrons between bases was very extensive throughout the war. In some cases the precise movement date is arbitrary as pilots would fly to the new aerodrome while ground crews followed on by road. At other times, aircraft were handed over to the incoming squadron and the change of fuselage codes did not always happen immediately.

Contents

Royal Air Force Fighter Command Headquarters

In 1936, as part of the major reorganisation and expansion programme of the Royal Air Force, the Air Ministry split the former Air Defence of Great Britain, which had been formed in 1925, into two separate formations covering the fighting and bombing roles. On July 14, RAF Fighter Command came into being with its headquarters at Bentley Priory and Air Marshal Sir Hugh Dowding as its first Air Officer Commanding-in-Chief.

Bentley Priory at Stanmore in Middlesex had been designed by Sir John Soane in 1788 and built to the order of the Hon. John James Hamilton, the 9th Earl and 1st Marquis of Abercorn. It became a mansion of great distinction and a rendezvous for many of the political and literary celebrities and statesmen of the day. On the death of the Marquis in 1818, the Priory passed into the hands of his grandson and first Duke of Abercorn, who lived there intermittently until

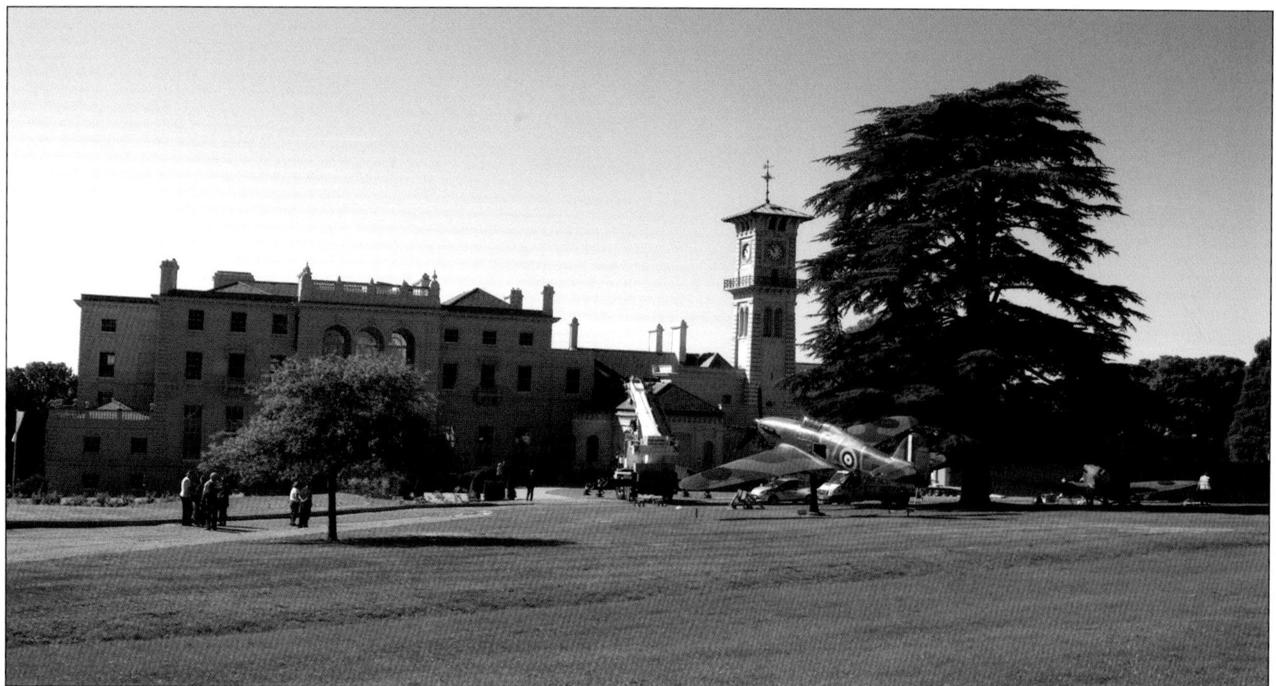

Royal Air Force Fighter Command existed for just 32 years but its legacy lives on: both in the exploits of those who served in its ranks and in the bases which sustained it. *Top:* Its headquarters was located at Bentley Priory at Stanmore in north London. The Air Ministry had purchased 40 acres of the estate in 1926 and initially the Priory was occupied by the Headquarters of Inland Area — a part of the organisation of the Air Defence of Great Britain out of which Fighter Command was born in July 1936. On April 1, 2000, Bentley Priory ceased to operate as a headquarters although it continued to house a number of independent units including the Institute of Flight Safety, the Directorate of Communications and Information Systems, the RAF Ceremonial Branch, the Air Historical Branch and an element of Strike Command based at High Wycombe. Seven years later the site was earmarked by the Ministry of Defence for disposal and in May 2008 the station finally closed, the RAF ensign being lowered in a sunset ceremony on the 30th. In 2010 it was agreed that the ground floor and basement of the Grade II* building would be dedicated to a museum run by the Bentley Priory Battle of Britain Trust while the upper floors would be converted into luxury flats. *Above:* In September 2012 the lease was signed by the Trust at which time a new fibreglass Spitfire and Hurricane were mounted outside the entrance.

1846. The widow of William IV, the Dowager Queen Adelaide then leased the Priory but died there three years later.

In 1862 the estate was purchased by Sir John Kelk — the railway engineer who had built the Albert Memorial in Hyde Park free for the nation — and it was during Sir John's ownership that the clock tower, terrace and ornamental lake were added.

A hotelier, Frederick Gordon, bought the property in 1882 with the intention of converting it into a residential hotel and to improve access he funded the extension of the railway line from Wealdstone to Stanmore but it appears that the venture was not a financial success and in 1908 the estate changed hands once again to become a girls' school. Tennis courts were laid out in front of the main entrance and modifications made to the interior to provide for classrooms and accommodation for 70 boarders. However, in the post-First World War depression, the school closed in 1924.

After standing empty for several months the estate was offered for sale in two lots, the Air Ministry purchasing 40 acres and the Priory for a sum believed to be £25,000 while the remaining 240 acres was sold for housing. On May 26, 1926, the headquarters of Inland Area (part of the organisation of the Air Defence of Great Britain) moved into the Priory from Uxbridge becoming the HQ for Fighter Command ten years later.

Work began to convert the mansion for its command role, initially by adapting the old billiards room and the ballroom to form a temporary Filter and Operations Room while a purpose-built underground structure was being designed.

As the inevitability of war came closer, windows were protected against blast with sandbags; trenches were dug, and trees cut down to give an all-round field of fire. The conservatory was demolished to provide more office space, the face of the clock painted black and the buildings sprayed in brown and green camouflage paint.

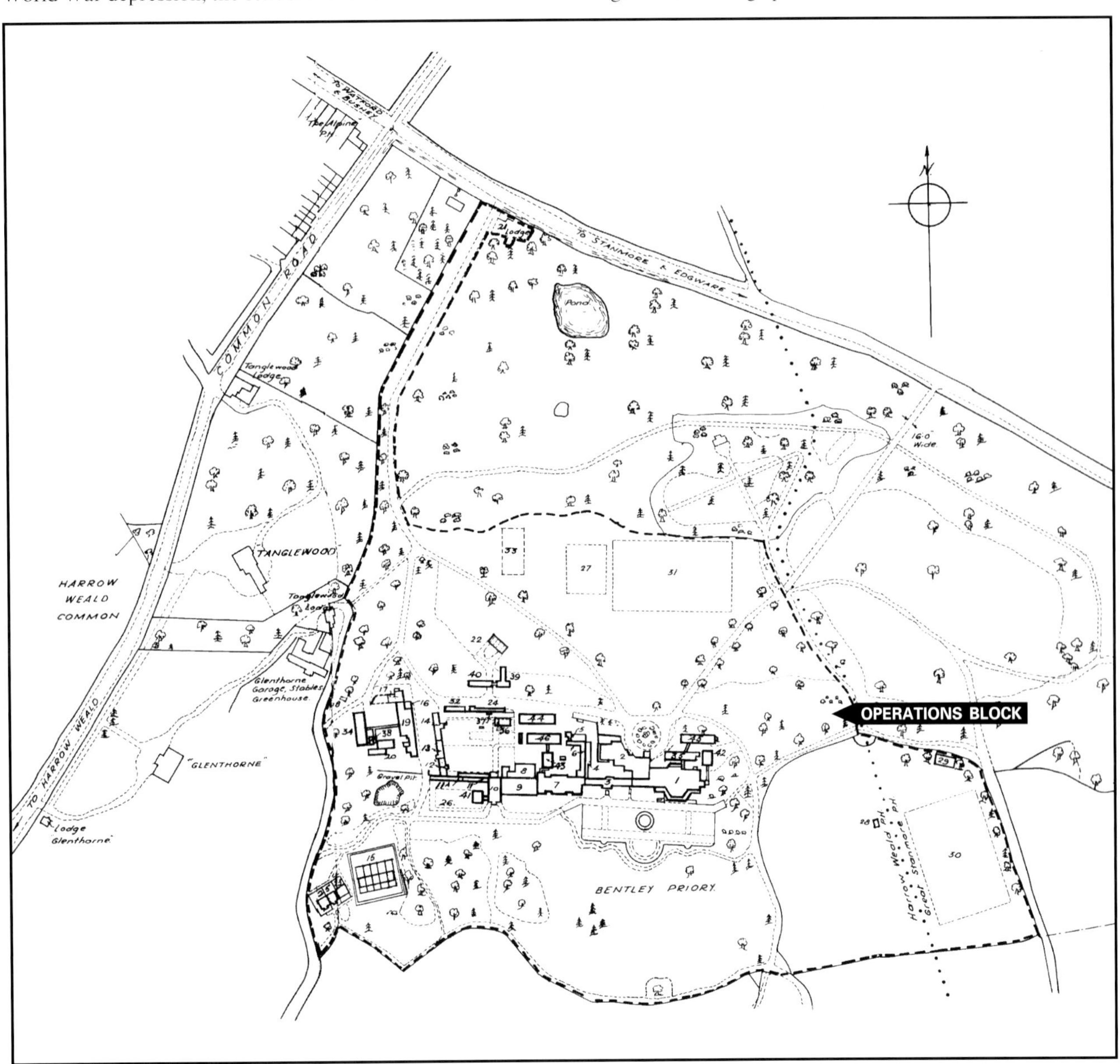

The layout of the headquarters in January 1939: [1] Headquarters Offices. [2] Officers' Mess. [3] Winter Garden. [4] Civilian Batmen's Quarters. [5] W/T Remote Control, Battery Charging Room and Coal/Coke Compound. [6] Batmen's Cleaning Quarters. [7] Single Officers' Quarters. [8] Airmen's Dining Room, Kitchen and Sergeants' Mess. [9] Airmen's Recreation Room. [10 and part of 11] Institute. [Part of 11, 11A and 12] Barrack Blocks. [13] Warrant Officers' Married Quarters. [14 and 15] Airmen's Married Quarters. [16] Motor Transport Workshop, A.O.C. and C.S.O.'s Garage. [17] Motor Transport Sheds. [18] Sub-Station. [19] Barracks, Car Shelter, Plumbers' Shop, Contractors' Workshop, Coal Store, N.A.A.F.I. Grocery Bar. [20] Officers' Garages. [21] Entrance Lodge (Gardeners' Cottage). [22] Fire Engine Pump House. [23] Warrant Officers' Married Quarters. [24] Clerk of Works Office, Electrician's Shop, Petrol Store. [25] Warrant Officers' Married Quarters. [26] Airmens' Tennis Courts. [27] Officers' Tennis Courts. [28] W/T Hut. [29] Recreation Hut. [30] Football Pitch. [31] Hockey Pitch. [32] Garage to Officers' Mess. [33] Airmens' Tennis Court. [34] Barrack Hut. [35] Offices for Intelligence Branch. [36] Squash Rackets Court. [37] Cycle Rack. [38] Bath House. [39] Sergeants' Mess. [40] Sergeants' Quarters. [41] Airmen's Games Room. [42] Offices for Central Registry. [43] Offices for Observer Corps. [44] Offices for Works Services. [45] Offices for Air Service Clerks. [46] Offices for Education Army and RAF.

Left: Hugh Caswall Tremenheere Dowding began his military career with the Royal Garrison Artillery on August 18, 1900 and in December 1913 gained Aviator's Certificate No. 711 at Brooklands. In August, 1914 he joined the Royal Flying Corps and was posted to No. 6 Squadron, being promoted to command No. 16 Squadron in the summer of 1915. When the RAF was created in 1918, he was employed in training, supply, development and research but in 1924 became Chief Staff Officer for the RAF in Iraq. His promotion to Air Vice-Marshal came in 1929 and he was made a member of the Air Council the following year. Raised to Air Marshal and knighted in 1933, on July 14, 1936, Dowding arrived at his new headquarters at Bentley Priory; Air Marshal Sir Peter Wykeham described what happened in his book *Fighter Command — a Study of Air Defence 1914-1960*: 'True to character from the first Dowding arrived at the gate sharp at nine o'clock in the morning. Equally true to character he was both unexpected and unaccompanied, and the guard only let him in after that solemn inspection of a pass that goes by the name of Security. No staff had yet arrived, and there was only a holding party under the command of the Camp Commandant but, as he was away for the day on business, the honours were done by Sergeant Cornthwaite, the N.C.O. in charge of the Orderly Room. Cornthwaite was not the sort of man to get flustered over a sudden visitation of this kind, but he was relieved to learn that the lack of a formal greeting suited Dowding perfectly, and that the Air Marshal would be content to look quietly round the premises under his guidance. Together they explored the Priory and grounds. Inland Area may have led an unexciting life, but they had certainly not neglected the magnificent surroundings entrusted to them. The great house still preserved the air of a nobleman's mansion, the lawns were shaved and the shrubs and hedges clipped. To the east of the house, a fine sports field was set against a background of splendid cedars. Mr. Hall, the gardener for many years, still served the Air Ministry as he had served the former owners. No huts had yet been put up, the great conservatory was still standing, and the vegetable gardens were full and prosperous with crops. Sergeant Cornthwaite showed his new chief over the house, from the attics that were once servants' bedrooms to the basement that was haunted by an elusive and indescribable, but not unpleasant smell. Dowding remarked that the basement was damp. When the tour was over the new Commander-in-Chief selected a room looking south that contained some office furniture, and told Cornthwaite to put his name on the door.'

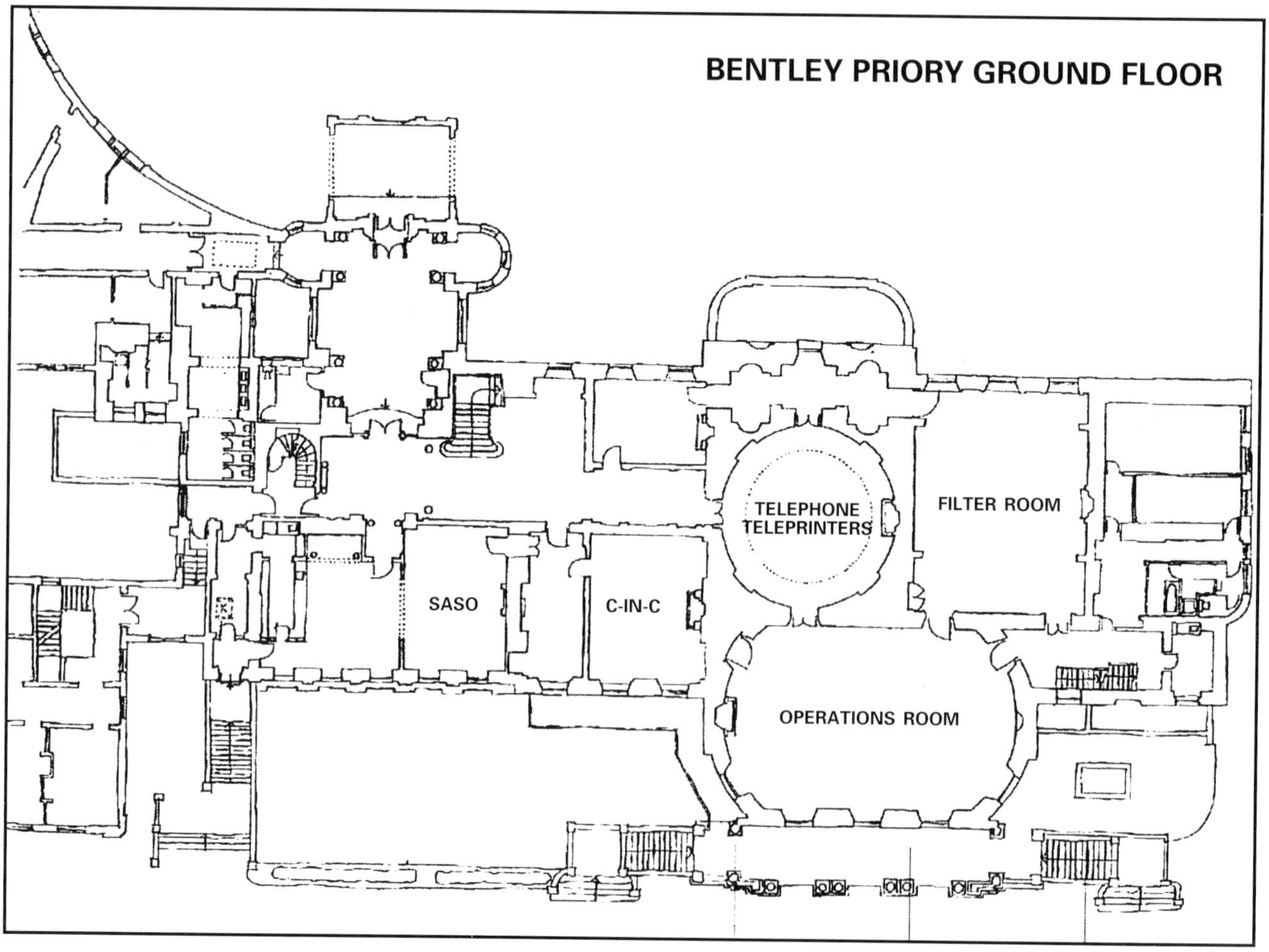

BENTLEY PRIORY GROUND FLOOR

TELEPHONE TELEPRINTERS

FILTER ROOM

SASO

C-IN-C

OPERATIONS ROOM

With the advantage of radio location, or radar, although in its infancy, there was now no need to mount standing patrols as in the First World War. In future it was hoped that fighters could be directed by VHF radio onto, or close to, their targets, helped by the eyes and ears of the Observer Corps. To assemble all this incoming information, Dowding envisaged it being displayed visually on a large map table. So, with a grant of £500 from the Air Ministry, the former ballroom overlooking the gardens was converted into a temporary Operations Room. Sir Peter Wykeham: 'When Air Vice-Marshal Keith Park became Senior Air Staff Officer (SASO) at Command and Dowding's right-hand man, he devised another table which should get all the information first, settle all queries rapidly, and produce a "clean" or "filtered" plot for passing to the main table. This filter table, as it was called, did not seem to find favour with Dowding when Park put forward his idea, so the wily Park set up his filter room in the basement, had the lines reconnected to suit, and all that the Commander-in-Chief noticed for some time was that his general situation map seemed to be much more readable, and his Operations Room far more quiet and well-regulated. When Park judged that the C-in-C was won over, he unveiled the secret and Dowding was convinced.'

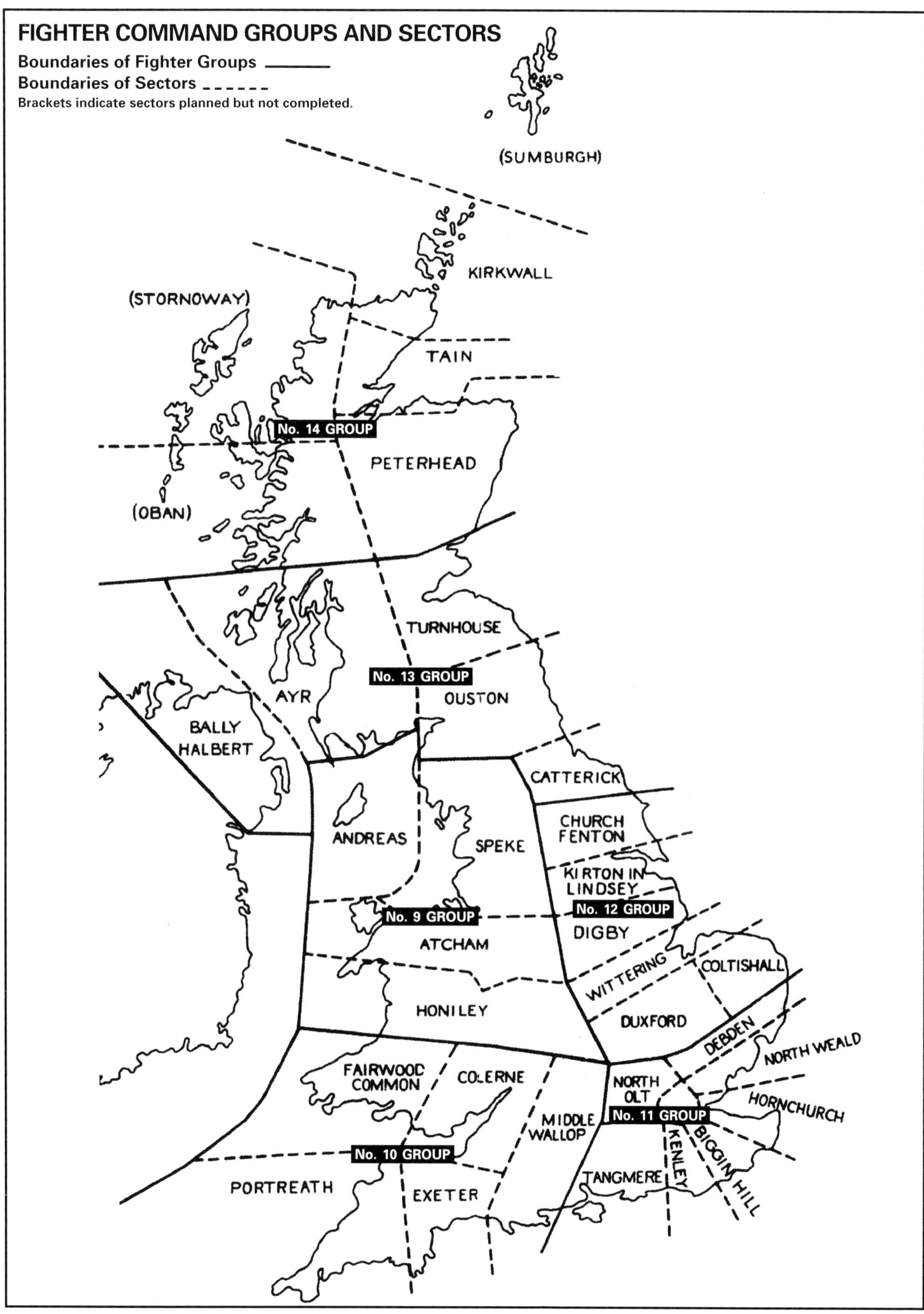

At first, for air defence, Great Britain was simply divided in half, No. 11 Group controlling the country south of Bedford and No. 12 Group that lying to the north, but it was soon appreciated that these areas were far too large so later No. 13 Group took over north of York and No. 10 Group west of Oxford. A further sub-division gave No. 9 Group control in north-west England and No. 14 Group those airfields north of the River Tay in Scotland. Each Group was further divided into sectors, one airfield in each becoming the Sector Station with its own dedicated Operations Room.

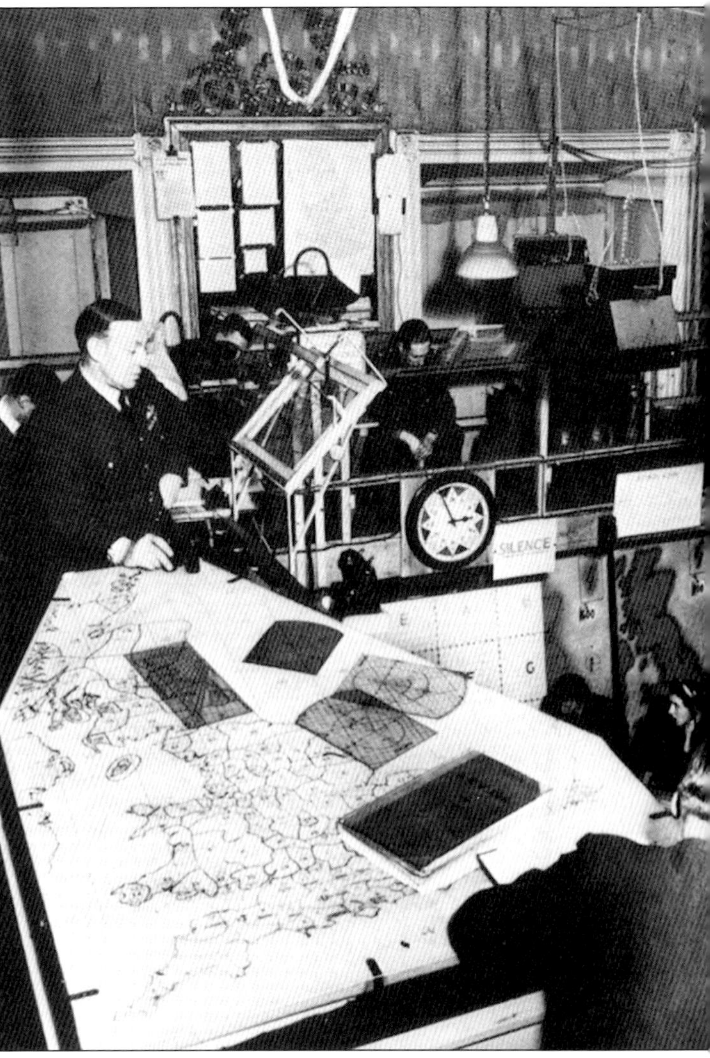

Once the idea of a separate filter room had been proven, it was later adopted by each Group as well, which cut out the bottle-neck by not having to pass down radar plots from Bentley Priory. The map tables at each Group covered just their area. Nevertheless, as these pictures show, the Fighter Command Operations Room was very much an improvisation so in September 1938 the Air Ministry provided £45,000 to begin the construction of an underground command centre.

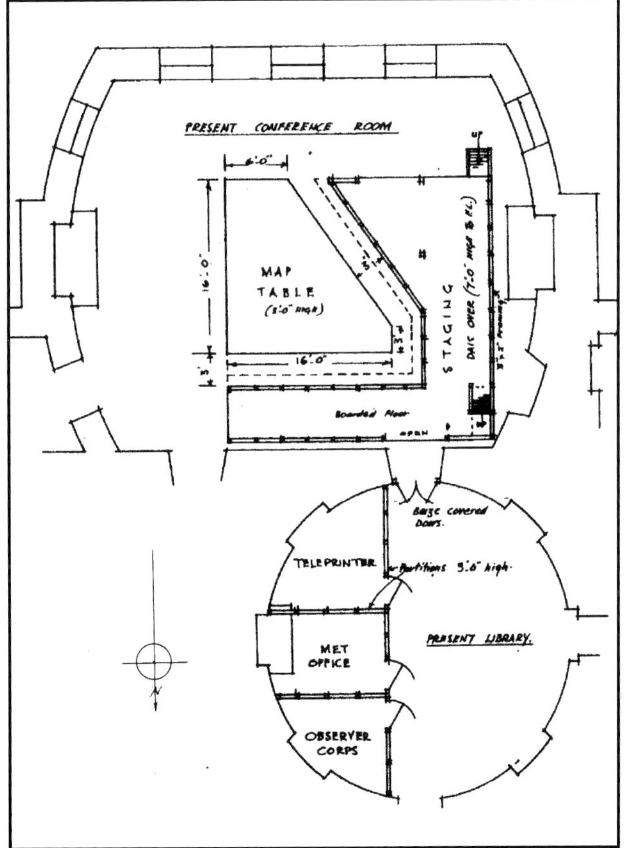

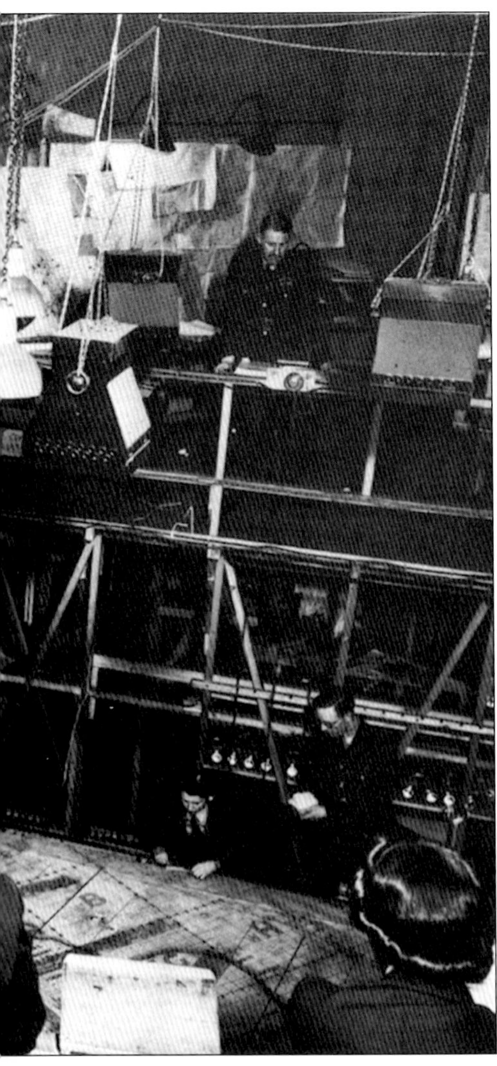

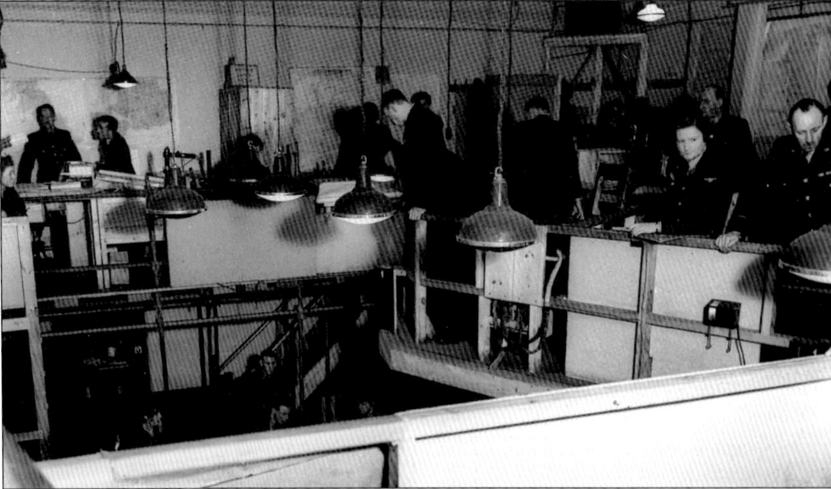

An L-shaped makeshift balcony was provided on the northern and western sides of the ballroom so that the controlling staff could get a clearer view of the plots on the map which were being moved by WAAFs below.

On March 10, 1947, the centre portion of the Priory, including the room above the ballroom and the offices on the floor above, were destroyed by fire. During the reconstruction a new bar was built in the sub-basement under the ballrooom, the old Operations Room then becoming the Ante-Room.

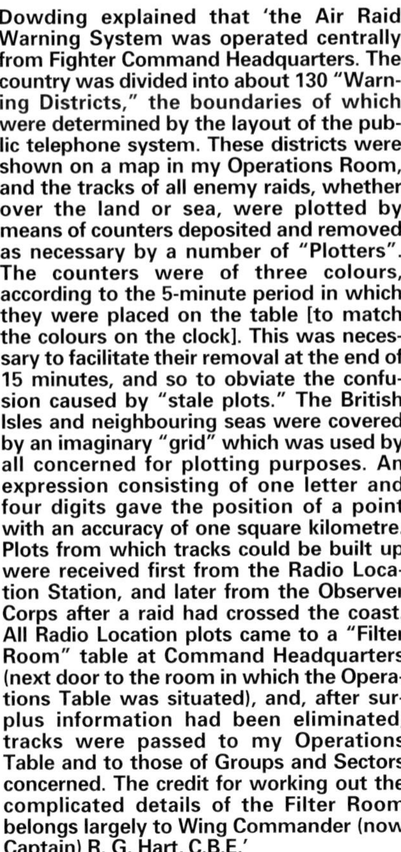

Dowding explained that 'the Air Raid Warning System was operated centrally from Fighter Command Headquarters. The country was divided into about 130 "Warning Districts," the boundaries of which were determined by the layout of the public telephone system. These districts were shown on a map in my Operations Room, and the tracks of all enemy raids, whether over the land or sea, were plotted by means of counters deposited and removed as necessary by a number of "Plotters". The counters were of three colours, according to the 5-minute period in which they were placed on the table [to match the colours on the clock]. This was necessary to facilitate their removal at the end of 15 minutes, and so to obviate the confusion caused by "stale plots." The British Isles and neighbouring seas were covered by an imaginary "grid" which was used by all concerned for plotting purposes. An expression consisting of one letter and four digits gave the position of a point with an accuracy of one square kilometre. Plots from which tracks could be built up were received first from the Radio Location Station, and later from the Observer Corps after a raid had crossed the coast. All Radio Location plots came to a "Filter Room" table at Command Headquarters (next door to the room in which the Operations Table was situated), and, after surplus information had been eliminated, tracks were passed to my Operations Table and to those of Groups and Sectors concerned. The credit for working out the complicated details of the Filter Room belongs largely to Wing Commander (now Captain) R. G. Hart, C.B.E.'

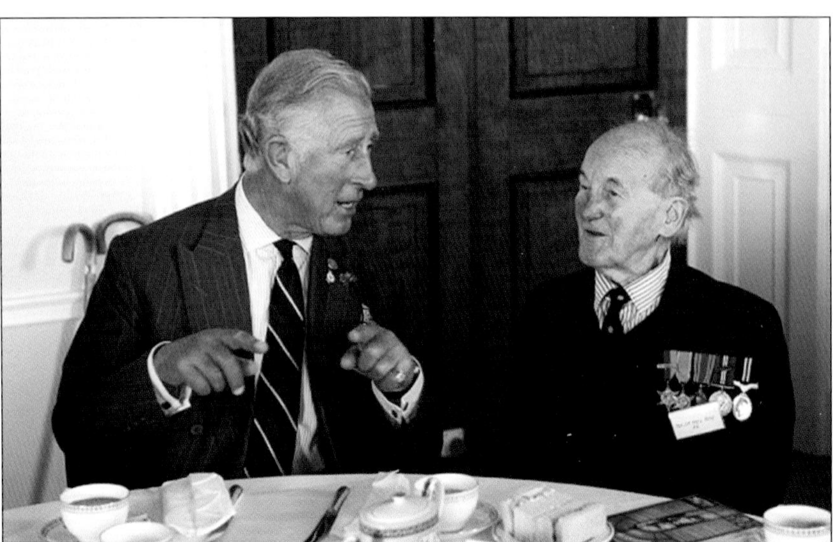

Following an extensive restoration by City and Country, the Priory was split into two parts: luxury apartments upstairs and the Bentley Priory Battle of Britain Museum on the ground floor. This was opened by the Prince of Wales and Duchess of Cornwall on September 12, 2013. Here Prince Charles chats to Squadron Leader Nigel Rose of No. 602 Squadron in the former Operations Room.

On March 10, 1935, Hermann Göring, the Reich President and head of the German Air Force, revealed the existence of the Luftwaffe in a flagrant breach of the Versailles Treaty, doubling the actual number of aircraft to impress. Then, in a clear portent of Germany's true intent, the Rhineland was suddenly occupied before the press on March 7, 1936. Soon thereafter the Luftwaffe sent aircraft to assist Generalissimo Francisco Franco in Spain.

So it was surely naïve for the Air Council to invite the leaders of the Luftwaffe to Britain to inspect the RAF, plus permitting a visit to the top secret headquarters at Bentley Priory. The delegation was led by Oberst Erhard Milch *(left)*, the head of the German Air Ministry, together with Generalleutnant Hans-Jürgen Stumpff, Chief of the German Air Staff *(centre)* and Generalmajor Ernst Udet *(right)*, the Director of Research and Development.

In 1933, Oberst Erhard Milch was appointed State Secretary of the Reichsluftfahrtministerium (RLM), the newly-formed German Air Ministry. Answering directly to the head of the embryo Luftwaffe Hermann Göring, Milch was instrumental in building up the air force together with one of the aces of the First World War Ernst Udet who became his Director of Research and Development.

In 1937, both officers visited Britain, touring RAF stations, shadow factories and even being entertained by Air Marshal Dowding at Bentley Priory. Then the Germans obtained a copy of a comprehensive publication on British industry which became the basis for a report titled *Studie Blau* (Blue Study) which became a standard reference work for the Luftwaffe.

On January 1, 1938, the Germans established the 5. Abteilung of the military intelligence branch of the Oberkommando der Luftwaffe with the brief to collate and prepare target information and plans on Germany's potential enemies. The small but highly efficient unit under Major Joseph 'Beppo' Schmid was based at the RLM building on the Wilhelmstrasse in Berlin although he had little time to coordinate all the elements to provide the Luftwaffe with the necessary material before Austria was annexed in March. The remainder of 1938 and early months of 1939 were devoted to preparing information on targets in Poland with a completion date of July 1.

Then, following an express order from Göring, Schmid turned his attention to Britain and by the outbreak of war, extensive target dossiers had been prepared on the RAF's aerodromes and other key targets such as docks, power stations, oil refineries and armament factories, etc. These files included aerial photographs taken covertly by specially converted Heinkel 111Cs wearing civilian markings under the direction of Oberst Theodor Rowehl, the founder of Germany's air reconnaissance programme. Operating under the guise of Hansa Luftbild G.m.b.H. and based at Berlin-Staaken on the western outskirts of Berlin, the excuse for the flights was given as 'civil route proving flights' in those countries where Lufthansa operated. The airship *Graf Zeppelin* was also useful in this respect.In January 1939, Rowehl was promoted to Oberstleutnant and formally put in charge of Kommando Rowehl which was later re-designated Aufklärungsgruppe Ob.d.L.

In July 1940, Schmid drew up a report on the Royal Air Force vis-à-vis the Luftwaffe. Concerning the airfields, he stated that 'there are a considerable number of airstrips in the southern part of the island and in some areas in the north.

The Germans flew into Croydon on Sunday, October 17, 1937 in a specially-converted Heinkel III, *Flight* commenting that it was powered by a pair of the new 'Daimler-Benz inverted Vees.' Milch is being welcomed by Air Vice-Marshal Sir Richard Peirse of the Air Staff. General Wenninger, the German Air Attaché, stands in front of the cabin door. Others in the party were Major Werner Kreipe, Major Andreas Nielsen and Oberleutnant Wilhelm Polte. During the tour the Germans (now in uniform) were presented to the King and were hosted to a cocktail party at the Carlton Hotel. Visits were made to Army Co-operation units at Odiham and RAF bases at Cranwell, Halton and Mildenhall, as well as aircraft factories in the Midlands. At the luncheon with Dowding and his staff at Bentley Priory, Milch stunned those present when he loudly declared: 'Now gentlemen, how are you getting on with your experiments in the radio detection of aircraft approaching your shores?'

It must have been an incredibly fruitful intelligence-gathering mission — and all through the courtesy of the Royal Air Force. No wonder Milch said in his closing speech that he would have a splendid report for General Göring on every phase of the visit! (On Hitler's birthday the following month, Milch was promoted to General der Flieger.) Now it was the turn of Major Joseph Schmid *(left)* and the 5. Abteilung of the Luftwaffe's Intelligence Branch who was tasked with producing target maps of every industrial and military installation in Britain. The job was masterminded by Oberst Theodor Rowehl *(right)* under the pretext of the German airline Hansa Luftbild carrying out proving flights for civilian operations. More than 1,700 potential targets in Great Britain were covered, each being given a unique reference number. And, as we will see in the following pages, every RAF aerodrome from Sumburgh in the Shetland Isles to St Mary's in the Scilly Isles was photographed and the target plans produced ready for war operations.

However, only a limited number can be considered as operational airfields with modern maintenance and supply installations. In general, the well-equipped operational airfields are used as take-off and landing bases, while the numerous smaller airfields located in the vicinity serve as alternative landing grounds and rest bases.'

The 5. Abteilung had produced target information on most of the RAF bases for the three Luftflotten attacking Britain, and this was updated as new recce photos became available once hostilities had begun. By August, Schmid claimed that the Luftwaffe had destroyed Driffield, Eastchurch, Gosport, Hawkinge, Lee-on-Solent, Lympne, Manston, Martlesham Heath, Portsmouth, Rochester and Tangmere, but was ignorant of the fact that only five of these were Fighter Command aerodromes. Nevertheless, between June and December 1940, the Luftwaffe had carried out 620 attacks on RAF bases (365 by day and 255 by night). This was in spite of the efforts carried out by the RAF to camouflage their airfields by painting field lines across them, identification still being made possible using Schmid's detailed target maps.

On September 7 the emphasis switched to attacking London and although airfield attacks continued — another 375 raids before the year was out — it proved a major tactical error. Back in June 1940 after the defeat in France, Dowding prophesied to his staff that now 'the nearness of London to German airfields will lose them the war'. And so it came to pass.

Meanwhile, at Bentley Priory, the excavation of a massive hole had begun in January 1939, just to the east of the Priory for the building of the bomb-proof command centre. Over 58,000 tons of spoil were excavated and 17,000 tons of reinforced concrete used in its construction, the whole complex being provided with its own services, filtration and gas-tight doors. It was completed by March 1940.

However, the creation of what was to become the physical nerve centre of Fighter Command was only one part of the overall plan; more important were the actual methods devised by Air Chief-Marshal Dowding to command and control the squadrons in action.

Fighter Command comprised several Groups covering the different areas of the country, each Group being subdivided into Sectors, both Groups and Sectors having their own Operations Rooms feeding into Bentley Priory. Information was received by the Filter Rooms attached to each Ops Room, primarily from radio-location posts and the Observer Corps. (Their headquarters was also located at Bentley Priory as was the HQ of Anti-Aircraft Command in a separate house which had been built in the grounds by Frederick Gordon.) The Filter Room was basically a telephone exchange or series of switchboards which collated, cross-checked and simplified the intelligence before passing it to the adjoining Operations Room for displaying visually on maps, blackboards and the 'ops table' on which was painted a simple outline map.

Specially adapted Heinkel He IIIs in civilian markings were employed in the photo reconnaissance missions over Britain.

Having been promoted to Air Chief Marshal in 1937, Sir Hugh had the pleasure of escorting King George VI and Queen Elizabeth on their visit to Bentley Priory in September 1940. Here, having toured the grounds, they are pictured returning to the terrace outside his office which overlooks the gardens at the rear.

Despite its importance, the Germans paid little attention to Bentley Priory throughout the war and the only damage was caused by two small bombs and the blast from a V1 in 1944, and a V2 in February 1945.

After the war, Bentley Priory continued to operate as the headquarters of Fighter Command until its merger with Bomber Command in April 1968. The new Strike Command headquarters was located in a new operations centre at High Wycombe while the Administrative Headquarters remained at Bentley Priory which also became the HQ for No. 11 Group covering the air defence of the United Kingdom. Until 1974, the Priory itself was used by the AOC and SASO (Senior Air Staff Officer) for their office accommodation and for the Officers' Mess.

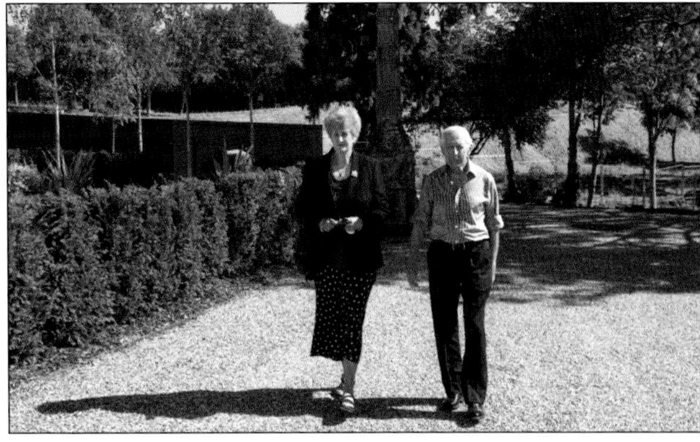

A highlight of their Majesty's tour was a visit to the underground Operations Block which had been completed in March 1940. This lies some 300 yards further to the east — see page 7. *Left:* Here Sir Hugh escorts them back to the Priory.

The underground Ops Room. Members of the Women's Royal Air Force were employed to move the markers on the map table.

By the 1960s the Operations Room had been converted with electronic screens more suited to the Cold War; in fact a Soviet target assesment of 1967 had earmarked Bentley Priory for two 1-3 megaton air-burst atomic bombs! *Left:* Having had its wartime appearance destroyed by its adaptation, it was decided that the bunker did not warrant preservation so the complex was filled in and sealed up in March 2010 *(right).*

The rear aspect as it appeared in 1928 shortly after the RAF had acquired Bentley Priory. One of the major alterations was the demolition of the conservatory to provide more office space. Air Chief Marshal Dowding's office is arrowed.

In February 1979, a £1 million programme was put in hand to restore the interior, replace rotting timbers in the floors and roof, and it was during the early stages of reconstruction, when the interior had been gutted, that the building caught fire. The alarm was raised shortly after 8.30 p.m. on June 21 but it was three and a half hours before the fire could be brought under control despite the attendance of 23 appliances. The fire completely destroyed the roof and three floors in the west wing, and the hall, stairway and clock tower were also badly damaged but fortunately all the contents and furnishings were in store at the time. After the damage was assessed, it was decided that the building could still be saved, the cost of the repairs being covered by the contractor's insurance, and work went ahead at a cost of over £3 million.

In July 2007, the headquarters — which then housed the Defence Aviation Safety Centre, the Air Historical Branch and RAF Ceremonial — was deemed by the Ministry of Defence to be surplus to requirements and it faced an uncertain future. Fortunately, with support from the Prince of Wales's Regeneration Trust, the Bentley Priory Battle of Britain Trust was formed with the remit of establishing a museum on the ground floor which would include Lord Dowding's office. The remainder of the Priory was to be converted into apartments with further housing being built in the grounds.

During renovation in 1979, the building caught fire but fortunately the contractor's insurance covered the repair.

September 2012 with work on the conversion into a museum and luxury apartments nearing completion.

The RAF preserved Dowding's office and in 1968, Spitfire Productions were given permission to film scenes there with Sir Laurence Olivier playing Dowding for the film *Battle of Britain*. Lord Dowding — then aged 86 and in a wheelchair — was invited to watch the proceedings and, on meeting him, Sir Laurence said that he had been sitting behind the original desk all day 'pretending to be you and making a mess of it too'. To this Dowding replied: 'Oh, I'm sure you are!' Then, as Dowding watched Olivier being filmed sitting behind his old desk, he shed a tear. *Below left:* In the final scene in the film, Sir Laurence walks out onto the balcony with the hope that the first massed attack on the East End, which took place on Saturday, September 7, 1940, might turn the tide of battle as the Luftwaffe now appeared to be concentrating on bombing London rather than his aerodromes. Although Dowding defeated the German attempt to invade Britain, controversially he was removed from office in November 1940 and never accorded the rank of Marshal of the Royal Air Force. He left the RAF in 1942 and died on February 15, 1970. *Below:* Forty-four years later, the final touches were carried out to the £3 million restoration project.

Aerodromes for Fighters

Hawkinge in Sector D of No. 11 Group had first been established in the Great War for the Royal Flying Corps, and it came into its own again as a front-line RAF aerodrome in 1940.

In 1914 the aeroplane was a new and almost entirely untested form of military technology. The advent of war that same year hastened both design and production of aircraft together with the formation of the Royal Flying Corps and the Royal Naval Air Service. The need for both organisations was the aerodrome: a large area of level grass where aircraft could take-off and land safely. The First World War saw the establishment of such airfields, many laid out hastily as the enemy attacks by German Zeppelins and giant Gotha bombers increased. In the February 15, 1916 edition of *Pearsons Weekly*, Noel Pemberton-Billing, one of the pioneers of aviation in the UK, wrote: 'There is only one real way of fighting aircraft and that is with aircraft'. Such thinking forced the pace of development, so much so that by the end of 1918, the rival air forces were deploying combined front-line strengths of over 10,000 machines. At this time Britain held supremacy in the air but despite Pemberton-Billing again writing in the magazine *English Review* and stating that 'I contemplate not hundreds but thousands of aeroplanes being required to gain and maintain for us the supremacy of the air. Build now, build quickly, build in immense numbers according to the best approved types', interest in military aviation at the end of 1918 was on the wane.

Following the end of the 'war to end all wars', Britain quickly slipped into a period of false delusion that such a terrible conflict would not be possible in the future. History did however repeat itself in 1939 but in between came the period known as 'the halcyon days of flying'. Pioneer aviators such as Sir Alan Cobham, Amy Johnson, Campbell Black and many others brought civil flying to the public notice. The National Aviation Day Displays, which ran from 1932 until 1935, arranged and led by Cobham, resulted in his attempts to persuade every large city or town to have its own airfield. He called it his 'Municipal Aerodrome Campaign' and were it not for many councils throughout the country taking up his idea, when the second conflict did begin, Britain may not have had as many aerodromes as we did. These however were mainly grass and of World War One vintage. They suited the purpose for flying biplanes and light aircraft but when it came to the more modern monoplane designs, they were found to be lacking in every way.

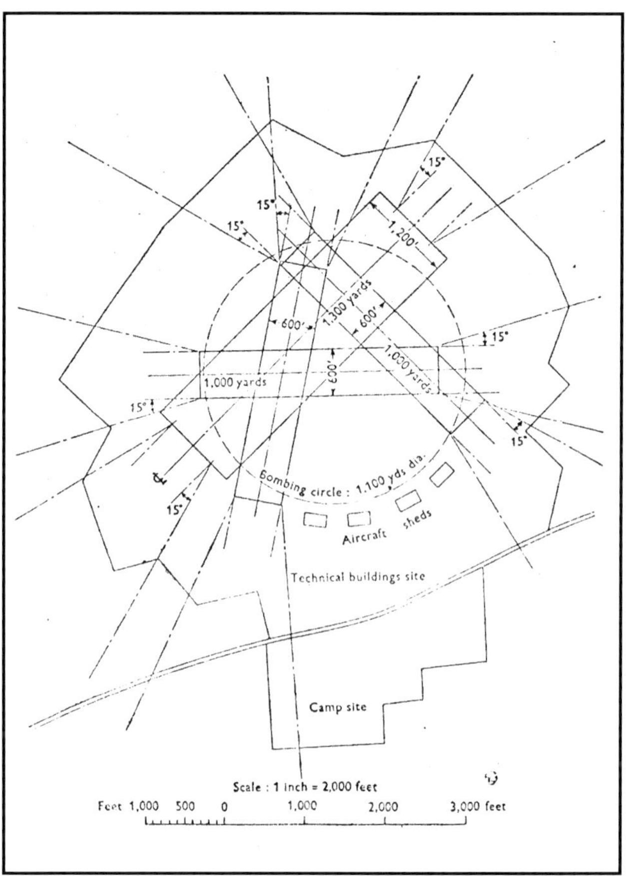

In 1939 most RAF aerodromes were grass and the diagram shows a typical layout before the construction of hard runways. The main strip gave a take-off distance of 1,300 yards by 400 yards and the subsidiaries 1,000 yards by 200 yards.

In 1934 there were 52 RAF aerodromes in the UK accommodating both fighter and bomber aircraft. With the signs of a new and sinister power rising in Germany, the Air Staff looked at this number together with the nature of the sites, and realised that if another war did occur, the country would not be able to mount a defence of the UK. Looking further ahead they estimated that by 1942 there would be a need for 700 aerodromes.

And so began the largest civil engineering project since the building of the railways. Known as the RAF Expansion Scheme, it began with the setting up of a committee in November 1933 to 'examine deficiencies in national and imperial defence'. One year later the Commander-in-Chief of Air Defence of Great Britain (ADGB), Air Chief- Marshal Sir Robert Brooke-Popham, devised the 're-orientation scheme' which was to kick start the programme. Under the new scheme the ADGB was to be scrapped in July 1936 to be replaced by four commands: Fighter, Bomber, Coastal and Training. Each would require its own type of airfield although the bias at this time was towards bomber airfields which would be needed to carry the war back to the enemy when required.

A series of alphabetical schemes indicating designs for airfields were started beginning with 'A' and continuing through to 'L'. Each letter carried various ideas and projections with each one improving on the previous. When it came to the letter 'L' it was the final scheme accepted for the period 1934 to 1939. In order to meet the requirements of the scheme, the Air Mininstry Aerodromes Board was formed within the Air Ministry Directorate of Works. This was headed by Air Vice-Marshal C. A. H. Longcroft and Air Commodore J. D. Boyle. The board worked closely with the Air Ministry Lands Branch whose duty was to handle the legal side of land acquisition. Sites chosen as eligible for selection as aerodromes had to be five miles apart, free from obstructions and above sea level but by no more than 600 feet. This was to reduce the risk of low cloud and fog. All of this came under the auspices of the Land Officer, a person required to judge the suitability of soils, the need for drainage and the adjustment of boundaries on large estates. As the work load increased additional officers were required. In 1939 the Emergency Powers (Defence) Act came into force. This gave the officers immediate power of requisition, something that did not go down well with farmers and the land-owners. However the offers of compensation for taking land was adequate for the time and softened the blow of losing good agricultural acreage.

Most of the new aerodromes initially followed a similar pattern with a grass landing area laid to a standard diameter of 1,100 yards. Surrounding this would be a circular track with buildings and hangars situated in one area and following the curve of the airfield perimeter. The aerodromes that were of World War One vintage required to be up-graded and in many cases, enlarged. Work on this scale could not be done by service personnel alone and so a large civilian labour force was recruited. Men who for some reason or other were not in military service began work on the construction of new aerodromes and the improvement of others. Most manual workers it must be said came from Ireland to find permanent work with civilian companies such as Wimpey and John Laing. Working under the control of the Royal Engineers and later the RAF Construction Service, between 1935 and 1939 they built 123 new aerodromes in addition to enlarging existing ones. The majority were grass, the building of a concrete runway taking priority at bomber stations due to the weight of the aircraft. Between 1939 and 1945, 444 new aerodromes were constructed showing that this work continued throughout the six years of war. It remains today one of Britain's foremost civil engineering feats.

On the other hand, Debden in Sector F of No. 11 Group was constructed during the pre-war 'expansion' period when additional airfields were provided for the RAF. When opened in 1937 Debden was a grass aerodrome but the so-called 'Phoney War' period gave a breathing space for two intersecting runways of 1,300 by 50 yards to be completed, linked by a 50-foot perimeter track.

The Battle Headquarters was the nerve centre of the ground defence at RAF aerodromes. This particular example can be seen at the No. 10 Group airfield at Perranporth in Cornwall (see page 95).

Airfield Defences

With the fall of France, the Air Ministry took a close look at the ground defences for its aerodromes as it was obvious that Britain now faced invasion with landings by paratroops highly likely. Thus a building programme was put in place to try to ensure that the airfields could be adequately defended. At first it was the army that was detailed to man the defence sites with assistance from ground gunners of the RAF but in February 1942 this task became the responsibility of the newly-formed RAF Regiment.

In order to safeguard the personnel engaged in airfield defence pillboxes were needed so in June 1940, Branch FW3 (Fortress Works Department 3), a department of the War Office's Directorate of Fortifications and Works, drew up various designs for brick-built structures. Known collectively as 'Types', they were designed to incorporate a 360-degree field of fire around an airfield perimeter. The Type 27 was hexagonal or octagonal and is the pillbox most commonly found on airfields today. Having an open, central well into which was mounted a machine gun (usually .303 Lewis or Bren), it was entered usually through a small steel door at the rear. When manned there was room for ten men armed with rifles.

The other common type is the smaller Type 22 (FW3/33). Hexagonal in shape, it was built to be bullet-proof and could accommodate six men although had no facility for a fixed machine gun. Further examples built during this period were Types 23 holding up to four men; the Type 24, which was a larger version of Type 22; a thick-walled Type 24 and a smaller round Type 25. The Type 28 was designed to anti-tank standard. Other less common types were the Oakington Mushroom Pillbox (Type 303/41), the Allan Williams Turret, the Tett Turret and the Pickett/Hamilton, more commonly known as the 'pop-up' pillbox.

The RAF Type 13313/40 came in three variations. Designed to rise up from ground level in the case of an enemy attack or landing, the elevating process was accomplished initially by a counterbalance weight inside the fort, but this was later replaced by an air cylinder and a hand-operated hydraulic pump to assist in the operation. When it needed to be lowered back into the outer concrete sleeve, the air was allowed to escape letting the fort sink to ground level. Usually placed alongside runways, the idea of a 'pop-up' fort attracted the attention of Winston Churchill who wrote to General Ismay on July 12, 1940: 'I saw these pillboxes for the first time when I visited Langley aerodrome last week. This design appears to afford an admirable means of anti-parachute defence and it should surely be adopted. Let me have a plan.'

Although none of the defences were tested in action, examples of pillboxes of several different types still stand mouldering at many Fighter Command airfields. ***Left:*** **This Type FW3/22 was sited to defend the Watch Office at Church Stanton (see page 65).** ***Right:*** **The remains of the rare Allan Williams Turret can still be seen at Harrowbeer (page 70).**

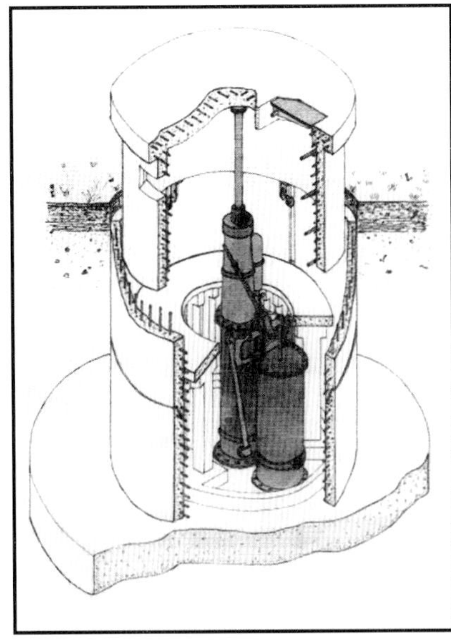

However, none of the structures can equal the elevating Pickett/Hamilton Fort for ingenuity. This example at Manston (see page 182) was selected by our author Robin Brooks, for removal and preservation as no working examples existed.

With this recommendation, most fighter airfields were to receive a maximum of three forts. Although by June 1941, 170 had been installed at 59 airfields, the final figure was 335. However, the drawbacks to the design soon became apparent, first the constant risk of flooding and also that further ammunition supplies for the men inside the fort would have to be carried across the airfield which might be under attack at the time. This, together with the fact that the conditions inside were very cramped, led to the realisation in 1942 that the Pickett/Hamilton Forts were not practical.

The other significant structure still to be seen on many Fighter Command aerodromes is the RAF Type 11008/41 Battle Headquarters. Not strictly a pillbox, the semi-sunk, reinforced concrete building was intended to permit the coordination of all the defence sites on and around the airfield should it come under attack. The standard type consisted of five rooms below ground level with a concrete mushroom-shaped cupola raised from the main structure to allow personnel an all-round view of the airfield.

When it came to the protection of ground crews, three main types of air raid shelters were provided. Still to be found on many airfields are the Stanton Shelters which consisted of a high-sided brick entrance that led to several steps going down to a concrete or asbestos chamber that could accommodate up to 50 personnel. The whole structure was then covered with soil.

Similar to a Nissen hut, the Summers Shelter (RAF Type 2091/39) was arch-shaped with a steel door. Other shelters were locally built and bore a similarity to the civilian Anderson shelter having earth banked up around the sides.

Barrack-blocks were also provided with basement shelters sealed by armoured doors.

Much of the initial construction work was undertaken by the Royal Engineers, but civilian contractors were also employed supervised by a military officer. Today signs of wartime defence lay scattered around the countryside both on and around various wartime airfields. All have stood the test of time well.

Robin approached 36 Engineer Regiment of the Royal Engineers based at Maidstone to see if they would help and in May 2006 a team of sappers arrived on site. Digging through chalk it took several hours before the JCB reached the base, some ten feet below ground. Having been lifted free, it was transported to the Lashenden Museum at Headcorn airfield in Kent where it has been restored to working condition. Robin was pleased that at least one of the unique Pop-up Forts has been preserved (see also *Afer the Battle* No. 135).

Although the RAF were only at Grove briefly in November 1942, we have deliberately included this shot to illustrate how sensitive the wartime censor was to releasing photographs showing airfields. The main purpose of this picture was to show the new Spitfire Mk XII with its Griffon engine, clipped wings and pointed rudder designed to improve low level fighting performance.

No. 9 GROUP

On the reverse of the photograph the censor has instructed that the photo was not to be published before the morning papers on Thursday, April 20, 1944 and that 'if the two airfields [the second one is Harwell, taken over after the war by Britain's Atomic Energy Authority] cannot be satisfactorily obliterated, the lower half of the picture must be cut'.

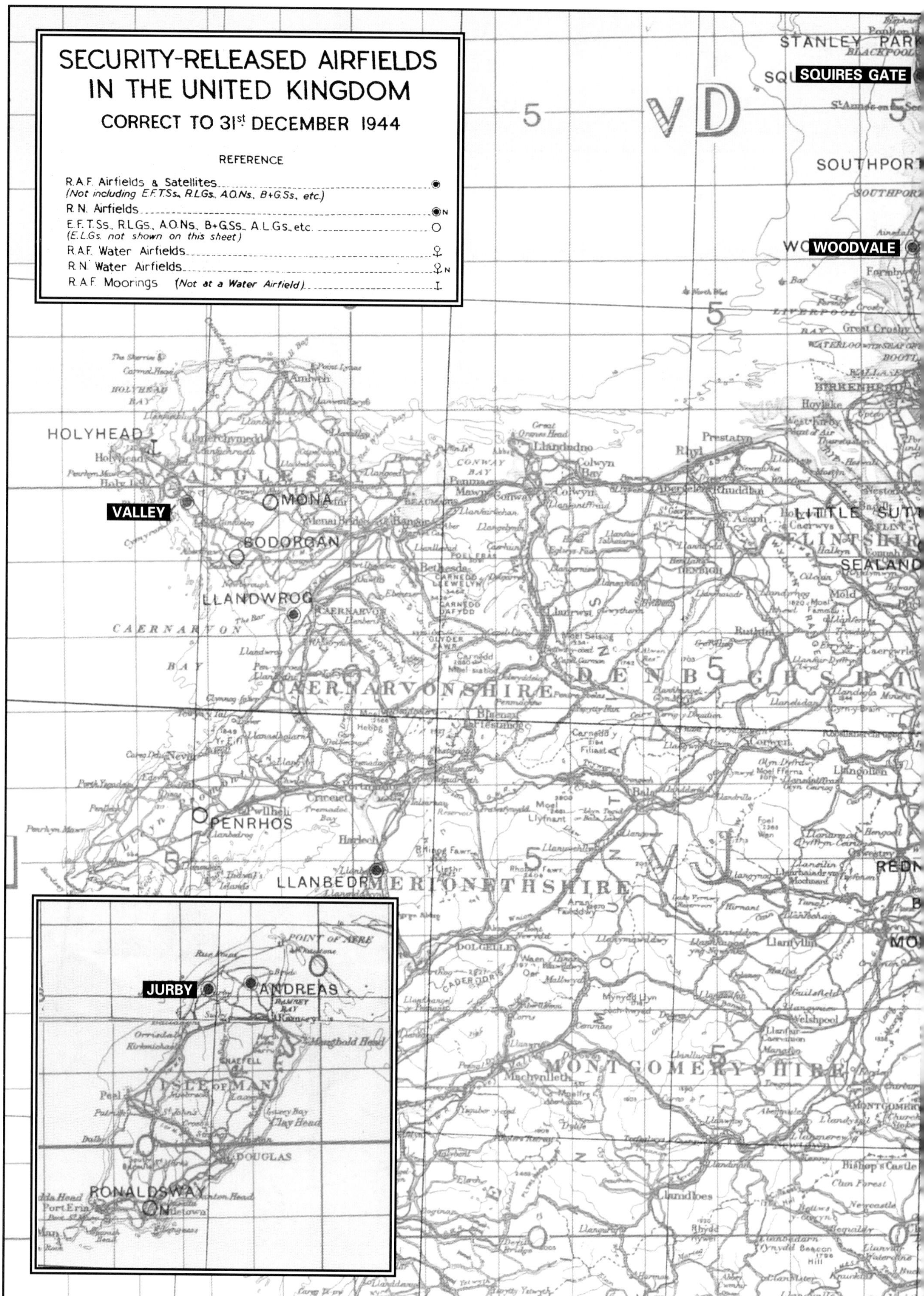
SECURITY-RELEASED AIRFIELDS IN THE UNITED KINGDOM
CORRECT TO 31st DECEMBER 1944
REFERENCE
R.A.F. Airfields & Satellites (Not including E.F.T.Ss., R.L.Gs., A.O.Ns., B+G.Ss., etc.)
R.N. Airfields
E.F.T.Ss., R.L.Gs., A.O.Ns., B+G.Ss., A.L.Gs., etc. (E.L.Gs. not shown on this sheet)
R.A.F. Water Airfields
R.N. Water Airfields
R.A.F. Moorings (Not at a Water Airfield)
STANLEY PARK
SQUIRES GATE
SOUTHPORT
WOODVALE
HOLYHEAD
VALLEY
MONA
BODORGAN
LLANDWROG
PENRHOS
LLANBEDR
LITTLE SUTTON
SEALAND
JURBY
ANDREAS
RONALDSWAY
ANGLESEY
CAERNARVONSHIRE
DENBIGHSHIRE
MERIONETHSHIRE
MONTGOMERYSHIRE
ISLE OF MAN
DOUGLAS

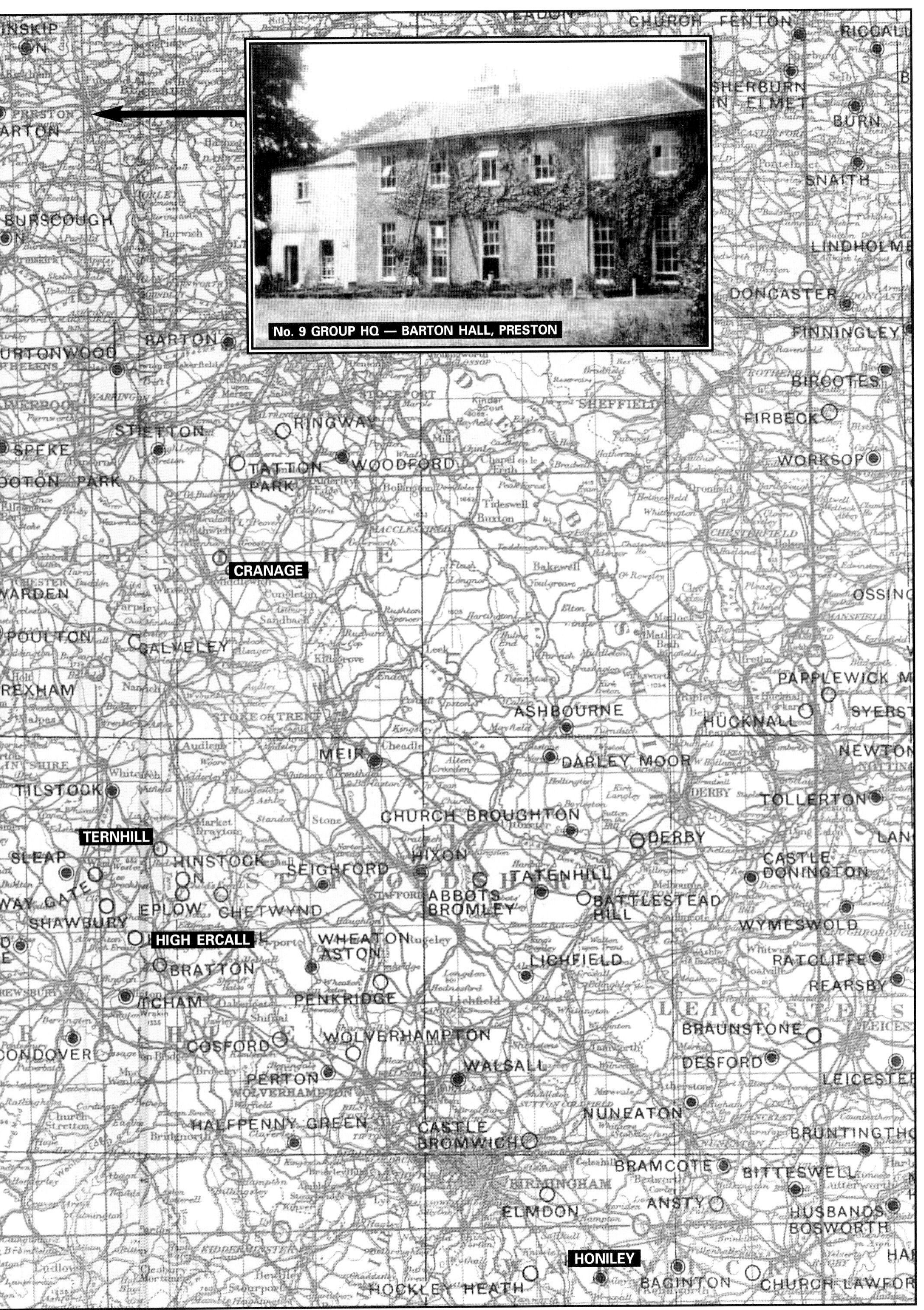

No. 9 GROUP HQ — BARTON HALL, PRESTON

On December 18, 1940, No. 96 Squadron was formed from No. 422 Flight at Cranage specifically to try to counter the night raids on Merseyside and it was hoped that this was the best airfield to catch the Luftwaffe inbound for Manchester and Liverpool.

CRANAGE

Work commenced on land just to the north of Middlewich in Cheshire in August 1939 to create a relief landing ground, its intended function being as a base for an air navigation school. Located at a height of 150 feet above sea level, the grass landing area measured N-S 1,200 yards, NE-SW 900 yards, E-W 1,400 yards and SE-NW 1,000 yards, three of the runways being laid with tracking in 1940 to provide all-weather capability. A 50-foot concrete perimeter track gave access to eight Bellman hangars and the flying control was equipped with wireless telephony and a 'Darky' direction-finding aid.

The airfield played no part in the opening phases of the war or the Battle of Britain. The first flying unit to be based there was No. 2 School of Air Navigation on October 21, 1940 equipped with Ansons. Changing its name in 1942 to the Central Navigation School, the aircraft strength increased to 58 Ansons with a number of Wellingtons joining later for the same role.

Now returned to agriculture, the most striking feature of Cranage today is the M6 motorway which slices across the north-eastern corner.

The squadron line-up photo — a pre-requisite of most units. These are the pilots and staff of No. 96 Squadron in December 1940.

Although operating within Flying Training Command, Cranage was also a fighter base, No. 96 Squadron reforming there on December 16, 1940, re-numbered from No. 422 Flight. Flying Hurricanes, the unit operated in the night defence role mainly for the protection of the industrial and port areas of Liverpool.

Situated close to Cranage at Byley was a small Vickers-Armstrong shadow factory assembling Wellingtons that were then towed to the airfield for flight testing and subsequent delivery to squadrons.

No. 96 Squadron was joined by a detachment from Jurby of No. 307 (Lwow) Polish Squadron flying the Boulton Paul Defiant, which was also tasked with the protection of the Liverpool area. In March 1941, No. 96 Squadron converted to the same type before switching back to the Hurricane six months later. They left for Wrexham on October 21, 1941, the Defiants having left eight months earlier.

Now devoid of fighting squadrons but still remaining a training school, Cranage entered a phase of experimental flying with the formation in July 1942 of No. 1531 Beam Approach Training Flight. Flying Airspeed Oxfords, the unit was tasked with teaching aircrew the techniques of using an airfield blind approach aid. In addition to the RAF units, the arrival of No. 14 Liaison Squadron saw an American presence at Cranage. Flying the Stinson L-5 Sentinel, they were used in a communications, medical and training role.

In May 1945, No. 190 Gliding School was based at Cranage, remaining for two years. Thereafter the airfield was used for storage and maintenance until it finally closed in 1958.

The Vickers-Armstrong Shadow factory at nearby Byley is now used by local industry.

With no buildings left standing, there is no chance of a meaningful comparison — hence this shot of the crumbling Battle Headquarters. As part of the ground defence each aerodrome was usually protected by a number of pillboxes co-ordinated by a Battle Headquarters — in the main a standardised design topped by a cupola with a horizontal aperture giving all-round observation. The accommodation below ground consisted of an office, sleeping quarters and toilet.

HIGH ERCALL

Although primarily a maintenance base, High Ercall was also a night fighter airfield in No. 9 Group of Fighter Command. Located five and a half miles north-west of Wellington in Shropshire, and 220 feet above sea level, it was an expansion airfield constructed by G. Walker and Slater Ltd. As well as a grass landing area, it had three tarmac runways built to a bomber airfield configuration necessary to deal with the different types of aircraft that would land either for storage or maintenance.

Dimensions for the grass were N-S 1,200 yards, NE-SW 1,400 yards, E-W 1,550 yards and SE-NW 1,200 yards whilst the tarmac runway lengths were 11-20 1,580 yards, 05-23 1,377 yards and 35-17 1,250 yards. The hangar accommodation was vast with eight 'L' types, three 'G's, one 'K', two Bellman, four Extra Over Blister and eight Over Blisters together with 12 pens.

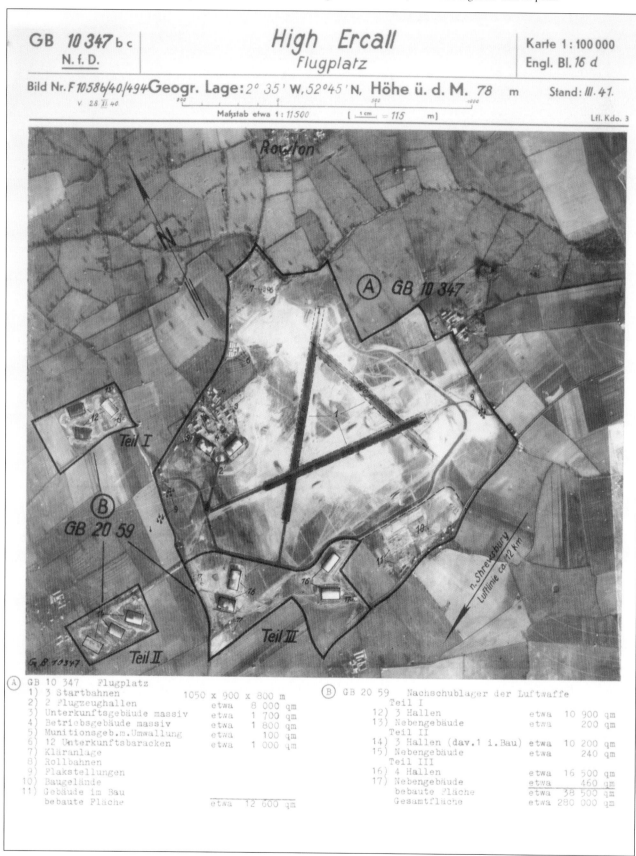

GB 10 347 b c | High Ercall | Karte 1 : 100 000
N. f. D. | Flugplatz | Engl. Bl. 16 d

Bild Nr. F 1058b/40/494 Geogr. Lage: 2° 35' W, 52° 45' N, Höhe ü. d. M. 78 m Stand: III. 41.
V 28 XI 40
Maßstab etwa 1 : 11500 [1 cm = 115 m] Lfl. Kdo. 3

Rowton
A GB 10 347
B GB 20 59
Teil I
Teil II
Teil III
n. Shrewsbury Luftlinie ca. 12 km
G. B. 10347

(A) GB 10 347 Flugplatz

1)	3 Startbahnen		1050 x 900 x 800 m
2)	2 Flugzeughallen	etwa	8 000 qm
3)	Unterkunftsgebäude massiv	etwa	1 700 qm
4)	Betriebsgebäude massiv	etwa	1 800 qm
5)	Munitionsgeb.m.Umwallung	etwa	100 qm
6)	12 Unterkunftsbaracken	etwa	1 000 qm
7)	Kläranlage		
8)	Rollbahnen		
9)	Flakstellungen		
10)	Baugelände		
11)	Gebäude im Bau		
	bebaute Fläche	etwa	12 600 qm

(B) GB 20 59 Nachschublager der Luftwaffe

	Teil I		
12)	3 Hallen	etwa	10 900 qm
13)	Nebengebäude	etwa	200 qm
	Teil II		
14)	3 Hallen (dav.1 i.Bau)	etwa	10 200 qm
15)	Nebengebäude	etwa	240 qm
	Teil III		
16)	4 Hallen	etwa	16 500 qm
17)	Nebengebäude	etwa	460 qm
	bebaute Fläche	etwa	38 500 qm
	Gesamtfläche	etwa	280 000 qm

Although not a front-line aerodrome as such, nevertheless the Luftwaffe still had it listed as Target GB 10 347.

Unfortunately this Mosquito is not identified other than it is standing outside one of the hangars of No. 29 Maintenance Unit.

Parented by nearby Atcham, in addition to being a major maintenance unit it was deemed an operational satellite or relief landing ground. Fuel storage was large with 90,000 gallons of aviation spirit and 10,000 gallons of MT petrol, all necessary for an airfield that was to handle many movements.

High Ercall played no part in the Battle of Britain although many aircraft passed through and were stored at No. 29 Maintenance Unit. March 7, 1941, saw an enemy attack on the airfield causing damage to several buildings. The expansion of No. 29 MU during 1941 saw it classified as operating within No. 51 Wing with its headquarters at Broughton Hall in Flintshire. Due to the number of aircraft requiring storage facilities, it also became necessary to establish further satellite landing grounds at Teddesley Park (SLG48), Ollerton (SLG21) and Brinklow (SLG46).

With night attacks on the Midlands cities and towns increasing, No. 68 Squadron brought their Blenheims in from Catterick on April 23, 1941. Converting to the Beaufighter a month later, they carried out many successful sorties from High Ercall before leaving for Coltishall on March 8, 1942. Six days earlier No. 255 Squadron had arrived from Coltishall to convert to the Beaufighter VIF before leaving for Honiley in June 1942.

Dozens of aircraft appear in this vertical taken in May 1946.

The contrast could not be greater with an airfield which was once a hive of industry with the servicing and repair of Fighter Command aircraft. Most of the subsidiary buildings have gone; only the hangars still stand.

Personnel of Fighter Command's No. 257 Squadron at High Ercall in June 1942 when they were equipped with the Hawker Hurricane.

With No. 29 MU ever-expanding with over 700 aircraft to disperse, the unit took over a further satellite at Weston Park (SLG33) during June. With the arrival of the Spitfire VBs of No. 257 (Burma) Squadron on June 6, High Ercall once again became operational. The month also saw No. 1456 Flight, known as a Turbinlite Flight, carry out experiments in night-fighting. Equipped with the Douglas Havoc fitted with an enormous searchlight in the nose, they hoped this would illuminate an enemy aircraft enabling an accompanying fighter to shoot it down. However the scheme was not a success and, with aircraft such as the Beaufighter and later the Mosquito carrying airborne radar, the idea was abandoned by late 1942.

The formation of No. 222 MU Aircraft Packing Depot at High Ercall coincided with the arrival of the American 309th Fighter Squadron, a unit within the 31st Fighter Group. Flying the Spitfire V instead of the intended P-39 which proved unsuitable for operations in Europe, they stayed for several weeks before moving to the Twelfth Air Force in North Africa.

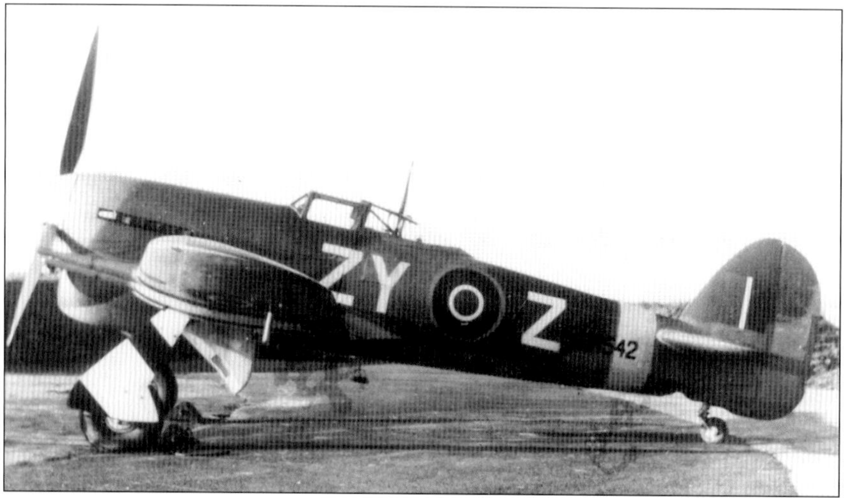

They re-equipped with Hawker Typhoon's the following month. This is DN542 which was hit by flak and crash-landed at Lympne in August 1943.

From swords to ploughshares — the flying field 70 years on . . . view taken looking towards The Wrekin.

On July 16, 1942 the airfield hosted Royal visitors as No. 1456 Flight was experimenting with a new method of countering night raiders using a 'Turbinlite' searchlight fitted to Douglas Bostons (the RAF called them Havocs). The flight was co-operating with the Hurricanes of No. 257 Squadron but in the end the idea was judged a failure and it was abandoned in January 1943.

No. 60 OTU formed at the station on May 17, 1942, with 24 Mosquitos, two Ansons and an Oxford, their duties being to train Mosquito aircrews. No. 257 Squadron, having converted to Typhoons, took part in the Dieppe operation in August before moving to Exeter on September 21. They were replaced by the Hurricanes IIB of No. 247 (China/British) Squadron. The Lockheed Lightnings of the 27th Fighter Squadron, 1st Fighter Group, of the US Eighth Air Force, arrived on August 21, for training and refitting before leaving in September.

In February 1943 the Spitfires of No. 41 Squadron arrived to carry out offensive patrols over the Irish Sea but they left in April. They were the last fighter squadron to be based at High Ercall but No. 29 MU continued to occupy the base until it closed in 1962.

The outline of the aerodrome still shows up midst the Shropshire countryside.

HONILEY

Construction of Honiley by John Laing and Sons Ltd took place during 1939-40 although the aerodrome was first known as RAF Ramsey. Situated 426 feet above sea level, off the A4177 road seven miles south-west of Coventry, it was initially intended to be used as a training base for Bomber Command but, as a result of the heavy night raids upon the Midlands over the winter of 1940-41, the Air Ministry changed its role to that of a fighter station. Honiley then became a sector station in No. 9 Group with satellite airfields at Baginton and Defford.

As with most aerodromes intended for heavy bomber use, Honiley had been provided with three hard runways in the familiar triangular configuration. Conforming to the standard lengths, the main measured 2,350 yards. Hangarage comprised three Bellmans and 12 Blisters. Unusually, the operations room was situated some distance away from the main airfield to ensure its safety.

The completion of the airfield allowed the Hurricanes of No. 605 (County of Warwick) Auxiliary Squadron to arrive on September 4, 1941 for a brief stay before embarking on HMS *Argus* for Malta. A similar procedure followed when No. 135 Squadron's Hurricanes arrived before being posted overseas on November 10.

Meanwhile the Hurricanes of No. 257 (Burma) Squadron had arrived on November 7 for night patrols, a stay that was to last six months. Whilst at Honiley they converted to various marks of Hurricanes before getting the Spitfire VB that they took to High

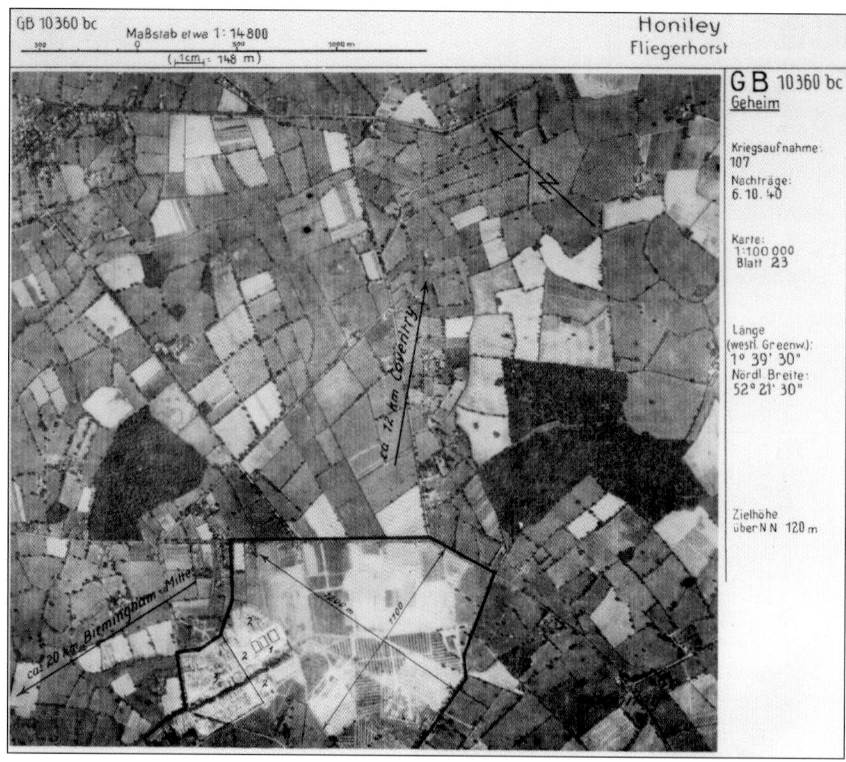

Situated some 15 miles to the south-east of Birmingham city centre, this aerodrome was first called Ramsey until its name was changed in August 1941 to Honiley. It is interesting to compare this October 1940 reconnaissance photo by Luftflotte Kommando 2 with the late-war Air Ministry schematic *(below)*.

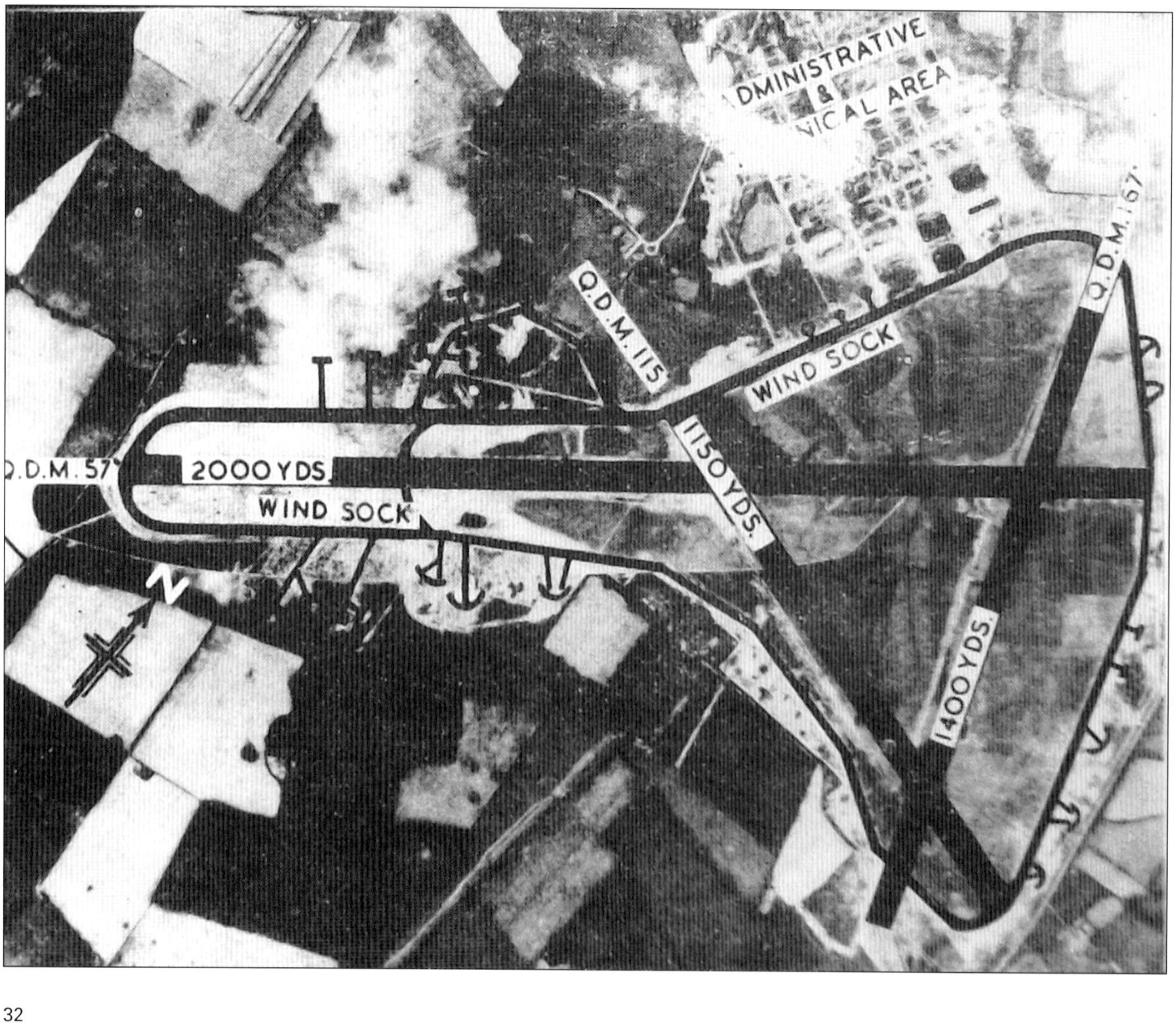

Ercall on June 6, 1942. Another night fighter unit was No. 1456 Turbinlite Flight that had formed at High Ercall and occasionally used Honiley to fly in co-operation with the Hurricanes of No. 257. Later to become No. 535 Squadron, like the other Turbinlite units, they had very little success with all such squadrons disbanding in January 1943.

A detachment of No. 285 Squadron, an Anti-Aircraft Co-Operation Flight of No. 9 Group, had arrived from Wrexham during December 1941 bringing with them a selection of aircraft comprising Blenheims, Hudsons, Lysanders, Oxfords, Defiants and Martinets. With the entire squadron arriving on October 29, 1942 they departed to Woodvale on August 23, 1943, a detachment remaining at the airfield until September.

The Beaufighters of No. 255 Squadron arrived on June 6, 1942 for a working up period prior to moving to Maison Blanche in North Africa. A brief visit by No. 32 Squadron on September 10 saw Hurricanes return to Honiley before the Beaufighters of No. 96 Squadron flew in on October 20, 1942. Taking the title of Honiley's longest-serving squadron, they carried out night intruder operations sending detachments to Tangmere and Ford until August 1943 when they moved to Church Fenton.

Unfortunately the name of this airman appears to have been lost to history, but this Hurricane IIA (Z2979) was on the strength of No. 135 Squadron when pictured at Honiley in October 1941.

By 1941, all stations were supposed to have been improved to the 'ideal' dimensions of one main runway of 2,000 yards and two subsidiaries 1,400 yards long. At minimum, the runways were to be 1,600 yards and 1,100 yards respectively with another 100 yards of cleared area at either end for overshoots. All were 50 yards wide, those at Honiley now being used as a 1.8 mile multi-surface motor test track by ProDrive which claims to give the 'ultimate driving experience' in Warwickshire.

The nine-month tenure of Honiley by No. 96 Squadron from October 1942 to August 1943 was the longest by any of the units stationed there, even though their night intruder ops were largely uneventful during that period.

Day fighters returned on April 20 when No. 91 (Nigeria) Squadron arrived to exchange their Spitfire VBs for the Mk XII before moving to Wittering on May 9. Two further Spitfire squadrons arrived for short stays, namely Nos. 130 (Punjab) and 234 before Honiley became devoid of operational aircraft. The reason was that with No. 9 Group assuming control of all Fighter Command Operational Training Units, the airfield was to become home to No. 63 OTU devoted to the task of training night fighter crews in airborne interception techniques. For this a selection of aircraft were used including Beaufighters, Beauforts and Blenheims, most having arrived by mid-August. Staying for seven months, the unit moved to Cranfield on March 21, 1944.

A brief visit by the Mosquitos of No. 219 Squadron saw the airfield return to active operations but with a change in policy at the Air Ministry, Honiley became an airfield within the Air Defence of Great Britain (ADGB). A detachment of Typhoons from No. 3 Tactical Exercise Unit arrived for a brief stay before a further switch in July 1944 saw Honiley transfer from the ADGB to No. 26 (Signals) Group of Bomber Command. Testing new radio equipment, it was renamed the Signals Flying Unit and remained until August 1946.

With the cessation of hostilities the airfield continued to be used for flying, becoming home to auxiliary squadrons and the Royal Naval Volunteer Reserve. In 1957 it was reduced to care and maintenance before finally closing on March 1, 1958.

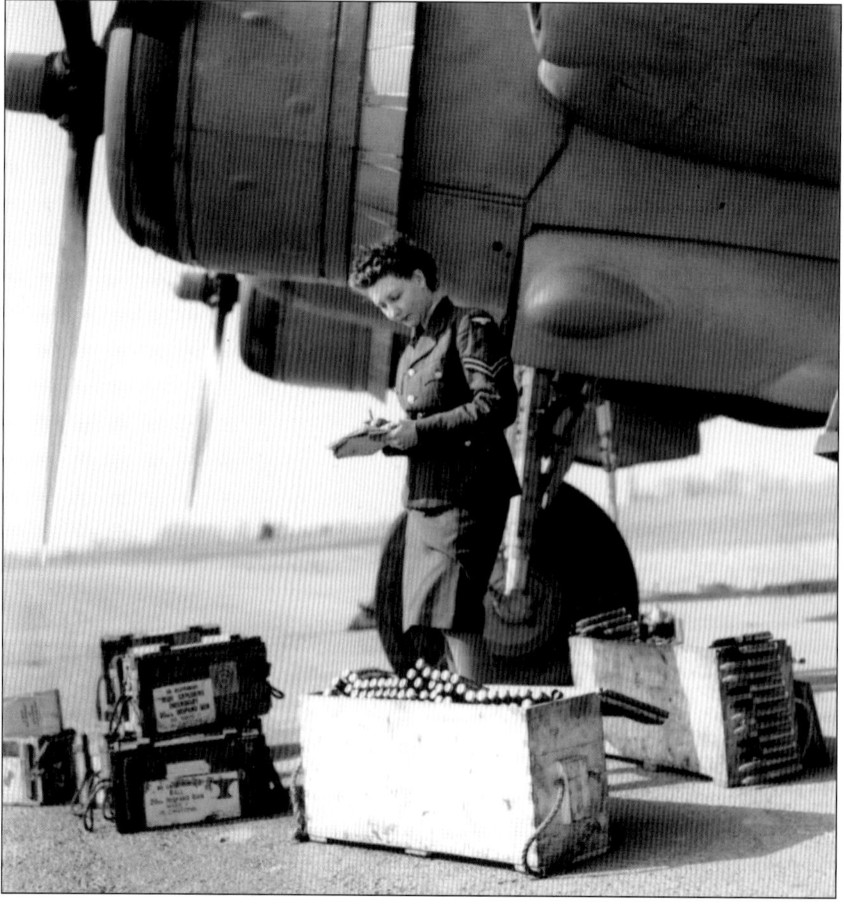

A WAAF corporal checks a delivery of 20mm Hispano cannon shells before armourers load the ammunition into one of the squadron's Bristol Beaufighter NF Mark VI.

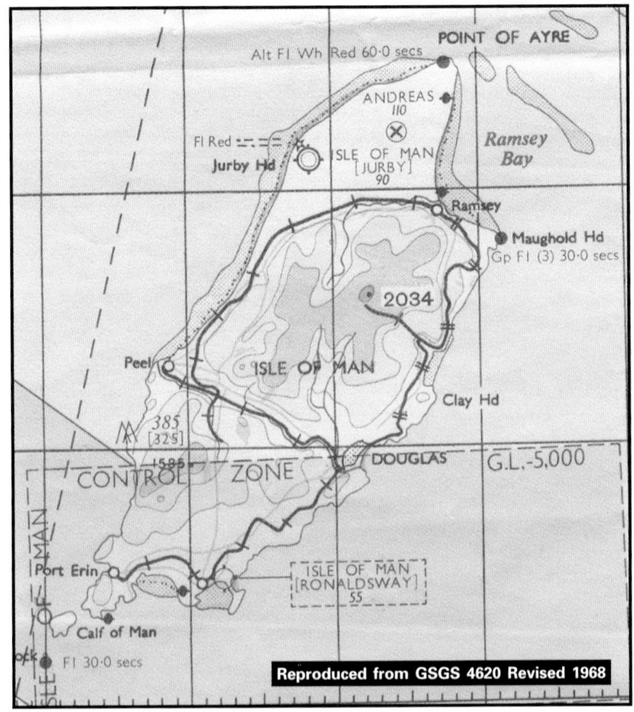

JURBY

During 1937, secret negotiations took place between the Air Ministry and the Manx government regarding the building of an airfield on the Isle of Man. Details were released in the Press in April 1938 about the land to be compulsory purchased which comprised an area of 305 acres at Jurby near the main Ballaugh-Jurby-Lhen road. It was also proposed to site a gunnery and bombing range close to the airfield, something that did not bode well with the local populace but, with legal arrangements settled, work began immediately.

A contract was issued to Land Cultivators Ltd of York to lay the grass surface for the landing ground, the dimensions of which were N-S 1,333 yards, NE-SW 1,100 yards, E-W 1,500 yards and SE-NW 1,000 yards with building construction going to Gerrard and Sons Ltd of Swanton, Manchester. On the technical site three Bellman hangars and a large former Admiralty seaplane shed were put up between the camp and the aerodrome together with a number of Blister hangars. A fourth Bellman hangar was added in 1940.

No. 457 Squadron arrived at Jurby on the Isle of Man on August 7, 1941 when they were operating Spitfire Mk Is. It then moved to RAF Andreas on October 3 where the only photographs of them were taken.

Its first six Spitfire Mk VBs flew into Andreas on December 11, this particular machine, R7348, arriving on the following day along with three others. It was written-off following a crash-landing at Heston on February 3, 1944 while on the strength of No. 315 (Polish) Squadron.

A Hampden (or possibly a Hereford) of No. 5 Air Observers School at Jurby in January 1942. Ivor Ramsden, who kindly took the comparison for us, adds that the hangar on the left is a Bellman while the one on the right is an ex-Admiralty seaplane shed adapted by the RAF as an F-type Aeroplane Shed. Ivor explains that he should be standing about 50 yards further back but the view from there would be obstructed by a high bank of spoil which has recently been placed there.

During that summer trench-type air raid shelters, each one designed to accommodate 50 people, were completed, and the following year a 1,200 x 50 yards tarmac runway together with a Watch Office were laid down by the Highway Board and the Penmaenmawr Trinidad Lake Asphalt Company.

By December 1939, No. 5 Bombing and Gunnery School was running two courses, one for Air Gunnery and the other for Air Observers and, by January 1940, 15 Battles, 21 Blenheims, 16 Henleys and a Magister were on station for the training school.

However, because of the shortage of fighter airfields around the Midlands and the north, in November 1940 the Air Ministry decided that fighter squadrons would also be deployed at Jurby coming under the control of the newly-formed No. 9 Group of Fighter Command. The prime role of these squadrons would be the daylight protection of convoys sailing through the Irish Sea. The first to arrive were the Defiants of No. 307 (Lwow) Polish Squadron. The advance party of eight officers and 59 men arrived by boat on November 7 with the aircraft and air transport party following the next day.

Although planned as a day fighter unit, the Poles were to train and operate both by day and night. Sending detachments to Cranage and Squires Gate, the main squadron flew day patrols over the Irish Sea until January 1941 when they took on a night fighter role. This continued until January 23, when they moved to Squires Gate, their replacements being the Hurricanes of No. 258 Squadron that arrived on February 2. They stayed for two months until No. 312 (Czech) Squadron took their place. No. 302 (Poznan) Polish Squadron then arrived on May 29 for a rest period, leaving for Church Stanton on August 7, 1941.

The only Spitfire unit to fly from Jurby arrived on the same day. No. 457 Squadron had formed at Baginton on June 16 with Australian pilots and RAF ground crews. With just the occasional scramble, it was a frustrating time for the squadron. They moved to Andreas on October 3 and were the last fighter unit to be stationed at the airfield.

Despite fewer aircraft being based there, training continued at Jurby throughout 1943. No. 5 Air Observers School closed down on February 1, 1944 and a new unit, the Air Navigation and Bombing School, formed in its place. With all basic navigation training having by then moved overseas with the Empire Training Scheme, the Jurby unit was the only one based in the UK.

From September 1946 No. 11 Air Gunnery School was at Jurby (from Andreas). It remained there until October 1947 when the airfield was reduced to care and maintenance. It was later re-activated for a training role until finally closing on April 30, 1964.

Later that year — on July 11 to be precise — Admiral Percy Noble was on the island for the King's Birthday Parade at HMS *St George*, the Royal Navy Boys' Training School in the capital Douglas. The pipe band leading the march past on the airfield is approaching the control tower.

Stand-down ceremony at Jurby in 1945. Ivor says that the building in the background is the NAAFI.

Ronaldsway in the south is the main airport on the Isle of Man, Jurby *(left)* having been completely closed to traffic and Andreas *(right)* restricted as an entry point under the Prevention of Terrorism legislation due to its proximity to Northern Ireland.

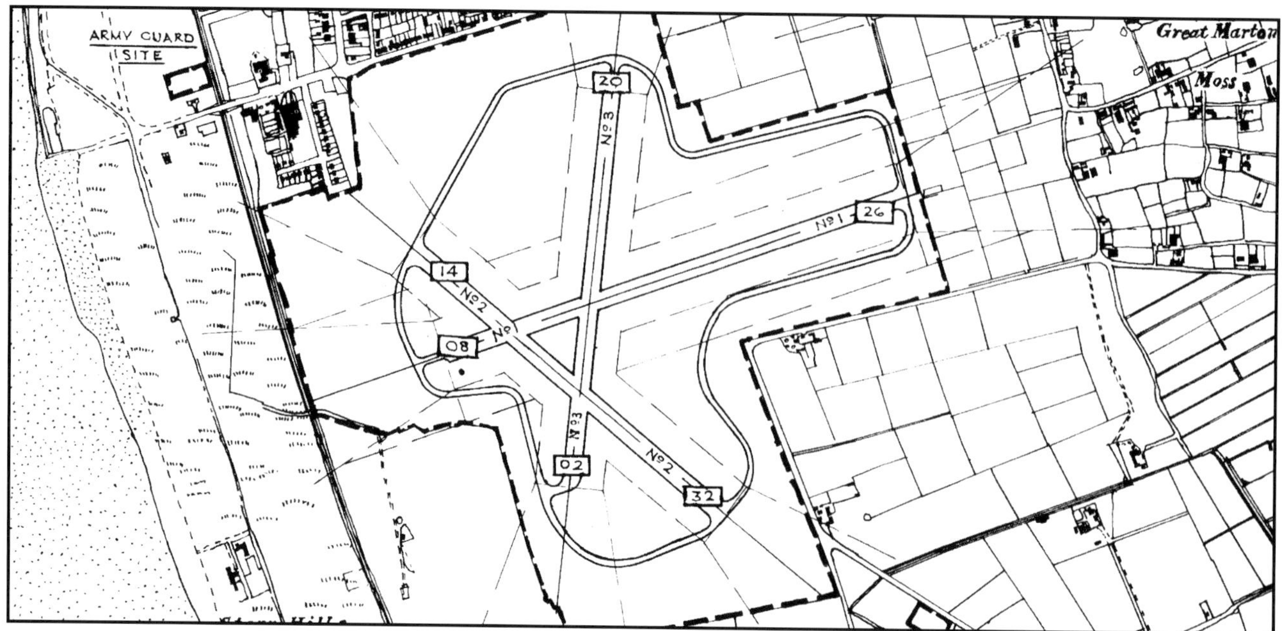

SQUIRES GATE

Squires Gate aerodrome as it appeared during the war. It closed as a military airfield in 1946 and, after the E-W runway had been lengthened to 2,000 yards, Squires Gate reopened in 1951 as Blackpool Airport.

Though encompassed within Coastal Command, Squires Gate was also used as a satellite by Fighter Command. With its first link to civilian flying dating back to 1909, the airfield is steeped in aviation history.

The original site was known as Stanley Park and was owned by Blackpool Corporation but in 1935 the airfield moved to a new and larger location one mile south-south-east of Blackpool from which scheduled and charter services could operate. When war seemed inevitable, a survey by the Air Ministry Directorate of Works considered it acceptable for a military airfield. Still going by the name of Stanley Park, the grass landing area at a height of just 34 feet above sea level measured N-S 1,250 yards, NE-SW 1,110 yards, E-W 1,400 yards and SE-NW 1,110 yards. During 1940 three hard runways were laid down using a mixture of sand and tarmac, the longest being 1,400 x 50 yards. Hangar accommodation was four Bellmans, two semi-permanent hangars and 19 Blisters with living accommodation sufficient to house 2,000 personnel. Drem night-landing facilities were installed and HF/DF and VHF radio. Fuel capacity stood at 94,000 gallons of aviation spirit and 1,000 gallons for motor transport.

In August 1939, No. 42 Elementary and Reserve Flying Training School, which was operated by the civilian firm of Reid & Sigrist, was forced to move out when the airfield's function was changed to that of a General Reconnaissance School. The first unit to arrive on September 17, 1939, was a detachment from No. 63 Squadron with Fairey Battles. Further detachments from Nos. 75 (New Zealand) and 215 Squadrons arrived at the same time, both flying Wellingtons.

The airfield was not used during the Battle of Britain although it was bombed on several occasions causing some damage. On Septem-

The runways in use today are the 10-28 (during the war designated 08-26) and the former 14-32, now corrected with magnetic variation to 13/31. The third wartime runway is no longer in use. The Vickers shadow factory lies to the north-east.

Defiant night fighters are the aircraft most associated with Squires Gate, this one, T4037, being on the strength of No. 256 Squadron.

ber 5, 1940, No. 308 (Krakow) Polish Squadron formed at the airfield with the official re-designation as RAF Squires Gate coming on December 1. To help defend Merseyside, in January 1941 No. 307 (Lwow) Polish Squadron arrived from Jurby with Defiants, exchanging places with No. 256 Squadron in March which was the last fighter squadron to be based at the airfield.

In addition to the flying units at Squires Gate, in 1939 the Ministry of Aircraft Production inspected the airfield as a possible site for a Vickers shadow factory. Once approved, construction of the buildings began in January 1940 alongside the north-eastern boundary with further facilities being built at the Stanley Park site. Meanwhile manufacture of Wellingtons began immediately using two of the Bellman hangars with the first aircraft leaving the airfield in September 1940. Production continued throughout the war, the factory finally closing on October 13, 1945 after some 2,584 Wellingtons had been built, flown and tested at Squires Gate. Other units at the airfield around this time were No. 9 Civilian Air Navigation School with Ansons together with a detachment of Battles used for drogue target-towing.

On January 7, 1941, Squires Gate recorded the tragic death of Amy Johnson, a pilot in the Air Transport Auxiliary. On a delivery flight from the airfield to Kidlington in Oxfordshire, her Airspeed Oxford was seen to crash way off course into the Thames Estuary. Her body was never recovered despite a long search.

May 1943 saw an Air-Sea Rescue school based at the airfield equipped with Ansons. They remained until the war ended, the last military unit based at Squires Gate being No. 1510 Flight which trained bomber crews in beam landing techniques. When the airfield closed in August 1946 it was transferred to the Civil Aviation Authority for conversion into the future Blackpool Airport.

And not forgetting the ground crews. The normal complement under a Flight Sergeant would include engine fitters, aircraft riggers, wireless mechanics, electricians, instrument repairers and armourers.

For more than 20 years, an Avro Vulcan which saw action in the Falklands War stood as the gate guardian to Blackpool Airport but in January 2006 it was unceremoniously scrapped.

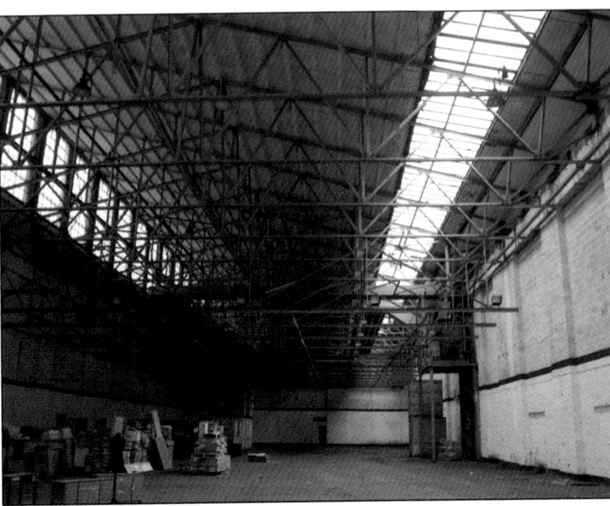

The buildings of the shadow factory, which turned out over 2,500 Wellington bombers during the war have now been sub-divided to provide a new lease of life for local industry.

From 1939 to 1945, 444 aerodromes were built for the RAF in the United Kingdom with paved runways and during the peak construction year of 1942, new airfields were being completed at an average rate of one every three days. In addition, over 60 major extensions were taking place to existing airfields although prior to 1939 only nine airfields had paved runways. Ternhill has been cleverly camouflaged so that even the hangars merged into the background in this photo taken by the Luftwaffe in September 1940.

TERNHILL

The oldest military airfield in Shropshire, Ternhill is situated four miles south-west of Market Drayton at 280 feet above sea level, the first site of over 300 acres being requisitioned by the War Office in 1916. It became a training depot, much of which was destroyed by a huge fire in March 1919. As a result the land was sold for agriculture but by 1935 the Air Ministry Directorate of Works had once more re-requisitioned the site and work began to enlarge the airfield. At this time the measurements of the grass landing area were N-S 1,050 yards, NE-SW 1,255 yards, E-W 1,000 yards and SE-NW 1,275 yards.

Initially, the airfield was earmarked for Flying Training Command, the first unit to arrive on December 15, 1936 being No. 10 Flying Training School with Avro Tutors and Hawker Harts. This heralded the long association that Ternhill would have with flying training.

The hangar accommodation comprised three 'C' Types, three Bellmans and three Blisters and several satellites were established at Chetwynd, Perton, Childs Ercall, Wheaton-Aston and Bratton. However, in the autumn of 1936, yet another fire began in one of the wooden huts which ended up destroying a large part of the living accommodation. Hastily rebuilt, by the outbreak of war, Ternhill was finally deemed ready to become operational.

Like many aerodromes located in the county, Ternhill was scheduled to house a maintenance unit and No. 24 MU was formed there on July 1, 1937 to carry out first line servicing and storage, additional 'C' Type, 'D' Type and Lamella hangars being erected to accommodate the increased number of aircraft.

The Whitleys of No. 78 Squadron arrived on June 1, 1939 remaining for most of 1940 and carrying out sorties in support of coastal operations. In addition, nightly infiltrations by the Luftwaffe forced the Air Ministry to base two Blenheims from No. 29 Squadron at Ternhill. Joining them in October 1939 came a Spitfire detachment from No. 611 (West Lancashire) Auxiliary Squadron to provide defence by day but they soon returned to Digby to be replaced by No. 306 (Torun) Polish Squadron bringing the first Hurricanes to the airfield.

Further expansion took place at No. 24 MU with the acquisition of land between Stoke Heath and Buntingsdale. Site 'A' refurbished Spitfires and Lancasters whilst Site 'B' catered mainly for Spitfires. Site 'C' was for the storage of Battles and Tiger Moths whilst Site 'D' repaired all types with various degrees of damage.

The Luftwaffe attacked Ternhill on October 16, 1940 causing major damage to the hangars. No. 10 FTS disbanded later that year before moving to Canada to be replaced by No. 5 FTS with Miles Masters. By now the number of movements and the size of aircraft being accommodated by No. 24 MU gave rise to the question of hard runways and by early 1941 two were under construction, both 1,000 x 50 yards. A further storage unit, known as Satellite Landing Ground 29 (SLG29), was established at Hodnet which soon became filled with Wellingtons, Hudsons, Ansons and Oxfords.

Several fighter squadrons were rested at Ternhill. No. 403 (Wolf) Canadian Squadron arrived on March 19, 1941 with Curtiss Tomahawks but converted progressively through various marks of Spitfires before moving to Hornchurch on August 4. Two days later No. 131 (County of Kent) arrived at the same time as the Polish squadron, No. 306, moved to Northolt. They had been in daily contact with the enemy over the Midlands.

Still in active use today, Ternhill has enjoyed nearly 80 years as an RAF aerodrome, runways having been added to cater for its use by heavier aircraft when the resident maintenance unit was tasked with the repair of Lancasters.

Thirteen days after the reconnaissance photo was taken, the Luftwaffe returned to bomb the airfield. The so-called 'Sunshine Hangar' was hit and later had to be demolished.

It stood here, the common reference point being the fire tender building on the extreme right. Ternhill has now become the headquarters of the Royal Irish Regiment.

This Turbinlite-equipped Boston Havoc was pictured on May 13, 1942, in front of the control tower during the brief period when this method of dealing with German night raiders was put into practice. Ten flights were created in 1941 in which a Hurricane night fighter would be paired with a Turbinlite aircraft, the idea being that once the Havoc had detected a raider using its Airborne Interception radar, it would illuminate it using its on-board searchlight. However, with only one enemy aircraft confirmed destroyed, the project was abandoned in January 1943.

Being basically a training station, several methods of simulating night flying were in place and, apart from the standard flare path, pupils either wore special goggles or aircraft were fitted with blue screens to simulate darkness.

In April 1942 No. 5 FTS became No. 5 (Pilots) Advanced Flying Unit (P) AFU while No. 24 MU was transferred to No. 43 Group the same month. By this time personnel at Ternhill amounted to over 2,000 including 400 women and civilian workers, the role of the airfield throughout the latter war years revolving around training and maintenance until No. 24 MU moved to Sealand in 1946.

Having built itself a fine reputation for training during wartime, Ternhill continued in peacetime until August 4, 1961. Although downgraded from this point on, training still continues to the present day with the Defence Helicopter Flying School based at nearby Shawbury using the airfield as a satellite. It is also the home of No. 632 Volunteer Gliding School giving air cadets their first experience of flying while the camp has been allocated to the 1st Royal Irish Regiment.

Touching down on the same spot — a Squirrel of the Defence Helicopter Flying School.

VALLEY

Another No. 9 Group airfield, the name Valley replaced the original Welsh name of Rhosneigr on April 5, 1941. Classified as a fighter and night fighter sector station, it lay one mile south of the village of Valley on the Isle of Anglesey at a height of 26 feet above sea level. The main task of the station was the air defence of Liverpool, the industrial north-west, and shipping in the Irish Sea.

From the beginning, Valley had three tarmac runways with 14-32 being the longest at 1,000 × 50 yards. Hangar accommodation was three Bellman, four Over Blisters and eight Extra-Over Blisters. The other intended functions for the station were air-sea rescue and target towing. With much activity by the Luftwaffe over the area during 1941, the airfield was supported by several radar stations plus a Ground Controlled Interception station at Trewan Sands.

Opening on February 1, 1941, the first arrival was No. 312 (Czech) Squadron with

By 1941, the number of Belgian pilots who had escaped to Britain was sufficient to be able to make up their own squadron — No. 350. They were formed at Valley on the Isle of Anglesey on November 12 equipped with Spitfire IIAs.

Hurricanes that flew in on March 3. Moving over to Jurby on April 18, three days later No. 615 (County of Surrey) Auxiliary Squadron replaced them from Kenley. During their tenure of four and a half months, they claimed to have shot down one Ju 88 and damaged three others.

To help counter attacks on Merseyside by night, a night fighter squadron was formed at Valley on June 30, 1941. No. 456 (Australian) Squadron was equipped with Defiants although it did not become operational until September 5 owing to a lack of aircrew. However, by that time the Defiants had been exchanged for Beaufighters enabling the squadron to claim its first enemy aircraft in January 1942.

Due to the number of training accidents causing aircraft to crash into the sea, No. 275 Air-Sea Rescue Squadron was based at Valley on October 15. Sending detachments to Andreas and Eglinton, the aircraft used were Lysanders and a Walrus. The Hurricanes of No. 242 (Canadian) Squadron flew in for day defence duties on September 16 but their stay was brief before they departed for the Far East on HMS *Argus*.

Although prone to sea fog in spring and autumn, Valley enjoyed reasonable weather which prompted a request for the main runway to be lengthened in order to facilitate its use as a future transatlantic airways route.

The departure of No. 242 Squadron saw No. 350 (Belgian) Squadron formed from a nucleus of Belgian pilots taken from No. 131 (County of Kent) Squadron with Spitfires on November 12, 1941. After training the squadron moved to Atcham in February 1942 to be replaced by the parent squadron, No. 131, the following month. However, they had a miserable time at Valley, experiencing problems with engines and guns so moved back to Llanbedr a month later.

In 2013 Valley hosted both No. 4 Flying Training School, equipped with the Hawk fast jet trainer, and C Flight of No. 22 Squadron with Sea King search and rescue helicopters.

Left: **The Americans pictured Valley in June 1943 when the airfield came into its own as a transport base for aircraft arriving from the States. The main runway had already been lengthened at its eastern end but further extensions have since been made to both ends to its current 2,500 yards.**

The New Year saw Ferry Command begin to make use of the new runways. Whilst still under the overall control of No. 9 Group, Valley was earmarked for use as a staging post for bombers arriving from the USA prior to being issued to units stationed in East Anglia and the Midlands. The first B-17 arrived on July 28, with many following over the coming months. Throughout the rest of 1943 and most of 1944 the airfield was devoted to American Ferry Services.

The departure of No. 456 Squadron in March 1943 saw more Beaufighters arrive belonging to No. 125 (Newfoundland) Squadron. The unit converted to the Mosquito before moving to Hurn. With the airfield now more of a transport base than a fighter station, Valley lost its sector status on November 1. No further fighter squadrons were based there leaving No. 275 (ASR) Squadron the sole resident.

Although Valley was placed on care and maintenance in June 1947, nevertheless it was scheduled to become a major training base as well as a Military Emergency Diversion Aerodrome. Both roles continue at the present time.

WOODVALE

One mile north of Formby, alongside the A565, lay the RAF's only fighter station in Lancashire. Sitting 37 feet above sea level, the site chosen for the airfield in 1940 was formerly a golf course and several acres of farmland. Designed and built primarily for the defence of Merseyside, by the time it was opened unfinished in October 1941 the immediate threat had passed. However, with the Air Ministry seeing a need for fighter cover in the area, Woodvale's function was to be as a sector airfield in No. 9 Group with satellites at Squires Gate, Wrexham and Stretton.

One hard runway of 1,600 yards had been laid by the time Woodvale opened on a bearing of 22-04. Two others followed, 17-35 at 1,100 yards and 09-27 at 1,170 yards. All were finished with tarmac with a similar 50-foot perimeter track. There were three Bellman hangars and nine Extra-Over Blisters. The domestic site was situated along the old Southport Road, a safe distance from the airfield should it be attacked. With the airfield prone to industrial haze, a Drem flarepath was installed.

The first airmen to arrive were the advance party of No. 308 (Krakow) Polish Squadron on December 12, 1941. They had seen some hard fighting with No. 11 Group and had come north to rest. However, they still managed to damage a Ju 88 while at Woodvale before they left for Exeter on April 1, 1942, Replaced by another Polish Squadron, No. 315 (Deblin) the same day, this unit had some success when they damaged a Ju 88 in conjunction with two other squadrons. Returning to Northolt on September 5, the night defence of Liverpool then fell to the Hurricanes, Beaufighters and Defiants of No. 256 Squadron which had flown in from Squires Gate on June 1, 1942. Converting to the Beaufighter VIF, they moved to Ford on April 24, 1943.

Yet another Polish squadron, No. 317 (Wilno), had arrived at Woodvale on September 5, 1942 although they achieved no successful interceptions. They moved to Kirton-in-Lindsey on February 13, 1943.

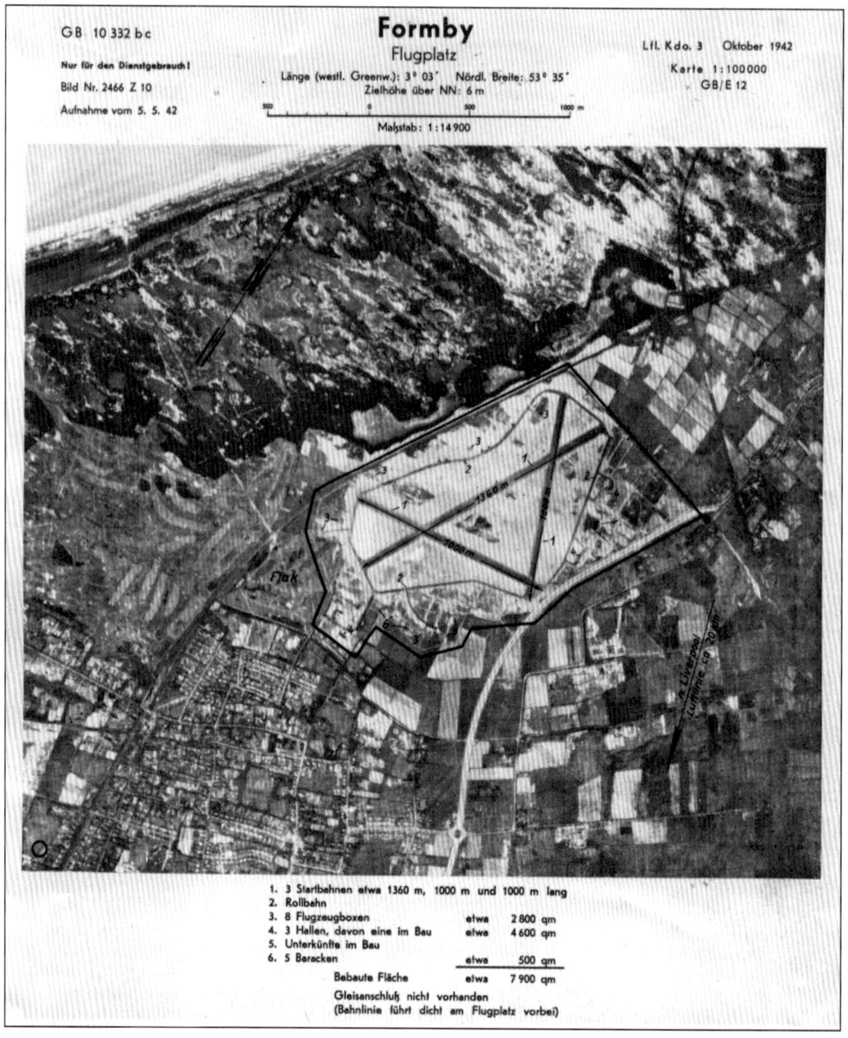

Woodvale, just behind the foreshore near Southport, was opened in October 1941 having been built as an all-weather station for the defence of Merseyside. The Luftwaffe photographed it in May 1942 calling it Formby after the nearest town.

The control tower lay alongside the New Bronk Farmhouse (left) which was retained as the radio repair shop. This oblique taken in 1943 shows the signals square with the landing 'T' and station identification code 'OD'. The barn (right) was utilised for crash vehicles and uniquely the plan of the airfield was painted on the rear of the tower.

The detachment of No. 285 Squadron that arrived from Wrexham was tasked with target-towing and anti-aircraft calibration duties, the remainder of the unit joining them on August 25, 1943, dispersing flights to High Ercall, Honiley, Croydon, Colerne and Fairwood Common. Previously flying Martinets, they progressed through Beaufighters and Hurricanes before moving to Andover on November 19, 1944.

Late 1942 saw a naval presence at the airfield when No. 776 Squadron of the Fleet Air Arm arrived with Skuas, Rocs, Seafires and Chesapeakes. The New Year began with two Typhoon squadrons, Nos. 195 and 198, moving in on February 12, and May 15, respectively. They completed a working up period before being sent south.

The formation of No. 322 (Dutch) Squadron on June 12, brought Spitfires back to Woodvale operating as part of the Merseyside day defences. They left for Hawkinge on December 31. The addition of Nos. 222 (Natal), 316 (Warsaw) Polish and 219 (Mysore) Squadrons saw the airfield operating at maximum capacity. This became

No. 256 Squadron moved in from Squires Gate in June 1942, this shot with one of their Beaufighters being taken in front of one of the Bellman hangars . . .

. . . and in front of a Mosquito just before the squadron moved south to Ford.

Today, still an RAF station, Woodvale hosts two university air squadrons which provide pre-service training to cadets prior to graduation and transfer to the officer course at Cranwell. So here, exactly 70 years later, cadets Danny Yeomans, Sarah Day and Niall Moroney of the Liverpool University Air Squadron line up in front of the same hangar.

In August 1944, the headquarters of No. 9 Group closed seeing the end of fighter squadrons being stationed at Woodvale. However, as it was situated close to the main USAAF depots at Burtonwood, Warton, and Langford Lodge in Northern Ireland, American aircraft became frequent visitors like this B-24 Liberator, one of which crashed on landing in bad weather on October 25, 1944. Of the 20 men on board from the 740th Bomb Squadron of the 446th Bomb Group, seven lost their lives.

In the picture at the top of the page, the control tower can be seen on the left. The basic wartime structure still stands albeit with a modern glasshouse on the roof.

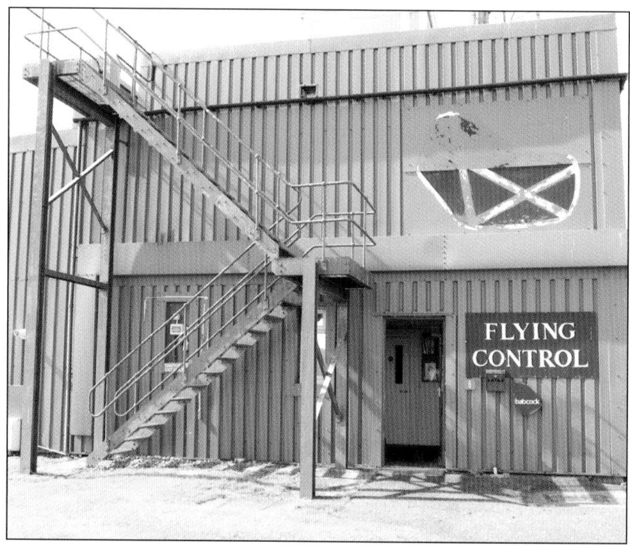

The map which had been painted on the rear wall was later rendered over but when a refurbishment was carried out after the war, it was discovered and reinstated.

more acute with the arrival of the Blenheims of No. 12 (P) Advanced Flying Unit and 'B' Flight of No. 650 Squadron as an additional target-tug unit.

By now the threat of attacks on Merseyside had receded so Woodvale supported no further operational squadrons. The United States Army Air Force used it for transport duties and for the repatriation of servicemen to the States before it was handed over to the Royal Navy. No. 776 Squadron was the first to arrive followed by No. 889. Further Fleet Air Arm units were Nos. 816 and 822 Squadrons.

Returned to the RAF, peacetime occupants were No. 186 Gliding School, Liverpool University Air Squadron and No. 19 Reserve Flying School. Currently Woodvale is home to Liverpool and Manchester University Air Squadrons, the Merseyside Police Air Support Group, No. 10 Air Experience Flight, and as a centre for the training of undergraduate student pilots to the RAF's Elementary Flying Training Scheme.

Woodvale pictured by the RAF in August 1942 looking north-west towards the Irish Sea. The aerodrome was squeezed in between the Liverpool-Southport railway and the A565.

Now the only active RAF base in north-western England, the airfield is also used by civilian organisations such as the West Lancs Aero Club and Woodvale Aviation.

No. 10 GROUP

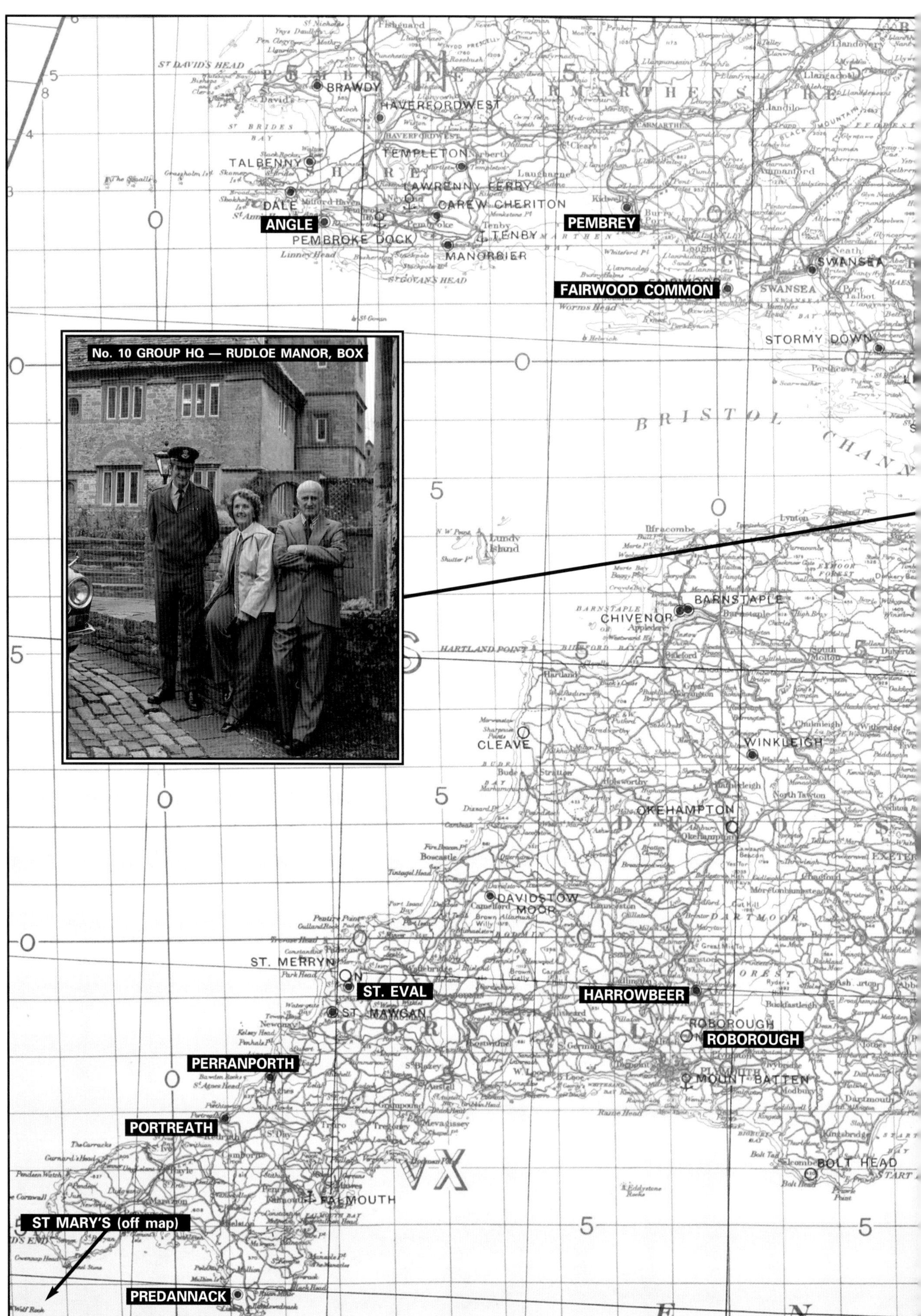
No. 10 GROUP HQ — RUDLOE MANOR, BOX
BRAWDY
HAVERFORDWEST
TEMPLETON
TALBENNY
LAWRENNY FERRY
DALE
CAREW CHERITON
ANGLE
PEMBROKE DOCK
TENBY
MANORBIER
PEMBREY
FAIRWOOD COMMON
SWANSEA
STORMY DOWN
BRISTOL CHANNEL
BARNSTAPLE
CHIVENOR
CLEAVE
WINKLEIGH
OKEHAMPTON
DAVIDSTOW MOOR
ST. MERRYN
ST. EVAL
ST. MAWGAN
HARROWBEER
ROBOROUGH
MOUNT BATTEN
PERRANPORTH
PORTREATH
FALMOUTH
BOLT HEAD
ST MARY'S (off map)
PREDANNACK

SECURITY-RELEASED AIRFIELDS
IN THE UNITED KINGDOM
CORRECT TO 31st DECEMBER 1944
REFERENCE
R.A.F. Airfields & Satellites
(Not including E.F.T.Ss., R.L.Gs., A.O.Ns., B+G.Ss., etc.)
R.N. Airfields
E.F.T.Ss., R.L.Gs., A.O.Ns., B+G.Ss., A.L.Gs., etc.
(E.L.Gs. not shown on this sheet)
R.A.F. Water Airfields
R.N. Water Airfields
R.A.F. Moorings (Not at a Water Airfield)
FILTON
COLERNE
CHARMY DOWN
BOSCOMBE DOWN
CHILBOLTON
MIDDLE WALLOP
CHURCH STANTON
IBSLEY
BEAULIEU
HOLMSLEY SOUTH
WARMWELL
EXETER
MADLEY
ST. JOHN
MORETON IN THE MARSH
CROUGHTON
STOKE ORCHARD
ENSTONE
UPPER HEYFORD
CHIPPING NORTON
STAVERTON
LITTLE RISSINGTON
BICESTER
KIDDINGTON
BROOKWORTH
NORTHLEACH
KIDLINGTON
WESTON ON THE GREEN
CHEDWORTH
AKEMAN STREET
OAKLEY
MORTON VALENCE
BIBURY
WINDRUSH
WITNEY
BROADWELL
BRIZE NORTON
STANTON HARCOURT
SOUTHROP
ASTON DOWN
KELMSCOTT
FAIRFORD
ABINGDON
KEMBLE
SOUTH CERNEY
DOWN AMPNEY
KINGSTON BAGPUIZE
BABDOWN FARM
SHELLINGFORD
MOUNT FARM
LONG NEWNTON
BLAKEHILL FARM
WATCHFIELD
GROVE
BENSON
HARWELL
HULLAVINGTON
WANBOROUGH
HAMPSTEAD NORRIS
CARDIFF
LYNEHAM
WROUGHTON
CASTLE COMBE
CLYFFE PYPARD
MEMBURY
WALTHAM ST. LAWRENCE
WELFORD
YATESBURY
RAMSBURY
CHARMY
THEALE
RHOOSE
OVERTON HEATH
WHITCHURCH
GREENHAM COMMON
ALDERMASTON
LULSGATE BOTTOM
WESTON-SUPER-MARE
ALTON BARNES
KEEVIL
UPAVON
NETHERAVON
NEW ZEALAND FARM
SHREWTON
ANDOVER
THRUXTON
LASHAM
OATLANDS HILL
HIGH POST
OLD SARUM
WESTON ZOYLAND
ZEALS
YEOVILTON
CHARLTON HORETHORNE
HENSTRIDGE
MERRYFIELD
EASTLEIGH
STONEY CROSS
UPOTTERY
HAMBLE
TARRANT RUSHTON
CALSHOT
HURN
CHRISTCHURCH
COWES
LEE ON SOLENT
GOSPORT
SANDOWN
BEMBRIDGE
PORTLAND
FRENCH LAMBERT ZONE

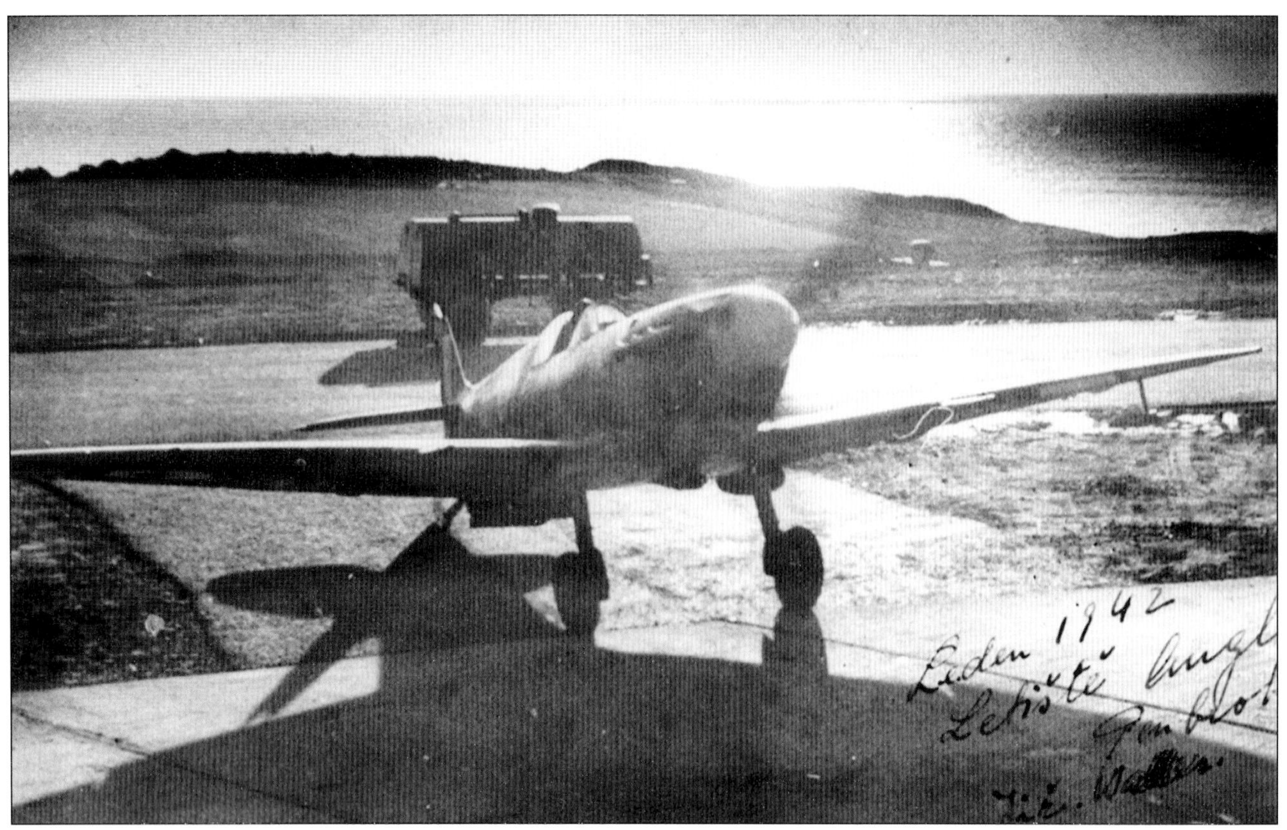

Squadron Leader M. A. Liskutin of No. 312 Squadron taxies his Spitfire VB into a revetment at Angle. The Czech squadron had moved there on January 1, 1942 to carry out convoy patrols.

ANGLE

Operating as a satellite to the parent station of Fairwood Common within No. 10 Group, Angle officially opened on December 1, 1941. Situated in the extreme southwest corner of Wales, some eight and three quarter miles west of Pembroke and 209 feet above sea level, three tarmac runways were constructed, the longest being 1,300 x 50 yards and the other two, 1,000 x 50 yards. A perimeter track 50 feet wide led to 12 pens and six hardstandings. Hangar accommodation was limited to just four Blisters with floodlights, gooseneck flares and Glim lamps for night landings.

First to arrive were the Hurricanes of No. 32 Squadron followed by those of 615 (County of Surrey) which arrived for convoy escort duties. Staying barely two months they were replaced by No. 312 (Czech) Squadron from Fairwood Common. Flying similar convoy sorties, they returned to the parent station on April 18, 1942.

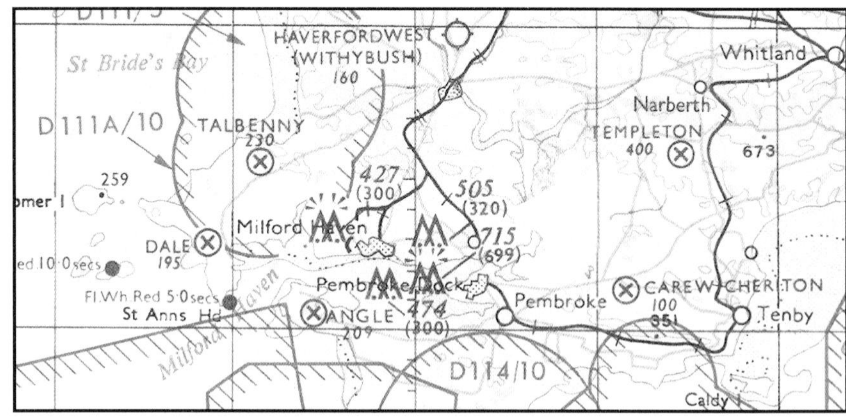

One of the most remarkable incidents to occur at any RAF airfield, took place at Angle on May 29, 1943 when a Sunderland flying boat landed on dry ground!

T9114 of No. 461 Squadron of the Royal Australian Air Force based at nearby Pembroke Dock was captained by Pilot Officer Gordon Singleton of St Kilda, Victoria, the mission being to rescue survivors from a Whitley and a Sunderland which had crashed in the Bay of Biscay. *Above left:* The 16 survivors from both aircraft were transferred to the French destroyer *La Combattante* by whaler. *Above right:* However, by the time this had been carried out, the heavy sea would have made a take-off dicey so the rescue aircraft was taken in tow. *Below left:* When Pilot Officer Singleton finally took off the hull was ruptured leaving a 7ft by 4ft gash below the water line. *Below right:* Gordon Singleton returned to Angle in June 2008 when he described what happened: 'In 1943 my Sunderland would have sunk immediately had I landed on water so I opted for the airfield. I did not aim for the runways but chose an area of grass which was much more forgiving. Lots of my squadron colleagues rushed out from Pembroke Dock expecting to see a big crash — instead my CO filmed a smooth landing!' This was the only time a Sunderland had been successfully dry-landed. T9114 was recovered from the airfield and six hedges were removed to tow it to the nearby beach but it never flew again, being scrapped there beside the sea.

In 1992 Gordon's remarkable landing was remembered on a plaque which was unveiled in West Angle Bay car park.

Angle made aviation history by being one of the few wartime bases to host the Westland Whirlwind — the first single-seat, twin-engined fighter to see service. Only two squadrons were equipped with this futuristic machine, one being No. 263 (Fellowship of the Bellows) which arrived at the airfield on April 18, 1942. Initially, the type had proved troublesome due to problems with the Rolls-Royce Peregrine engines but, once solved, it was to become a superb ground-attack aircraft. Whilst at Angle the squadron was engaged on shipping protection over the Welsh coast and Irish Sea. Later sorties included 'Ramrods'— bomber raids escorted by fighters. Sending a detachment to Portreath, the squadron finally left for Colerne on August 15, 1942.

Nos. 152 (Hyderabad) and 421 (Red Indian) Canadian Squadron spent short periods at the station together with No. 412 (Falcon), another Canadian squadron. After the latter departed on February 8, 1943 for Fairwood Common, no further operational units were based at Angle for several months. A detachment of Whitley bombers and Horsa gliders arrived some time later to work in conjunction with an army exercise for a short period before a lone Mosquito appeared to carry out tests with the 'Highball' weapon which was similar to the 'bouncing bomb' used in the raid against the Ruhr dams. A rather unusual use was made of Angle's landing area when on May 29, 1943, a damaged Sunderland flying boat of No. 461 Squadron made the first landing on a hard surface.

Loaned temporarily to the Royal Navy, July 1,1943 saw the Naval Air Firing Unit arrive in the form of No. 794 Squadron of the Fleet Air Arm. This establishment consisted of 16 Sea Hurricanes, four Master IIs, two Defiants and eight Martinets which acted as a target-towing and air-firing training unit in conjunction with the Fighter School at Yeovilton. Moving to Dale on September 10, 1943, Angle was then occupied by the Coastal Command Development Unit which remained until January 1945. With no further use for the airfield, the runways were soon ploughed up and much of the site returned to agriculture.

Situated on the extreme western tip of south Wales, Angle, like so many Second World War aerodromes, has now returned to agriculture.

BEAULIEU

Aerodromes listed in this book were by no means the exclusive use of Fighter Command and Beaulieu is a good example. It was built as a standard bomber airfield but first used by Coastal Command then Bomber Command before switching to Fighter Command early in 1944. Then it was handed over to the Americans for the invasion of Normandy. This P-47D, of the 386th Fighter Squadron of the US Ninth Air Force came a cropper when landing on the main runway with its bomb hung up. As the pilot touched down, the bomb released and exploded.

Although a landing ground known as Beaulieu was used during the First World War, and later as a civilian airfield, the location of the Second World War site was a short distance away from the original. The new airfield lay four miles north-east of Lymington in Hampshire, alongside the B3055 road at a height of 130 feet above sea level. It was originally intended to become a satellite of Thorney Island but once built it initially came under Coastal Command.

Construction began in the spring of 1942 to Class A standard with three hard runways. The longest was 09-27 at 1,970 yards with 03-21 and 15-33 being 1,400 yards, all 50 yards wide. Initially there no hangars but later two T2s and a Blister were added together with 50 hardstandings. The plan was for Beaulieu to accommodate one general reconnaissance squadron while building work continued to provide for a second. Nevertheless by October the airfield was still classed as open for full operational use.

With the U-Boat situation in the Bay of Biscay critical, immediate use was made of Beaulieu when No. 224 Squadron with Liberators moved in from Tiree on September 10. The situation in the Bay was so dire that Bomber Command was even forced to switch some of their aircraft to Coastal Command, with No. 405 (Vancouver) Squadron from the Royal Canadian Air Force, and a detachment from No. 158 Squadron, being sent to Beaulieu with Halifaxes. Arriving in October, they were soon involved in anti-shipping strikes using St. Eval as a forward base. After much success, No. 158 left for Rufforth on December 6, whilst No. 405 stayed until they returned to Bomber Command on March 1, 1943.

A Czech squadron, No. 311, bought their Wellingtons to Beaulieu on May 26, 1942. Exchanging their aircraft for Liberators in June, they were joined by the Liberators of No. 53 Squadron on September 25, 1943, followed by No. 1 (Coastal) Liberator OTU for pilot training. With the increase in squadrons and movements at Beaulieu, petrol storage was increased from 24,000 gallons to 72,000 gallons with improvements to night landing facilities.

When the Ninth Air Force units quit the base for airfields in France, the Airborne Forces Experimental Establishment arrived in December 1944 and some particularly rare types were seen at the airfield like this Sikorski R-4.

This vertical was taken by the 30th Photographic Reconnaissance Squadron based at Chalgrove on March 4, 1944.

By February 1944 the Liberators had departed and Typhoons occupied the airfield for the next few months. Nos. 257 (Burma) and 263 (Fellowship of the Bellows) Squadrons had arrived in January to commence attacks on V1 sites and bomber escort operations. Known as the Beaulieu Wing, No. 257 swapped places with No. 486 Squadron in late January, the latter bringing the first Tempests to the base. On March 1, Beaulieu was transferred out of Coastal Command to No. 10 Group under the auspices of the Air Defence of Great Britain.

In readiness for the coming invasion of France, Beaulieu was now handed over to the US Ninth Air Force, becoming Station 408, the transfer of the 365th Fighter Group from Gosfield taking place on March 5-6. The group was equipped with P-47 Thunderbolts and comprised the 386th, 387th and 388th Fighter Squadrons. All were active in the run-up to D-Day with bomber escorts and dive-bombing sorties attacking gun

The perimeter tracks remain and a memorial to Squadron Leader David Mackie Sleep, who served with No. 224 Squadron at Beaulieu, was placed on the main runway by his widow after he passed away in June 1989 aged 74.

After Beaulieu was taken over by the Forestry Commision, all the buildings were demolished and parking areas were provided for picnickers. Yet flying still continues at the airfield, albeit of the model kind!

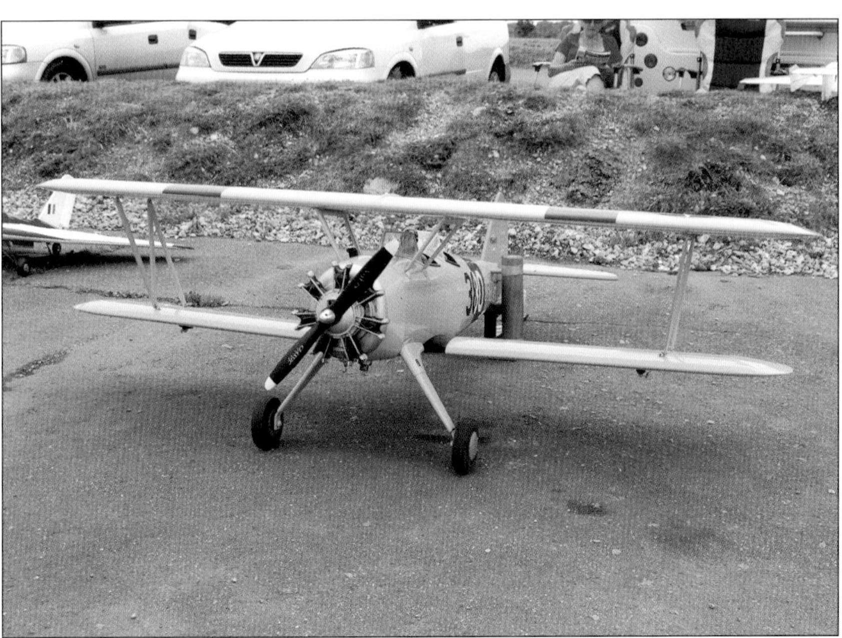

emplacements and enemy communications, losing seven aircraft over the few days of intensive operations. They operated from Beaulieu for four months and were credited with a total of 29 enemy aircraft destroyed. Beginning the move to French airstrips, they were the first group to take up residence at Azeville (A-71) on June 26.

Their exodus left the way clear for the B-26 Marauders of the 323rd Bombardment Group to fly in from Earls Colne. With over 60 aircraft in residence, the airfield became very crowded. During the five weeks they stayed at Beaulieu, 28 missions were flown without loss.

When the 323rd moved to the Continent later in August, Beaulieu was returned to the RAF on September 27, 1944. The airfield remained empty until December when the Airborne Forces Experimental Establishment arrived, eventually remaining for six years. After the organization moved to Boscombe Down in September 1950, the airfield was put on care and maintenance pending a possible return by the United States Air Force. However this did not materialise although Beaulieu remained in military hands until November 1959 when control was finally relinquished.

S.R.

BOSCOMBE DOWN

From a grass field . . . to a high-tech testing ground. And it was from here that Flight Lieutenant James Nicolson took off on August 16, 1940 on an exploit which would earn him — and Fighter Command's — only Victoria Cross of the war.

Google

Flight Lieutenant James Nicolson, yet to wear his VC ribbon, pictured in November 1940 while recovering from the wounds he received on August 16. The photo was taken at the RAF hospital at Torquay which was bombed by the Luftwaffe on October 25, 1942 killing over 20 aircrew (see *After the Battle* No. 118).

Made by Hancock and Co. from bronze removed from Russian guns captured in the Crimea, Nicolson's Victoria Cross is inscribed with the enigmatic '10 NOV 1940' which is neither the date of the action for which it was awarded nor the date of promulgation in the *London Gazette*.

Boscombe Down then with the Anson of No. 51 Squadron . . .

Boscombe Down entered the history books when the only Victoria Cross of Fighter Command was awarded to a pilot flying from the airfield.

First opened in 1917 as a training station, the airfield sat 378 feet above sea level one and a half miles east-south-east of Amesbury in Wiltshire. With the Armistice in 1918, Boscombe Down closed only to re-open in 1930 to become a permanent station in Bomber Command. Briefly handed over to Coastal Command in February 1937, two general reconnaissance squadrons arrived, these being Nos. 217 and 224, both flying Ansons. Staying for a brief period, the airfield soon returned to Bomber Command and No. 4 Group, later moving to No. 1 Group.

The Fairey Battles of Nos. 88 (Hong Kong) and 218 (Gold Coast) Squadrons arrived on July 17, 1937, and April 22, 1938, respectively, but by September 1939 both had been sent to France as part of the Advanced Air Striking Force.

The Ansons of No. 58 Squadron occupied the station for seven months, converting to the Whitley before moving to Linton-on-Ouse, only to return to Boscombe Down on September 30, 1939. Their role this time was anti-submarine patrols in the English Channel, a duty they carried out for five months.

Further extensions were forthcoming at the airfield before No. 249 (Gold Coast) Squadron bought their Hurricanes in from Church Fenton on August 14, 1940. Two days later Flight Lieutenant James Nicolson, leading Red Section of No. 249, was patrolling between Poole and Romsey when they were bounced by enemy fighters, all three aircraft being hit. Although gravely wounded after his aircraft had been struck by cannon shells and set on fire, Nicolson was about to abandon his burning Hurricane when he spotted an enemy fighter which he promptly attacked. As a result he sustained serious burns. Finally managing to leave his doomed machine, while suspended on his parachute he was further wounded by a blast from a shotgun fired from the ground. Taken to the Royal Southampton Hospital, he was later transferred to Torquay to convalesce where he learned that he had been awarded the Victoria Cross. Nicolson was later to die in a Liberator crash on May 2, 1945.

After a brief stay, the squadron was replaced by No. 56 (Punjab) also flying Hurricanes on September 1. They were the last fighter squadron to fly from Boscombe Down before it assumed its new role as the Aeroplane and Armament Experimental Establishment. The first unit to arrive was the Bomber Development Unit followed by the High Altitude Flight in 1941.

Still a grass airfield measuring N-S 1,300 yards, NE-SW 1,900 yards, E-W 1,660 yards and SE-NW 1,300 yards, by this time a perimeter track had been laid to allow for the better movement of heavier aircraft.

Boscombe Down came to the attention of the Luftwaffe in October 1941 when a serious raid destroyed one of the experimental aircraft and damaged the landing area. Several other minor attacks also took place.

The introduction of the Intensive Flying Development Flight was followed by the Test Pilots Training Flight, later renamed the Empire Test Pilots School. From this time on, many experimental flights were conducted at Boscombe Down. The construction of the first hard runway, promised over a year before, was carried out by Sir Alfred McAlpine and Sons Ltd which by late 1944 allowed experimental flying with jet-powered aircraft to begin. The end of the war and peacetime saw test flying in its heyday, a tradition that Boscombe Down still carries on today.

. . . and now with the cadets of the Essex wing of the Air Training Corps.

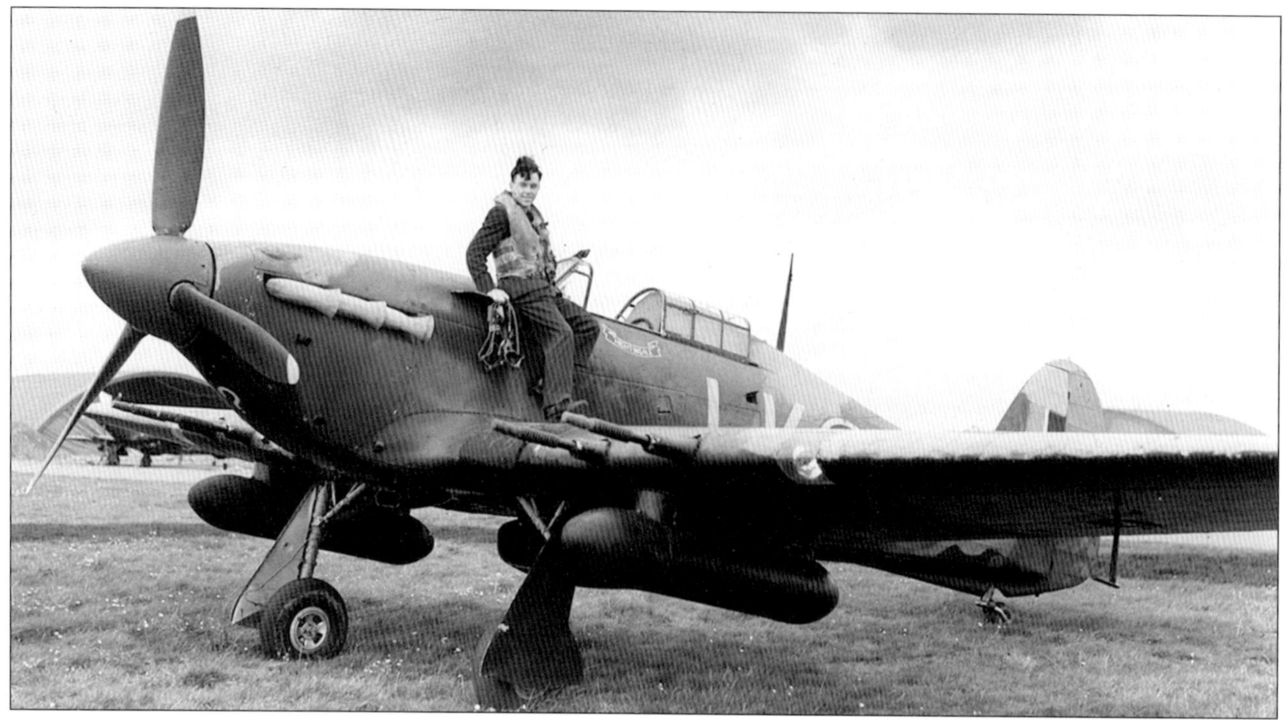

No. 87 Squadron were stationed at Charmy Down for night fighter operations. This Hurricane, HL864, was purchased for the RAF by the readers of the *Nursing Mirror* and christened 'Nightingale' — an apt title as the main Rolls-Royce works in Derby were on Nightingale Road! The machine ended its days in Russia.

CHARMY DOWN

Lying four miles north-east of Bath on a high ridge 688 feet above sea level, Charmy Down was classified as a satellite to Colerne. Opened in late 1940, it was originally a grass airfield with dimensions of N-S 950 yards, NE-SW 1,375 yards, E-W 1,450 yards and SE-NW 1,375 yards. The perimeter track led to 39 aircraft dispersals consisting of 12 double and 15 single pens. Although the grass surface was reasonably free draining, in early 1941 three runways were laid: 13-31 of 1,450 yards, 17-25 1,350 yards and 01-19 933 yards. A Bellman and 12 Blisters were added later.

The initial role of Charmy Down was as a night-fighter base for the protection of Bath and Bristol, heralded by the arrival of No. 87 Squadron at the end of November. Although their Hurricanes were not really suitable for night fighting, the CO, Squadron Leader Gleed , claimed a Do 17 during a night sortie the following May. The squadron also became the longest serving Hurricane night fighter squadron, remaining at Charmy Down until August 1941 when they moved to Colerne.

Although not yet fully operational, the next residents were No. 125 (Newfoundland) Squadron with Defiants and No. 263 with Whirlwinds. Both were at Charmy Down for working up with a nucleus being taken from the latter to form the second Whirlwind squadron, No. 137. Reformed at the airfield in February 1941, they moved to Coltishall in November.

In January 1942 No. 1454 Flight formed with Douglas Havocs fitted with Turbinlites for operations in conjunction with the Hurri-

A US 7th Photo Group picture taken on December 4, 1943 as the airfield had been chosen as a base for the US Army Air Force.

Charmy Down is one of the highest aerodromes in Britain lying on a 688-foot-high, flat-topped hill north of Bath. Later in the war it was earmarked for the USAAF's first night fighter group in Europe but in the event no P-61s were ever based there.

Unfortunately none of the Blister hangars seen in the background of the Hurricane photo opposite survive but several brick structures like the control tower still remain to be seen on Hartley Farm.

canes of No. 87 Squadron but, after several abortive attempts at finding the enemy, the idea was discontinued in January 1943.

Away from the main area of activity, the Somerset airfield was fairly safe from the enemy and during 1941 to 1943, the station was an ideal base for units working up for operational duties, and visiting squadrons included Nos. 234 (Madras Presidency), No. 245 (Northern Rhodesia) and Nos. 417 (City of Windsor) and 421 (Red Indian) Squadrons of the RCAF. Two Boston detachments also arrived from Nos. 88 (Hong Kong) and 107 Squadrons for operations. And in February 1943, the Fighter Leaders School — part of No. 52 OTU — took up residence for training flight and squadron commanders.

Later that year, Charmy Down was allocated for use by the American Ninth Air Force. Becoming Station 487 and intended for use by the 4th Tactical Air Depot, their operation was transferred to Kingston Bagpuise in Oxfordshire and instead the airfield was allocated as a base for three American night fighter squadrons. The first personnel of the 422nd Night Fighter Squadron arrived on March 7, 1944 but as their P-61 Black Widow aircraft had not yet materialised, the aircrews spent their time flying various communications aircraft. Joined by the 423rd Night Fighter Squadron on April 18, the following month the 422nd were transferred to Scorton where they eventually got to fly the Black Widow. Meanwhile the 423rd were moved to Chalgrove on May 10 and assigned to the 10th Photographic Group equipped with the Douglas A-20 Havoc. When the 425th Squadron arrived at Charmy Down there were still no Black Widows forthcoming so the original plan for all three squadrons to be trained on P-61s by D-Day never came to fruition.

During the spring of 1944 a Ninth Air Force Troop Carrier Service Wing was formed. This was in support of the troop-carrier units in south-west England. It remained at Charmy until September 1944 when the airfield was returned to RAF control. Several clandestine operations over France were carried out before No. 15 (P) Advanced Flying Unit and 'B' Flight of No. 3 (P) Advanced Flying Unit brought their Oxfords in from Castle Combe. When they left in May 1945, Charmy Down was retained on a care and maintenance basis and was used by trainees of No. 92 Gliding School for Air Cadets, and as a re-settlement centre for Australian personnel. It finally closed in October 1946.

Today, although the main concrete has been removed, the outline remains clearly identifiable.

CHILBOLTON

No. 54 Squadron had a chequered career beginning in 1916 on the Western Front. Following disbandment after the First World War, it was reformed at Hornchurch in 1930 but was posted to Australia in 1942. Stood down at Melbourne in October 1945, it was re-established at Chilbolton in November by renumbering No. 183 Squadron which had returned to the UK from Germany. This is one of their Bristol Centaurus-engined Tempest F.2s (MW795) — the RAF's last piston-engined fighter before the jet age.

In 1939, work began levelling 145 acres of land belonging to Manor Farm which lay one mile south of Chilbolton village in Hampshire to create an airfield sitting 300 feet above sea level. As part of the RAF's expansion plan, Chilbolton was intended to act as a dispersal aerodrome and satellite to the bomber base at Middle Wallop. However, with a change in policy, for a short period the latter became operational as a training airfield before being transferred to Fighter Command and No. 10 Group.

With Middle Wallop being designated a station controlling Sector Y, three squadrons in residence caused severe overcrowding. Consequently, No. 238 Squadron with Hurricanes was dispersed to Chilbolton on September 30, 1940. They were soon in action almost every day and by the end of the Battle of Britain the squadron had lost 17 Hurricanes. The squadron remained at Chilbolton until January 1941 when they returned to Middle Wallop.

The next month they returned to convert to the Mk IIA Hurricane before departing to Pembrey on April 1, 1941 prior to going overseas. This left Chilbolton clear to receive the Poles of No. 308 (Krakow) Squadron who brought in their Spitfires from Baginton on May 31. Converting to the Mk IIA, they left soon after to be replaced by No. 501 (County of Gloucester) Auxiliary Squadron also flying Spitfire IIAs. A stay of a month saw them carrying out convoy patrols before moving over to Ibsley. Their replacement was another auxiliary squadron, No. 504 (County of Nottingham) flying Hurricane IIBs but their stay was also brief as after two weeks they left for Ballyhalbert in County Down, Northern Ireland. During this period of

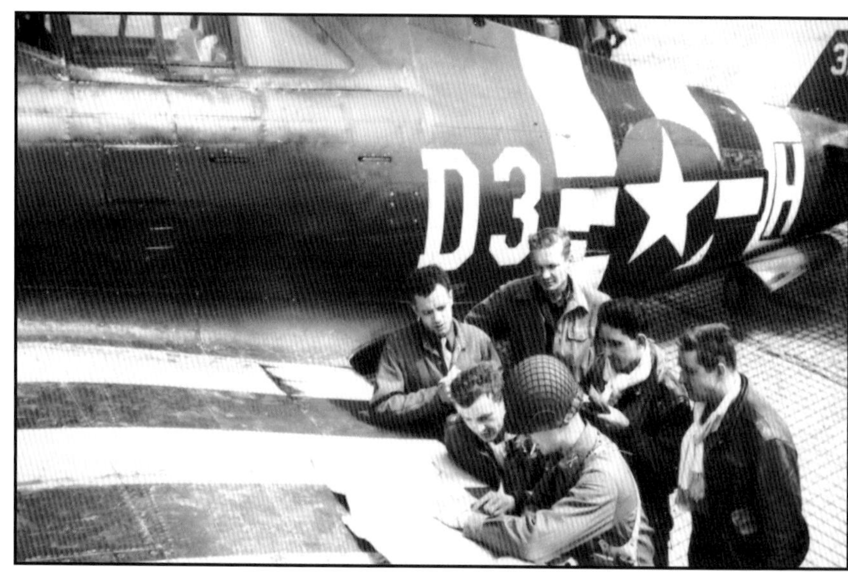

And this is a P-47 of the 397th Fighter Squadron of the 368th Fighter Group.

The fighters may have flown away but a grass strip, some 450 yards long, is now maintained at Chilbolton for light aircraft.

rapid squadron changes, No. 245 (Northern Rhodesia) Squadron arrived to commence offensive operations with their Hurricane IIBs. They carried out several ops over Northern France before moving to the parent station of Middle Wallop in December 1941.

There now came a period of upgrading for Chilbolton. Although the landing area was to remain grass, a concrete perimeter track was added with a number of hardstandings together with three Blister hangars, the completion of which saw the aerodrome become a full No. 10 Group satellite in April 1942.

Ready now to accept a full unit, the Army Co-operation Tomahawks of No. 41 Operational Training Unit moved in from Old Sarum from May till November. However another change in policy saw Chilbolton transferred to No. 70 Group and put on care and maintenance. This however proved to be brief and on December 7 No. 38 Wing took over the aerodrome and it became designated a satellite to Netheravon in place of Shrewton.

It remained in Army hands with the Night Flying Unit of the Glider Pilots Exercise Unit in residence flying Tiger Moths until June 1943 when the aerodrome reverted back to No. 10 Group, Fighter Command. A further period of re-development took place prior to handing Chilbolton over to the US Ninth Air Force to house the 5th Tactical Air Depot. Concrete runways were laid, the first being 1,800 yards aligned 12-30, the second of 1,600 yards on 02-20, and the third 1,400 yards on 07-25. Now known as Station 404, the unit was later joined by the 368th Fighter Group from Greenham Common which arrived on March 15, 1944. The three squadrons in the group — the 395th, 396th and 397th — flew P-47 Thunderbolts and were soon engaged in bombing and strafing airfields, bridges, trains and V-weapon sites in Northern France. After they transferred

From a simple grass field in 1940 to a fully-fledged aerodrome by 1944.

Save for the ghostly imprint of loop dispersals showing through the newly-tilled soil, Chilbolton has returned to farmland . . .

to an airstrip in Normandy, Chilbolton was clear to receive USAAF transport aircraft bringing wounded American servicemen from the European Theater. The 442nd Troop Carrier Group moved in on September 11 and began to run supply flights to the advancing troops in Normandy. Six days later, 45 C-47s took off carrying troops to Holland on Operation 'Market-Garden'. The group moved to the Continent in October 1944 with ambulance flights continuing to use Chilbolton until 1945.

Returned to the RAF and Fighter Command in March of that year, it was used by No. 41 OTU flying Hurricanes, Spitfires, Masters and Martinets. A forward airfield in Sector 'Y' of No. 11 Group, it was used consecutively by Nos. 26, 183 and 247 Squadrons.

With the coming of peace, an experimental role was found for the aerodrome when Vickers Supermarine arrived in 1947 for test flying the Attacker and the Swift. Joined by Folland Aircraft Ltd for testing their Midge jet trainer, the former departed in 1957 leaving Folland to carry out development on their new Gnat.

Experimental work is still carried on there today with the establishment of a radio research station and the Chilbolton Observatory. Subsequently most of the airfield was sold off but a section of one runway was reserved for continued flying. In 1979 a crop-spraying firm, Agricopters Ltd, bought a three and a half acre plot for the use of their helicopters. The domestic site retains many wartime buildings now used as industrial units.

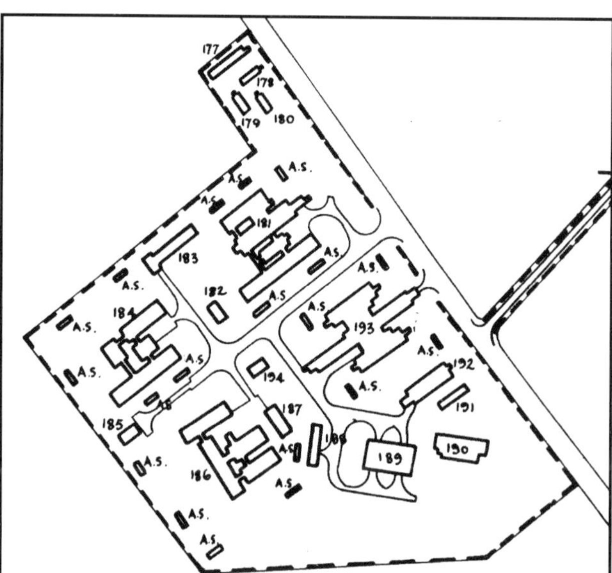

. . . but the Communal Site (No. 2) has survived the intervening years almost unchanged, as can be seen in this oblique shot taken by Geoffrey Hall. [177] W.A.A.F. Decontamination Baths, [178-180] W.A.A.F. Barrack Blocks, [181] Sergeants Mess for 500, [182] Squash Court, [183] Officers & Sergeants Showers and Boiler Room, [184] Officers Mess for 150, [185] C.O.'s Quarters, [186] N.A.A.F.I.'s Institute, [187] N.A.A.F.I.'s Quarters, [188] Ration Store, [189] Fuel Compound, [190] Gymnasium, [191] Airmen's Latrine Block, [192] Airmen's Showers, Ablutions and Decontamination, [193] Airmen's Dining Room.

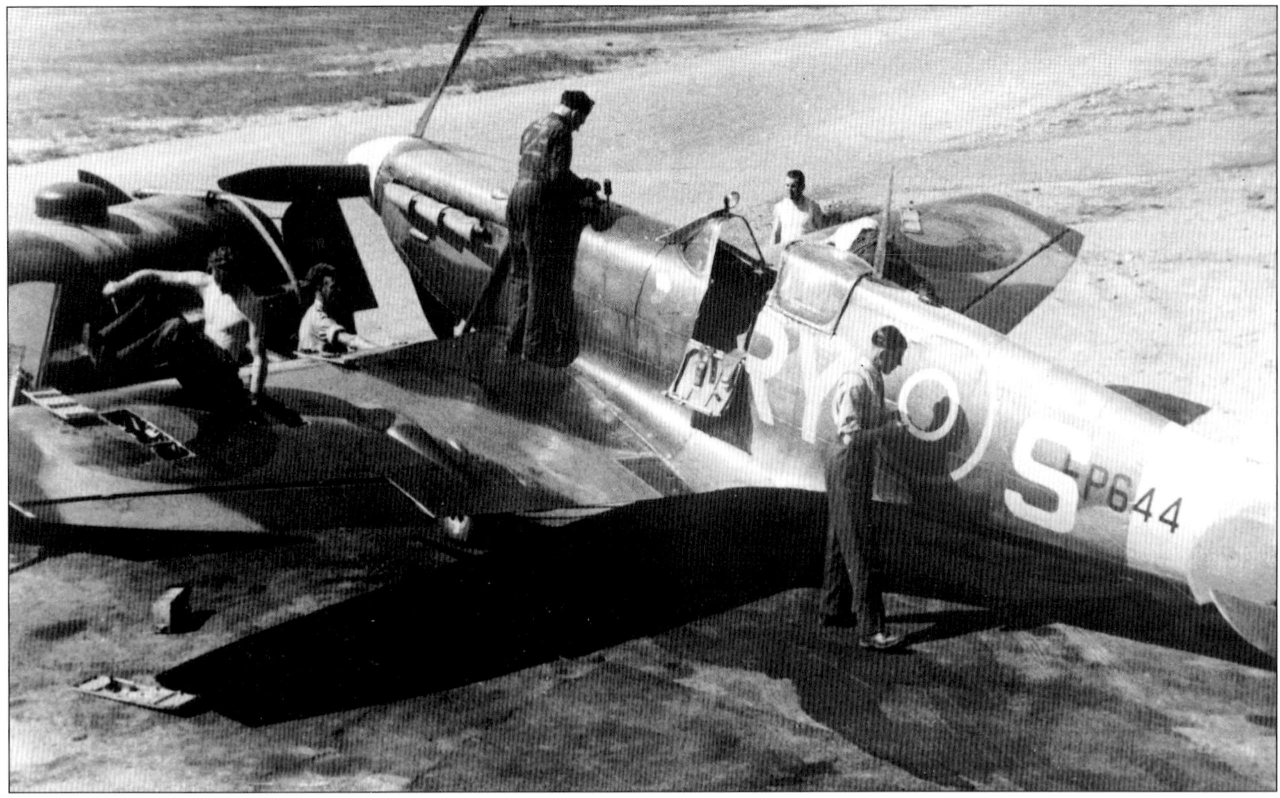

During its wartime service, Church Stanton — or Culmhead as it was known from December 22, 1943 — hosted Polish, Czechoslovakian, Royal Air Force and Fleet Air Arm squadrons. Pictured in the spring of 1943, this Spitfire Mk VB bears the code-letters of No. 313 (Czech) Squadron.

CHURCH STANTON

This Somerset airfield was originally known as Church Stanton but it was renamed Culmhead in December 1943 to avoid possible confusion with the many other airfields that had the prefix 'Church'. Situated eight miles south of Taunton at 865 feet above sea level, it was classified as an operational satellite to Exeter within the confines of No. 10 Group, Fighter Command. Begun in 1940, it consisted of three runways, the longest being 04-22 (1,400 x 50 yards), 15-33 (1,300 x 50 yards) and the shortest 10-28 (1,100 x 50 yards). A tarmac perimeter track led to double blast pens situated around the airfield together with ten Blister hangars.

Opened on August 1, 1941, the first unit to arrive the next day was a Polish squadron, No. 316 (Warsaw), followed by another Polish unit, No. 302 (Poznan) on August 7. Both were flying Hurricanes until the former converted to Spitfires during October. Together they formed No. 2 Polish Fighter Wing, Church Stanton soon being dubbed the 'Polish airfield', convoy patrols and occasional escort duties being the normal activities of

No. 131 Squadron arrived at Church Stanton/Culmhead in September 1943 where they remained until February the following year.

Left: **Both the early Type 17658/40 watch office provided for satellite aerodromes and the later Type 12779/41** *(right)* **still stand.**

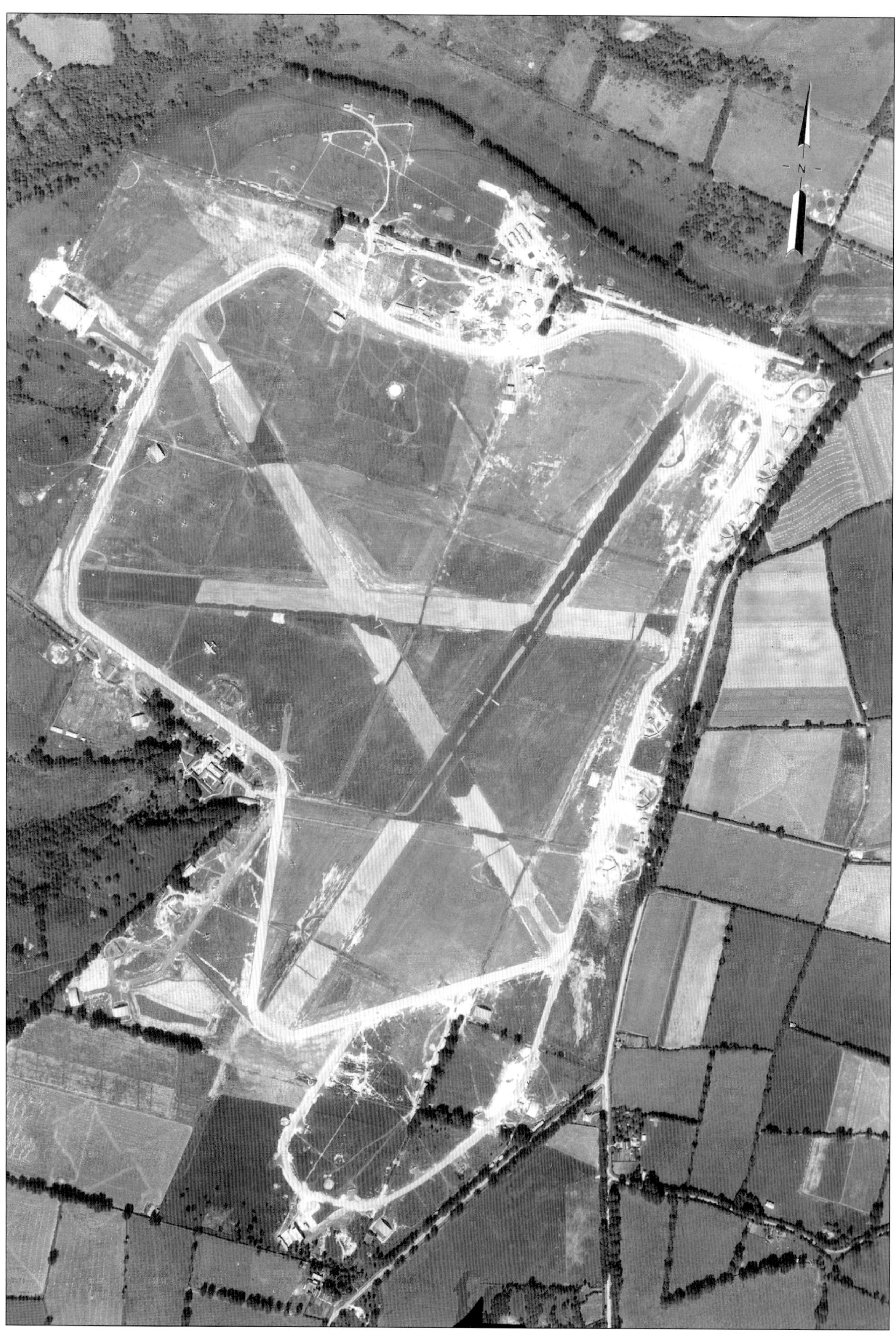

Devoid of any aircraft, the aerodrome photographed from 12,000 feet in August 1943, shortly before No. 131 Squadron arrived.

In the centre of the airfield lies the Culmhead Business Park with quite formidable fencing but this is a leftover from when it was the location for a GCHQ Cheltenham listening station which closed in the 1990s.

the wing. No. 316 moved to Northolt in December to be replaced by No. 306 (Torun) Squadron..

In February 1942 Battles and Wellingtons flew in from the Royal Aircraft Establishment at Farnborough to carry out test flights with equipment designed to cut balloon cables. Later that year the Poles were replaced by two Czechoslovakian squadrons, No. 313 arriving in June and No. 312 in October, both carrying out offensive operations over France. Remaining until June 1943, they took their Spitfires to Peterhead and Warmwell respectively.

Short stays were forthcoming for the Spitfires of No. 66 Squadron and No. 504 (County of Nottinghamshire) Auxiliary Squadron in June but thereafter very little activity took place until No. 131 (County of Kent) and No. 165 (Ceylon) arrived in September. Carrying out sweeps over occupied Europe, No. 165 remained at Culmhead, as it then was, before being posted to Colerne with No. 131 Squadron in February 1944.

With D-Day fast approaching, a brief visit by No. 286 Squadron flying Martinets also saw No. 587 Squadron arrive from Weston Zoyland in April with a variety of aircraft. A mixture of Oxfords, Henleys, Hurricanes and Martinets were now seen at the airfield, while more Oxfords and Fairey Fireflies — the two-seat carrier fighter — joined them from the Fleet Air Arm to form No. 790 (Naval Fighter Direction School).

However, by August, with Culmhead devoid of any units, it was put under care and maintenance until December when it was transferred to No. 23 Group allowing a detachment of No. 3 Glider Training School to move in with Masters and Hotspur gliders. After they left in January 1945 the airfield was used for a short period for storage under the auspices of Maintenance Command before finally closing in August 1946.

The aerodrome remains very intact. It is owned by Rupert Phillips of Burnworthy Manor although rented out to various farmers.

Squadron Leader Ian 'Widge' Gleed touches down at Colerne. He was the CO of No. 87 Squadron from December 1940 until the following November. By 1943 he had been promoted to Wing Commander but lost his life in North Africa in April that year.

COLERNE

Colerne was one of the few wartime airfields to share its facilities with a BOAC repair unit. This civilian status however changed in March 1942 when the unit, which had been repairing and assembling fighter aircraft, was taken over by RAF personnel to become No. 218 Maintenance Unit. Despite its split use, Colerne was still a sector station in Fighter Command in late 1940 with satellites at Filton, Charmy Down and Lulsgate Bottom. Its function was stated as a maintenance unit and night fighter station.

Lying eight miles west-south-west of Chippenham at 595 feet above sea level, the grass landing ground became soft after heavy rain so the addition of three tarmac runways were necessary to give Colerne all-weather capability. The main was 1,600 yards and the secondaries 1,250 and 1,200, all 50 yards wide joined by a 50-foot perimeter track. Being a maintenance unit, the extensive hangarage consisted of one 'J' type, three 'K' types, five 'L' types, a Blister and six Robins. Being one of the last expansion airfields to be built, it was still under construction at the outbreak of war.

Officially opening on January 1, 1940 as a maintenance unit within No. 41 Group, its status as a sector station began on November 27 when the Hurricanes of No. 87 Squadron arrived for a short stay. However it was not until April 27, 1941 that a squadron was posted in for a longer period. This was No. 600 (City of London) Auxiliary Squadron which flew in with Beaufighters. Sending a detachment to Predannack, the entire squadron moved there on October 6.

The arrival of the BOAC repair facility in 1941 coincided with the arrival of the Hurricane Is of No. 316 (Warsaw) Squadron which flew in on June 18. The Poles converted to the Mk IIA and IIB and carried out convoy escort work, claiming a Bf 109 destroyed on June 21 before moving over to Church Stanton. The Whirlwinds of No. 263 (Fellowship of the Bellows-Argentina) arrived for night patrols on

The Air Ministry wartime schematic diagram outlining the three tarmac runways, the main on a bearing of 064 degrees and the secondaries on 004 and 010.

Robin Brooks touching down on the main runway on a rainy day 70 years later.

Left: **Sergeants Jankowiak and Lipinski of No. 307 Polish Squadron with their Defiant night fighter in a sandbagged dispersal in April 1942.** *Right:* **Dispersals still remain although no guarantee that this is exactly the same one.**

January 28, 1942, being joined by the Defiants of No. 264 (Madras Presidency) Squadron. However the lack of success in finding the enemy by night saw the squadron convert to Mosquito IIs during May with detachments being sent to Bradwell Bay, Treblezue and Portreath. Staying for nearly a year at Colerne, they achieved considerable success before departing to Predannack on April 30. Further Mosquito IIs arrived with No. 151 Squadron but a conversion to the Mk XII saw them depart to Middle Wallop on August 16.

The arrival of the Typhoon IBs of No. 183 (Gold Coast) Squadron on May 30 saw Colerne at full squadron strength, and the arrival of an American unit, the 27th Fighter Squadron of the 1st Fighter Group, made dispersal places a premium. Their P-38 Lightnings stayed for two months before moving overseas. The return of No. 151 Squadron on November 17, 1943 heralded conversion to the Mosquito XIII allowing them further success with six aircraft claimed shot down. Moving to Predannack in March 1944, the gap was filled for one month by the Mosquito XVIIs of No. 219 (Mysore) Squadron. With their departure, the Martinets of No. 286 Squadron arrived for two months joined by a detachment of Hurricane IICs of No. 587 Squadron.

The approach of D-Day saw the maintenance unit very busy preparing and storing aircraft needed for the invasion. The two squadrons departed on July 28 and October 1 respectively, leaving the maintenance unit the main occupant. Later arrivals were No. 410 (Cougar) Canadian Squadron; No. 488 Squadron; No. 604 (County of Middlesex) Auxiliary Squadron, and No. 264 Squadron. All spent brief periods at Colerne but by December 1944 they had all departed and it was No. 616 (South Yorkshire) Auxiliary Squadron that brought the first sounds of the jet engine to the airfield. They had re-equipped with the Meteor I at Culmhead in July 1944 to become the first jet-powered squadron in the RAF. When they arrived at Colerne on January 17, 1945, they converted to the Meteor III before taking them to Andrewsfield in Essex on February 28.

By 1946 Colerne had transferred to No. 41 Group and housed Nos. 39 and 218 Maintenance Units until October 1953. Thereafter the airfield became a major transport base until it closed on March 31, 1976.

After the RAF relinquished the base, the Army took it over as a training facility for the Junior Leaders Regiment of the Royal Corps of Transport. Today, it is still very much an active airfield being the home of 21 Signal Regiment, No. 93 (City of Bath) Air Training Corps and the Bristol University Air Squadron which operates a training facility for the RAF alongside No. 3 Air Experience Flight.

EXETER

Situated four miles east of Exeter in Devon, this grass airfield was opened in May 1937 with the dimensions of N-S 850 yards, NE-SW 1,050 yards, E-W 1,500 yards and SE-NW 1,100 yards. Known as Exeter Airport, scheduled domestic flights began the following month. By July 1939, No. 37 Elementary & Reserve Flying Training School run by the Straight Corporation had formed there equipped with Tiger Moths but when war broke out, the training school closed and, with the airfield taken over by the RAF, it became a sector station in No. 10 Group. Extensions to the grass landing area were carried out together with the laying of an asphalt perimeter track and several hardstandings. A Type I Watch Office was added together with three hangars and Drem airfield lighting for night use. Unusually, Exeter was allocated six satellites: Bolt Head, Church Stanton, Harrowbeer, Dunkleigh, Dunkeswell, and Charlton Horethorne.

Initially the airfield was home to a detachment from the Royal Aircraft Establishment at Farnborough which arrived in September 1939 and stayed until February 1942. It was however during July 1940 and the start of the Battle of Britain that the first of several Hurricane fighter squadrons arrived.

No.213 (Ceylon) Squadron flew in during June 1940 to be joined by No. 87 (United Provinces) which sent detachments to Hullavington and Bibury. Both had been driven out of France and were to continue the fight from Exeter until No. 213 moved to Tangmere on September 7 followed by No. 87 on November 28 with a move to Colerne.

No. 601 (County of London) Auxiliary Squadron, fresh from fighting in the Battle of Britain, arrived in September. Known as the 'millionaires squadron' due to the number of wealthy pilots within its ranks, one being Flying Officer Whitney W. Straight, founder of the Straight Corporation, the pre-war owners of Exeter Airport. They spent a very unhappy two months at the 'drome, suffering several accidents, before moving to Northolt on December 17.

The Whirlwinds of No. 263 (Fellowship of the Bellows) Squadron arrived before No. 601 left. Sending a detachment to St Eval, they were mainly engaged on seeking out E-boats in the English Channel that were employed on picking up downed Luftwaffe crews. Pilot Officer J. Stein claimed a probable Ju 88 with a confirmed victory coming on February 8, 1941 when an Ar 196 was shot down by Pilot Officer K. A. Graham. Sadly he was seen to crash into the sea shortly afterwards.

No. 263 were replaced by further Hurricane and Spitfire squadrons: No. 504 (County of Nottingham) arrived in December 1940, remaining until July 1941; No. 66 came in February and left in April 1941, with the Defiants of No. 307 (Lwow) Polish Squadron arriving on April 26. Sending a detachment to Pembrey, they had originally formed as a day fighter squadron but with little success in this role, the Defiants were painted black and their role changed to night fighting and during their first sortie from Exeter, Sergeants Jankowiak and Lipinski flying Defiant N3315 shot down a Ju 88. Conversion to the Beaufighter during August saw further success when a Do 217 and a Ju 88 were shot down in November. Leaving Exeter on April 15, 1943, during their stay they witnessed the upgrading of the airfield when John Laing and Sons arrived in 1942 to construct three runways, the longest being 3,000 yards, second 1,450 yards and third 1,000 yards. A perimeter track 50 yards wide and several hardstandings were built at the same time.

The airfield looking south-west in June 1941.

Exeter at war and peace. Ground crews from No. 601 (County of London) Squadron swarm over one of the unit's Hurricanes on the eastern fringe of the perimeter sometime after the squadron's withdrawal from Tangmere in September 1940.

The airfield was attacked several times, the heaviest being on April 5, 1941 when a hangar and 16 aircraft were badly damaged. In July 1941 another Polish squadron, No. 317 (Wilno) replaced No. 504. Arriving with Hurricanes, it converted to Spitfires to form the No. 2 Polish Wing with Nos. 302 (Poznan) and 316 (Warsaw) Squadrons. When No. 317 moved out to Northolt during April 1942, they were replaced by yet another Polish squadron, No. 308 (Krakow). This period also saw the beginning of the Baedeker raids. These were retaliation raids by the Luftwaffe on English cities, the targets supposedly drawn from the guide books published by Karl Baedeker. Exeter was one of the cities on the list and squadrons operating from Exeter saw the destruction at first hand.

When No. 308 Squadron moved to Hutton Cranswick during May they were replaced by No. 310 (Czech) Squadron flying Spitfire VBs. With a detachment at Bolt Head, the squadron claimed one Do 17 before moving to Castletown in June 1943.

Hurricanes returned to Exeter on May 17, 1942 when No. 247 (China-British) Squadron was posted in. Sending detachments to Predannack, Middle Wallop and Charmy Down, they carried out 'Roadstead' operations before moving to High Ercall in September.

The Typhoons of No. 266 (Rhodesia) Squadron flew in on January 8, 1943. Sending a detachment to Warmwell, the Exeter-based aircraft achieved success when on January 10, Flying Officer Small shot down a FW 190 followed by two similar aircraft on March 13 with further claims later in the month. Leaving Exeter on September 7 for Gravesend, they were to return for a few days on September 10.

An increase in E-boat activity in the Channel during 1943 saw units from the Fleet Air Arm based at the airfield. Nos. 825, 834 and 816 Squadrons were equipped with black-painted Swordfish while No. 841 had Alba-

core torpedo bombers. However the difficulty in finding targets made for a frustrating time for all these squadrons.

Arriving in April 1943, No. 125 (Newfoundland) Squadron added Air-Sea Rescue duties to their workload. Flying Beaufighters, they still achieved success at night when on June 13, Pilot Officer McLachlin and Pilot Officer W.E. Pettifer managed to shoot down a Ju 88 over Devon. Moving to Valley in November 1943, they were replaced by the Canadians of No. 406 (Lynx) Squadron which converted to the Mosquito XII for the build-up to D-Day.

Spitfires based at Exeter over this period belonged to the auxiliary squadrons of Nos. 616 (South Yorkshire) and 610 (County of Chester). Although all the three fighter squadrons were to take part in the invasion, by April 1944 they had been withdrawn as Exeter was being handed over to the USAAF. Now Station 463, the arrival of the 440th Troop Carrier Group on April 15 saw a large number of C-47s arrive. They carried out drops on D-Day itself and backed up the operation with fuel and ammunition supply over the following days. Remaining until August 7, they moved to Ramsbury before returning to Exeter on August 23. Finally leaving in September, the airfield was then used for receiving evacuated wounded troops from France.

Returned to the RAF, the rest of the war saw Exeter used as an Air-Sea Rescue base until 1945, remaining in Fighter Command until transferred to the Ministry of Civil Aviation in 1947 to become a commercial airport once again.

Above: **This is Exeter at the end of the war.** *Below:* **The main runway has since been lengthened to 2,277 yards.**

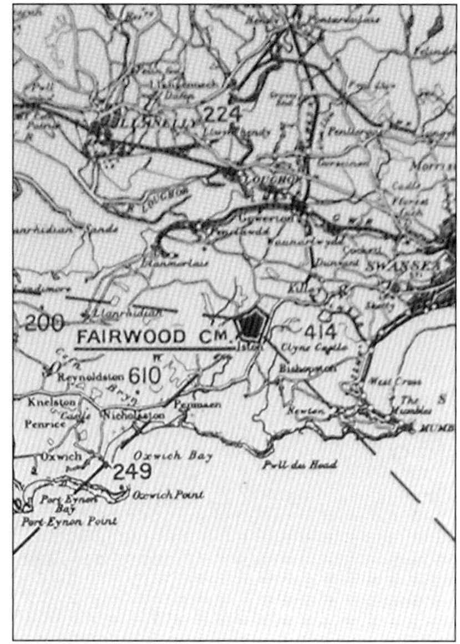

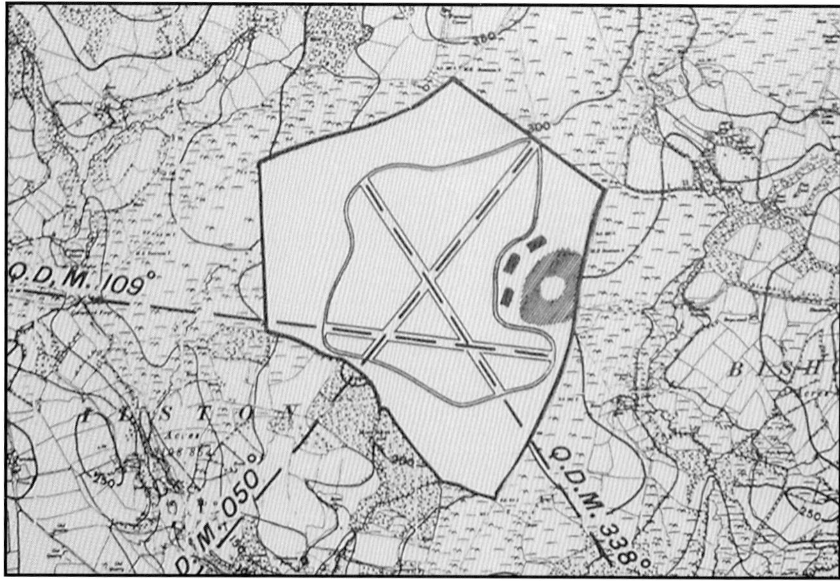

FAIRWOOD COMMON

Sitting 272 feet above sea level, Fairwood Common lay four miles west of Swansea in Glamorgan, alongside the A4118 road. After extensive levelling and the filling of boggy land, the airfield opened as a fighter station in No. 10 Group on June 15, 1941. By October its function changed to that of a sector station with satellites at Angle and Pembrey. Three hard runways were laid, all 1,100 yards but later the main was extended to 1,600 yards and the second to 1,300 yards. A 50-foot perimeter track led to three aeroplane sheds and four Blister hangars. A Type I Flying Control was built and a Drem lighting system installed.

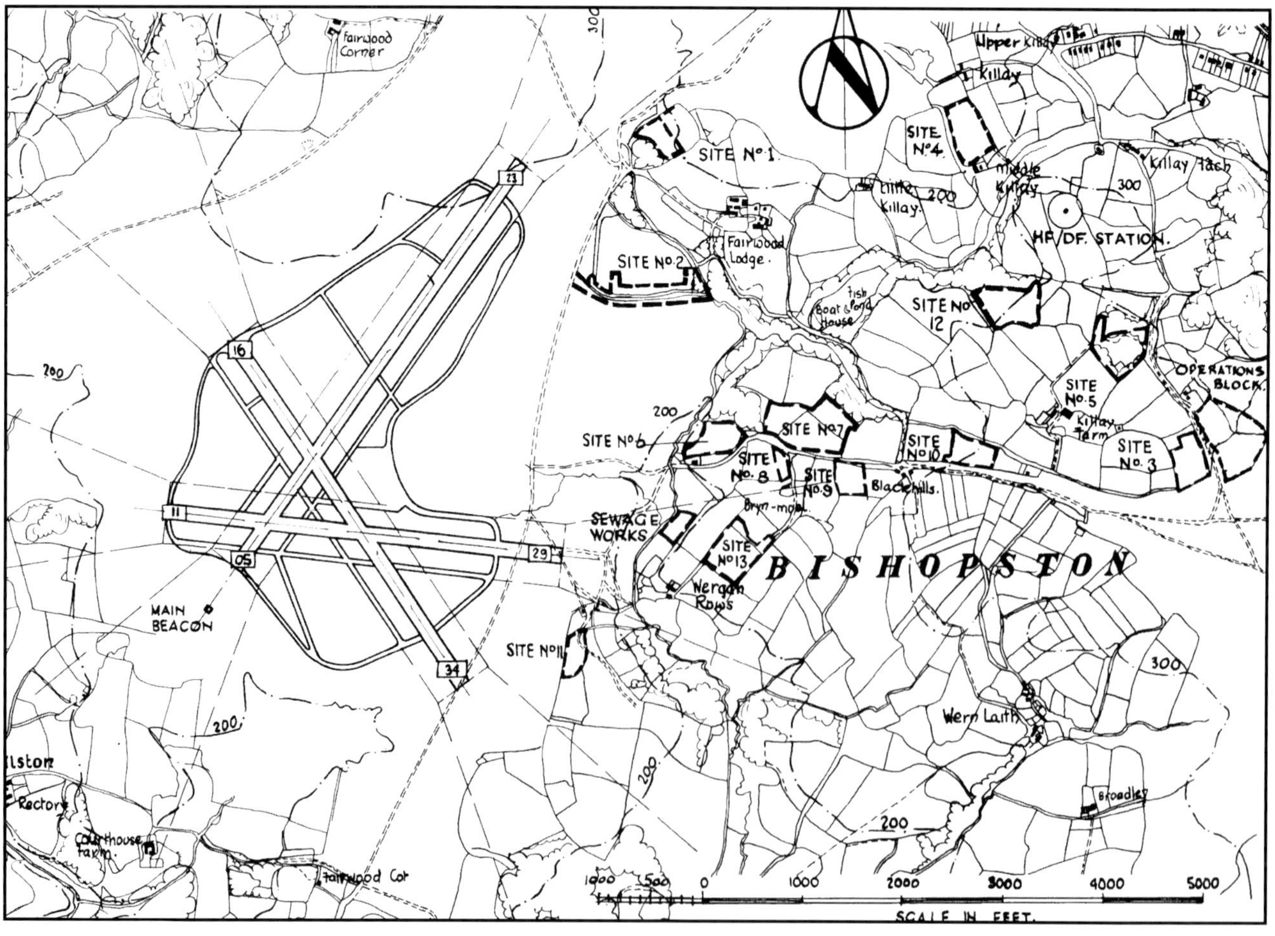

The transition from a Fighter Command station to a civil airport. Fairwood Common was opened in 1941 with three 1,100-yard runways but, like at most other aerodromes, these had to be progressively increased to cater for the advances in aircraft development. The magnetic heading of each runway (QDM) had to be changed over the years depending on the shift in magnetic variation.

By 1945 the main 05-23 had been lengthened to 1,600 yards and the secondaries 16-34 and 11-29 by an additional 200 yards at their eastern ends. All purpose-built wartime aerodromes were provided with a number of dispersed sites so as not to provide easy targets for administration and living areas. Fairwood Common had 13 such sites. No. 1: Officers latrines, Sergeants and airmen's quarters. No. 2: Ditto plus works and stores. No. 3: Living quarters for officers, NCOs and airmen. Nos. 4 and 5: WAAF quarters. No. 6: Quarters for all ranks. No. 7: Communal site — dining, gym, NAAFI, barber, tailor and shoemaker, etc. No. 8: Sergeants' Mess and bath house. No. 9: Officers' Mess and baths plus tennis and squash courts. No. 10: Sick quarters, ambulance, mortuary, fire pool. Nos. 11, 12 and 13: All ranks quarters and latrines.

Today, although the main runway (04-22) of what is now Swansea Airport appears longer, its useable length is listed as 1,476 yards and the secondary 10-28 at 937 yards.

First to be stationed there were the Hurricanes of No. 79 (Madras Presidency) Squadron which transferred from Pembrey in June. They were based at Fairwood Common primarily for the defence of Wales but saw little action. Two days after their arrival they were joined by the Beaufighter IIFs of No. 600 (City of London) Auxiliary Squadron. Sending a detachment to Predannack, this unit moved to Colerne nine days later. Their replacement was the City of Wilno Squadron of the Polish Air Force, No. 317. Having worked up on Hurricane Is at Colerne they moved to Fairwood Common. A quick conversion to the Hurricane IIB saw success when the squadron shot down a Ju 88 before moving to Exeter on July 21.

A similar conversion from Hurricane Is to IIBs came to No. 504 (County of Nottingham) Auxiliary Squadron who flew in the same day. Staying barely three weeks, they departed before Fairwood Common was upgraded to sector status. A flurry of activity around this time saw No. 79 leave with Nos. 312 (Czech), 615 (County of Surrey) and 263 (Fellowship of the Bellows) Squadrons coming and going, the latter leaving on April 18, 1942, eight days before the second Baedeker raid took place on nearby Bath.

No. 125 (Newfoundland) Squadron arrived on September 24, 1941 with Defiant Is. Conversion to Defiant IIs saw them scrambled several times over Bristol and South Wales. Moving to Colerne on January 25, 1942, they left a detachment behind at Fairwood Common. By February they had converted to Beaufighter IIFs with the entire squadron returning on May 14. During a sortie on June 27, Squadron Leader F. D. Hughes shot down a Ju 88 which crashed into the sea off County Wickford, Eire. July saw further kills when Pilot Officer G. E. Jameson shot down a He 111 over Cemaes Head, Pembrokshire, on the night of July 27/28. One month later another He 111 fell to the guns of No. 125 Squadron. Conversion to the Beaufighter VIF in September saw the squadron send detachments to Peterhead and Sumburgh. The month also saw further kills when a Ju 88 and an Ar 196 were shot down. With a further two Dorniers to their credit, the squadron moved to Exeter in April 1943.

Shortly after they left, No. 307 (Lwow) Squadron arrived with the first Mosquitos to be based at Fairwood. They commenced night operations followed by daylight patrols before leaving for Predannack in August. The airfield saw further Mosquito squadrons based there with No. 264 (Madras Presidency) arriving in July and departing in November, being replaced by No. 456 (Australian) Squadron which remained until February 1944, having re-equipped with the Mosquito XVII.

Beaufighters returned on March 1 when No. 68 Squadron flew in from Coleby Grange. Sadly a mock dogfight over the airfield ended in tragedy when one Beaufighter shot down another, killing two crew members.This was the last fighter squadron to be based at Fairwood Common as it thereafter became a training station, hosting several Armament Practice Camps. Other detachments followed before it closed as an operational RAF station in October 1946. Fairwood later re-opened as Swansea Airport.

The Bellman hangar was designed in 1936 by Mr N. S. Bellman of the Directorate of Works, some 400 being manufactured by Head Wrightson & Co. of Teeside. Although they were only intended to be temporary, one still remains in use at Swansea.

FILTON

This Hurricane was on the strength of No. 504 Squadron when it was pictured at Filton in 1940. This particular aircraft, L1590, is listed as being struck off charge in May that year.

During the First World War, Filton was used as a base for squadrons destined for France and also as an aircraft acceptance park. Between the wars it continued its flying activities with the establishment of No. 2 Elementary & Reserve Flying Training School and also as a base for No. 501 (County of Gloucester) Auxiliary Squadron.

Lying four and three quarter miles north-west of Bristol at 250 feet above sea level, Filton became an operational satellite to Colerne during 1939. Initially it had a grass-surfaced landing area with dimensions of 2,000 yards N-S and E-W; 1,700 NE-SW and 1,000 yards SE-NW, but by 1941 it had a single tarmac runway 1,000 x 50 yards. A 35-foot perimeter track and five 'B' Type hangars were built as well as 12 pens, four huts and four sleeping shelters. Noted obstructions were a balloon barrage for the defence of Bristol.

No. 263 (Fellowship of the Bellows) Squadron reformed as a fighter unit on October 2, 1939 with biplane Gladiators. They worked up at Filton carrying out several scrambles before being earmarked to go to Norway. Leaving on April 24, 1940, the Hurricanes of No. 504 (County of Nottingham) Squadron arrived on September 26. After a short stay they departed for Exeter on December 18. The next day the Hurricanes of No. 501 (County of Gloucester) Auxiliary Squadron, now a fighter unit, arrived from Kenley where they had been engaged during the Battle of Britain. They left to convert to the Spitfire at Colerne in April 1941.

With the Bristol Aeroplane and Engine Company sharing the airfield, the production of the Bristol Blenheim necessitated the setting up of a ferry flight. Formed in 1939, it later adopted the name of No. 2 Ferry Pilots Pool. Despite the danger of the balloon barrage around Bristol, the Luftwaffe paid several visits to Filton, the first on June 24, 1940. With the main target being the aeroplane works, the worst raid came on September 27 when 60 aircraft crossed the coast at Weymouth and attacked the factory. Estimations at the time gave 60 dead with 150 injured, all the casualties being the result of two direct hits on air raid shelters. Resident at the time was No. 504 Squadron which was scrambled when raiders appeared over the Parnall Aircraft Works at Yate near Bristol. In the ensuing dogfight, the squadron claimed five enemy aircraft either shot down or damaged. By December 18 they had moved to Exeter.

No. 501 Squadron came back again before finally leaving in April 1941. That same month, No. 263 Squadron, which had returned from Norway in June 1940 and had converted to the Whirlwind, arrived to commence convoy patrols. However,very little success in engaging the enemy saw them move to Charmy Down in August. This was the last fighter squadron to be based at Filton as a change from No. 10 Group to No. 44 Group saw the airfield become an overseas aircraft preparation unit. Changing its name to No. 2 Aircraft Preparation Unit during 1942, No. 528 Squadron formed at Filton on June 15, 1943 flying Blenheim IVs and Hornet Moths for the purpose of calibrating the local radar stations. Remaining until September 1944, they were absorbed into No. 527 Squadron.

With the Ferry Flight remaining, contractors moved in to extend the main runway in preparation for test flying the mighty Bristol Brabazon airliner. Additional buildings were also constructed when the airfield was transferred to the Ministry of Supply on August 7, 1946. Elements of the RAF remained, part of No. 62 Group, Reserve Command, to give Air Cadets air experience flights and until 1957 Filton was also the home of the newly-reformed No. 501 (County of Gloucester) Auxiliary Squadron. The airfield was also shared between British Aerospace and Rolls-Royce for test and flight evaluation purposes but it was announced by BAE Systems in 2011 that Filton would close in December 2012.

The beginning . . . and the end. Most of the wartime buildings have since been demolished and the airfield is currently owned by British Aerospace. The first flight of the Concorde prototype (002) took place at Filton on April 9, 1969, and all other British-built Concordes used the main runway for their first flights. The last by the supersonic airliner on November 26, 2003 also took place at Filton.

Above: **Filton suffered a heavy raid on September 27, 1940, the Luftwaffe taking this picture in the aftermath of the attack. The airfield was then grass but by December 1943** ***(right)*****, two runways had been laid down.**

The main runway was lengthened in 1949 for the maiden flight of the Bristol Brabazon and was extended again in the late 1960s to 1½ miles for the Concorde. It is also one of the widest in Britain at 100 yards. The airfield served as a dispersed site for V-Bombers during the Cold War, and Vulcan bombers were stationed there during the Cuban Missile Crisis in October 1962.

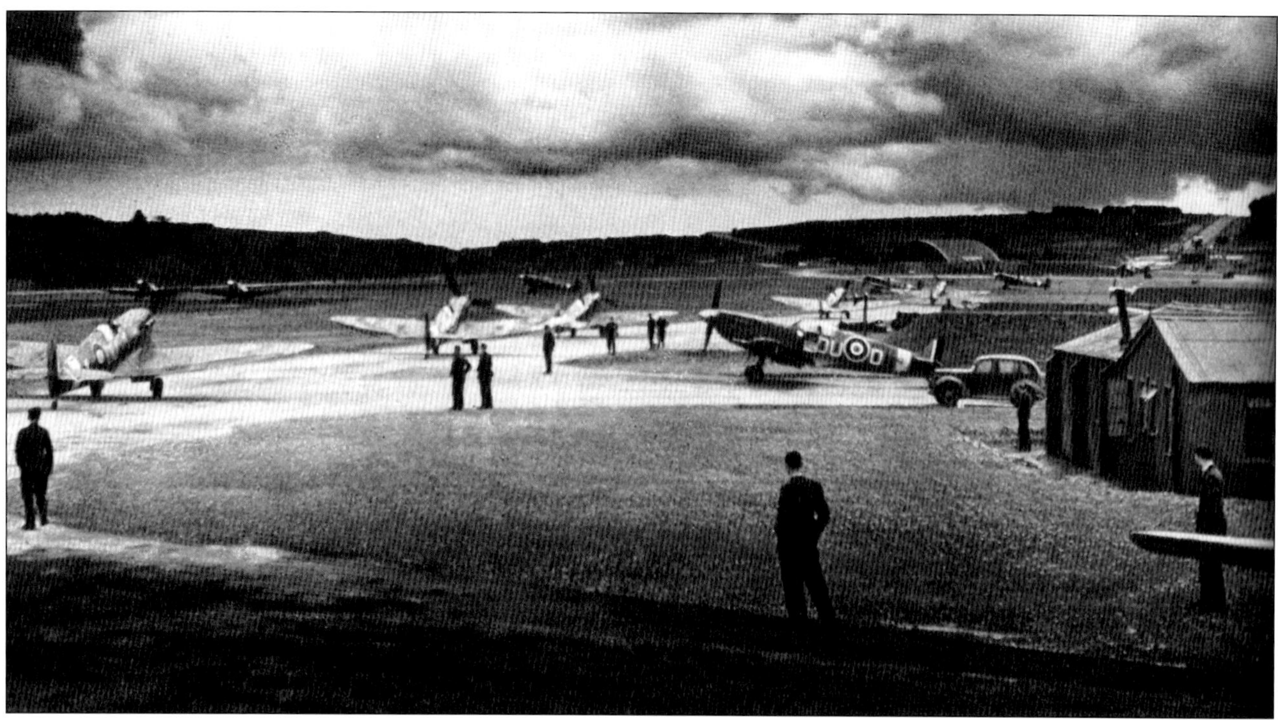

HARROWBEER

No. 312 (which had been formed in August 1940 at Duxford) was a Czech squadron which served at over 20 Fighter Command stations apart from Harrowbeer where it was pictured in 1942.

Classified as a forward fighter aerodrome in Fighter Command, Harrowbeer's other functions were air-sea rescue and calibration. Located six miles south-east of Tavistock in Devon, the airfield lay 640 feet above sea level and at this height was prevalent to 40 per cent risk of sea fog. With construction beginning in late 1940, three tarmac runways were laid on a hardcore base of rubble from blitzed buildings in the Plymouth area. The main was 1,300 yards and the secondaries 1,100 and 900 yards, all 50 yards wide. A 35-foot perimeter track led to shelter bays and two Bellman and four Over Blisters. Night landing facilities were Glim lights and Goose Neck flares. A large house named 'Ravenscroft' served as the station headquarters whilst another served as a temporary watch office before a purpose-built one was erected in late 1941.

Officially opening on August 15, 1941, first in was a detachment from No. 500 (County of Kent) Auxiliary Squadron with Blenheims. Then in October came the Spitfires IIs of No. 130 (Punjab) Squadron tasked with shipping patrols and occasional bomber escort duties. Converting quickly through the Spitfire VA to the VB, the squadron was posted to Warmwell on November 30.

With its secondary function as an air-sea rescue station, No. 276 Squadron formed at Harrowbeer on October 21, 1941 equipped with Lysanders and Hurricanes. The addition of a Walrus in 1942 saw detachments sent to Portreath, Warmwell, Perranporth and Fairwood Common. Later years saw Spitfires, Defiants, Ansons and a Sea Otter join the squadron before it finally left for Portreath in April 1944.

With the arrival of No. 302 (Poznan) Squadron on November 1, 1941, Harrowbeer began a period of intensive operations comprising bomber escort and convoy patrols, their Hurricanes having now been exchanged for Spitfires. Moving to Warmwell on April 27, 1942, they returned to Harrowbeer a month later for five days. That month also saw an attack on the airfield but with little material damage.

As No. 302 left, No. 312 (Czech) Squadron arrived from Fairwood Common with Spitfire VBs. This was the first of several stays during the summer of 1942 leaving finally on August 20.

Hurricanes returned with No. 175 Squadron. Flying the IIBs in the fighter-bomber role, a two-month stay from October 1942 saw them depart to Gatwick. Replacing

The foundation of the huts are in the trees on the right and those of the Blister hangar lie beyond the trees in the middle distance.

One of the squadron's Spitfires — a Mk V — prepares for another operation.

the Hurricanes were the Typhoons of No. 193 (Brazil) Squadron. They formed at Harrowbeer on December 18, 1942 as a fighter-bomber, ground attack squadron. A brief move to Gravesend in August 1943 saw them back at Harrowbeer on September 18 having become fully operational. Joined by the Whirlwinds of No. 263 Squadron for a month, both squadrons were flying low-level strikes against targets in France.

No. 183 Squadron, which arrived with Typhoons on June 5, 1943 and stayed for two months, carried out attacks on marshalling yards and railways. By August the Typhoon squadrons had left with No. 193 returning to partner No. 266 (Rhodesia) Squadron. The two units then formed the Harrowbeer Wing and were tasked with operations against the V1 sites in France. In the run-up to D-Day, Harrowbeer saw frequent squadron changes with Nos. 263 (Fellowship of the Bellows), 610 (County of Chester), 193 (Brazil), 64 and 611 (West Lancs) Squadrons arrive at various periods for anti-shipping sorties. Two months after D-Day, Harrowbeer was placed on care and maintenance, being used occasionally by the US Navy.

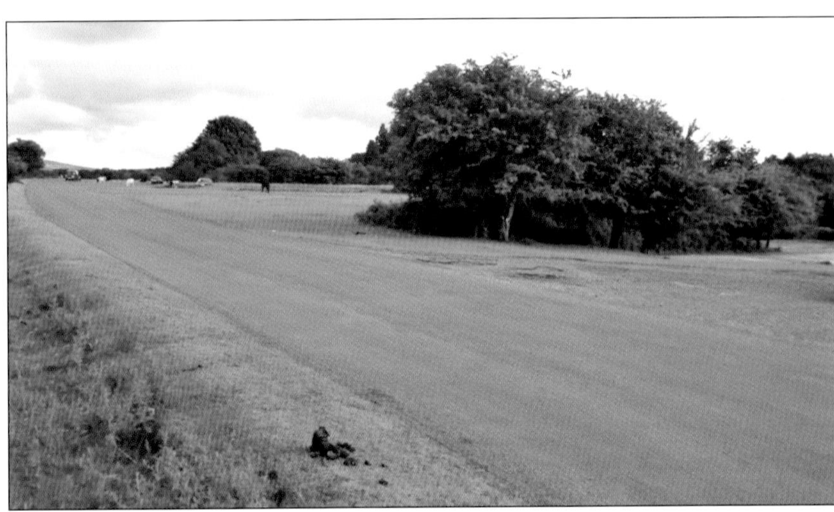

Steve Casely explored Harrowbeer and matched up the wartime shot.

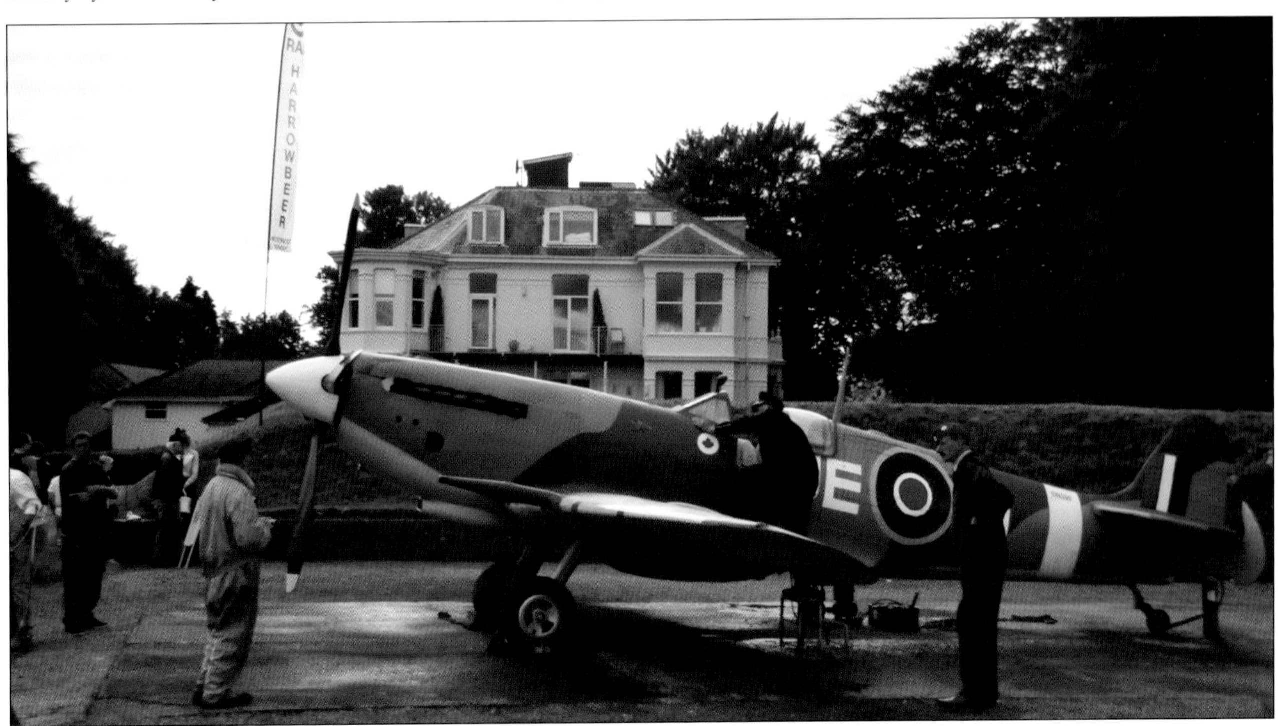

In August 2013, a Spitfire — albeit a replica fitted with a Rolls-Royce Meteor tank engine — was once again to be seen at Harrowbeer, brought in for a special event marking the 1940s. Visitors could pay to sit in the cockpit while the engine was fired up. The white building known as Ravenscroft was the headquarters of No. 276 (ASR) Squadron.

Members of No. 276 Squadron outside Ravenscroft. Then it was the squadron HQ but now it is a nursing home.

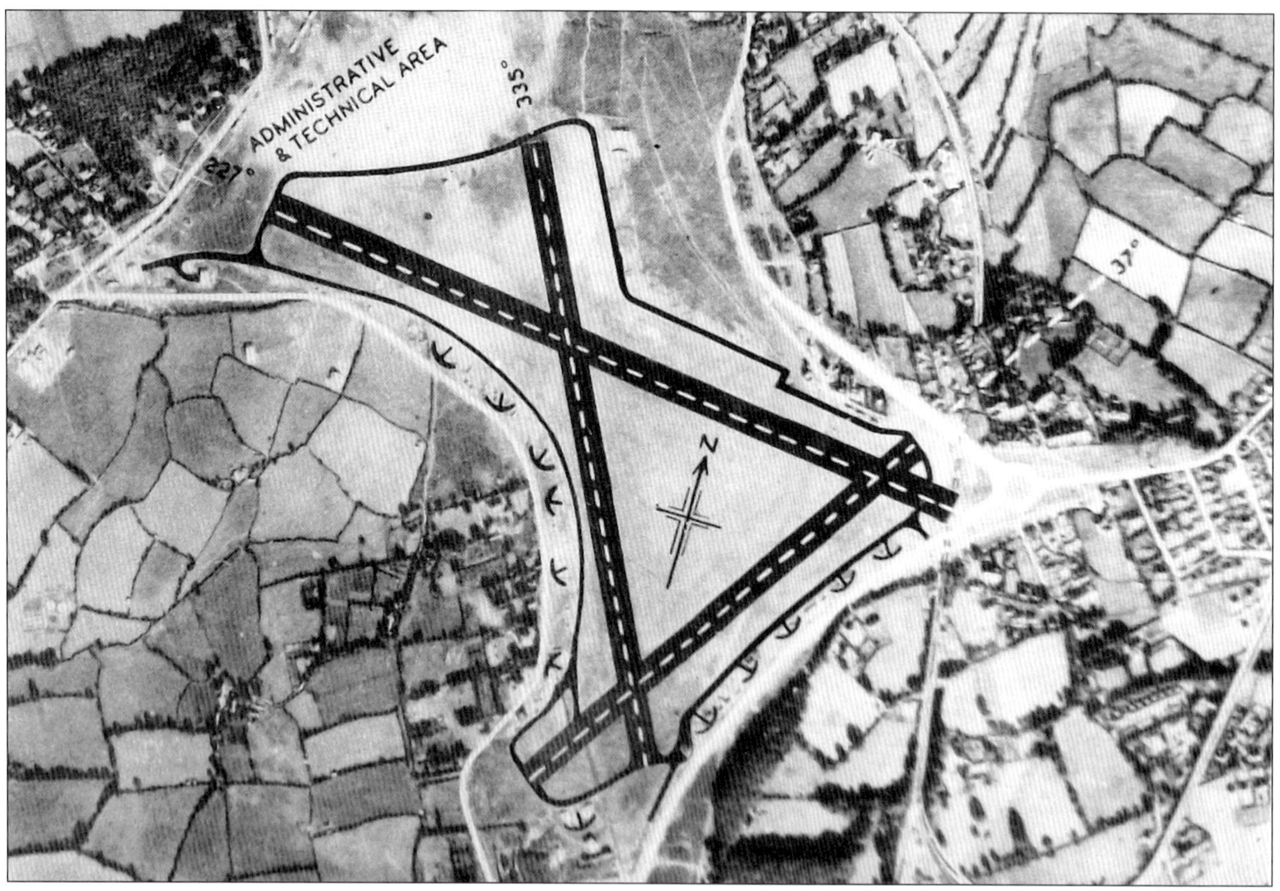

In 1942 the Duke of Kent visited Harrowbeer and was photographed with members of the Czech squadron. This is the left-hand butressed hut seen in the photo on page 78.

Because the impressions of the three butresses which strengthened the walls were still apparent in the concrete base, Steve Casely was able to take an exact match.

No. 193 Squadron was inaugurated at Harrowbeer in December 1942 when it was earmarked to be equipped with Typhoons. Initial attacks on V1 sites in France were followed by air support for the armies on the Continent.

A new lease of life came in January 1945 when No. 275 (ASR) Squadron arrived with Walrus aircraft together with No. 26 (South African) Squadron with Mustangs and No. 691 Squadron equipped with Barracudas, Defiants, Hurricanes and Oxfords. The latter squadron soon added Spitfires and Vengeance to its stable. With the South Africans leaving for Chilbolton on May 23 and No. 691 departing for Exeter on August 1, the airfield reverted back to care and maintenance, finally closing on May 13, 1946. The military returned in 1947 when a communications flight arrived with Ansons and Dominies but was placed back on care and maintenance in 1948, Transferred to the Ministry of Civil Aviation, it was hoped that the site could become Plymouth Airport. However local opposition defeated the plan and Harrowbeer returned to agriculture. In 1981, a granite memorial was erected as a tribute to all the military personnel who had served there with Plymouth Airport becoming established at Roborough airfield.

HOLMSLEY SOUTH

Holmsley South was one of over a dozen airfields in the New Forest area, including Beaulieu, Bisterne, Christchurch, Hurn, Ibsley, Lymington, Stoney Cross, Warmwell and Winkton, which all played an important part in the run up to D-Day.

Five miles north-east of Christchurch on the A35 road in Hampshire can be found the remains of Holmsley South. Designated an airfield in Coastal Command in 1942, it was built to Class A standard with three converging hard runways, each 50 yards wide. The longest, 07-25, was 1,970 yards, 12-30 was 1,400 yards and 18-36 was 1,370 yards. A 50-foot perimeter track led to panhandle dispersals with hangarage consisting of two T2s, one with 23 bays the other of 13 bays. Domestic accommodation consisted mainly of Maycrete and Nissen huts to provide for the expected 2,963 personnel.

With construction beginning in 1941, the North African landings forced the work ahead when the airfield became needed for the support of Operation 'Torch'. Finally opening in summer 1942, though far from complete, Holmsley South was delegated to No. 19 Group, Coastal Command. The primitive facilities allowed a detachment of Whitleys of No. 502 (Ulster) Squadron to arrive during late summer followed by the formation of No. 547 Squadron on October 22, with Wellington VIIIs. Used in an anti-shipping role, they moved to Chivenor on December 10.

Preparations for 'Torch' also saw the arrival of the USAAF when the B-24 Liberators of the 330th Squadron, 93rd Bomb Group, arrived to assist in anti-U-boat operations prior to the landings but once 'Torch' was over the unit moved back to Alconbury.

Mosquito Mk VI, believed to belong to the Canadian squadron, No. 418 (City of Edmonton), at Holmsley South. The squadron was stationed there from April to July 1944 during which time they claimed their 100th victory.

The end of 1942 also saw further Whitleys arrive when No. 58 Squadron left Stornoway for Holmsley South. Arriving on December 2, they converted to Halifax IIs before leaving for St Eval and returning to Holmsley South in June 1943.

Having converted to the Halifax II at St Eval, the rest of No. 502 Squadron moved to join the detachment at Holmsley South on March 2, 1943. Two weeks later it returned to St Eval before coming back on June 30.

Although the runways are derelict and taken over by the Forestry Commission, several camping sites and a caravan park have been established on the airfield.

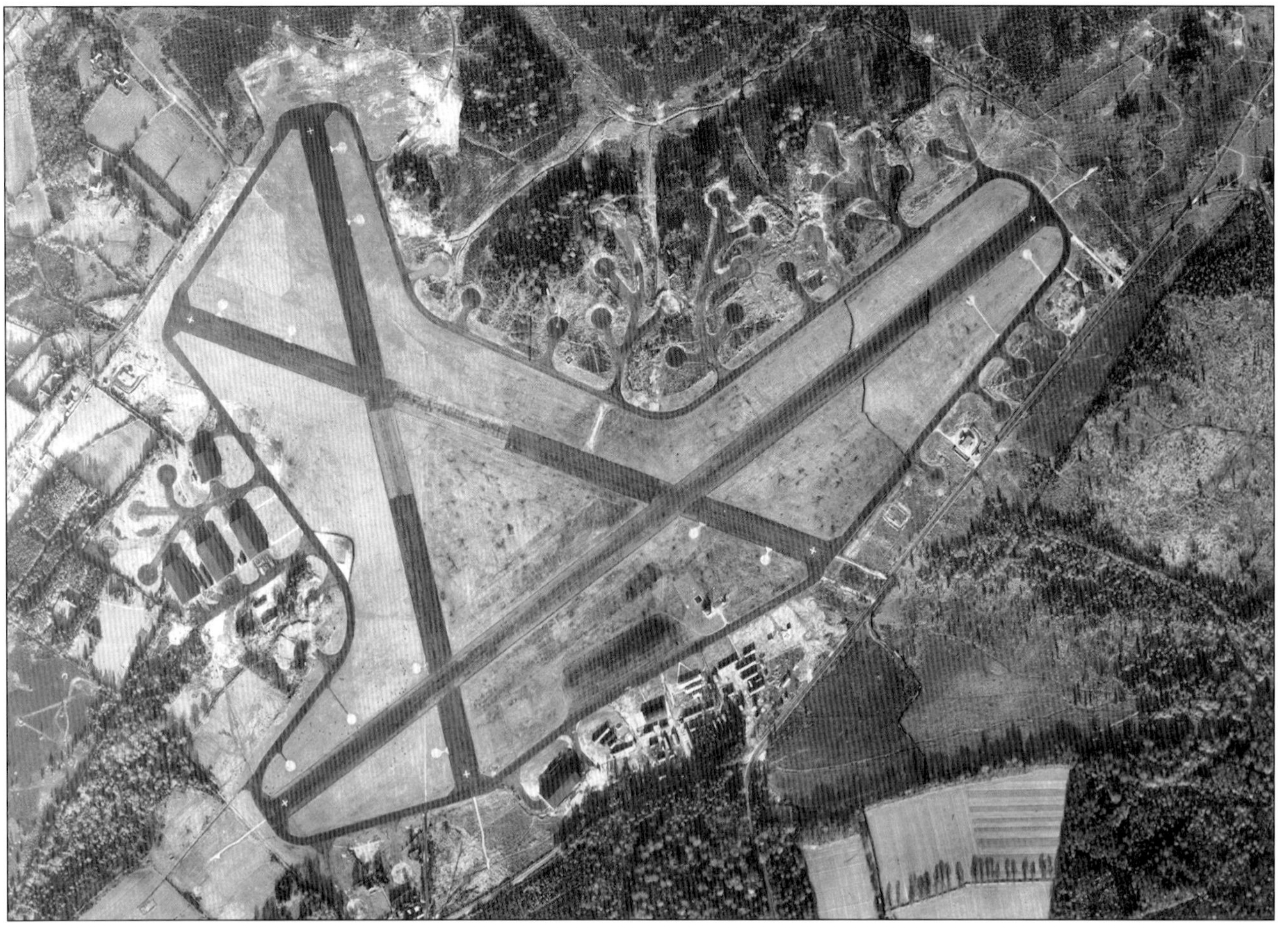

Above: **Holmsley South as it appeared in December 1946, then relegated to care and maintenance status.**

Below: **With much of the concrete removed, nature is reclaiming what remains.**

In July 1944 the airfield was handed over to the US Ninth Air Force and the 394th Bomb Group moved in with Marauders. *Above:* **Armourers fitting tail fins to 500lb bombs on a hardstanding in the north-eastern corner. The aircraft belongs to the 586th Bomb Squadron.** *Right:* **Bombing up 43-34194 K5✪S of the 584th Bomb Squadron.**

Further Halifax aircraft flew in on May 1, 1943 when the Mk Vs of No. 295 Squadron came in from Netheravon. Holmsley South now became a conversion airfield for Whitley squadrons re-equipping with the Halifax. A one-month stay by No. 295 saw a detachment of touring gliders to Goubrine in North Africa before the rest of the squadron left for Hurn. By the end of the year the Halifax squadrons had all departed and the station was transferred to No. 10 Group, Fighter Command.

Now classified as a fighter station, Nos. 441 (Silver Fox), 442 (Caribou) and 443 (Hornet) Squadrons of the RCAF arrived on March 18, 1944 with Spitfires. Forming No. 144 Wing, their stay at Holmsley South was only for a brief working up period before they left, being replaced by No. 121 Wing consisting of Nos. 174 (Mauritius), 175 and 245 (Northern Rhodesia) Squadrons. Flying Typhoon IBs, they arrived during April for pre-D-Day operations. On D-Day itself the wing was busy in support of the landings but once the Allies had established a foothold, it moved to Camilly in Normandy in mid-June.

The first Mosquitos had flown in from Ford on April 8. The Canadian No. 418 (City of Edmonton) Squadron had claimed its hundredth victory flying from there with the intruder operations continuing from Holmsley South over D-Day. Their stay also included flying night patrols against the flying bombs. A move to Hurn on July 14 later saw them attacking the V2 rocket sites.The Mustangs of Nos. 129 (Mysore), 306 (Torun) and 315 (Deblin) Squadrons arrived from the Advanced Landing Ground at Coolham on June 22. All three remained for a few days carrying out several patrols against the V-weapons before moving on to Ford.

When they left, Holmsley South became Station 455 of the US Ninth Air Force. That prompted the arrival of the 584th, 585th, 586th and 587th Bomb Squadrons of the 394th Bomb Group. Operating B-26 Marauders, they arrived over the four days from July 24-28. Commencing light bomber operations over France, the group received a Distinguished Unit Citation for its work against rail bridges and ammunition dumps. In one raid, Captain Darrell R. Lindsey was awarded a posthumous Medal of Honor when he stayed with his damaged aircraft during a bomb run and then ordered his crew to bale out whilst he continued to control the aircraft. The group had moved onto the Continent by August 31.

For just over a month Holmsley South had no units and further aircraft did not arrive until October when it was transferred to No. 116 Wing, Transport Command. No. 167 Squadron reformed there with Warwicks in November 1944 to begin transport services to France. Liberators also returned when No. 246 Squadron came in from Lyneham to begin services to the Middle and Far East. Additional aircraft flown were Halifax IIIs, Yorks and finally in April 1945 Skymasters. Holmsley South was placed into care and maintenance on October 16, 1946, the site later being reclaimed by the Forestry Commission.

A memorial now stands at the western end of the old main runway (accessible from the A35) to remember all those who served at the 12 airfields situated in the New Forest area.

IBSLEY

One of the first airfields to be built within the New Forest in Hampshire, Ibsley officially opened on February 15, 1941. Early morning fog was a problem as it lay on meadowland only 80 feet above sea level. The main contractor was John Mowlem & Company and, once completed, it was given satellite status to Middle Wallop.

Although originally a grass airfield, three asphalt runways were added later in the year, the longest being 1,200 x 50 yards with the other two 1,000 x 50 yards. Initially a Type 17658/40 Watch Office for fighter satellite stations was built but this was later demolished and replaced by a Type 518/40 incorporating a meteorological section. The addition of a concrete floor later classified it as a Type 8936/40 Watch Office. Two Bellman Hangars and 12 Blister Hangars of various sizes were built with double fighter pens added at a later date. Shortly after Ibsley had opened, a film crew arrived to shoot many of the scenes featured in the film *The First of the Few*.

Ibsley came to the attention of the Luftwaffe and was attacked on the night of March 13, 1941, damaging a Hurricane of No. 32 Squadron which moved to Pembrey the following month. At the same time, the Spitfire IIAs of No. 118 Squadron flew in from Warmwell. This was the start of a long association between the squadron and Ibsley with detachments being sent to Perranporth and Predannack. Converting through the Spitfire marks to the VB, operational patrols began initially with disastrous results. On May 4, in a friendly fire incident, a Whitley was shot down in error, fortunately with the

Ibsley began life as a grass airfield, captured forever on film in October 1941.

British Aviation Pictures Ltd wanted footage taken at a fighter station for their film *The First of the Few* which told the story of R. J. MItchell's invention of the Supermarine Spitfire. No. 501 Squadron were then based at Ibsley and their Operations Record Book states that on October 22, 1941, their CO, Squadron Leader Christopher Currant went to Denham Studios to discuss the filming. Mitchell was portrayed by Leslie Howard, who also directed the film and David Niven was released from his contract with Sam Goldwyn in the States to play Squadron Leader Geoffrey Crisp, an amalgam of the Vickers' test pilots Jeffrey Quill and 'Mutt' Summers. *Above:* Niven is seen explaining to a group of pilots (of whom Tony Bartley and Brian Kingcombe (with pipe) are recognisable) how the Spitfire came to be created. Although Howard uses poetic license in the film (showing Mitchell meeting Willy Messerschmitt which he never did) nevertheless *The First of the Few* stands as a fine movie record of action at a real Fighter Command aerodrome. Released in 1942, Sam Goldwyn, who had distribution rights for the film in the US, was not pleased to see his star cast in a secondary role and we are told that he personally edited out 40 minutes before reissuing the film in America with a new title *Spitfire*. (Leslie Howard lost his life on June 1, 1943 when the civilian airliner in which he was a passenger was shot down over the Bay of Biscay.)

crew managing to bale out. With better fortune, a Ju 88 was damaged the same month and a change of duty to escorting Beauforts saw Squadron Leader F. J. Howell shoot down a He 111 during the night of July 7/8.

The previous day saw No. 501 (County of Gloucester) Auxiliary Squadron bring in their Spitfire IIAs. This squadron had enjoyed much success during the Battle of Britain claiming to have destroyed 149 enemy aircraft. Staying at Ibsley until January 25, 1942, a brief move to Warmwell saw them back at Ibsley 13 days later with Spitfire VBs.

The squadron had been joined by No. 234 (Madras Presidency) in November 1941. Also equipped with the Mk VB, they alternated between Ibsley, Predannack and Warmwell then back to Ibsley until April 27, 1942 when they left for Portreath. Arriving to take their place the same day was No. 66 Squadron which followed a similar pattern of postings with short stays between Ibsley, Tangmere, Zeals and Skeabrae.

After the airfield was allocated to the USAAF to become Station 347, an advance party of the 1st Fighter Group moved in on August 24, 1942 prior to the arrival of the P-38 Lightnings of the 71st and 94th Fighter Squadrons. They commenced fighter sweeps and escort duties before leaving for North Africa in October. Returned to the RAF and No. 10 Group, December saw Nos. 66 and 118 return to Ibsley. They were joined on February 13, 1943 by Nos. 504 (County of Nottingham) and 616 (South Yorks) Auxiliary Squadrons together with No. 129 (Mysore). Operating as a wing, they began an intensive period of 'Circus' operations to try to entice the Luftwaffe to battle. They were replaced in mid September by a Czechoslovakian wing comprising Nos. 310, 312 and 313 Czech Squadrons flying Spitfire VCs. The latter part of the year saw the Czechs carrying out various duties but achieving very little in the way of contact with the enemy. Joined by No. 263 (Argentina) Squadron in December 1943 to work up on their Typhoons, all the units had left by February 1944 as Ibsley once again became Station 347 of the USAAF.

More excitement at Ibsley when No. 1426 Enemy Aircraft Flight flew in from its Collyweston base with a Junkers Ju 88A-6. Note the Messerschmitt Bf 110 in the background.

The intention was to give the American pilots of the 1st Fighter Group first-hand experience of German types. This Heinkel He 111 of 5./KG26 had forced landed at North Berwick on February 9, 1940. It later crashed at Polebrook on November 10, 1943.

Today the derelict control tower stares with empty eyes at the total loss of the flying field to the mining of aggregate.

With extensions to the runway carried out, the 48th Fighter Group moved in on March 29. The 492nd, 493rd and 494th Fighter Squadrons, flying P-47 Thunderbolts, then carried out fighter-bomber operations and fighter sweeps in the run-up to D-Day. The arrival of the 31st Fighter Group from Bisterne doubled the amount of aircraft flying from Ibsley until May 14 when they returned to their own base. Meanwhile the 48th continued pre-D-Day attacks and on June 6 flew convoy and beach cover. By the time they moved to France on June 18 they had lost a total of eight P-47s but had accounted for five enemy aircraft over the D-Day period. Further American occupants were the 14th Liaison Squadron with Sentinels and the P-38 Lightnings of the 367th Fighter Group, but with the latter leaving between July 27 and 31, Ibsley returned to Fighter Command.

The Oxfords of No. 7 Flying Instructors School became temporary residents until March 1945 when the airfield was transferred to No. 46 Group, Transport Command. Ibsley then became a satellite to Stoney Cross and Holmsley South and was used by a Glider Pick-up Training Flight with Dakotas and Hadrian gliders. Late 1945 saw the airfield in care and maintenance and within a year it had been returned to agriculture. With the runways removed during the 1960s, Amey Roadstone purchased the entire site for gravel extraction.

With the transfer of the airfield to the US Ninth Air Force, the main runway was increased to 1,600 yards.

MIDDLE WALLOP

First conceived for Royal Air Force Bomber Command, Middle Wallop was just completed in time for it to play its part as the headquarters aerodrome for Sector Y in No. 10 Group.

Middle Wallop, one of the largest grass airfields in Britain, was originally planned as a bomber station. Situated five miles west of Andover in Hampshire, a compulsory purchase was made of Ringwould Farm and Hungary Hunt to allow the Raynor Brothers to begin clearance. Once completed, Messrs Higgs and Hill moved in to construct the airfield which lay 296 feet above sea level. With heavy rain during November 1938, the station headquarters was not established until April 16, 1940 and by the time the Battle of Britain started in July, the site was still far from complete. Satellite airfields were located at Chilbolton, Warmwell, Ibsley, Hurn, Christchurch and Holmsley South.

The grass landing area measured 1,200 yards N-S (later extended to 1,600 yards), NE-SW 1,400 yards (later extended to 1,900 yards), E-W 1,250 yards and SE-NW 1,000 yards. A 50-foot concrete perimeter track was laid down together with the construction of five 'C' Type hangars plus a Type I Watch Office. Radio facilities were Fighter Command VHF, Bomber and Coastal Darky (a position-finding aid), and HF/DF.

Although still incomplete, Middle Wallop became officially operational on June 12, 1940, but not as a bomber station. Instead it became a sector airfield in control of Sector 'Y' in No. 10 Group. The first occupant was No. 15 Flying Training School but it moved out as No. 601 (County of London) Auxiliary Squadron arrived from France with their battle-scarred Hurricanes. Arriving on June 1, they only stayed for 17 days before moving on but by August there were three squadrons on strength: Nos. 238 and 609 (West Riding) Auxiliary Squadrons with Spitfires and

The station under construction seen from a window of Station Headquarters — a scene largely unchanged 70 years later.

The Luftwaffe already had the airfield in its sights and a heavy raid on August 13, 1940 wrecked Hangars 4 and 5.

No. 604 (County of Middlesex) Auxiliary Squadron with Blenheims.

Middle Wallop first attracted the attention of the Luftwaffe on August 8. A further attack followed on August 13 with the worst raid coming the following day. Around 5 p.m. a mixed force of He IIIs and Ju 88s scored direct hits on two of the hangars, an air raid shelter, the station headquarters, and the sector control room. A further raid later saw a string of delayed-action bombs dropped.

As work continued to repair the extensive damage, No. 238 moved out in September to the satellite at Chilbolton. By the end of the Battle of Britain, deemed to be at the end of October, No. 56 (Punjab) Squadron transferred from Boscombe Down to Middle Wallop on November 29 with Hurricanes whilst No. 604 had exchanged their Blenheims for the Beaufighter IF.

With the coming of winter Middle Wallop entered a phase of experimental flying. No. 93 Squadron reformed at the airfield flying the aged Handley Page Harrow bomber and the Douglas Havoc. They arrived to work in conjunction with Operation 'Mutton' which was a scheme whereby small mines were suspended on 2,000 feet of piano wire attached to a parachute. The idea was that they would be dropped from a Harrow in front of an approaching enemy bomber force. However no record of success is recorded. Another experimental unit arrived in October 1941, when No. 1458 Flight was created from a nucleus of No. 93 Squadron and equipped with Havocs to be used in Turbinlite operations using airborne searchlights..

Further attacks on the airfield in 1941 led to the operations room being moved to Wallop House, a large mansion a short distance

Today the aerodrome is the headquarters of the Army Air Corps with the Apache helicopter its main equipment.

There is some controversy as to where the picture of the men of No. 609 Squadron was taken: either at Middle Wallop, where they moved to from Northolt on July 4, 1940, or at Warmwell later in the year. However, Air Commodore David Roberts, who was then Wing Commander and Officer Commanding Middle Wallop, told us that he was of the opinion that it was taken there. He explained that this bungalow, which still stands beside the perimeter track, served as their dispersal.

away. On December 19 that year the Hurricanes of No. 245 (Northern Rhodesia) Squadron arrived, sending a detachment to Shoreham. They began offensive operations over France as well as using Hurricanes to accompany the night-fighter Havocs. The end of 1942 saw two Sommerfeld Track runways laid, the N-S extending 4,800 feet and the SW-NE to some 5,500 feet.

Mustangs arrived next with the Canadian No. 400 (City of Toronto) Squadron followed by two auxiliary squadrons, Nos. 501 (County of Gloucester) and 504 (County of Nottingham), both flying Spitfires. Then in December 1942 another Canadian unit, No. 406 (Lynx), were posted in with their Beaufighters for a three-month stay.

Rapid changes were the order of the day in early 1943 with Nos. 414 (Sarnia Imperials), 19, 182, 247 (China-British) and 456 Squadrons arriving and departing. Flying Hurricanes, Spitfires and Typhoons, by April they had all left to be replaced by No. 169 Squadron with Mustangs. No. 151 Squadron brought their Mosquitos to Middle Wallop in August, remaining until their move to Colerne three months later.

During preparations for the invasion of Europe, Middle Wallop was handed over to the United States Army Air Force as Station 449. It also became the Ninth Air Force Fighter Command headquarters in November 1943 when the 67th Reconnaissance Group arrived. Flying the P-38 Lightning and the P-51 Mustang, their missions included low-level armed sorties and visual and photographic reconnaissance in the run-up to D-Day. Units involved were 107th and 109th Reconnaissance Squadrons, the 30th Photographic Squadron and the 9th Weather Reconnaissance Squadron. After the group moved to Normandy, Middle Wallop was returned to the RAF on July 7.

On July 30, 1944 the Mosquitos of No. 125 (Newfoundland) Squadron arrived for operations directed against the flying bomb. They were joined by a Canadian squadron, No. 418 (City of Edmonton), which was also equipped with the Mossie, and by the end of August they had claimed 90 V1s shot down. Further detachments of Hurricanes came and went until No. 3501 Central Servicing Unit arrived to carry out servicing for the Second Tactical Air Force. This work continued until February 16, 1945 when Middle Wallop was transferred to the Royal Navy, being renamed HMS *Flycatcher*.

The base was handed back to the RAF in April 1946 to host further Spitfire and Typhoon squadrons until September 1958 when it was given to the Army Air Corps. Today, still a large grass airfield, it is the Corps' main helicopter base and the home of the Museum of Army Flying.

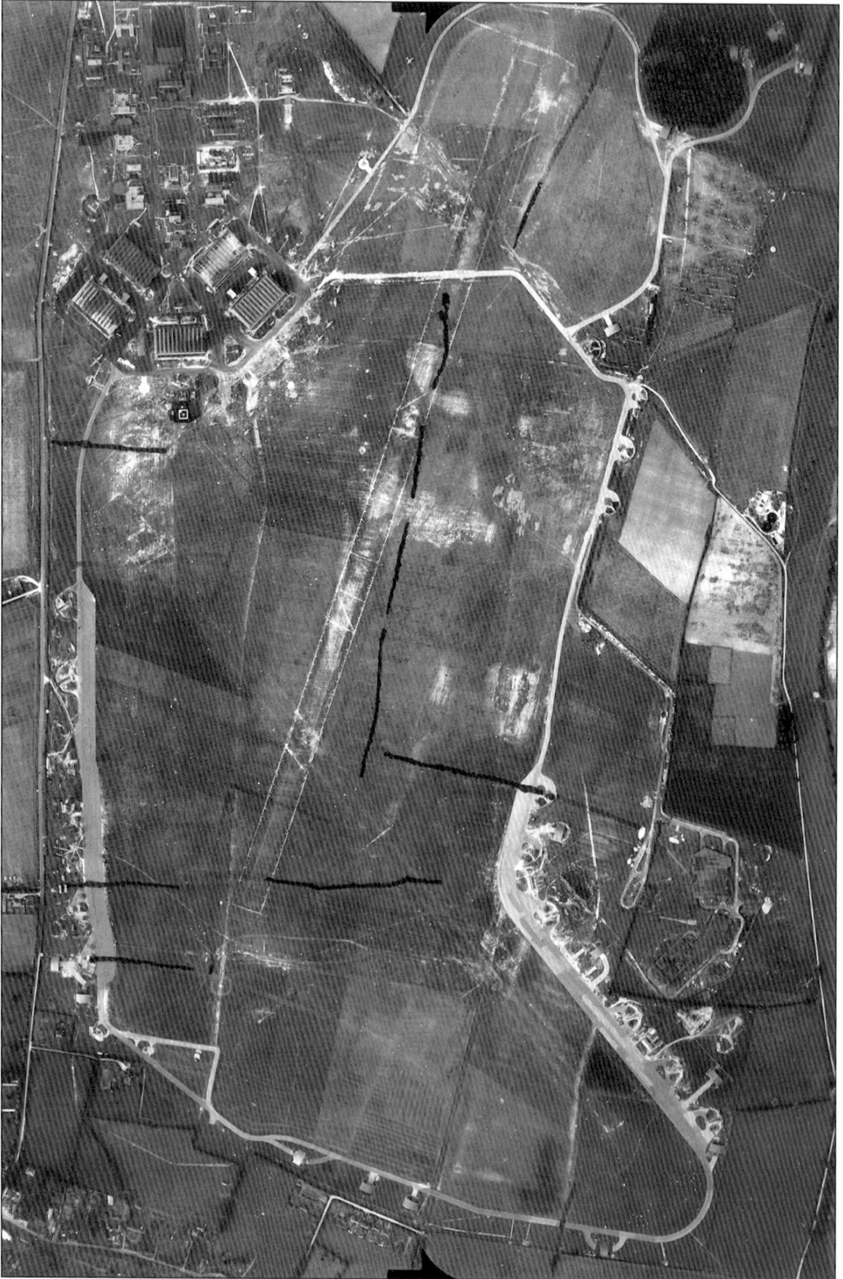

In November 1943 the airfield was handed over to the USAAF to become the headquarters of IX Fighter Command to control all Ninth Air Force fighter and tactical reconnaisance groups for the invasion of Europe. The Americans took this photo of Middle Wallop — greatly expanded since 1940 — in September 1943.

In February 1945, a further handover took place when the Mobile Naval Airfields Organisation moved from RNAS Ludham.

Under Admiralty control, the aerodrome became known as HMS *Flycatcher* until handed back to the RAF in April 1946.

Google

The Army Air Corps took over in September 1958, later establishing the Museum of Army Flying alongside the airfield.

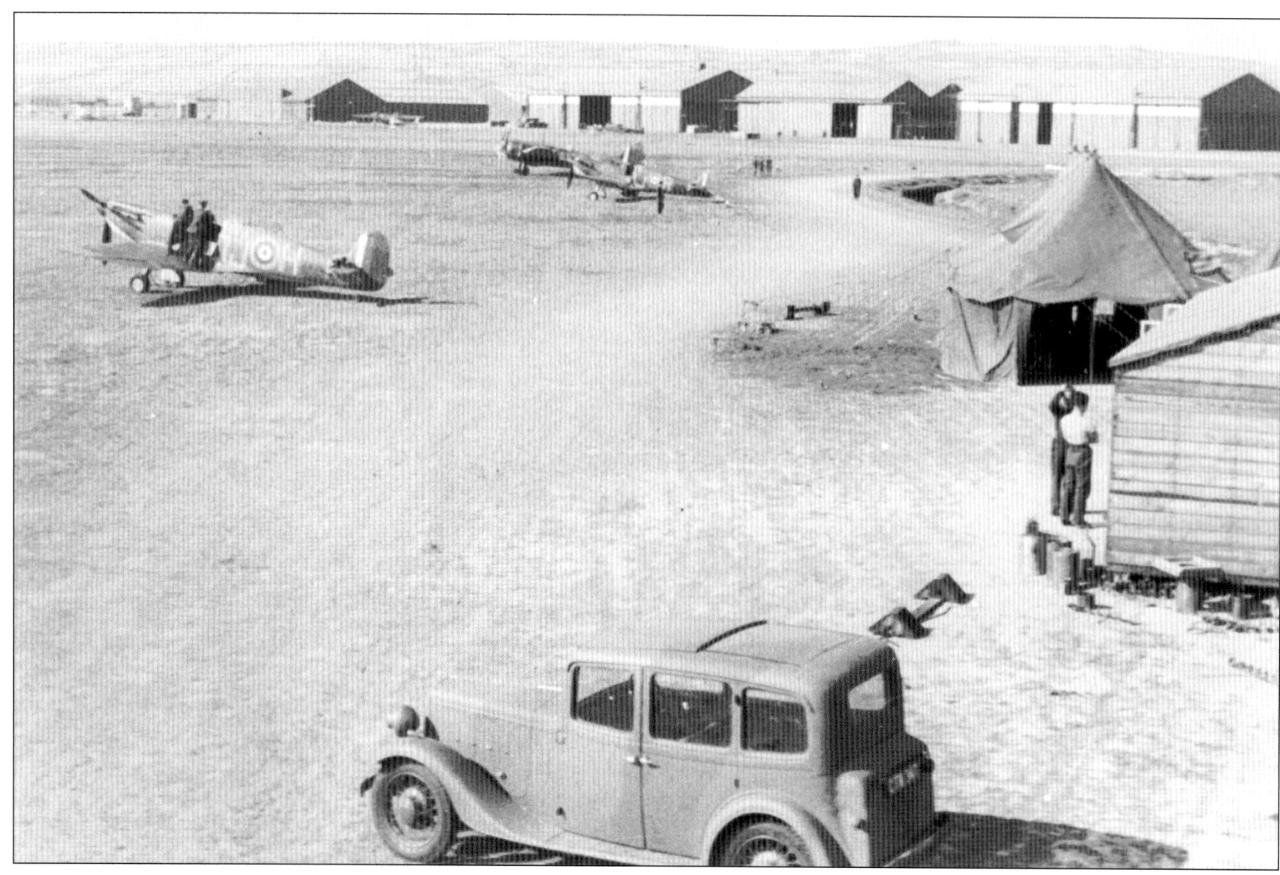

Spitfires of No. 92 Squadron at readiness during the summer of 1940 at the south Wales airfield at Pembrey where they carried out convoy patrols over the Channel. They then moved to Biggin Hill and the thick of the Battle of Britain in September.

PEMBREY

In June 1942 Pembrey entered the history books when Oberleutnant Arnim Faber presented the RAF with a unique prize! On the 23rd, the German pilot had taken off in his FW 190 from the French airfield at Morlaix but, becoming disoriented in a dogfight with Spitfires, ended up mistaking the Bristol Channel for the English Channel. Thinking he was over his home airfield, he landed at RAF Pembrey and promptly got himself arrested.

Although allocated for flying training, the airfield was temporarily handed over to Fighter Command as a night fighter satellite to Fairwood Common. Originally a grass airfield measuring N-S 1,200 yards, NE-SW 640 yards, E-W 1,300 yards and SE-NW 1,180 yards, the addition of two Macadam runways with concrete extensions and one of concrete ensured better serviceability. A 35-foot perimeter track and four 'F' Type and three smaller hangars were constructed together with a 150 x 95 feet workshop. Night landing facilities consisted of Glim Lamps and Gooseneck flares.

Opening in May 1940, No. 92 (East India) Squadron arrived a month later for a rest period but managed to carry out several convoy patrols during their stay. Leaving on September 8 for Biggin Hill and back to the Battle of Britain, they exchanged bases with the Hurricanes of No. 79 (Madras Presidency) Squadron who flew

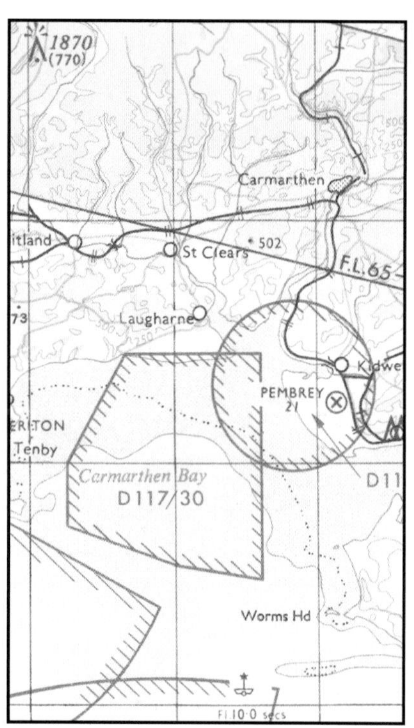

Being situated close to the Pembrey Sands Firing Range, the airfield is used by the military. These Chinooks of No. 18 Squadron from Odiham have dropped in to refuel.

By the autumn of 1941, the fighter side of the air war had taken a dramatic turn in favour of the Luftwaffe with the introduction of the Focke-Wulf FW 190. This radial-engined fighter appeared to completely outclass the RAF's Spitifire VBs and Typhoons, a worrying superiority which was to remain in Germany's favour for some two years. The FW 190A-3 was regarded by both sides as the Luftwaffe's best fighter ever, and RAF intelligence was desperate to obtain one in flying condition to assess its performance and discover any weaknesses. As the weeks passed by with none being shot down over Britain, the problem became so serious that when Captain Philip Pinckney of E Troop, No. 12 Commando, proposed that he go to France to capture one, his idea was given serious consideration. His friend, Jeffrey Quill, the Supermarine test pilot, was inveigled to go along and fly the aircraft back to Britain, but on the very day the plan was put forward to Combined Operations — June 23 — Oberleutnant Arnim Faber did the job for them. Faber was the adjutant of the III Gruppe JG2 based at the French coastal aerodrome at Morlaix. After dogfighting with Spitfires over the Bristol Channel, Faber mistook South Wales for France and, we are told, after performing a victory roll and cockily extending his wheels while inverted, he touched down at RAF Pembrey.

One can imagine the jubilation at Fighter Command on hearing of the gift, and the aircraft was quickly dismantled and taken to Farnborough. On July 3 it made its maiden flight under RAF colours, but continuous rough running of the BMW engine — which was normal according to PoWs — curtailed the tests.

west the same day having seen heavy fighting throughout May, June and August. Although their main duties were convoy patrols, success came to Flight Lieutenant G. D. L. Haysom when he shot down a Ju 88 on November 20. Further Hurricanes arrived on April 17, 1941 when No. 32 arrived for a two-month stay, a detachment being sent to Carew Cheriton before the squadron moved to Angle.

'City of Warsaw' was the name given to No. 316 Squadron when formed at Pembrey on February 15, 1941. Flying Hurricanes, the Poles claimed success when on the night of April 1/2, Flying Officer B. Anders and Flying Officer A. Gabszewicz forced a He 111 to land in County Wexford, Ireland. The squadron was later joined by a detachment of No. 307 (Lwow) Squadron before they moved to Colerne in June. The period also saw a brief stay by the Defiants of No. 256 Squadron.

By June, Fighter Command had relinquished Pembrey and it became home to No. 1 Air Gunnery School whose Lysanders and Blenheims, superseded by Ansons, later became familiar sights over Wales. In addition the airfield was used for trials of equipment and aircraft before they entered service with the RAF.

By 1944 the ageing Ansons had been replaced by Wellingtons, Spitfires and Martinets that continued with the school until its disbandment on June 14, 1945. A brief visit by No. 595 Squadron in October 1946 saw Pembrey enter peacetime service and once again become a fighter airfield in Fighter Command. This continued until the 1950s when Pembrey became surplus to requirements and closed. The firing range close by is still operational and is used by modern day jet aircraft.

The RAF quit Pembrey in 1957 but 40 years later — in August 1997 — the airfield was given a brand new lease of life when the Secretary of State for Wales opened it as Pembrey South Wales Airport. The main runway 04/22 was extended to its current length of 2,650 feet with South Western Airlines as a resident operator.

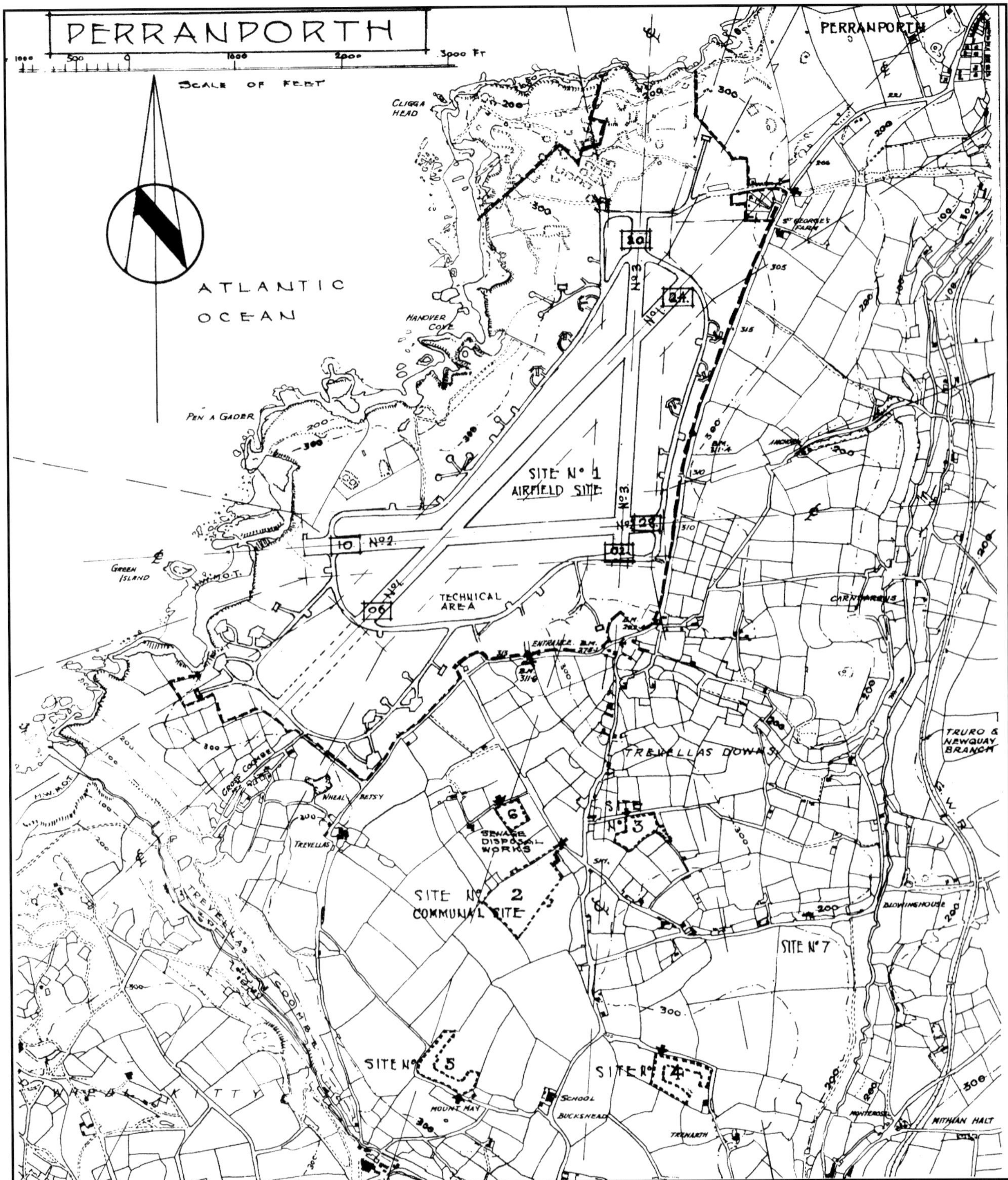

PERRANPORTH

With its stated function as an operational satellite to nearby Portreath, Perranporth lay one and a half miles south-west of the village of that name. However, sitting on a cliff top 300 feet above sea level, it was prone to sea fog and the grass landing area was constantly soft. This was rectified when three tarmac runways were laid, the longest being 1,400 x 50 yards and the other two 1,100 x 50 yards. The perimeter track was well over two miles long yet hangarage was minimal with just one T2 and four Blisters.

Open by April 1941, the first squadron based there was No. 66 with Spitfires. For a year they were to operate between Perranporth, Portreath and Warmwell, finally leaving in April 1942. By this time Nos. 19, 310 (Czech) and 234 (Madras Presidency) Squadrons had rotated through Perranporth in similar vein with time spent at other West Country airfields.

The Canadian Falcon Squadron, No. 412, had moved to No. 9 Group in the spring of 1943 and by April had arrived back at the airfield flying Spitfire VBs. They were joined by No. 610 (County of Chester) Auxiliary Squadron on April 30. Converting from the Spitfire VB to the VC, they flew to Bolt Head on June 26 with No. 412 moving to Friston at the same time.

After extending the main runway, a Polish wing arrived with Spitfires. Nos. 302 (Poznan) and 317 (Wilno) Squadrons flew in to join a detachment of No. 307 (Lwow) that had been at Predannack since April. A three-month stay saw them carrying out bomber escorts but with very little contact with the enemy.

The first Typhoons to use Perranporth were No. 183 (Gold Coast) Squadron who arrived during September flying the fighter-bomber version. Most operations however were flown from other West Country airfields due to restrictions on sorties caused by the size of Perranporth. They had been preceded by No. 453 (Australian) Squadron when their Spitfire VBs and VCs moved in from Ibsley. They claimed their first victory on October 8 when, in conjunction with 610 Squadron, seven Bf 110s fell to the guns of the two squadrons. The Australians moved north to the Shetlands shortly afterwards.

Mechanics servicing a Spitfire VB of No. 453 Squadron in the south-western corner of the aerodrome in 1943. This unit was formed in Australia in July 1941 for the defence of Malaya but, after losing virtually all its aircraft during the Japanese attacks in December, it was disbanded in March 1942 only to be reformed in Britain in June at Drem in Scotland.

Two French squadrons, Nos. 340 (GC IV/2 'Ile de France') and 341 (GC III/2 'Alsace') arrived to replace them. As plans for D-Day were being finalised, both were heavily engaged in low flying patrols to soften up the enemy defences. Joined by another French squadron, No. 329 (GC I/2 Cigognes) on January 22, 1944, all three formed No. 145 Wing before moving to the forward coastal airfield at Merston during April.

That month also saw a change from Fighter to Coastal Command with Perranporth becoming an airfield within No. 19 Group. This saw Nos. 816, 849 and 859 Squadrons of the Fleet Air Arm fly in and commence anti-E-boat operations as a prelude to the invasion. Avengers and Swordfish now replaced the Spitfires until August when No. 816 Squadron disbanded and the other two squadrons moved on to other naval airfields.

The distinctive outcrop of rock in the south-western corner of the airfield makes for a perfect comparison.

Perranporth, seven miles south-west of Newquay on the north Cornish coast, remains fully operational, albeit with no military presence since the end of the war. Today only two of its runways are licensed, 05-23 reduced to 1,000 yards and 09-27 now only 810 yards as indicated by the painted lines. The old N-S runway (01-19) is no longer used.

Perranporth was placed under care and maintenance on September 1, 1944. A month later it was re-activated to become part of No. 46 Group and a Command Staging Post but by May 1, 1945 it had returned to care and maintenance and in this state became home to No. 95 Air Cadet Gliding School. The airfield finally closed as a military unit on April 6, 1946.

After a brief period as a small civil airport from 1950 to 1952, Perranporth closed once again until it became the home of the Cornish Gliding and Flying Club in 1957. It is currently up for sale with an asking price of £1.49 million. English Heritage have also put a preservation order on the airfeild.

Evidence of its wartime history *(left)* the old battle headquarters and *(right)* the memorial close to the control tower.

PORTREATH

Another aerodrome on the north Cornish coast was Portreath, pictured here from an altitude of 2,000 feet in December 1943 at which time Beaufighters were in residence. Several can be seen dispersed alongside the perimeter track.

Portreath was one of the earliest aerodromes to be planned in Cornwall. Lying 295 feet above sea level, it was located on farmland a mile north-east of the town. The site was requisitioned in 1940 to allow Richard Costain Ltd to start levelling and infilling ditches prior to beginning building work. Four tarmac runways were laid down, the main being 1,300 yards with three secondaries of 1,000 yards, all 50 yards wide. Four T2 and four Over Blister hangars completed the original work and, although far from complete, the airfield opened in the spring of 1941.

Classified as a fighter sector station with satellites at Perranporth and Predannack, its other function was that of an Overseas Air Despatch Unit and the base for No. 44 Ferry Group. A brief stay by the Whirlwinds of No. 263 (Argentina) Squadron from St Eval was followed on April 9 by the arrival of No. 152 (Hyderabad) Squadron with Spitfires. They remained for four months before moving to Snailwell, carrying out convoy patrols and the occasional night sortie, although their main task was flying escort duties to bombers attacking targets in north-western France.

The first of several Luftwaffe attacks on Portreath were made during April with the worst taking place on May 9 resulting in the death of an airman with a further three wounded. In the same attack two aircraft were destroyed with several damaged.

The formation of No. 130 (Punjab) Squadron on June 16 with Spitfire IIAs saw it become operational ten weeks later. Together with the Spitfire IIAs of No. 313 (Czech) Squadron that had arrived in August, their main duties were shipping patrols. The squadron moved to Harrowbeer on October 25 whilst No. 313 converted to the Spitfire VB before leaving on November 23 for Warmwell.

Today access to the airfield is restricted as it is the location of one of the RAF's Surveillance and Control Systems which monitors all aircraft flying in and around the United Kingdom Air Defence Region.

This Spitfire IIA was pictured in a sandbagged revetment soon after B Flight of No. 130 Squadron were established at Portreath in 1941. After the war the aerodrome continued to be used by the RAF until May 1950 when it was handed over to the Ministry of Supply. This was the beginning of the Cold War and a remote location was required for the development of chemical weapons and their antidotes. The Chemical Defence Establishment, CDE Nancekuke, opened a pilot plant on the airfield in 1954 to produce sarin nerve gas and over the next two years approximately 20 tons of the agent were produced. With the cessation of the UK's offensive chemical weapons programme in 1956, production was switched to CS gas and chemical warfare counter-measures including the development of protective clothing to be worn in the case of a poison gas attack. In 1976 work was transferred to the main establishment at Porton Down at which point most of the wartime buildings were demolished.

October 1941 also saw a detachment of No. 276 Squadron arrive for air-sea rescue duties with Lysanders, Hurricanes and a Walrus. In April 1944 they would be joined by the rest of the squadron before moving to Querqueville in France in September 1944.

No. 66 Squadron flew in on December 14, 1941 for a short stay. Moving to Warmwell on February 8, 1942, they were back at Portreath on the 22nd to convert to the Spitfire VA, VB and VC. Remaining until April 27, a move to Ibsley saw them replaced by No. 234 (Madras Presidency) with Spitfire VBs the same day. Patrols were carried out with the squadron alternating between Portreath and Perranporth.

Various units now arrived in preparation for overseas duties with Blenheims, B-17s, Hudsons and Beaufighters. At the same time a detachment of No. 248 Squadron with Blenheims was posted in to counteract enemy activity around the Scilly Isles. Conversion to Beaufighters saw these move to Dyce in February 1942.

Operation 'Cackle' — the movement of USAAF supplies and aircraft involved in Operation 'Torch'— the Allied landings in North Africa, saw much work for the station during 1942. However Portreath was to prove a difficult airfield for heavy aircraft flown by inexperienced crews, sometimes leading to incidents and fatalities. Protection during the initial stages of the long flights was provided by a detachment of No. 400 (City of Toronto) Canadian Squadron as their long-range Mustang Is proved ideal for the task. Arriving on December 4, 1942, they moved to Dunsfold just over a year later.

With No. 234 Squadron leaving in December, the base was now only being used for ferry movements. Not until July 1943 did fighters return in the form of No. 613 (City of Manchester) Auxiliary Squadron and No. 414 (Sarnia Imperials) Canadian Squadron. Once again their Mustangs were involved in escorting aircraft for part of long overseas journies. Staying for a brief period, a return to fighter operations saw the Beaufighter VICs of No. 235 Squadron fly in from Leuchars on August 29. Joined by the Beaufighter XIs of No. 143 Squadron in September, they carried out long-range, anti-aircraft patrols from Portreath with both squadrons converting to the Beaufighter X in October. They remained until February 1944 although No. 235 were to return on March 27 to convert to the Beaufighter XI and finally to the Mosquito V. They left for Banff on September 6, 1944.

The Mosquito XVIIIs of No. 248 Squadron had also been posted in on February 17, 1944 and flew together with the aforementioned squadrons on anti-U-Boat operations. However, by the end of September all the Coastal Command squadrons had left and with No. 276 (ASR) Squadron now based in France, rescue coverage was transferred to a detachment of No. 275 Squadron and one from No. 277 Squadron with Warwicks. They remained until February 1945 after which Portreath was transferred to No. 44 Group, Transport Command.

When they transferred to St Mawgan in September, the airfield was put to care and maintenance. Re-activated later for Technical Training Command, it was used by No. 7 (Polish) Resettlement Unit until 1949 when the Ministry of Supply acquired Portreath for a station within the Chemical Defence Establishment. Amid intense secrecy, the CDE carried out experiments similar to those at Porton Down until its closure in 1978.

On October 1, 1980, Portreath was again re-opened as a Control Reporting Post within the UK Surveillance and Control System.

A fine memorial to all who served at Portreath.

PREDANNACK DOWN

Situated 285 feet above sea level, Predannack often presented problems to those pilots who were unfamiliar with the airfield and for several reasons. Tregonning Hill, 635 feet high, lay ten miles north-north-west; there was an experimental kite balloon station at Mullion, three and a half miles away; there were 690-foot WT masts nearby, and finally two 'Q' site decoy airfields lay in close proximity.

Building work for a night fighter base to protect the nearby ports of Falmouth and Penzance began in 1940. Categorised as a satellite to Portreath, as the grass surface was marshland and prone to waterlogging, four tarmac runways were laid down, the main being 1,750 x 50 yards. The secondaries were two at 1,400 and one of 1,000 yards, each runway having a 45-foot hard core border to prevent aircraft becoming stuck in the marshy ground should they run off the centre line. There was a Bellman hangar and six Blisters and 24 hardstandings.

Predannack opened in May 1941 but was still far from complete with local buildings having to be requisitioned for personnel and certain trades. The first squadron to take up residence was No. 247 (China-British) which arrived with Hurricane IIAs on June 18. Converting to the IIB and the IIC in August,

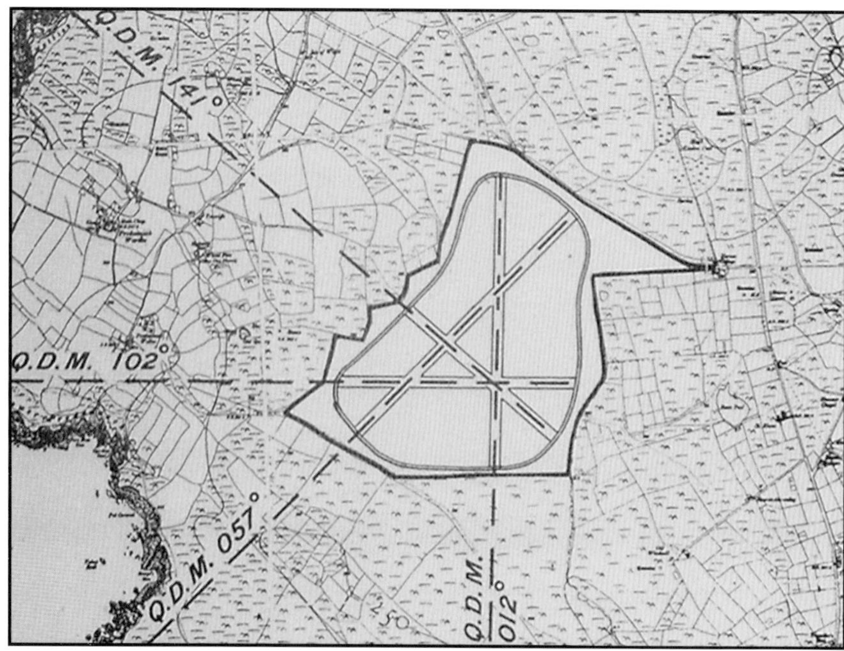

Predannack Down lies on the southern coast of Cornwall and it is interesting to see the progression of an aerodrome from planning through to its development. The magnetic headings (QDM) of the runways would change over the years.

This is how the airfield appeared in 1943 when the runways were in the process of being lengthened.

Two Spitfire IXs (the further machine being MK426 coded SK:D) of No. 165 Squadron based at Predannack just prior to D-Day in 1944. Both are standing plugged in to trolley accumulators ready to scramble at a moment's notice to patrol the Western Approaches to the English Channel.

a detachment was sent to Exeter while the rest of the squadron began intruder operations during which they claimed an He III. In September a detachment from No. 118 Squadron flying Spitfire VBs joined them. Also the same month saw No. 1457 Turbinlite Flight arrive with Havocs which were to work in company with a Hurricane from 247 Squadron. Like the rest of the Turbinlite units, the airborne searchlight scheme had little success. Reformed at Predannack on September 2, 1942 as No. 536 Squadron, they moved to Fairwood Common before disbanding on January 25, 1943.

October 6, 1941 had seen No. 600 (City of London) Auxiliary Squadron posted in with Beaufighters. Three months later the Luftwaffe attacked Predannack although only minor damage was inflicted. In March the squadron claimed an He 115 and in June a Ju 88D-5 was brought down in the sea although the attacking Beaufighter was hit and had to ditch, the crew taking to their dinghy. In September, No. 600 Squadron left for Church Fenton..

Their replacement was No. 406 (Lynx) Canadian Squadron, also equipped with Beaufighters. Flying in on September 4, 1942, after three months without any success, they moved to Middle Wallop.

Anti-shipping strikes became routine when a detachment of Whirlwinds from No. 263 (Argentina) Squadron arrived from Warmwell during September. Joined by No. 604 (County of Middlesex) Auxiliary Squadron on December 7 and No. 248 on January 18, 1943, Predannack gained a reputation for operations against enemy shipping.

Wing Commander 'Bob' Braham was a fine night fighter pilot when flying with No. 29 Squadron at West Malling in Kent. Now in command of No. 141 Squadron equipped with Beaufighters, he brought them to Predannack on February 18, 1943. Night landing facilities at this time consisted of Drem lighting but the arrival of a full night fighter squadron saw the addition of an AI Homer Beacon together with further runway lights to try to ensure safety from the surrounding danger zones.

No. 248 Squadron claimed success on the night of March 11/12 when a Ju 88 was destroyed. No. 263 Squadron returned the same month together with No. 264 (Madras Presidency) that introduced the first Mosquitos to Predannack. Together with detachments from No. 307 (Lwow) Polish and No. 456 (Australian) Squadrons, this was a period of fighter interception of enemy aircraft attacking shipping in the Bay of Biscay.

A detachment of No. 618 Squadron arrived later in the year equipped with the latest version of the Mosquito. Attached for anti-U-boat operations, the fire-power of the Mk XVIII proved fatal to many enemy submarines. This period also saw extensions to the runways to allow larger types of aircraft to use the airfield such as the Wellington XIVs of No. 304 (Silesian) Squadron. They arrived on December 13. The aircraft were equipped with powerful Leigh Lights in the nose to illuminate U-boats at night and one sinking was obtained before the squadron left for Chivenor on February 19, 1944. Four days later the Liberator Vs of No. 311 (Czech) Squadron carried out similar duties. Joined by the Mosquito XIIIs of No. 151 Squadron on March 25, the latter celebrated the magic score of 100 enemy aircraft shot down before leaving for Castle Camps on October 8.

April 1944 also saw the return of Spitfires to Predannack with Nos. 1 and 165 (Ceylon) Squadrons working anti-shipping operations. Also returning were the Leigh Light Wellingtons, this time from No. 179 Squadron, to join the Liberators on operations to stop U-boats entering the English Channel and Irish Sea. As this threat moved away during the summer, so did the larger aircraft with No. 311 leaving for Tain in August and No. 179 for Chivenor on September 6. At the same time Predannack saw Nos. 264 (Madras Presidency) and 604 (County of Middlesex) Auxiliary Squadron arrive for rest periods until

Today Predannack is still operational, also serving as a satellite to the Royal Navy Air Station at nearby Culdrose, although the only fighters present today are these redundant Harriers used for fire practice.

Taken looking south, this shot shows just how close the aerodrome is to the coast.

December when Nos. 33 and 222 (Natal) Squadrons flew in to convert from Spitfires to Tempest Vs. However, both had left by February 1945 with Predannack being placed into care and maintenance on June 1, 1946.

In 1951, the airfield was used for experimental purposes by Vickers under the supervision of Barnes Wallis before being taken over by the Royal Navy on December 15, 1958 and re-designated HMS *Seahawk*. Today Predannack is a satellite to nearby RNAS Culdrose. Its main duty is intensive helicopter training with the airfield also home to No. 626 Volunteer Gliding School. A memorial was unveiled at the main gate in June 2002.

In November 1943, No. 157 Squadron, commanded by Wing Commander J. Mackie, arrived to carry out shipping patrols over the Western Approaches and it was during a practice flight on February 26, 1944 that one of their Mosquitos came to grief right on the aerodrome. The aircraft was being piloted by Flying Officer John Clifton with Flying Officer Scobie as observer when it piled in from 200 feet. The Mosquito burst into flames and as firemen covered the aircraft with foam, officers rushed to the rescue. In this dramatic photo, Wing Commander Mackie can be seen with a Czechoslovakian RAF doctor attempting to release the crew but it was difficult as the observer had been thrown across the pilot making it very awkward to reach their harnesses in the excessive heat. On the right is the station padre, Squadron Leader Brown. The crew were eventually cut free, Flying Officer Scobie surviving though badly injured. Tragically Flying Officer Clifton could not be saved and his grave (No. 34) can now be found in Row C of the north-western section of Helston Cemetery.

Four runways were laid down to cater for the unpredictable nature of the prevailing wind on the exposed cliff-top.

ROBOROUGH

Roborough, alias Plymouth Airport, lies on the northern outskirts of the city and it was here that No. 247 Squadron — the China-British squadron — were posted in 1940, thereafter serving at several West Country airfields.

Roborough was initially a small municipal airport established in 1925, being formerly opened by the Prince of Wales (later Edward VII) in July 1931. It was first managed by the Plymouth and District Aero Club on behalf of Plymouth City Council, and used by Railway Air Services and Jersey Airlines. It was also used for exercises by some auxiliary squadrons and the Fleet Air Arm. The landing area was grass measuring 833 yards from N-S; 950 yards NE-SW; just 554 yards from E-W, and 833 yards NW-SE, at 488 feet above sea level.

Requisitioned by the Admiralty in1937 and renamed HMS *Drake*, the first aircraft to arrive were the Ospreys and Swordfish of Nos. 801 and 810 Squadrons. Further Fleet Air Arm squadrons arrived for short periods until June 1939 when Roborough was effectively taken over by Coastal Command, though still under Admiralty control.

Parented by Mount Batten, its functions were as a communications and target-towing base in No. 15 Group. Three small hangars were constructed with an additional one added later. The Watch Office was sited on a corner of the main hangar and although Glim Lamps were available, a regulation stated that 'night landings were safe only to experienced pilots used to Roborough'.

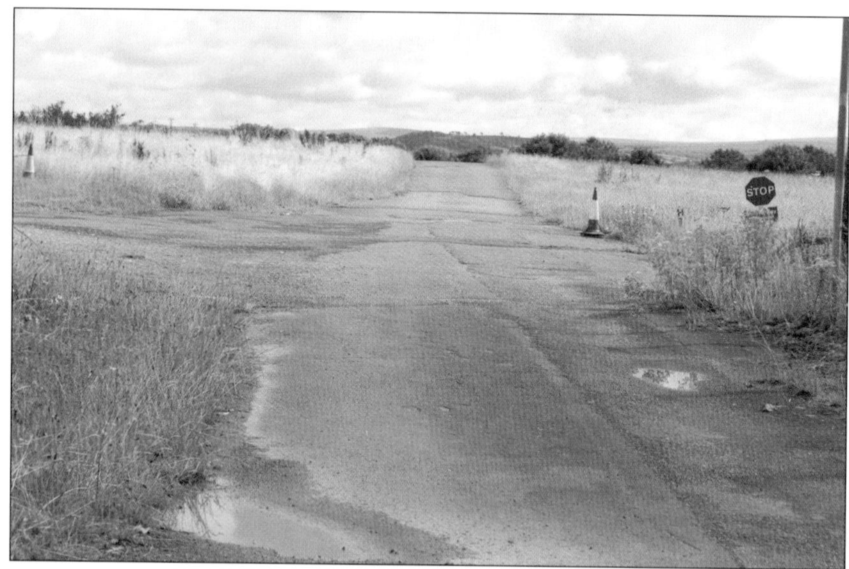

Nothing more sad than an aerodrome with no aircraft. When the last airline service ceased in 2011, the airport closed down, the area above and part of the runway being scheduled for housing.

A communications flight from No. 15 Group was established during June 1940 with a Vega Gull, an Envoy and a Magister. By this time the civilian companies had moved out as No. 247 (China-British) Squadron reformed at the airfield on August 1. Previously known as the Sumburgh Fighter Flight, it was equipped with two Gloster Gladiators before a conversion to the Hurricane was made in January 1941 when they departed to St Eval.

A detachment of Lysanders from No. 16 Squadron based at Weston Zoyland arrived in October 1940 to carry out coastal patrols on behalf of the army. They had a rather tragic time at Roborough when a Lysander piloted by the CO crashed on take-off, killing both occupants. By June 1941 they had left for Okehampton.

The new headquarters of No. 19 Group of Coastal Command at Mount Batten saw the replacement of the 15 Group communications flight by its own on February 14 that year. Another arrival was No. 2 Anti-aircraft Co-operation Unit flying aged Hectors and Gladiators for target-towing duties. There were no further changes until control of Roborough was transferred from the Admiralty to the Air Ministry in May 1942. Still used by No. 2 AACU, now with additional aircraft such as Defiants and Battles, the forming of No. 691 Squadron on December 1, 1943 saw Barrucudas, Defiants, Hurricanes and Oxfords crowding the small grass airfield. Used for gun-laying exercises, the squadron remained until February 1945.

Roborough was then left with a detachment of No. 3 Armament Practice Camp flying Martinets. When they left in May, usage of the airfield fell to just the No. 19 Group communications flight and No. 82 Air Cadet Gliding School.

Relinquished by the military in 1946, civil flying resumed with the airport once again being operated by Plymouth and District Aero Club on behalf of the council. Although the aircraft operator Sutton Harbour Holdings announced a significant growth in 2008-9, the withdrawal of the service to London sounded the death knell and the airport closed in December 2011.

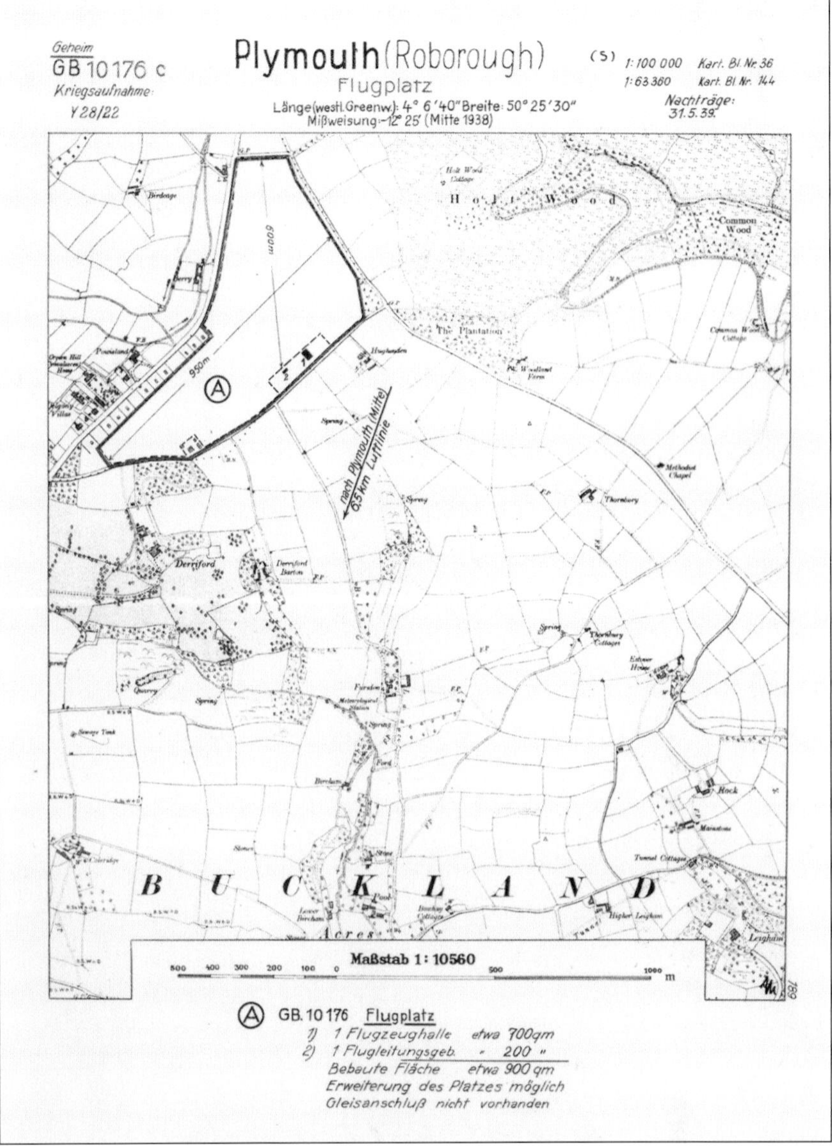

Roborough as the Luftwaffe depicted it on their 1939 target map and as it appeared in its heyday below.

ST EVAL

Sergeant John Shepherd was serving with No. 234 Squadron at St Eval when he was pictured there with his Hillman 'Aero' Minx. John became the CO of No. 41 Squadron in Germany in April 1945 but was killed in a flying accident in January 1946.

Unique due to the fact that it was one of the largest Coastal Command bases in the area and also a fighter sector station, St Eval was one of the first sites chosen for the rapidly expanding RAF in the late 1930s. The site was six miles north-east of Newquay in Cornwall, and was a large grass area of some 290 acres. This allowed a landing area measuring 1,050 yards from N-S, 1,200 yards NE-SW, 1,000 yards E-W and 1,080 yards SE-NW, surrounded by a 70-foot perimeter track. Groundwork was carried out by G. Wallace Ltd and involved the removal of drystone walls and the demolition of a small village. Only the church was allowed to remain standing.

Hangar accommodation was good with four large 'C' Types and several Bessoneaux. A Type 1 Watch Office controlled the landing facilities which included night landing aids of Drem lighting, electric flare path and Glim lamps, electric wind tee, obstruction lights, aerodrome landmark beacon and Chance lights. Radio facilities were on the same level with HF and DF frequencies together with radar, St Eval being one of the first Coastal Command airfields to have such a facility. At first personnel accommodation was sparse comprising wooden huts until brick buildings could be built.

St Eval opened on October 2, 1939 within No. 15 Group with the arrival of the Ansons of No. 217 Squadron for anti-U-Boat operations. With a detachment at Carew Cheriton, a conversion to Bristol Beauforts in September 1940 saw similar duties continuing.

A rather unusual unit of six Hornet Moth biplanes also arrived at the same time. Known as No. 6 Coastal Patrol Flight, their remit was to fly over the sea in the hope of spotting U-Boats. Patrols began in December but bad weather conditions forced a premature halt to further flights.

Steve Casely replicates the shot with Dawn on exactly the same spot in 2013.

An early shot showing the attempts to break up the outline and camouflage St Eval with painted tar lines.

With the Beauforts continuing coastal and anti-submarine patrols, a temporary transfer of some Bomber Command aircraft saw a detachment of Whitleys from No. 58 Squadron fly into St Eval. This was the first of several Whitley detachments, though all had little success in spotting and attacking U-Boats.

June 1940 saw the aerodrome become a sector station within the newly-formed No. 10 Group. Spitfire Is of No. 234 (Madras Presidency) Squadron came in from Church Fenton on June 18 to carry out convoy protection. It was during one such operation that the squadron claimed its first success when a Ju 88 was shot down on July 8. The squadron moved to Middle Wallop on August 14 before returning in September.

With the arrival of the Spitfires came a series of enemy attacks. During the afternoon of July 12, a single Ju 88 dropped eight bombs causing minor damage. On August 21, 22nd, 23rd and 26th, the airfield suffered further attacks resulting in damage to hangars and the loss of three Blenheims. A detachment of Blenheims from No. 236 Squadron flew in to St Eval in July followed by the entire squadron in August. Classified as a fighter reconnaissance unit, they carried out escort duties to Sunderlands and Beauforts attacking shipping in the Bay of Biscay.

As the Spitfires of 234 left they were replaced by the Hurricanes of No. 238 Squadron on August 14. The same month a detachment of Gladiator IIs from No. 247 (China-British) Squadron arrived from Roborough to carry out night patrols. A move for 238 Squadron back to Middle Wallop on September 10 saw No. 234 return at the time when construction of three hard runways was underway. The main was 1,200 yards with the secondaries both 1,000 yards. And with so many aircraft now using the airfield, aviation fuel storage was increased to 144,000 gallons and MT petrol to 10,000 gallons.

With German capital ships sitting in Brest, several sorties were carried out by the Fleet Air Arm flying from St Eval although with little success. Nos. 812 and 829 Squadron flying Albacores and Swordfish flew nightly raids from November 10 for several weeks before being replaced by Nos. 801, 809 and 816. The three squadrons carried out similar attacks before the FAA left St Eval for good.

St Eval has a very varied wartime career having hosted some 80 squadrons belonging to both Fighter and Coastal Commands with other squadrons being seconded to the station from Bomber Command as well as from the USAAF. This shot dates from December 1943 when dozens of aircraft were dispersed around the airfield.

Attacks by the Luftwaffe were renewed during 1941 with devastating results and on January 25 a shelter was hit by a 250kg bomb, killing 21 personnel. Further raids saw damage to buildings resulting in some essential services being forced to move into domestic premises in the nearest village.

Meanwhile attacks on the German ships continued. A detachment of Beaufort 1s from No. 22 Squadron had arrived during April 1940. Armed with torpedoes, their instructions were to pursue the attacks previously attempted by the FAA. By April 1941, photographs had shown that the *Gneisenau* had left dry dock. The detachment was therefore tasked with carrying out an attack but, out of the six aircraft detailed, only two reached the target and just one dropped a torpedo. This Beaufort, piloted by Flying Officer K. Campbell, was hit by flak and crashed into the sea but not before the torpedo struck the *Gneisenau* causing severe damage. For his exploit, Flying Officer Campbell was awarded a posthumous Victoria Cross.

A transfer to No. 19 Group and Coastal Command in February 1941 saw the penultimate fighter unit arrive at St Eval. Joining a detachment that had arrived at the airfield in November 1940, the rest of the Whirlwinds of No. 263 (Argentina) Squadron stayed barely a month before moving to Portreath on March 18. More Whitleys arrived when several were detached from No. 502 (Ulster) Auxiliary Squadron, the first of several postings to St Eval. Both units were joined by another detachment, this time of Hurricane Is from No. 247 (China-British) Squadron. They arrived in February and departed in May for Portreath.

That month also saw renewed enemy attacks on the aerodrome with two heavy ones resulting in the destruction of three Blenheims and damage to many others. Two of the 'C' Type hangars were severely damaged resulting in canvas Bessonneau hangars having to be erected within their walls.

St Eval was now the major airfield in the Group with Hudsons of No. 206 Squadron and Beauforts of Nos. 217 and 22 Squadrons hunting for U-Boats and enemy shipping. Later the detachment from No. 22 was joined by the remainder of the squadron before moving to Thorney Island prior to being posted overseas. No. 206 was sent to Aldergrove in August but was not replaced by the Hudson Vs of No. 224 Squadron until December. They remained until moving to Limavady in February 1942.

As a break-out from Brest of the battlecruisers *Scharnhorst* and *Gneisenau*, (now repaired after the attack by No. 22 Squadron) was expected at any time, the Beaufort crews were at full readiness each day during this period. However the ships departed during the night of February 11/12, remaining undetected for 12 hours, too late for the Beauforts to mount an attack. In the event, a Swordfish flight from No. 825 Squadron flying from Manston in Kent attacked and crippled the *Scharnhorst* earning Lieutenant-Commander Eugene Esmonde, the CO, a posthumous Victoria Cross for courage.

Having converted to the Whitley VII, the remainder of No. 502 Squadron arrived to join the detachment on February 22. They converted to the Halifax II and moved to Holmsley South in March 1943.

The spring of 1942 saw the Whitleys of No. 58 Squadron touch down at St Eval on April 8 followed by the Hudsons of No. 53 Squadron on May 10. With the increase in U-Boat activity it was felt necessary to base an Operational Training Unit at St Eval. A detachment of No. 10 OTU arrived during August to train aircrew for U-Boat sorties. Another detachment in October was one of Spitfires from No. 543 Squadron for photographic reconnaissance but they disbanded a year later.

Such was the reputation gained by the squadrons operating from St Eval in U-Boat operations that the B-24 Liberators of the 409th Squadron, 93rd Bomb Group of the USAAF arrived for training and experience flights during the summer. Leaving after a stay of a month, the 1st Anti-Submarine Squadron came in to gain experience followed by the 2nd Anti-Submarine Unit but all the American units had left for North Africa by early March 1943.

Joining them during this period were the first Lancasters to fly from the airfield when a detachment of No. 61 Squadron arrived. With the majority of the squadron remaining at Syerston, the St Eval unit achieved success when the U-751 was destroyed in the Bay of Biscay on July 17. After flying 90 sorties from St Eval, they moved to Skellingthorpe in November 1943.

The Halifaxes of No. 58 Squadron left Holmsley South and arrived on March 31, 1943. They joined those of No. 502 Squadron that had recently converted from the ageing Whitleys. This formidible force of Halifaxes roamed far and wide seeking, attacking and sinking several U-Boats. The USAAF returned when the anti-submarine command formed the 479th Anti-Submarine Group at St Eval in July. Four squadrons of long-range

A book of remembrance and this memorial window can be seen in St Ulveus Church at St Eval.

B-24 Liberators — known as the 1st Anti-Submarine (Provisional) Group — patrolled far into the Atlantic and the Bay of Biscay. However their stay proved to be short as the unit moved to Dunkeswell on August 6. That same month a Whitley of No. 10 OTU and a B-24 collided on the runway killing both crews, the inquiry blamed the poor runway layout.

January 1943 had seen the arrival of a Beaufighter detachment from No. 235 Squadron which was followed by another from No. 143 Squadron in August. Providing air cover for the Halifax and Liberators, both had moved on by September.

With the airfield being prone to fog and sea mist, a FIDO (Fog Investigation and Dispersal Operation) facility was installed along the length of the main runway. Pipelines carrying petrol under pressure were ignited at intervals which generated heat to burn off the fog. First to use the system was a Wellington from No. 304 Squadron that had to divert from Chivenor.

By January 1944, St Eval was an all-Liberator base. Nos. 53, 224 and 547 Squadrons were joined by the returning 206 Squadron to form the St Eval Liberator Wing. Remaining over the spring and early summer period, the decline in U-Boat sightings saw them move away as the importance of St Eval as an anti-submarine base declined. This did not stop the Warwicks of No. 282 Squadron coming in from Davidstow Moor on September 19, 1944 with detachments at St Mawgan, Gt Orton and Exeter. Working in the air-sea rescue role with the addition of a Walrus and Sea Otter, they disbanded as the war ended.

The month also saw Wellingtons return when No. 179 Squadron arrived to convert to the Warwick. Further Wellingtons came with No. 304 (Silesian) Polish Squadron on March 6, 1945. They became the last squadron to record a U-Boat kill when Warrant Officer R. Marczak's crew sunk the U-321 off the Irish Coast. Moving to North Weald on July 9, the Liberator VIIIs of No. 224 Squadron returned on July 20. Conversion to the Lancaster GR3 saw them disband on November 10, 1947.

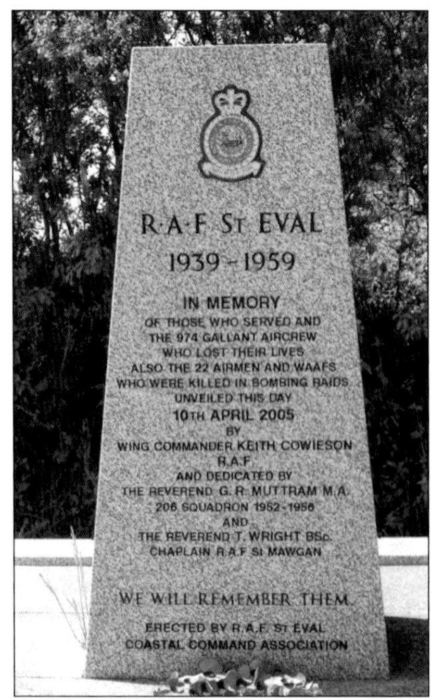

This memorial was also erected to commemorate all those servicemen who lost their lives while serving at the aerodrome.

St Eval now became a Master Diversion Airfield and home to several Shackleton squadrons. However when No. 206 Squadron left in 1958, it entered a period of care and maintenance, finally closing on March 6, 1959.

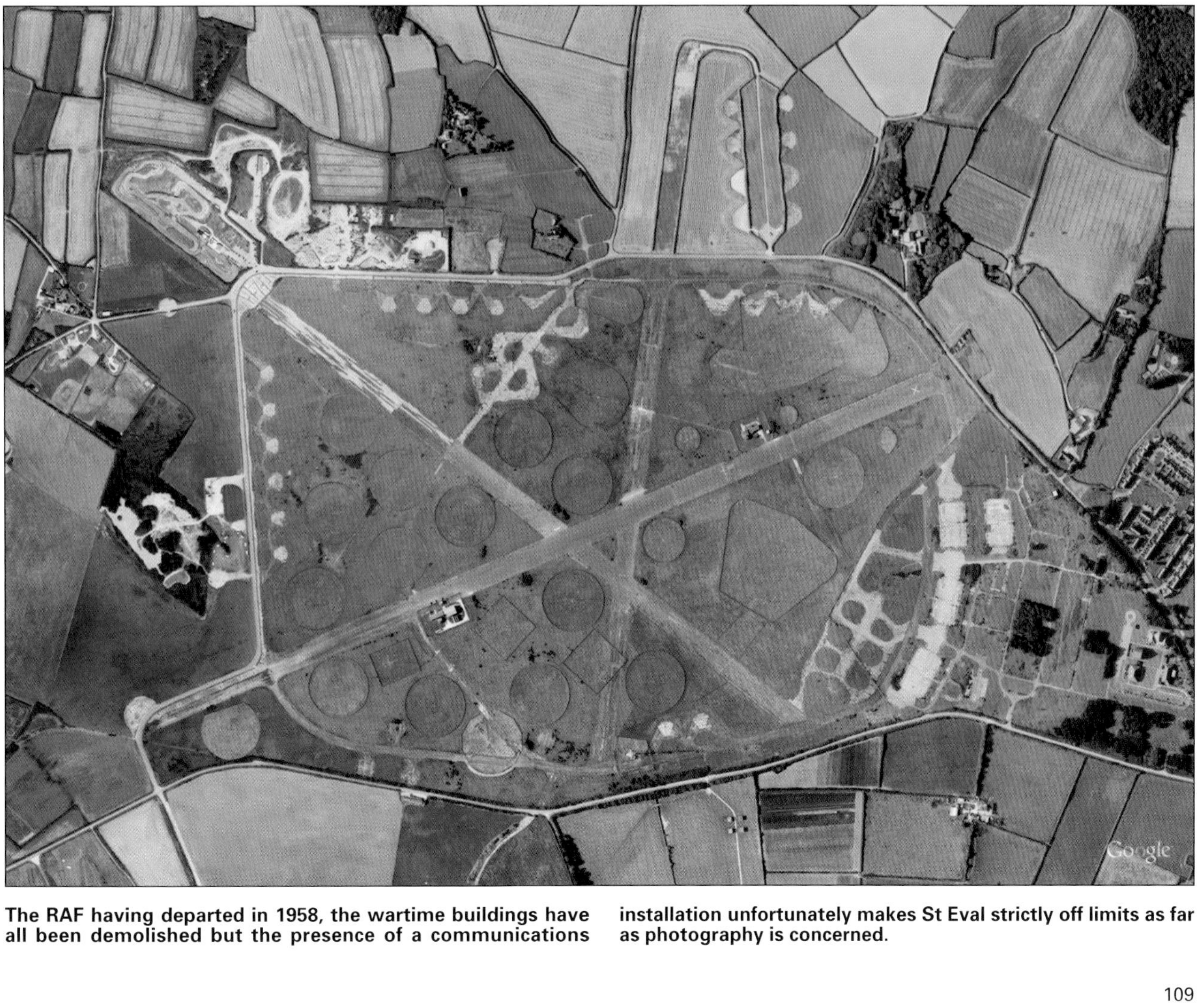

The RAF having departed in 1958, the wartime buildings have all been demolished but the presence of a communications installation unfortunately makes St Eval strictly off limits as far as photography is concerned.

During the war there were three grass strips at St Mary's on the Scilly Isles *(below left)* but today the aerodrome is dominated by the new runway laid down in 1991. The terminal building was added in 1975.

ST MARY'S

Lying one mile east of Hugh Town and 116 feet above sea level, the area of St Mary's saw service during 1917 when flying boats and seaplanes of the 34th Squadron of the Royal Naval Air Service used an area known as Porthmellon. The first landing strip was established on a local golf course with commercial flights beginning in 1937. Two years later High Cross Farm was converted to an airfield which was used by the Great Western and Southern Airways flying Dragon Rapides. However, with the outbreak of war, civil flying ceased and the aerodrome was earmarked to become a military airfield within No. 10 Group.

Accordingly three grass runways were laid out with the longest being 618 x 22 yards, second 566 x 20 yards and third just 530 x 22 yards. Despite being small, a detachment of Hurricane 1s from No. 87 (United Provinces) Squadron arrived at St Mary's from Charmy Down during December 1940. Led by the CO, Squadron Leader Ian Gleed, they found landing and taking off required a certain amount of skill due to the small size of the airfield and also the fact that it was severely 'hump-backed' in the middle! First contact

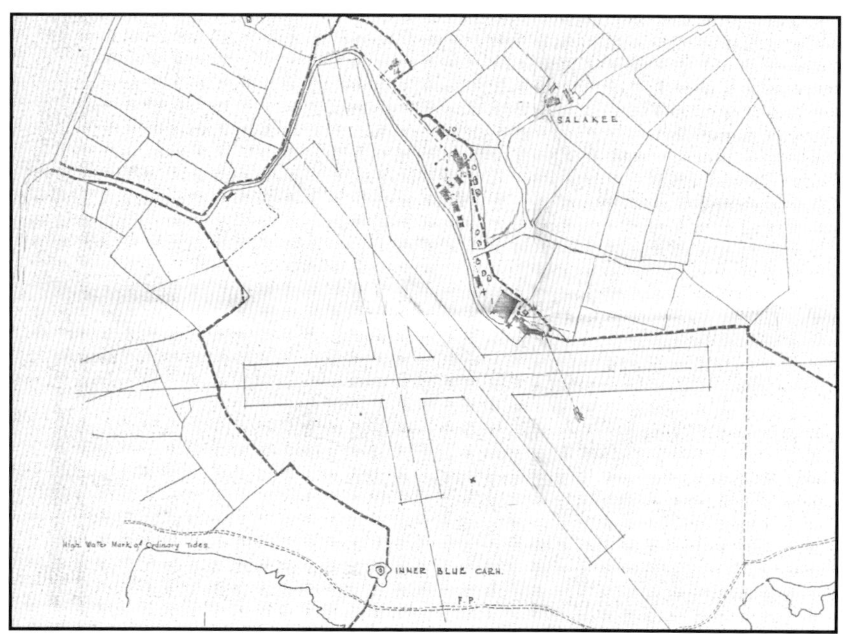

Pilots were told to exercise extreme caution as the airfield was severely hump-backed!

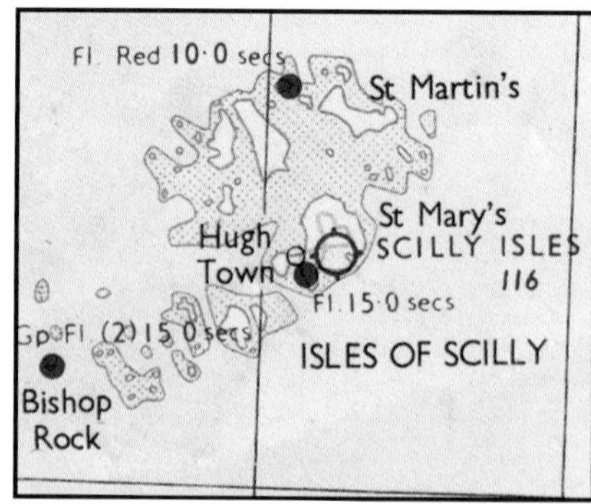

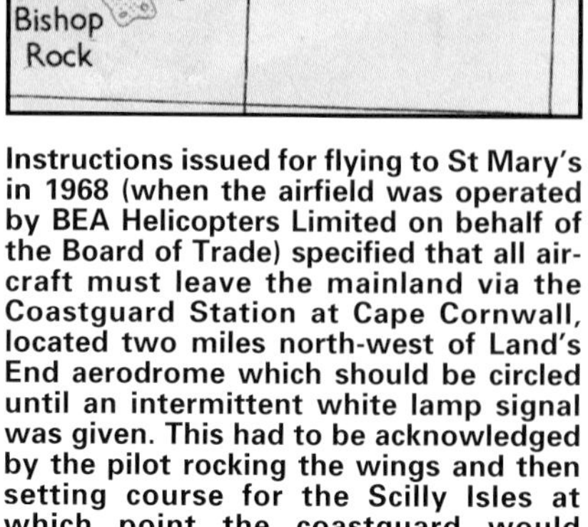

Instructions issued for flying to St Mary's in 1968 (when the airfield was operated by BEA Helicopters Limited on behalf of the Board of Trade) specified that all aircraft must leave the mainland via the Coastguard Station at Cape Cornwall, located two miles north-west of Land's End aerodrome which should be circled until an intermittent white lamp signal was given. This had to be acknowledged by the pilot rocking the wings and then setting course for the Scilly Isles at which point the coastguard would inform St Mary's to expect its arrival.

Responsibility for air defence over the Scilly Isles was entrusted to No. 87 Squadron which sent a detachment from its B Flight to St Mary's. Here Sergeant Ken Hughes takes a lunch break. Hurricane P3149 LK-P in the background.

with the enemy came in May 1941 when the squadron claimed a Do 18 flying boat and on July 18 an He 111 from 1./KG28 was shared by Sergeant A. H. Thom and Flying Officer G. L. Roscoe. Another Ju 88 was claimed by the squadron on August 18. Further patrols continued through the autumn and winter with the detachment becoming No. 1449 Flight in April 1942.

With the primitive conditions on the airfield, the personnel took it upon themselves to improve their lives. The tents were exchanged for Nissen Huts; a Blister hangar was erected for aircraft servicing requirements; a wooden Watch Tower was constructed for airfield control, and a tarmac extension was added to the 10-28 runway.

Although patrols continued throughout 1942 and 1943, just the occasional contact with the enemy was forthcoming with no positive results. By 1944, with the Allies established in France, No. 1449 Flight was disbanded and all military flying at St Mary's ceased as it was relegated to care and maintenance. Scheduled civil services resumed in 1945 with the airfield being operated by the Council of the Isles of Scilly, and in 2009 it was claimed to be the tenth busiest regional airport in the UK.

On standby ready for the call to scramble.

Left: Pilot Officer Ivor Badger pictured enjoying his cup of victory tea after having destroyed an Arado 196 on May 19, 1944.

Right: From this nice post-war shot, we can see that the picture was taken beside the old watch office.

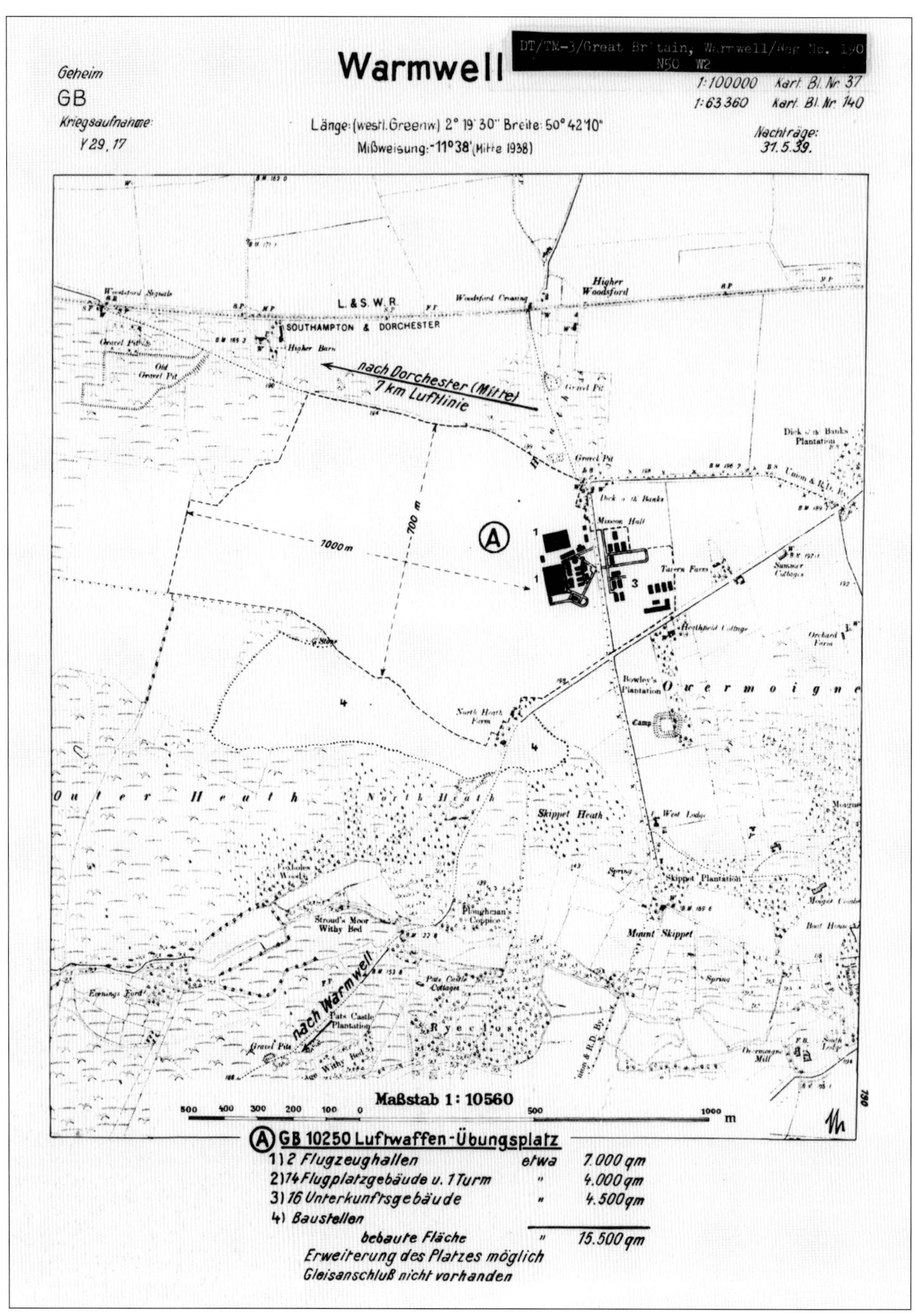

In the run up to the Second World War, the Luftwaffe had prepared hundreds of target folders covering a wide variety of installations in Britain. Each were given separate reference numbers — Warmwell aerodrome, then a grass field, being Target No. 250 — all airfields being classified as Group 10 (viz: GB 10 250). Other target groups were: Oil Tanks 21; Harbours 45; Wireless Stations 49; Power Stations 50; Gasworks 52; Ironworks 70; Munitions factories 76; Aircraft factories 82, and so on.

WARMWELL

Warmwell situated on Woodsford Heath sat on a rich deposit of gravel and the planning authorities decreed that if runways were laid down, the gravel should be first extracted but, in the event, hard runways were never constructed.

Known initially as RAF Woodsford in the county of Dorset, Warmwell officially opened in May 1937 as one of the new aerodromes created under the RAF expansion plans. Situated to the south of the Wareham to Dorchester railway line and 203 feet above sea level, the grass landing area measured 1,900 yards from both NE-SW and SE-NW, and 1,750 yards E-W although the N-S direction was just 800 yards. Its function was as an operational satellite to Middle Wallop. Hangar accommodation consisted of two Bellman and eight Blisters together with storage of 34,000 gallons of aviation spirit and 5,000 gallons of motor fuel. Night landing facilities were limited to a Glim Lamp flarepath whilst radio facilities were VHF and DF. Six double pens, 12 single pens and 18 small pan-type hardstandings were sited around the perimeter with accommodation for 1,675 personnel.

With the Chesil Beach bombing and gunnery range close by, the first occupant was No. 6 Armament Training Camp under the control of No. 25 Group Training Command. A station flight was formed in July 1937 with Avro Tutors and Westland Wallaces. A change in name to No. 6 Armament Training School coincided with Woodsford also being renamed RAF Warmwell.

In May 1940 the station switched from Training Command to Fighter Command and was classed as a forward aerodrome in Middle Wallop Sector 'Y' in No. 10 Group. The Spitfires of No. 609 (West Riding) Auxiliary Squadron used Warmwell as a day base flying over from Middle Wallop at dawn but on October 2, 1940, they made Warmwell their permanent home. Joined by No. 152 (Hyderabad) Squadron with Spitfire Is on July 12, the two squadrons were to fly from Warmwell for the rest of the summer months.

The formation of No. 10 Bombing and Gunnery School and the Central Gunnery School saw Warmwell become a very busy station as squadrons rotated through on courses. An attack on the airfield on August 25 saw some 20 bombs dropped destroying the station sick quarters, damaging hangars and several buildings and leaving large craters on the landing ground. The rest of the year saw both squadrons still based at the airfield with No. 609 leaving for Biggin Hill on February 24, 1941. In March, No. 152 converted to the Spitfire IIA and moved out to Portreath on April 9. No. 234 (Madras Presidency) Squadron had been posted in from St Eval on February 24, with Spitfire Is converting to the Mk IIA in March and Mk VB in September. Joining them for a few days were No. 118 Squadron who flew into Warmwell on April 9, leaving for Ibsley nine days later.

With the departure of the Central Gunnery School to Northern Ireland, No. 1487 Target Towing Flight formed at Warmwell on November 20, 1941 to take their place. The 12 Lysanders were converted for towing and remained at the station until September 1943. A change in type saw Hurricanes at Warmwell with No. 302 (Poznan) Polish

In 1940 facilities were primitive and this tent pictured on the northern dispersal area served as the crew room for pilots of No. 609 Squadron. Calls of nature had to be carried out across the road!

And we must not forget the ground crews, seen here labouring in the mud in October 1940.

Squadron on September 5, followed by those of No. 402 (Winnipeg Bear) Canadian Squadron on November 6. Another unit to form at Warmwell was No. 175 Squadron in March 1942. They flew the Hurricane IIB converted to carry a bomb under each wing, the 'Hurribombers' finding success when they sank two enemy minesweepers during May. Operation 'Jubilee' the Dieppe operation, saw further success for the squadron when, in the attacking role, the Hurricanes claimed a He III and an Fw 190 destroyed.

With the Canadians leaving in March 1942 for Colerne, No. 175 Squadron returned as the resident squadron until No. 266 (Rhodesia) Squadron brought their Typhoons in from Duxford on September 21. Two days before it was the twin-engined Westland Whirlwind that No. 263 (Fellowship of the Bellows-Argentina) Squadron flew in to Warmwell. With both squadrons sending detachments to Predannack, the rest of the aircraft managed to sink a considerable amount of enemy shipping. Taking their Whirlwinds to Harrowbeer in February 1943, the Typhoons returned in the form of No. 257 (Burma) Squadron in January 1943, with the Hurricanes of No. 164 Squadron arriving in June. By August both squadrons had left.

Warmwell had originally been allocated to the USAAF back in August 1942 but American units had not taken up permanent residence. It had been used on a few occasions as a forward landing ground for aircraft of the Eighth Air Force but was now to become Station 454 in the Ninth Air

Now it is November 1941 and No. 402 Squadron have moved in with their Hurribombers, seen here receiving 250-pounders.

An American oblique taken looking towards the east when Warmwell became Station 454 of the US Ninth Air Force.

Force.The first airmen arrived on March 12, 1944, part of the 474th Fighter Group. The group's three squadrons were equipped with the Lockheed P-38 Lightning, and they were to fly from Warmwell for four months completing 108 missions and losing 27 aircraft in the process. Flying their final sortie from Warmwell on August 5, they were the last of the Ninth's 18 fighter groups to move into France. After it was handed back to the RAF, No. 17 Armament Practice Camp arrived to provide gunnery training for the squadrons of the Second Tactical Air Force.

Over the years various air-sea rescue detachments had been based at Warmwell. These were Nos. 276, 275 and 277 flying an assortment of aircraft such as Lysanders, Hurricanes, Ansons, Defiants and Walrus. When No. 277 detachment disbanded on February 15, 1945, the airfield was left to care and maintenance before finally being sold in 1950.

Exactly the same view today. Over the past 50 years, over 350 acres have been mined for gravel, totally obliterating the aerodrome.

No. 11 GROUP

Back in the 1920s, the original Operations Room controlling the Air Defence of Great Britain had been located in a building in the grounds of Hillingdon House at Uxbridge which the Air Ministry had purchased in 1915. After No. 11 Group was brought into being in 1936, work to construct a new underground complex over 60 feet below ground began in February 1939, being completed just before the outbreak of war.

On April 22, 1958, Air Chief Marshal Lord Dowding was given the honour of unveiling a commemorative marker over the bunker . . . and then inspecting the restored interior.

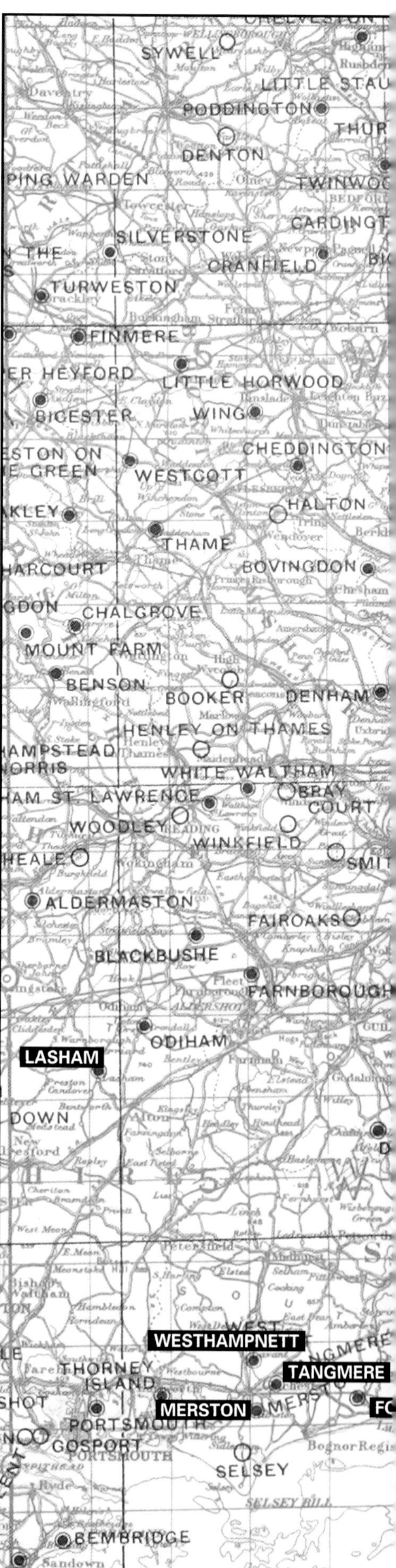

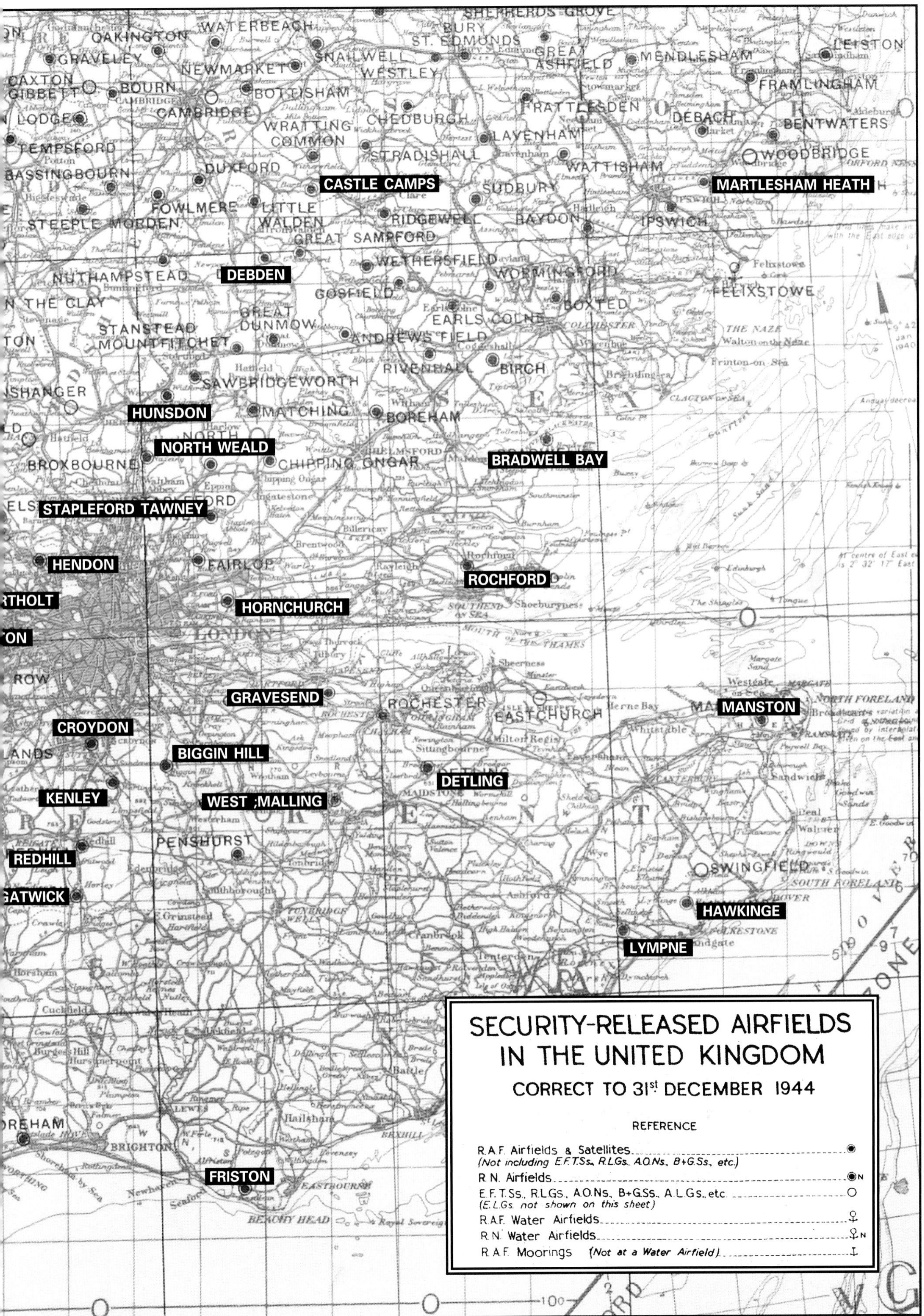
SECURITY-RELEASED AIRFIELDS
IN THE UNITED KINGDOM
CORRECT TO 31st DECEMBER 1944
REFERENCE
R.A.F. Airfields & Satellites
(Not including E.F.T.Ss., R.L.Gs., A.O.Ns., B+G.Ss., etc.)
R.N. Airfields
E.F.T.Ss., R.L.Gs., A.O.Ns., B+G.Ss., A.L.G.s., etc
(E.L.Gs. not shown on this sheet)
R.A.F. Water Airfields
R.N. Water Airfields
R.A.F. Moorings (Not at a Water Airfield)
CASTLE CAMPS
MARTLESHAM HEATH
DEBDEN
HUNSDON
NORTH WEALD
BRADWELL BAY
STAPLEFORD TAWNEY
HENDON
ROCHFORD
HORNCHURCH
GRAVESEND
MANSTON
CROYDON
BIGGIN HILL
DETLING
KENLEY
WEST ;MALLING
REDHILL
GATWICK
HAWKINGE
LYMPNE
FRISTON
OAKINGTON
WATERBEACH
GRAVELEY
NEWMARKET
BOURN
BOTTISHAM
CAMBRIDGE
WRATTING COMMON
CHEDBURGH
TEMPSFORD
STRADISHALL
BASSINGBOURN
DUXFORD
FOWLMERE
LITTLE WALDEN
STEEPLE MORDEN
RIDGEWELL
GREAT SAMPFORD
NUTHAMPSTEAD
WETHERSFIELD
WORMINGFORD
GOSFIELD
BOXTED
STANSTEAD MOUNTFITCHET
GREAT DUNMOW
EARLS COLNE
ANDREWS FIELD
RIVENHALL
BIRCH
SAWBRIDGEWORTH
MATCHING
BOREHAM
BROXBOURNE
CHIPPING ONGAR
FAIRLOP
ROCHESTER
EASTCHURCH
PENSHURST
SWINGFIELD
BURY ST. EDMUNDS
SNAILWELL
WESTLEY
GREAT ASHFIELD
MENDLESHAM
LEISTON
FRAMLINGHAM
RATTLESDEN
DEBACH
BENTWATERS
LAVENHAM
WOODBRIDGE
WATTISHAM
SUDBURY
RAYDON
IPSWICH
FELIXSTOWE
LONDON
BEACHY HEAD

BIGGIN HILL

As part of the pre-war intelligence gathering operation by the Luftwaffe on RAF bases, photographs would be taken from German aircraft on scheduled flights — in this case most probably en route to Croydon Airport.

Situated north of Biggin Hill village in Kent, and on the eastern side of the A233 road, the airfield lay 600 feet above sea level on a high plateau of the North Downs. It was originally an experimental site telephony before it became an air force station in 1916 with the arrival of No. 39 Squadron. No. 141 were stationed there in February 1918. The grass landing area measured N-S 1,660 yards, NE-SW 1,337 yards, E-W 710 yards and SW-NE 2,000 yards, but part of the reconstruction during the expansion period included laying down a tarmac runway running 03-21 measuring 1,600 x 50 yards.

Biggin Hill was to become a pivotal sector station in Sector 'C' of Fighter Command. The commencement of hostilities saw the Hurricanes of Nos. 32 and 79 (Madras Presidency) Squadrons and the Blenheims of No. 601 (County of London) Auxiliary Squadron in residence. With very little action during the 'Phoney War', 601 Squadron moved to Manston, 32 to Gravesend and 79 to Manston whilst further construction work was carried out. Returning to Biggin in early March 1940, Nos. 32 and 79 Squadrons commenced Channel convoy patrols before the latter was sent to France as part of the Air Component of the British Expeditionary Force. Their replacement was No. 610 (County of Chester) Auxiliary Squadron bringing the first Spitfires to the airfield.

With the evacuation of the BEF from France, No. 79 Squadron returned to Biggin but was then sent north to rest together with No. 32 Squadron. Their place was taken by a Hurricane detachment of No. 213 (Ceylon) Squadron and No. 242 (Canadian) Squadron. Meanwhile No. 610 Squadron had moved to Gravesend for the evacuation with all squadrons seeing plenty of action over the Dunkirk beaches.

Since the war, the southern side of Biggin Hill has been developed into a major business airport while the RAF maintained a separate presence in the North Camp on the north-western corner until the station was closed in 1992.

Biggin Hill

Flugplatz

Länge (ostw. Greenw.): 0° 02′ Nördl. Breite: 51° 19′ 30″

Zielhöhe über NN 177 m

Maßstab etwa: 1 : 18 500

Lfl. Kdo. 3 Juli 1941

Karte 1 : 100000

GB/E 34 b/d

After war broke out Luftwaffe reconnaisance aircraft updated their target files, this shot being taken in July 1941.

The month of June saw Nos. 32 and 79 back for brief periods and, as the Battle of Britain commenced, No. 610 Squadron returned to be joined by No. 141 with the Defiant turreted fighter on July 8. However, on their first operation flying from the forward airfield of Hawkinge, the squadron lost six aircraft with four pilots and five gunners killed and other aircraft damaged and aircrew injured. Consequently, the Defiant was withdrawn from day operations and the remainder of the squadron were posted north to Prestwick.

The rest of the month saw Nos. 32 and 610 Squadrons in daily contact with the enemy. August also saw several heavy enemy attacks on Biggin rendering the airfield almost unserviceable. Only with the operations room being relocated to a large house nearby was it able to carry on with the vital task of directing squadrons.

The departure of No. 32 Squadron on August 27 heralded the return of No. 79 Squadron. Two days after their arrival the airfield was subjected to another heavy enemy attack during the course of which further damage was sustained on the runways and buildings.

When No. 610 Squadron were rested on August 31, No. 72 (Basutoland) Squadron came to replace them. Flying Spitfires, they fought alongside No. 79 Squadron until the state of the battered airfield forced them to move to Croydon. Further enemy attacks reduced Biggin Hill to a shell yet it still remained operational. The Luftwaffe's change of tactics in early September to the bombing of cities instead of airfields came just in time as work commenced to repair the damage. This allowed No. 92 (East India) Squadron to fly in from Pembrey on September 8. The return of No. 141 Squadron, still flying Defiants, though now in a night-fighter role, brought Biggin Hill once again to full squadron strength even though repair work continued.

Although the hut has long gone, and the aircraft are no longer Spitfires of No. 124 Squadron, the same E-pen remains as a reminder of wartime Biggin. This unit was stationed at the airfield from November 1941 to May 1942.

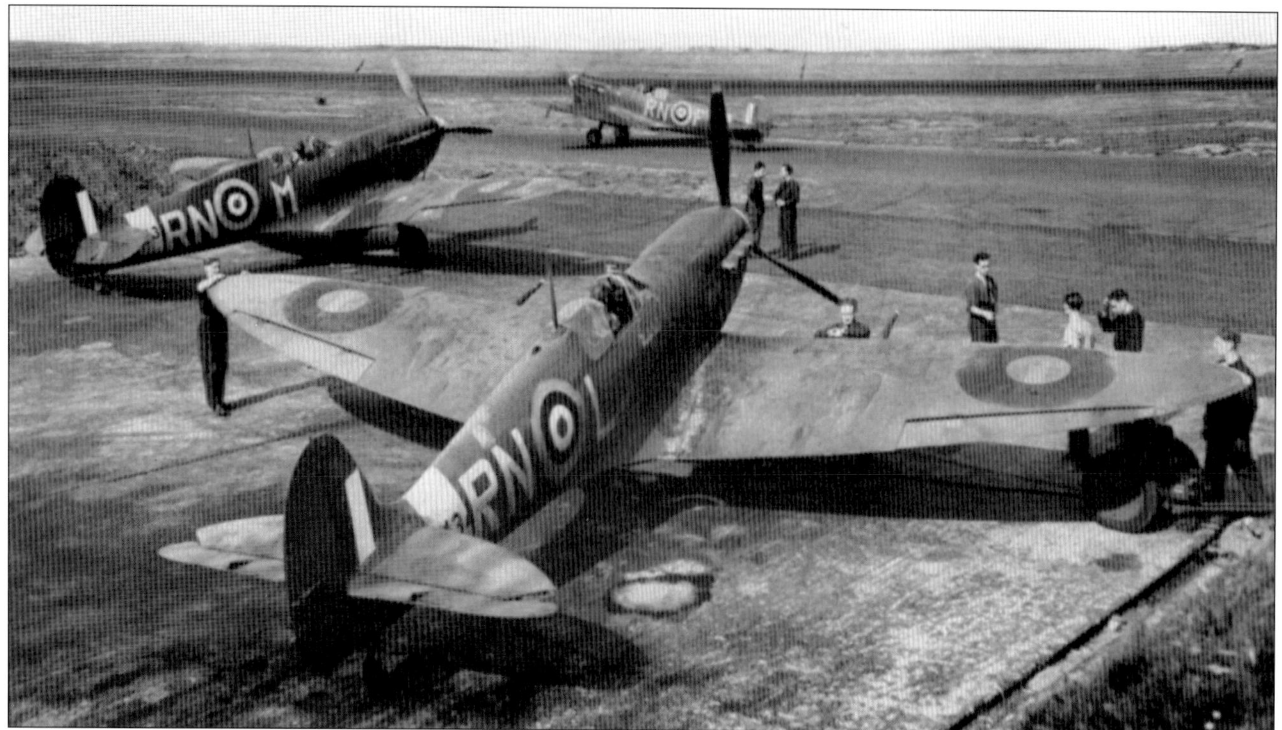

Spitfires of No. 72 Squadron pictured in August 1941. The pilots of RN-L and RN-M of B Flight wait for RN-F of A Flight to taxi past before starting their engines.

On October 15, No. 72 was replaced by No. 74 'Tiger' Squadron equipped with Spitfire IIAs and led by Squadron Leader 'Sailor' Malan. With the raids on Fighter Command airfields now less frequent, Biggin Hill, like many others, was set to become a major airfield in the offensive role. An extra squadron, No. 66, flew in from West Malling on November 7 just as Biggin became the first station to claim 600 kills.

The New Year saw many changes. No. 74 Squadron moved to Manston to be replaced by No. 92 Squadron whilst No. 66 was posted to Exeter. No. 609 (West Riding) Squadron arrived on February 24 quickly converting from the Spitfire I to the IIA and eventually to the Spitfire VB. This period also saw the formation of the Biggin Hill Wing, led by Wing Commander Malan, which consisted of Nos. 92, 609 and 74 Squadrons. Over the coming months the Wing was to carry out many 'Rhubarb' sorties (low-level strike operations against targets in occupied Europe) in conjunction with 'Circus' operations (fighter-escorted bombing raids designed to attract a response from the Luftwaffe). In May the Biggin Wing claimed 17 enemy aircraft destroyed with a further seven damaged, the airfield now having become known as 'Britain's Premier Fighter Station'.

The end of July saw No. 609 take their Spitfires to Gravesend whilst No. 92 converted to the Spitfire VB and No. 72 returned. In September No. 92 and 609 switched stations with each other, Biggin Hill seeing the arrival of No. 401 (Ram) Squadron of the RCAF on October 20. No. 124 (Baroda) Squadron then took over the Spitfire VBs of No. 609 when the latter left for Digby on November 19.

No further changes took place until May 3, 1942 when the third Eagle Squadron — No. 133 — took over the dispersal recently vacated by No. 124 Squadron. Now famil-

A wonderful comparison with the Mk1 Spitfire from the Biggin Hill Heritage Hangar standing in the same blast pen.

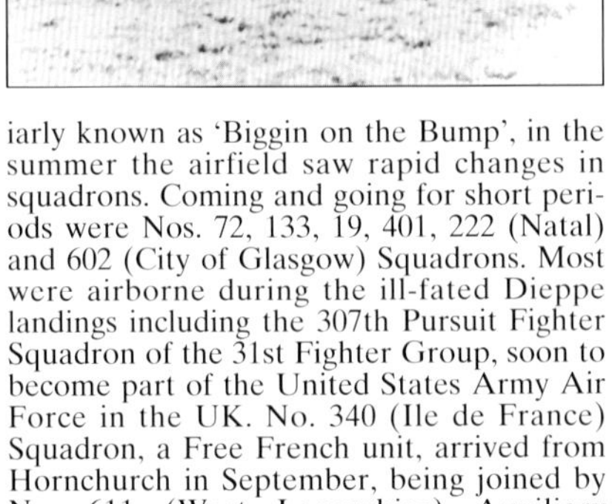

A new taxiway has been added since the Hurricane of No. 32 Squadron was photographed about to touch down in August 1940.

iarly known as 'Biggin on the Bump', in the summer the airfield saw rapid changes in squadrons. Coming and going for short periods were Nos. 72, 133, 19, 401, 222 (Natal) and 602 (City of Glasgow) Squadrons. Most were airborne during the ill-fated Dieppe landings including the 307th Pursuit Fighter Squadron of the 31st Fighter Group, soon to become part of the United States Army Air Force in the UK. No. 340 (Ile de France) Squadron, a Free French unit, arrived from Hornchurch in September, being joined by No. 611 (West Lancashire) Auxiliary Squadron on the same day.

The New Year saw an enemy attack approach Biggin Hill, the first in over two years. Twenty FW 190s carrying bombs and flying at zero feet overshot the airfield and dropped bombs in nearby Catford, sadly hitting a school killing teachers and pupils.

Typhoons arrived at Biggin on February 9 when No. 1 Squadron stayed for two weeks working up on the type before leaving for Lympne. Another Free French unit, No. 341 (GCIII/2 Alsace) Squadron, arrived on March 21. On May 15 the station claimed its 1,000th victory when Squadron Leader Jack Charles of No. 611 Squadron and Commandant Rene Mouchotte of No. 341 Squadron shared the honour.

High summer saw No. 485 (RNZAF) arrive to replace No. 611 before the airfield came under the umbrella of the Second Tactical Air Force. At the end of the year the Free French and New Zealand squadrons were posted away as Biggin Hill became No. 126 Airfield of the 17th (Fighter) Wing of the RCAF controlled by No. 83 Group. As a result it now became an all-Canadian station as Nos. 401 (Ram), 411 (Grizzly Bear) and 412 (Falcon) Squadrons arrived, the Wing carrying out sweeps and escort duties prior to D-Day. As June approached, the squadrons moved down to Tangmere on the south coast and Biggin Hill was downgraded to a sector station in No. 24 (Base Defence) Wing of No. 85 (Base) Group of the Allied Expeditionary Force.

With the advent of the V1 attacks, the airfield was used as a barrage balloon base until the end of 1944 when it became a transport command terminal. A brief stay by No. 340 (GC IV/2 Ile de France) Squadron during November 1944 saw them become the last fighter squadron to use the airfield during the war.

Peacetime saw Biggin Hill become both a major fighter station and also the Aircrew Selection Centre but with 41 Squadron leaving in 1958 and the Selection Centre moving to Cranwell in 1995, the RAF formally quit the airfield. Today it operates as a major civil airport with memories of its wartime role being maintained in the magnificent St George's Chapel flanked by a replica Hurricane and Spitfire.

Spitfire IXs of No. 611 Squadron cross the North Camp in December 1942. Below them stands the remains of the triple-bay hangar bombed back in 1940.

The large hangar partially masking the present-day view belongs to the Formula 1 chief Bernie Ecclestone.

BRADWELL BAY

In April 1942, No. 418 Squadron of the Royal Canadian Air Force was operating American Douglas Boston IIIs on night intruder sorties from Bradwell Bay using their ventral gun pack comprising four 20mm cannons.

Originally a grass airfield, Bradwell Bay was used for re-arming and refuelling aircraft using the nearby firing ranges at Dengie Flats. The outbreak of war saw it earmarked for development as a fighter aerodrome eventually becoming a satellite to the parent station of North Weald..

Situated nine miles south-east of Southminster, the major reconstruction began during 1941 when a grass surface measuring 1,400 yards SE-NW and 1,000 yards N-S, E-W and NE-SW was levelled ready for three tarmac runways. A Bellman hangar and 12 Extra Over Blisters were erected and a Watch Office was added later in the year.

Despite two small attacks by the enemy, and although not complete, the airfield was sufficiently finished to allow a detachment of Douglas Havocs from No. 23 Squadron to arrive at the end of 1941. However, the first full squadron to be based there was the Canadian No. 418 (City of Edmonton). They bought their matt-black Douglas Bostons in on April 15, 1942. Detailed to carry out night intruder operations over France, Holland and Belgium, they became very proficient at attacking targets at low level.

No. 23 converted from the Boston to the Mosquito before the entire squadron moved from Manston to join the detachment at Bradwell Bay on August 14. Joining them were further Mosquitos from No. 264 (Madras Presidency) Squadron. They remained until rejoining the rest of the squadron for a move to Predannack on April 30, 1943.

The idea of collecting funds for the purchase of presentation aircraft for the Royal Air Force was extremely popular as it gave cities, towns, counties, businesses and even individuals the ability to 'do their bit' and help the war effort in a positive way. £40,000 would provide a four-engined bomber; £20,000 a twin and £5,000 a single-seater fighter. On December 11, 1944, six Spitfires IXs were ceremoniously presented to the RAF on behalf of the Persian Gulf Spitfire Fund. Here Squadron Leader J. A. 'Johnny' Plagis of No. 126 Squadron extends an introduction to Lady Fowle, widow of Sir Trenchard Fowle, the former British Resident Minister in the Persian Gulf. Presentation Spitfires were by far the most numerous aircraft, £5,000 then being the equivalent of £800,000 today. After the war, the Air Ministry sold them off for £100!

Most of the airfield buildings have disappeared at Bradwell but the control tower has a new lease of life as a private dwelling.

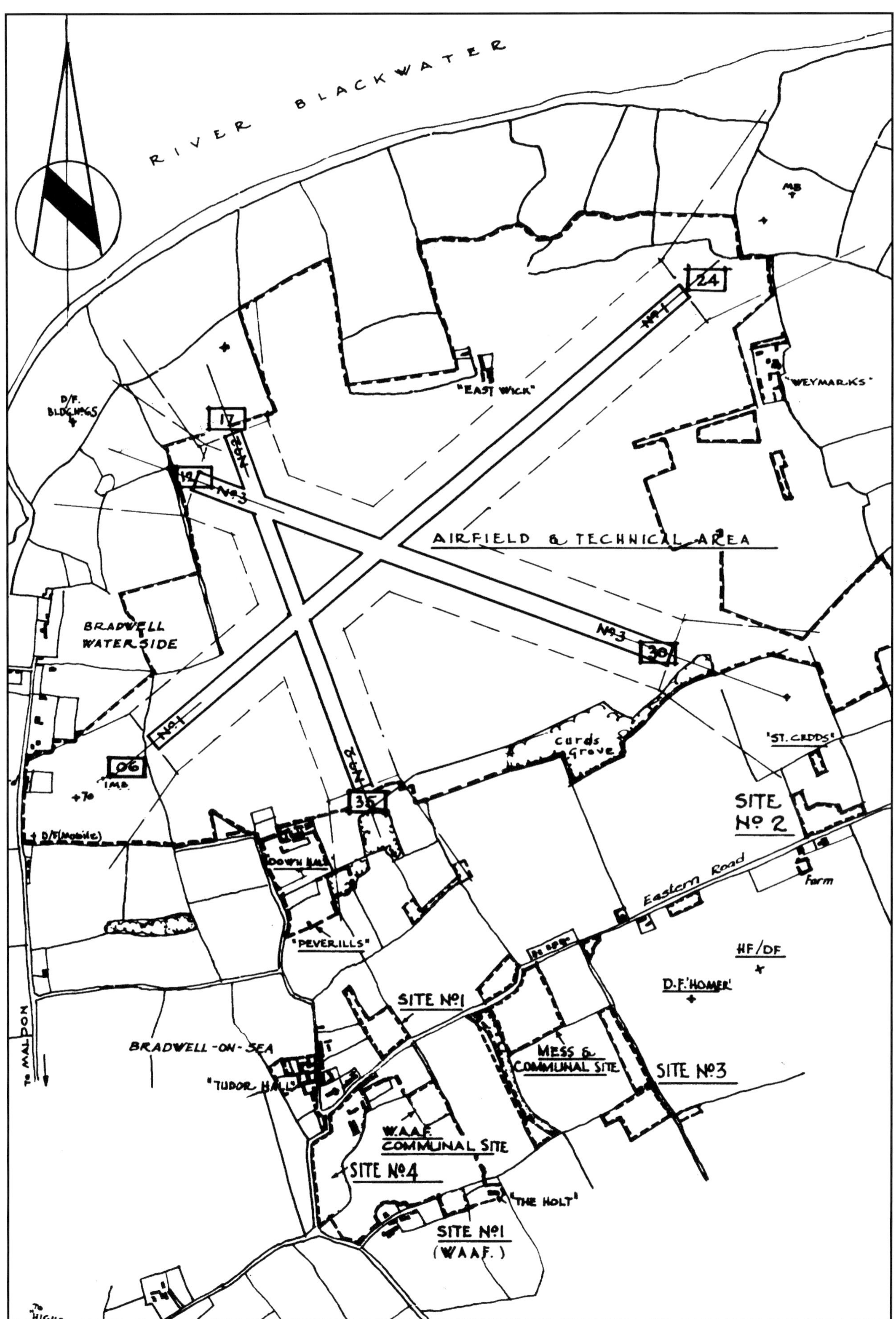

Plan of the aerodrome produced by the Air Ministry in April 1945.

Located just a few hundred yards from the Essex coast, Bradwell Bay proved to be a godsend to aircraft limping home across the Channel. Flying Officer Roy Calvert successfully landed this Lancaster (R5702) of No. 50 Squadron based at Skellingthorpe (see *Bases of Bomber Command Then and Now*) after being badly shot up on a raid to Hamburg on November 9, 1942.

No. 157 Squadron with their Mosquitos had spent several months training for night operations at Castle Camps. Arriving at Bradwell Bay on March 15, they carried out their first night sortie on the 23rd. Three weeks later success came their way when a FW 190 was shot down at night by which time the squadron had moved to Hunsdon.

As they left the Beaufighters of No. 29 Squadron flew in. Conversion to the Mosquito XII in May and the Mosquito VI in July saw several operations carried out before they moved south to Ford on September 3.

The first of several Typhoon squadrons had arrived on June 4 when No. 247 (China-British) came in from Gravesend. Followed by Nos. 198 on August 19 and 56 (Punjab) four days later, by October they had departed to be replaced once again by Mosquitos. First to fly in were the Mosquito XIIs of No. 488 (RNZAF) Squadron on September 3 followed by the Mosquito VIs of No. 605 (County of Warwick) Auxiliary Squadron on October 6. Both squadrons found success

Then . . . and now . . . from Air Ministry files to Google Earth.

The aerodrome today is overshadowed by the now-defunct nuclear power station.

Men of the RAF Regiment on patrol at Bradwell pass a Douglas Havoc — the fighter version of the Boston.

whilst at Bradwell, most notable being the night of March 14-15, 1944 when a Ju 88 was shot down and the night of March 21-22 when three Ju 88s fell to the guns of No. 488 Squadron. They converted to the Mosquito XIII leaving for Colerne on May 3 whilst No. 605 left for Manston on April 7.

For a brief period the Tempest Vs of No. 3 Squadron came to stay but they left as work began to install the FIDO fog dispersal system. This was to prove invaluable for American and British bombers returning to East Anglia and finding their home bases shrouded in fog.

Spitfire VIIs belonging to No. 124 (Baroda) Squadron arrived on April 23 from Church Fenton. They commenced bomber escort duties leaving for Detling on July 26 to become part of the Detling Wing.

Mid-1944 was to prove a busy time for the base as Nos. 64, 126 (Persian Gulf) and 611 (West Lancashire) Squadrons arrived with Spitfires on August 30 to form the Bradwell Bay Fighter Wing for bomber escort and anti-V1 operations. At this period it was felt necessary to base an air-sea rescue squadron at the airfield, so the Ansons of No. 278 were posted in on April 21. Quickly becoming obsolete, the squadron were re-equipped with Spitfires and a Warwick. Sending detachments to Martlesham Heath and Hornchurch, they left for Thorney Island during March 1945.

No. 611 took their Spitfires to Skeabrae on October 3 leaving the other two squadrons to convert to Mustangs but by December 1944 both had left leaving just No. 501 in situ until March 1945.

The last year of war saw Nos. 310, 312 and 313 (Czech) Squadrons form a Spitfire wing and carry out further patrols to counter the V-weapons. Arriving in January they left for Manston the following month whereupon several squadrons arrived for brief periods with Nos. 151, 456 (RAAF) and 25 Squadrons all seeing the war out at Bradwell Bay.

By 1946 the Air Ministry had relinquished control of the airfield and it rapidly reverted back to farming although part of the site was used for building one of Britain's first nuclear power stations.

The Magnox plant became operational in 1962 but was closed down in 2002. The site will not be decontaminated until 2083.

A memorial commemorating all those who flew or were killed whilst stationed at the airfield has been erected in one corner.

One of the most striking memorials to fighting men. Crowned with a fallen Mosquito, the panels are inscribed with the names of 121 servicemen of the Royal Air Force, Royal Canadian Air Force and Royal New Zealand Air Force, who failed to return.

In July 1940, an American magazine wanted to obtain photographs for an article on the RAF, its pilots and aircraft fighting in the Battle of Britain which had just begun. They chose to feature Castle Camps which had just become operational the previous month, this shot showing 'a Hurricane of No. 85 Squadron and the huts where the pilots live, the nearest one being the bar and recreation room. Ground crews had tents along the edge of the field as the aerodrome was just grass.'

CASTLE CAMPS

Built over the period 1939-40, the airfield was to be an operational satellite to Debden in Essex. Three miles south-east of Bartlow and 420 feet above sea level, the grass surface measured 1,400 yards NE-SW, 1,100 yards E-W and 1,000 yards N-S and SE-NW. Four Blister hangars and a Flying Control together with a 36-foot perimeter track were ready by June 27, 1940 to allow No. 85 Squadron to send a detachment of Hurricanes to Castle Camps. Although accommodation was in tents, the entire squadron arrived from Croydon before moving to Church Fenton. Further Hurricanes came on September 5 when No. 73 Squadron arrived. Having been very active during the Battle of France, the move to Castle Camps proved a failure when five Hurricanes fell with the loss of two pilots. The squadron left on November 6 for the Middle East.

Even though the aerodrome had been camouflaged with tar lines to break up the outline, the Luftwaffe still found the new airfield and photographed it on August 30, 1940. Several barrack huts can be seen around the perimeter.

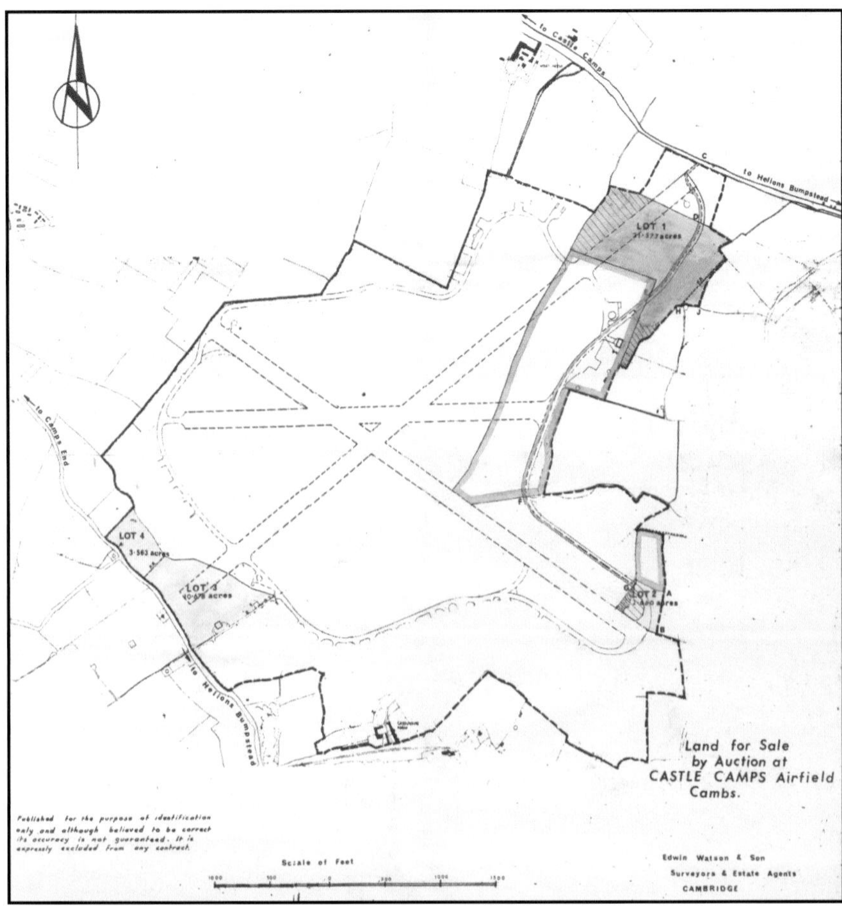

The end of an aerodrome. Greatly enlarged since 1940 with hard runways, first came the disposal by auction . . . then the inevitable demolitions.

With no resident squadron, contractors moved in to improve conditions. Three tarmac runways were laid with the longest being 1,600 x 50 yards and secondaries 950 x 50 yards. More permanent accommodation was built and several hardstandings for aircraft dispersal were laid down. Once completed the advance party of No. 157 Squadron, which had reformed at the parent station of Debden, arrived on December 18, 1941. They were the first fighter squadron to be equipped with the Mosquito II, the aircraft arriving at Castle Camps in January 1942. Undertaking a period of night fighter training, several claims were made with the first positive kill coming on the night of August 22-23 when Wing Commander R. G. Slade and his navigator, Pilot Officer P. Truscott, shot down a Do 217 over Suffolk. The squadron left for Bradwell Bay on March 15, 1943.

Their place was taken the same day by No. 605 (County of Warwick) Auxiliary Squadron, also flying Mosquitos. Converting to the Mk VI variant, they began intruder flights with some of the aircraft carrying bombs. A move to Bradwell Bay on October 6 saw the forming of No. 527 Radar Calibration Squadron at Castle Camps on June 15. Equipped with Hurricanes, Blenheims and a Hornet Moth, the unit gave sterling service to the radar sites within the area before moving to Snailwell on February 28, 1944.

Mosquitos returned on December 30, 1943 when No. 410 (Cougar) Canadian Squadron bought their Mk XIIIs in. However, achieving little success in meeting the enemy at this stage of the war, they moved back to Hunsdon on April 29, 1944.

A stay of just a month allowed No. 91 Squadron to convert from the Spitfire XII to the Mk XIV variant over the period February-March 1944. When they left for Drem on March 17, Tempests of No. 486 (RNZAF) Squadron spent a similar period at Castle Camps. Arriving on March 6 they departed to Ayr on the 21st only to return eight days later for a further month.

Not until June 23 did fighters return when No. 68 Squadron flew in from Fairwood Common. Though still equipped with the Beaufighter VIF, they quickly converted to the Mosquito XVII and XIX to begin patrols against the V1. Moving to Coltishall on October 28, similar patrols were carried out by the Mosquitos of Nos. 151 and 25 Squadrons. With both squadrons arriving as No. 68 Squadron departed, No. 151 quickly left for Hunsdon on November 19 although No. 25 squadron stayed until July 1945.

With victory in sight, sojourns were undertaken by Nos. 307 (Lwow) Polish and 85 Squadrons before Castle Camps finally closed during the summer of 1946. A brick memorial now marks the airfield that has returned to agriculture.

Croydon was officially opened by Lady Maud Hoare, the wife of the Secretary of State for Air, on May 2, 1928. With its impressive terminal building and associated hotel, it was a modern thriving centre for air travel to Europe.

CROYDON

Formed after the First World War by the merger of Beddington and Wadden airfields, during the inter-war years Croydon had been the hub for Imperial Airways and smaller airlines. But the coming of war effectively brought about a premature merger of them all when they were taken over by the Air Ministry on September 5, 1939. By the end of the year, the airfield — previously known as Croydon London Airport — had become the assembly point for RAF machines, supplies and personnel, intended for the Air Component of the British Expeditionary Force in France.

A large grass aerodrome situated south-west of Croydon between the B271 and B272, it lay just 20 minutes from the centre of London. Between the wars more land had been acquired for the ever-expanding airport, so much so that by August 1939, four landing strips had been laid out for its anticipated RAF use. The two longest, each of 1,200 yards, ran N-S and NE-SW. The E-W runway had a length of 1,120 yards whilst the SE-NW one was only 966 yards. Three fuel dumps were installed, one for 46,000 gallons of aviation spirit, another for 2,000 gallons of MT fuel and finally one for 2,000 gallons of oil.

It opened as a semi-permanent airfield in No. 11 Group Fighter Command with its parent station at nearby Kenley. The day before war started saw No. 3 Squadron bring their Hurricane Is into the newly-established airfield. They were to alternate between Croydon, Manston and Merville in France until May 30, 1940, when they left for Wick. Joining them at Croydon was No. 615 (County of Surrey) Auxiliary Squadron, then still equipped with the Gladiator biplane. One month later No. 145 Squadron reformed at Croydon with the first Bristol Blenheim IFs.

The departure of No. 3 Squadron to Hawkinge in December saw another Blenheim squadron arrive, No. 92 (East India). They left a detachment at Gatwick with the squadron converting to the Spitfire before leaving for Northolt on May 9, 1940. Not to be outdone, No. 145 Squadron exchanged their Blenheims for the newer Hurricane at the same time. In the meantime No. 615 Squadron had departed to France in November as part of the Air Component of the British Expeditionary Force. Not until May 22, would they return to the UK.

The evacuation at Dunkirk saw a flurry of activity at Croydon as No. 145 Squadron left for Filton and the remnants of No. 607 (County of Durham) Auxiliary Squadron arrived at Croydon after being hurriedly forced to leave the Continent.

With the Battle of France lost, No. 111 Squadron arrived from North Weald on June 4, 1940 having been very active over the beaches at Dunkirk. Joined by the Hurricanes of No. 501 (County of Gloucester) Auxiliary Squadron on June 21, which had left Jersey just before the Germans arrived to occupy the Channel Islands. Both squadrons moved on a month later.

The arrival of No. 1 (Canadian) Squadron coincided with the first of several Luftwaffe attacks on the airfield. At 6.20 p.m. on August 15, 15 Bf 110s and eight Bf 109s of Erprobungs Gruppe 210 crossed the coast and headed for Kenley. A mistake in navigation cost the force dearly as they mistook Croydon for Kenley and they unleashed their bombs on the grass airfield. Attacked by Nos. 111 and 32 Squadrons, they lost seven aircraft including the commander Hauptmann Walter Rubensdorffer. Nevertheless, the airfield suffered badly with the armoury receiving a direct hit; several buildings including the Officer's Mess, shelters and the MT petrol

The terminal building pictured just prior to the war, the exterior of which is unchanged since its halcyon days as London's main airport.

dump being damaged as well as hangars and the loss of several aircraft. The landing ground was also pockmarked with craters. The estimated death toll was given as 62 killed and 37 seriously injured.

August 18 saw another attack when once again the intended targets were Kenley and Biggin Hill. In the space of five minutes, 11 high explosive bombs and many incendiaries fell damaging a hangar and destroying a Hurricane of No. 111 Squadron. The next day they left for Debden to be replaced by the Hurricanes of No. 85 Squadron.

Due to the recent attacks, it was now felt prudent to disperse the aircraft around the perimeter and not in the hangars. Accordingly, the machines were placed on the western side of the airfield with the officers and men billeted in requisitioned houses in nearby Forresters Drive.

On September 1 the Hurricanes were joined by the Spitfires of No. 72 (Basutoland) Squadron with No. 85 Squadron departing for Castle Camps two days later. No. 111 Squadron returned from Debden at a time when a change in policy by the German High Command saw the major raids suddenly switch from the airfields to London. Both squadrons were in action during the first daylight raids on the capital with No. 111 moving to Drem on September 8. Their replacement was No. 605 (County of Warwick) Auxiliary Squadron. They often flew with the two Kenley squadrons, becoming known as a Hurricane Wing and both were in action on Sunday, September 15, 1940 for the climax of the Battle.

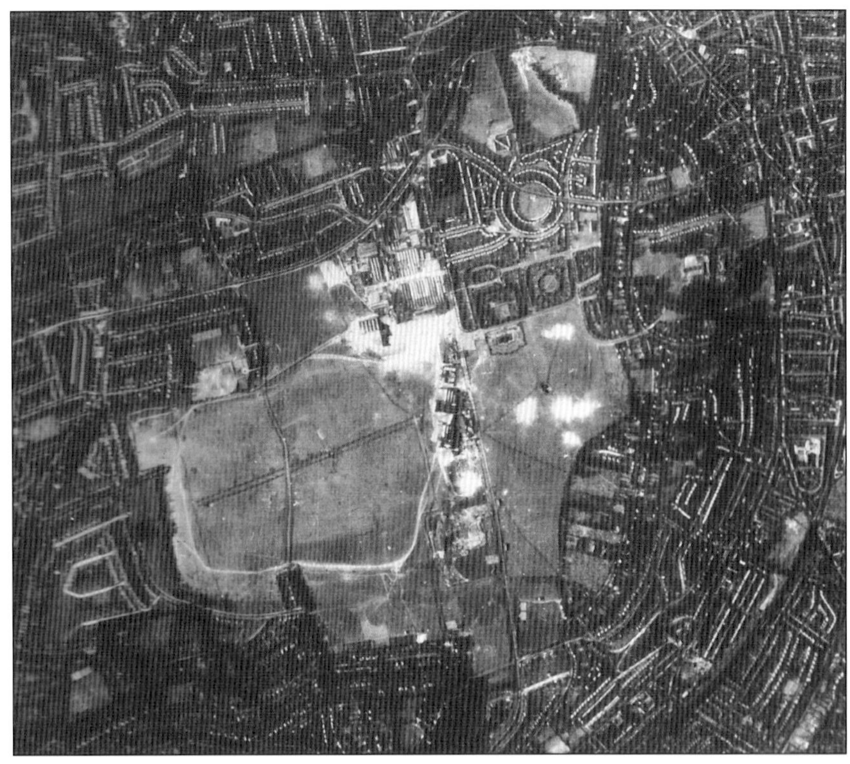

The aerodrome pictured under attack by the Luftwaffe in 1940.

Wartime dispersals are still evident in this picture taken two years after hostilities ceased.

In 1944 the aerodrome was transferred from Fighter to Transport Command and on February 6, 1946 its C-in-C, Air Marshal The Hon. Sir Ralph Cockrane, addressed the personnel of No. 110 Wing at the formal hand-over to British European Airways.

As the daylight raids on London were causing the Luftwaffe severe losses, the attacks switched to nights. It was the beginning of the Blitz proper although the Croydon squadrons were still fighting off sporadic airfield raids.

When the daylight raids petered out, squadron changes became rapid as Fighter Command moved to offensive operations. The main ones to effect Croydon were No. 605 re-equipping with Hurricane IIAs and, after a working up period, moving on to Martlesham Heath on February 25, 1941, plus brief stays by Nos. 17 and 1 Squadrons. With their departure the importance of Croydon as a front line fighter airfield began to diminish. As a further indication of this downgrading, No. 287 Squadron formed at Croydon on November 19, 1941. This was an Anti-Aircraft Co-operation unit from No. 11 Group flying many different types of aircraft including Masters, Defiants, Martinets and Spitfires. Joined by No. 116 Squadron on December 12, 1942, also operating different types of aircraft, both sent detachments to various airfields before leaving in July 1944.

No. 414 (Sarnie Imperials) Squadron of the Royal Canadian Air Force was formed on August 12, 1941 with Lysander IIIs and Tomahawk I and IIs. Their duties were

This monument on the edge of the flying field records the presence of the Royal Air Force at the airfield but, of all the Fighter Command bases, Croydon is quite unique in that the terminal building, now beautifully restored, has seen a host of stars, celebrities, statesmen and aviation pioneers passing through its doors . . .

. . . that is until December 1958 when it was announced that it was to be closed to flying. Amid huge protests, it was a case that the historic London airport — still a grass airfield — was just too small to cater for modern aircraft.

mainly army co-operation but conversion to the Mustang in June 1942 enabled the squadron to take part in the Dieppe operation when it claimed a Focke-Wulf 190. They remained at Croydon until December 5, before moving to Dunsfold. During July the Canadians had been joined by two Polish squadrons, No. 302 (Poznan) and No. 317 (Lwow) equipped with Spitfire VBs. They carried out several offensive sweeps before moving to Northolt.

The status of Croydon changed on September 5, 1944 from that of Fighter Command to Transport Command with the reforming of No. 147 Squadron with Dakotas and Ansons. Part of their remit was to establish a route for bringing back personnel from Allied-occupied Europe. Together with the establishment of the British Overseas Aircraft Corporation, this saw the beginning of a resurgence of civilian use for Croydon although this was short-lived as Heathrow and Gatwick had been selected for London's post-war airports.

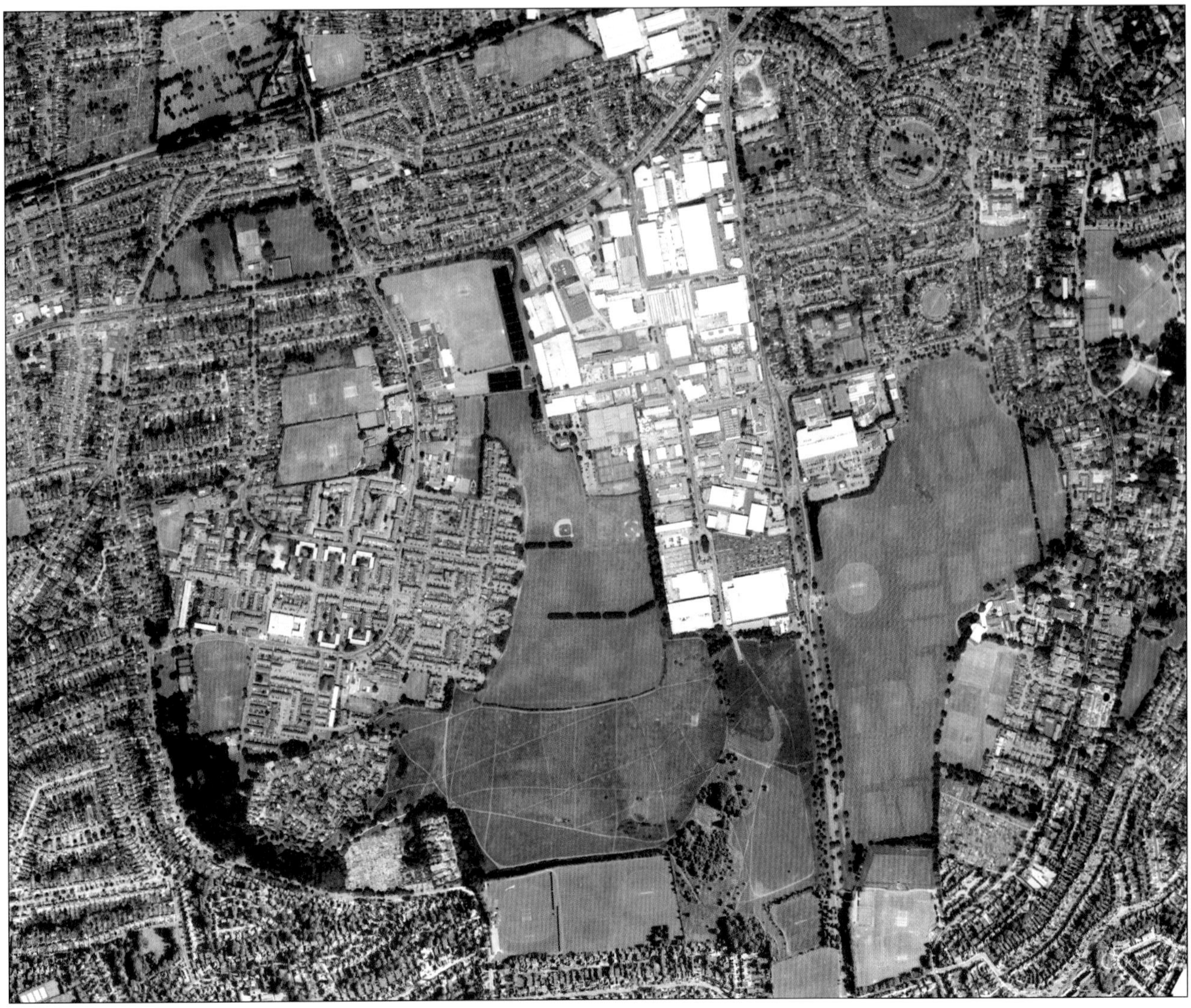

Fifty years later, housing and commercial developments have slowly spread their tentacles across the flying field.

In 1937 three squadrons arrived at Debden, No. 87 being the first flying the Hawker Fury but very quickly re-equipping with the Gloster Gladiator and occupying No. 3 hangar. No. 80 Squadron followed taking No. 1 hangar, with No. 73 using hangar No. 2.

DEBDEN

Initially a sector station in No. 12 Group of Fighter Command, Debden airfield in Essex lay three miles south of Saffron Walden at a height of 395 feet above sea level. Opening in April 1937, it was still being extended in 1940 with the construction of two concrete runways and additional taxiways. The original grass landing area provided four take-off and landing directions: N-S 1,600 yards, NE-SW 1,150 yards, E-W 1,200 yards and SE-NW 1,250 yards. When completed, the intersecting runways 50 yards wide ran 1,300 yards from E-W and N-S, the E-W runway being extended to 1,600 yards later. Three C- type hangars provided aircraft accommodation and workshop space. Night landing facilities were by Drem lighting with the fuel storage standing at 72,000 gallons of aviation spirit and 5,000 gallons of MT petrol.

With satellites or Relief Landing Grounds at Castle Camps, Great Sampford, Martlesham Heath and Ipswich, in September 1939 Debden was transferred to No. 11 Group in control of Sector 'F'. At this point Nos. 85 and 87 (United Provinces) Squadrons were flying Hurricanes; then No. 29 equipped with Blenheims arrived. With the need for more squadrons in France, the Hurricanes soon departed to be replaced by Nos. 17 and 504 (County of Nottingham) Squadrons, the latter alternating between Debden and Martlesham Heath until May 12, 1940, when they too moved to France.

The return of No. 85 Squadron on May 23, saw Squadron Leader Peter Townsend leading the squadron as the first phase of the Battle of Britain began. July and August saw much success for the squadron before it moved south to Croydon on August 19. Three days previous their replacement, No. 257 (Burma) Squadron, had flown in with Hurricanes. Joined by No. 601 (County of London) Auxiliary Squadron also with Hurricanes, they arrived at a period of intense raids on the airfield. Despite these attacks, Debden squadrons claimed 35 victories for the loss of seven Hurricanes during the month of August.

The winter of 1940-41 saw Debden almost entirely devoted to night fighting as the daylight squadrons moved out. Beaufighters, Defiants and Hurricanes of various squadrons were flying most moonlit nights. An incident of note took place on February 14, 1941 when a Heinkel He III landed and taxied up to the control tower but, quickly realising his mistake, the pilot turned about and took off before anyone on the station could take action.

In September 1975, Debden was transferred to the Army department of the Ministry of Defence prior to its re-opening as Carver Barracks (named after Field-Marshal Lord Carver).

Unfortunately this meant the end of several of the RAF buildings including the hangars to make way for facilities more suited to the needs of the Army.

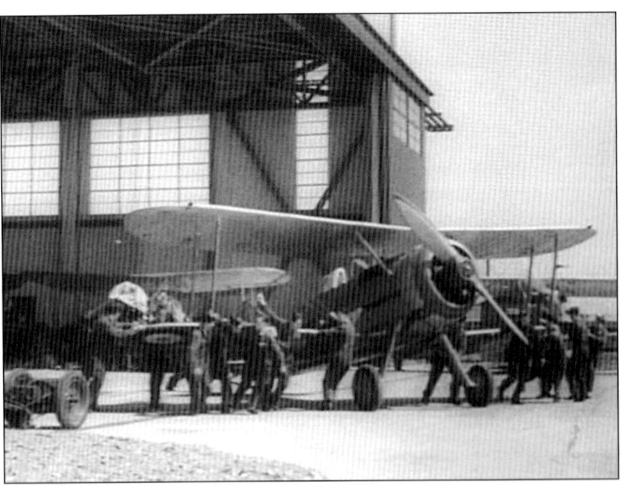

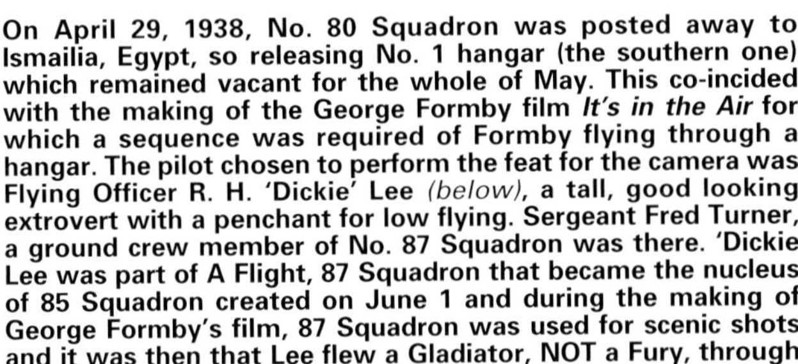

On April 29, 1938, No. 80 Squadron was posted away to Ismailia, Egypt, so releasing No. 1 hangar (the southern one) which remained vacant for the whole of May. This co-incided with the making of the George Formby film *It's in the Air* for which a sequence was required of Formby flying through a hangar. The pilot chosen to perform the feat for the camera was Flying Officer R. H. 'Dickie' Lee *(below)*, a tall, good looking extrovert with a penchant for low flying. Sergeant Fred Turner, a ground crew member of No. 87 Squadron was there. 'Dickie Lee was part of A Flight, 87 Squadron that became the nucleus of 85 Squadron created on June 1 and during the making of George Formby's film, 87 Squadron was used for scenic shots and it was then that Lee flew a Gladiator, NOT a Fury, through No. 1 hangar, which had been vacated by 80 Squadron. The event took place at around 12.30 lunchtime, just when the airmen were being marched off for feeding! The approach was made from the airfield side and after exit from the hangar, Lee pulled up and banked over the Parade Ground.' Sadly, this talented, if headstrong pilot failed to return on August 18, 1940. Squadron Leader Peter Townsend last saw him ten miles north-east of Foulness Point chasing Messerschmitt 109s out across the Channel. '"Come back, Dickie", I called out but he was drawing away. Again and again I called, but he kept on. Something had got into Dickie and there was no stopping him.' Already awarded the DSO and DFC, Lee's body was never found and he is now commemorated on the memorial at Brookwood.

However some things are never quite as they seem. Although we described the hangar exploit in two previous books, in those days the film was not available on video for us to check. Now *It's in the Air* has been released on DVD and all is not as we first thought. The opening sequence *(top left)*, shot from the control tower, certainly shows Gladiators of No. 87 Squadron at Debden, but instead we see Formby climbing into a Hawker Audax K8334 *(right)*. That aircraft was issued to No. 5 Elementary and Reserve Flying Training School then based at Hanworth Air Park at Feltham, Middlesex. We believe that the Air Ministry forbade the inclusion of Lee flying through the Debden hangar as it might encourage other pilots to have a go, so instead the sequence was created by using a model and the split screen technique, as our movie expert Trevor Popple explains: 'Given the limitations of the day, they tried to attain the best effect possible. The shot *(below left)* in which the Audax passes low over the airmen and turns an almost flat left into the hangar *(below right)* contains a horizontal split-screen. The lower image contains airmen in front of the hangar running and throwing themselves down as the Audax dives on them. Whilst the upper image shot separately is of the model Audax, and a section of a model hangar. When the two images were joined together the model upper section of the hangar lined up with the lower section of the real hangar at Feltham. Regrettably there is a horizontal white line denoting the join.'

Although the Brazilian dictatorship was unwilling to get deeply involved in the Allied war effort, nevertheless it was the only independent country in South America to send troops to fight in the war, the air force component being formed in 1943. However, British citizens in both Brazil and Argentina formed groups called the Fellowship of the Bellows to raise funds for the purchase of presentation aircraft for the Royal Air Force. The difference in their scheme was that each member agreed to donate a fixed sum for every Axis plane brought down during the month. Thus, on June 12, 1942, Spitfire BM634 named 'O Bandierante' (the name translating as 'The man who carries the flag') was presented to Treble One Squadron at Debden by the Brazilian Ambassador José Joachim de Lima E'Silva de Aragao. (It was shot down on July 18, 1943 when on the strength of No. 122 Squadron.)

The establishment of No. 52 OTU brought Hurricanes back to Debden together with the formation of a Canadian squadron, No. 418 (City of Edmonton), equipped with the Boston light bomber. Commencing operations at the end of November 1941, they moved to Bradwell Bay on April 15, 1942.

The formation of the Debden Wing in 1942 saw several Spitfire squadrons arrive. These included Nos. 65 (East India), 350 (Belgian) and 71 (Eagle) Squadrons. Joined later by Nos. 121 and 133 (Eagle) Squadrons, all three American units were transferred to the United States Army Air Force on September 29, 1942, with Debden becoming Station 356 and the home of the 4th Fighter Group. The airfield now became a showplace for the Eighth Fighter Command with the group becoming the highest scoring unit within the European Theater. Flying Spitfires, P-47 Thunderbolts and P-51 Mustangs, the group achieved great success with over 1,000 victories claimed by the end of the war.

When they left Debden in 1945, the airfield was returned to the RAF to become part of Technical Training Command until June 1975 when it closed. Today in Army hands, it has been renamed Carver Barracks and is home to 33 Engineer Regiment whose task is Explosive Ordnance Disposal. Although the hangars have been demolished and replaced with accommodation more suited to motor transport, the airfield and technical site remain in a good state of repair with a memorial to the 4th Fighter Group near the main gate.

Prior to the entry of the United States into the war, many American pilots had volunteered to join the RAF or the Royal Canadian Air Force. Wearing RAF uniform with the Eagle patch, 244 pilots were assigned to three Fighter Command squadrons: No. 71, 121 and 133. In 1942, Brigadier General Frank Hunter (rear right) had been put in charge of US Fighter Command and it was on his recommendation that the three Eagle squadrons should become the US 4th Fighter Group based at Debden under the US Eighth Air Force chief, General Carl Spaatz (rear left). No. 71 Squadron then became the US 334th Fighter Squadron; No. 121 became the 335th, and No. 133 the 336th. On September 29, 1942, Debden was formally handed over to the Americans by Air Chief Marshal Sir Sholto Douglas, the AOC-in-C of Fighter Command.

By the end of the war the 4th Fighter Group had become the highest scoring unit of the United States Army Air Force with 583½ air victories and 469 enemy aircraft destroyed on the ground, first with Spitfires, then the P-47 Thunderbolt and finally the P-51 Mustang. On April 11, 1944, General Eisenhower visited Station 356 during a pre-D-Day inspection tour of Eighth Air Force bases. He presented Distinguished Service Crosses to Lieutenant Colonel Donald Blakeslee, the CO of the 4th Fighter Group (right) and Captain Don Gentile, one of the leading fighter aces. The Americans finally left Debden in September 1945 but the memorial to their tenure stands just inside the main gate.

From RAF Debden as it appeared at the end of the war . . . to Carver Barracks 60 years later.

DETLING

Detling opens for business. The first squadron to be stationed there in 1939 was No. 500 with Avro Ansons. They remained at the aerodrome for seven months but their memorial lives on at the Kent County Showground.

Lying two and half miles north-east of Maidstone and sited 600 feet above sea level on the top of the North Downs in Kent, Detling was subject to hill fog throughout its existence, a problem that caused many incidents.

It was surveyed in 1915 by the Directorate of Works, first becoming home to the War Flight RNAS later No. 3 Wing of the Royal Naval Air Service, but a move to Manston put Detling into care and maintenance until transferred to the Royal Flying Corps on April 3, 1917. Used by various squadrons for the defence of London, the airfield was abandoned in December 1920 but later selected as part of the RAF's expansion scheme. The station was rebuilt with the technical and domestic site located near the ancient manor house of Binbury. The airfield was all grass, the dimensions being N-S 1,035 yards, NE-SW 1,250 yards, E-W 1,014 yards and SE-NW 1,020 yards. Hangarage comprised one Bellman and four Blisters with petrol storage at 48,000 gallons of aviation spirit and 1,750 gallons of MT fuel.

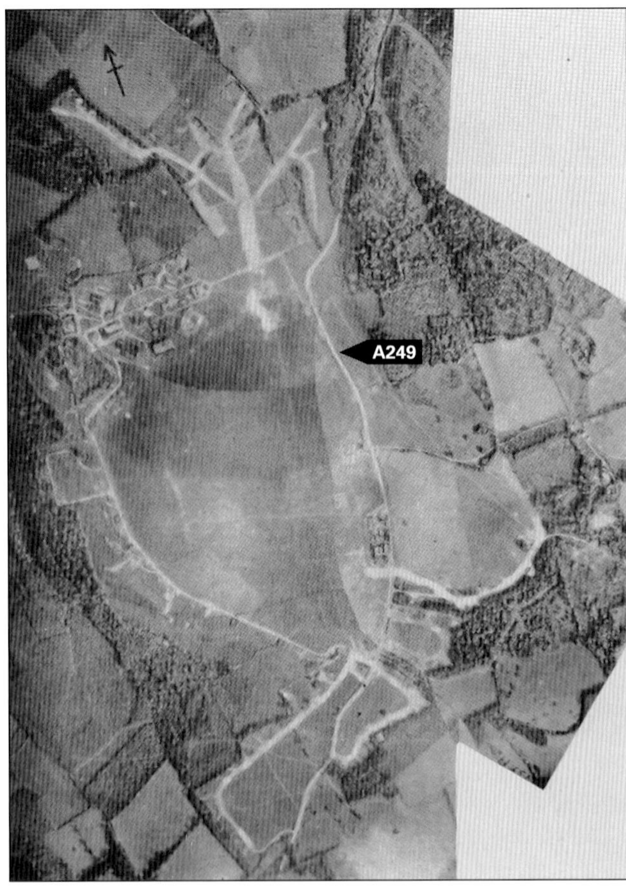

During the war, extra dispersals were provided to the north and south and east of the A249.

Today the southern half of the airfield is used as the Kent County Showground.

Embodied into Coastal Command and No. 16 (General Reconnaissance) Group with its headquarters at nearby Chatham, the first squadron to arrive was No. 500 (County of Kent) Auxiliary Squadron equipped with Avro Ansons. During its stay which lasted until April 8, 1941, the squadron achieved acclaim when a Bf 109 and a He III fell to the additional fire-power of the Ansons. These extra guns included machine guns fitted to fire through the glazed cockpit windows and a cannon fitted to fire through the floor of the aircraft.

August 13, 1940 saw a devastating raid on the airfield by Stukas of Lehrgeschwader I escorted by Bf 109s. The accuracy of the raid was good with the hangars blasted and set on fire, a total of 22 aircraft destroyed or damaged and 67 personnel killed including the Commanding Officer, Group Captain Edward Davis, together with a further 90 injured. Two WAAFs were honoured for courage they displayed during the raid, Corporal Josie Robins and Sergeant Sheila Youle both being later awarded the Military Medal.

Further Coastal Command units were based at Detling including No. 53 Squadron with Blenheims, No. 280 (ASR) with Ansons, and No. 816X Flight of the Fleet Air Arm with Swordfish. Transferred to Army Co-operation Command on January 1, 1943, No. 26 Squadron flew in their Mustangs on January 13 with a Polish unit, No. 318 (Danzig) Squadron forming with Hurricanes on March 20. However, with the disbandment of the command, the airfield was transferred to No. 11 Group, Fighter Command on June 1.

The Spitfires of Nos. 132 (City of Bombay), 184 and 602 (City of Glasgow) Auxiliary Squadron arrived on October 12 that year to form No. 125 Airfield which was transferred to the Second Tactical Air Force on November 15. The squadrons carried out

No. 132 (Bombay) Squadron — then part of the Second Tactical Air Force — at Detling in 1944.

The section of the airfield where the squadron was pictured has now been returned to agriculture.

The technical site as it appeared when occupied by the Home Command Gliding School.

Geoffrey Hall took this low level comparison of the site today.

The south-western end of the landing ground has now become the Kent County Showground.

bomber escort duties before commencing attacks upon V1 launch pads but January 18, 1944 saw Nos. 132 and 602 Squadrons leave to be replaced by Nos. 118 and 453 Squadrons. The return of 132 and 602 in March saw further flying bomb attacks until the Detling Wing, as it was now known, moved to Ford on April 18. A month later Nos. 80, 229 and 274 Squadrons arrived as a Spitfire wing within the Air Defence of Great Britain to commence escort work in addition to fighter sweeps.

On June 21, 1944, a V1 landed on the perimeter of the airfield causing major damage to the domestic site. Next day the fighter wing moved out and was replaced by Nos. 1 and 165 Squadrons to commence patrols to attempt to destroy V1s in the air. Both squadrons returned to Lympne in mid-July to be replaced by Nos. 118, 124 (Baroda) and 504 (County of Nottingham) Squadrons which carried out escort duties for day bomber raids before moving out on August 9 at which point Nos. 1 and 165 Squadrons returned.

Escort duties during Operation 'Market-Garden', the Arnhem landings, proved to be the last wartime operations flown from Detling and on January 1, 1945 the airfield was put under care and maintenance.

During this period, No. 1336 Wing of the RAF Regiment arrived to run an Air Disarmament School before being taken over on October 1, 1945 by No. 60 Group of No. 75 Signals Wing which remained until June 1947. For a period of eight years Detling then became the Home Command Gliding School before finally being de-requisitioned on October 1, 1959. Part of the disused airfield now forms the Kent Showground yet much still remains of the wartime buildings and constructions.

The Air Ministry relinquished Detling in the 1960s and 40 years later this fine memorial to all the units which had served there was unveiled in Detling village.

FORD

With wonderful shots like these of personnel of No. 315 Squadron at Ford in 1944, it was extremely frustrating not to be able to match them up because the old technical site has now been absorbed within a Home Office prison.

First known as Ford Junction or Yapton, the airfield was one of several training stations built during 1917. Closed in 1920, it was re-opened during the 1930s and became the headquarters for Sir Alan Cobham's company holding National Aviation Days. It was also used by several auxiliary squadrons for summer camps. It became RAF Ford on December 1, 1937 as part of No. 17 (Training) Group, Coastal Command. On May 24, 1939, the airfield was handed over to the Admiralty to become HMS *Peregrine*. Three naval squadrons arrived at the same time, these being Nos. 750, 751 and 752. They commenced coastal patrols before moving to Yeovilton in May 1940.

A flat grass area measuring 1,300 yards NE-SW, 1,100 yards SE-NW and 1,000 yards from N-S and E-W, Ford was situated two and a quarter miles from Arundel. Being a coastal airfield it soon came under attack, the first large raid coming on August 18, 1940. Ju 87 dive-bombers carried out a devastating attack hitting fuel dumps, accommodation buildings and hangars. Seventeen aircraft were wrecked which led the Navy to quit the base.

When Ford returned to the RAF it was to No. 11 Group on October 1, 1940, Blenheims and Beaufighters of the Fighter Interception Unit arrived to begin a long stay, carrying out intensive trials in fighter tactics. Designated an operational satellite to nearby Tangmere, the construction of a Type II Flying Control and further hangars to replace those damaged in the August raid, saw No. 23 Squadron bring their Blenheim IFs in from Wittering on September 12. Re-equipping with Havoc Is in March 1941, detachments were sent to Manston, Tangmere, Bradwell Bay and Middle Wallop. The squadron began intensive intruder patrols over French airfields with later conversions to Boston IIIs and in June 1942, the Mosquito I.

In order to provide all weather serviceability, two tarmac runways were laid down, the NE-SW being 2,000 x 50 yards and SE-NW being 1,600 x 50 yards. After a successful stay at Ford, No. 23 Squadron took their Mosquitos to Manston leaving the Havocs and Bostons to newly-formed No. 605 (County of Warwick) Auxiliary Squadron on June 7, 1942. Sending a detachment to Hunsdon, they also began operations over France.

Operation 'Jubilee', the Dieppe landings, saw a Boston detachment from No. 88 Squadron arrive together with further Bostons from No. 107 Squadron and 418 (City of Edmonton) Canadian Squadron. Joined by the Hurricane IIBs of No. 174 (Mauritius) Squadron, all the units took part in the operation. As the detachments departed they were replaced by the Beaufighter IFs of No. 141 Squadron on August 10. During the month the squadron claimed success when Sergeants Clee and Grant shot down a Ju 88 into the sea off Selsey. A change of tactics saw the squadron begin day scrambles against low flying enemy aircraft, although the only success was on December 16 when a Do 217 crashed into a gasometer in Bognor after being chased by a Beaufighter flown by Flying Officer Cook and Flight Sergeant Warner.

The squadron exchanged places with No. 604 (County of Middlesex) Auxiliary Squadron on February 18, 1943, the latter bringing their Beaufighter IFs in from Predannack. The departure of No. 605

Nevertheless, there is irony in the situation. On August 18, 1940 the aerodrome was the target of a devastating attack by Ju 87 dive-bombers of Stukageschwader 77 scoring direct hits on the installations including the fuel store.

Squadron to Castle Camps saw No. 418 (City of Edmonton) Canadian Squadron return and convert to Mosquitos. They remained until April 8, 1944. Enjoying a period of success at Ford, No. 604 was replaced by No. 256 Squadron flying the Beaufighter VIF on April 24, 1943. A conversion to the Mosquito XII during May saw them depart to Woodvale on August 25. More Mosquito XIIs arrived on September 3 when No. 29 Squadron flew in from Bradwell Bay for a six-month stay. They enjoyed great success, claiming several enemy aircraft, with the night of February 23/24 1944 proving exceptional when five were shot down, a sortie from which the CO, Wing Commander R. E. Mack DFC did not return. Posted to Drem on March 1, No. 29 Squadron were replaced by No. 456 (Australian) equipped with Mosquito XVIIs, Flight Lieutenant C. L. Brooks and Warrant Officer R. J. Forbes, claiming an Me 410-A on the night of April 19/20.

At this time Ford entered a period of intense security as plans for the invasion of Europe developed. The FIU moved out to Wittering and the airfield became No. 122 Airfield under the umbrella of No. 83 Group of the Allied Expeditionary Air Force. By April, Nos. 19, 65 (East India), 122 and 132 (Bombay) Squadrons had arrived from Gravesend and Detling all flying the Merlin-engined Mustang III. Beginning operations over France, some sorties stretched out as far as the Swiss border. Bomb racks were fitted during April to enable the aircraft to carry

Seventy years later a blaze again from the technical site as inmates of the prison started a riot after they objected to undergo breathalyser tests for contraband alcohol.

Apart from the prison which was built in 1960, industrial estates have now spread across the airfield.

out attacks on marshalling yards and enemy gun positions. Rapid changes saw Nos. 65 and 122 Squadrons depart to Funtington on May 14 only to return to Ford on June 15. No 19 moved to Southend on May 12 and returned on June 15. In between, the Spitfire IXBs of No. 125 Airfield arrived from Detling on April 18. Comprising Nos. 132 (City of Bombay), 453 (Australian) and 602 (City of Glasgow) Squadrons, sorties carried out included attacks on V-weapon sites. Prior to D-Day the airfield saw No. 144 Wing of the RCAF; Nos. 441 (Silver Fox), 442 (Caribou) and 443 (Hornet) Squadrons flying in from Funtington with Spitfire IXBs. Arriving on May 13 and 15, in addition to flying bomb targets, railways, highways and enemy radar sites were also attacked.

On June 15, No.144 Wing left for Normandy with No. 125 Airfield going over the Channel on the 25th. No. 96 Squadron arrived at Ford from West Malling with Mosquito XIIIs on June 20 and, together with still resident 456 Squadron, commenced operations against the V1s. The arrival of No. 129 (Mysore) Squadron on June 24 followed by the Polish Nos. 306 (Torun) and 315 (Deblin) Squadrons a day later saw Mustangs return to Ford. Flying offensive patrols over enemy lines, the Polish squadrons moved to the Advanced Landing Ground at Brenzett in early July. Replaced by the Polish No. 131 Wing comprising Nos. 302 (Poznan), 308 (Krakow) and 317 (Wilno) Squadrons, a few intensive operations were carried out before they too moved to the Continent on August 3. A brief visit by No. 132 Wing with Nos. 66, 127, 331 (Norwegian) and 332 (Norwegian) Squadrons with Spitfire IXs saw them depart to France on August 20. Left once again with No. 96 and 456 Squadrons, the former left for Odiham on September 24 just as the FIU returned. Arriving with a detachment of No. 746 Naval Squadron, the unit was now renamed the Night Fighter Development Wing. Flying a mixture of Mosquitos, Beaufighters and several naval Fireflies and Hellcats, they carried out experiments in airborne and carrier-borne radars.

No. 456 Squadron finally left for Church Fenton on December 31, 1944. With the end of hostilities Ford ceased to be a No. 11 Group station, and with the experimental wing moving to Tangmere, the airfield was

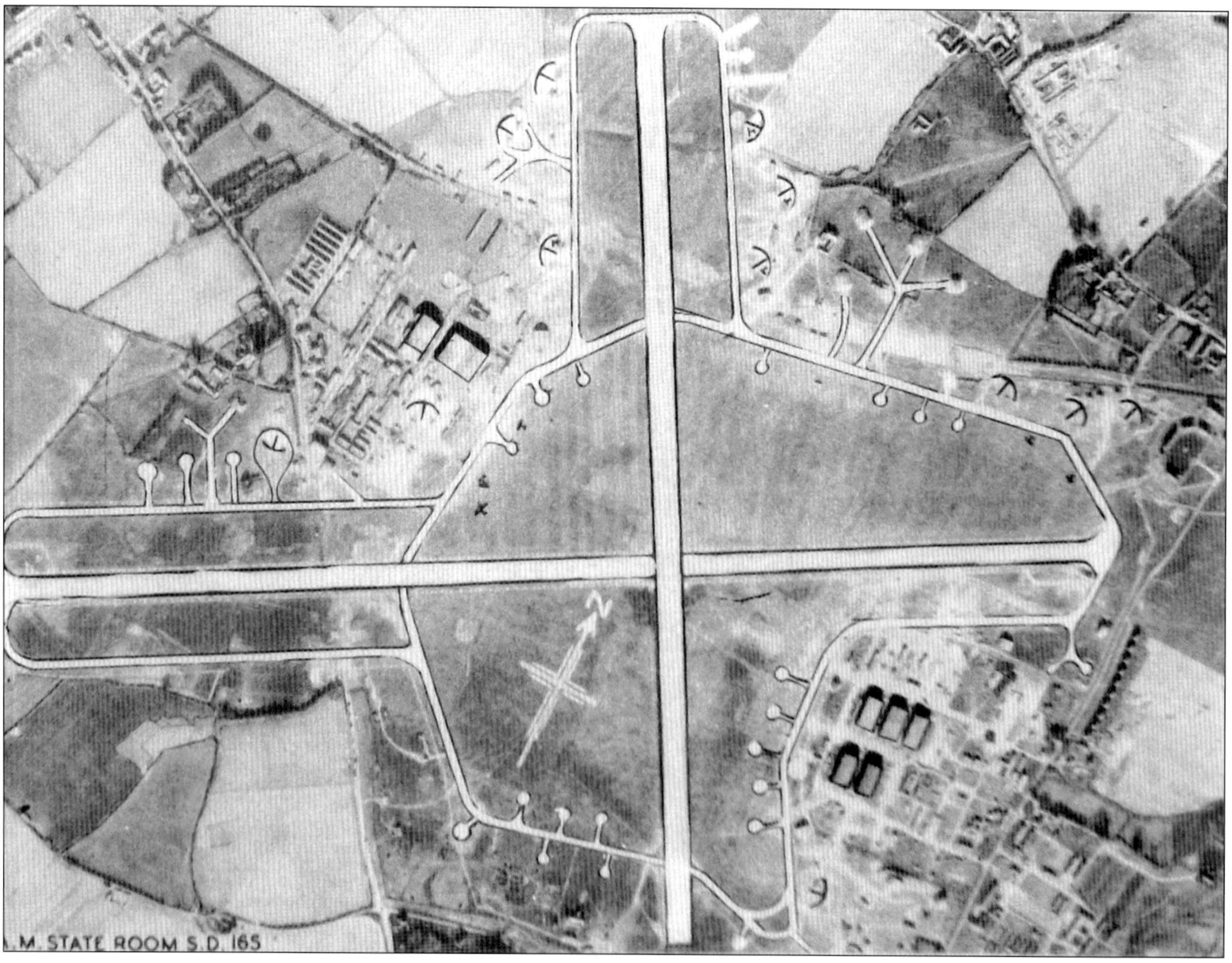

This formerly secret plan was reproduced in the Air Ministry publication *Airfields and Flying Boat Bases in the United Kingdom*.

transferred back to the Admiralty, once more becoming HMS *Peregrine*. Its main function was to act as a shore-based training establishment for squadrons temporarily disembarked from carriers. This use continued until 1958 when Ford closed. The site was later transferred to the Home Office for development as an open prison.

A gate guardian of a Royal Navy Hawker Hunter preserves the tenure of Ford as HMS *Peregrine*, photographed here by Geoffrey Hall on a low-level fly-by.

FRISTON

In February 1943, No. 41 Squadron was re-equipped with the Griffon-engined Spitfire MkXII, designed primarily for operations against low-level raiders which were striking at towns on the south coast. They were based at Friston for three weeks.

Lying 230 feet above sea level on the Seven Sisters cliffs along the Sussex Downs, Friston was designated a forward aerodrome in No. 11 Group. Originally known as either Gayles or East Dean, it was a grass-surfaced airfield on good chalk sub-soil, the land being owned by the Church Commissioners.

Two landing lanes were marked out, one 1,750 x 150 yards, the other 1,000 x 200 yards. There was no perimeter track. Being a forward aerodrome, facilities were minimal with just two Blister hangars and 11,000 gallons of fuel. It was controlled by a forward relay system from sector operations at Kenley.

Friston was in use prior to the war, being used for air exercises during 1936. However from 1940 it lay dormant as its first use was as a decoy airfield with dummy aircraft erected on site. It would appear that this failed to fool the Germans so the dummies were removed and replaced by real Hurricanes: those of No. 253 Squadron which arrived from Hilbastow on June 14, 1942. Joined the same day by the Hurricanes of No. 32 Squadron from West Malling, both carried out sorties against the guns around Dieppe.

The two squadrons left Friston on July 7 but it seems that the ruse of it being a decoy airfield now worked, as two bomb-carrying Bf 109s carried out an attack on July 10 causing some damage to one of the landing lanes and one of the Blister hangars.

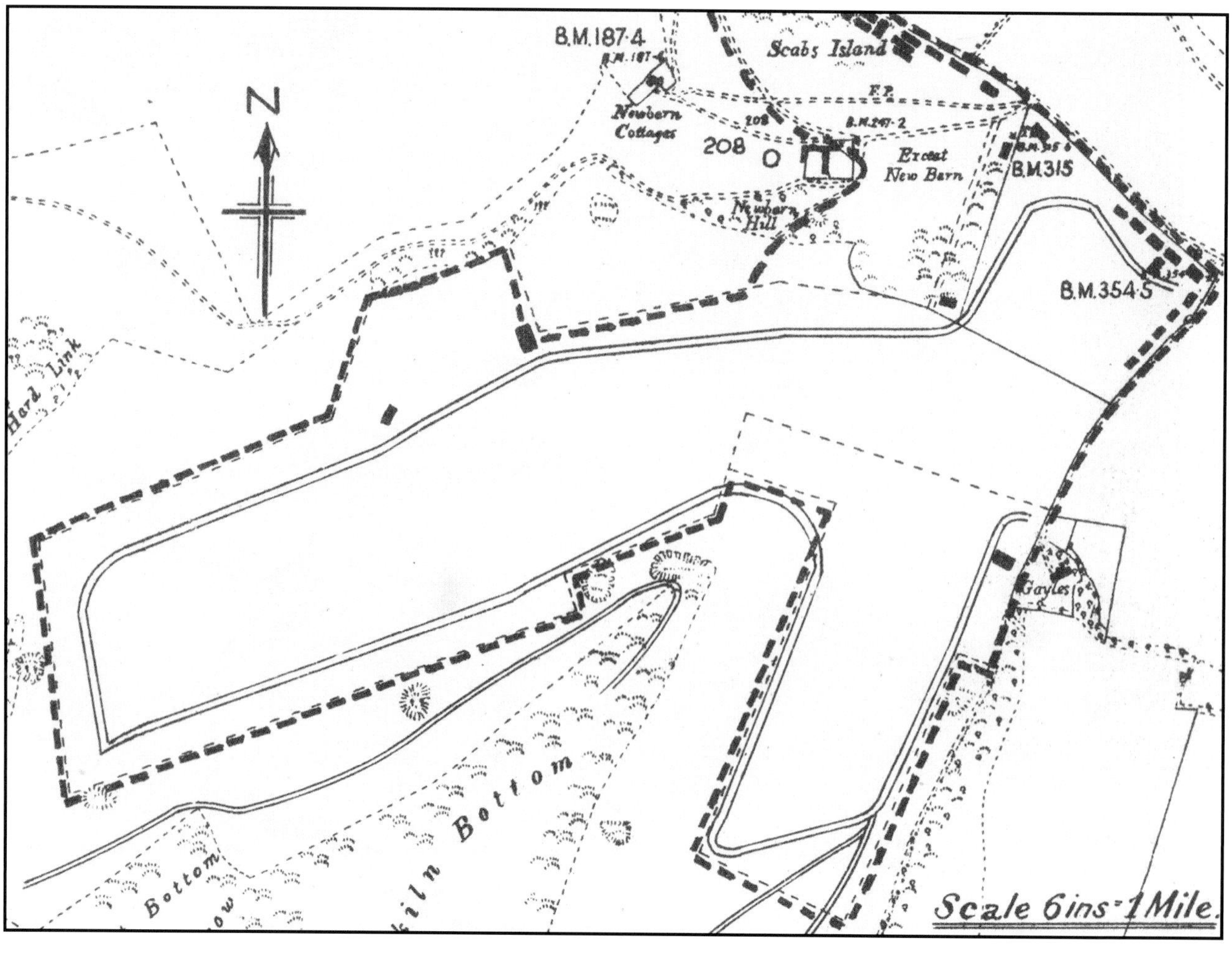

The following month, several detachments from the Kenley Wing used the sparse facilities during the Dieppe landings. However it was not until May 27, 1943 that a resident squadron arrived. No. 41 bought their Spitfire XIIs in from Biggin Hill to counter the many low-level fighter-bomber attacks on coastal airfields in Kent and Sussex. Leaving for Westhampnett on June 21, they were replaced by the Canadian No. 412 (Falcon) Squadron although they did not stay long, moving to Redhill on July 14.

A brief stay by No. 306 (Torun) Polish Squadron from Gravesend saw them working up in preparation to join the Second Tactical Air Force but they left for Heston on September 22. A six-day visit that month by another Polish squadron, No. 308 (Krakow) flying Spitfire IIs saw them follow a similar pattern.

One of the two Belgian squadrons in Fighter Command, No. 349, arrived on November 10 with Spitfire VCs. Re-equipping with the LF IXE variant in February 1944, they became an integral part of No.135 Wing and commenced flying sweeps over France, moving to Hornchurch on March 11. No.41 Squadron returned the same day, staying only until April 29.

The second Belgian squadron, No. 350, arrived on April 25. With Fighter Command now called the Air Defence of Great Britain, the arrival of No. 501 (County of Gloucester) Auxiliary Squadron saw the two units carry out Army co-operation exercises prior to D-Day. On June 6 both covered the landing troops though with little contact with the enemy. All three squadrons left at the beginning of July.

No. 610 (County of Chester) Squadron arrived on July 2 followed the next day with the return of No. 41 Squadron. Their stay was once again very brief as they moved to Lympne a week later, No. 316 (Warsaw) Polish Squadron arriving on July 11. Flying Mustangs on operations against the flying bombs, the squadron claimed it had destroyed 50 V1s by the end of July. They remained until August 27 to be replaced by No. 131 (County of Kent) Fighter Squadron carrying out similar duties. When they left in November it marked a gradual run-down for Friston. Relegated to an ELG status, No. 7 Fighter Command Servicing Unit took up residence in early 1945 whilst in April the Auster Vs of No. 666 Canadian Squadron moved in for just over a month. However, by May 25 the airfield was reduced to care and maintenance with the site finally being de-requisitioned and the land returned to the Church Commissioners on April 8, 1946. Some four decades later, the airfield was the setting for some scenes in the TV series *Piece of Cake* but very little of the site remains today.

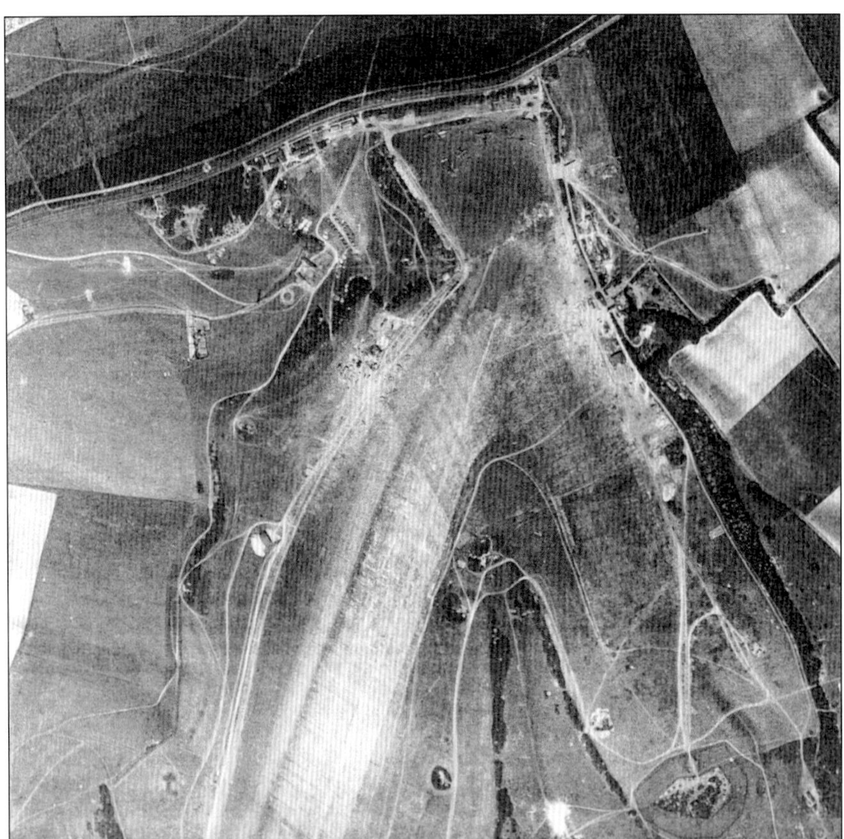

Located five miles west of Eastbourne, right on the edge of the cliffs bordering the Channel, Friston was photographed by the US 7th Photo Group on May 29, 1944 when its forward position was to be a vital element in support of the landings in Normandy.

Today the feint outline of the aerodrome can still be discerned.

In 1891 Gatwick Racecourse was opened beside the London to Brighton railway with its own dedicated station, and in the late 1920s land alongside was utilised as a private landing ground. This was formalised in August 1930 after an entrepreneur, Ronald Waters, wrote to the Air Ministry promoting the site as an alternative to Croydon as the latter was subject to fog. Three years later the Ministry approved Gatwick for commercial operations and the aerodrome closed in July 1935 for the building of a circular passenger terminal known as 'The Beehive'. The new airport was to be quite revolutionary in design. Apart from being the first one in the British Isles to have its own dedicated railway station, it included a control terminal and administrative building from which six covered passage-ways radiated to aircraft stands. A seventh passageway linked the railway station and passenger building via a subterranean tunnel. Passengers would therefore be able to move from the station into the airport, check-in and reach the aircraft steps completely under cover. The passageways were designed to reduce aircraft congestion to a minimum.

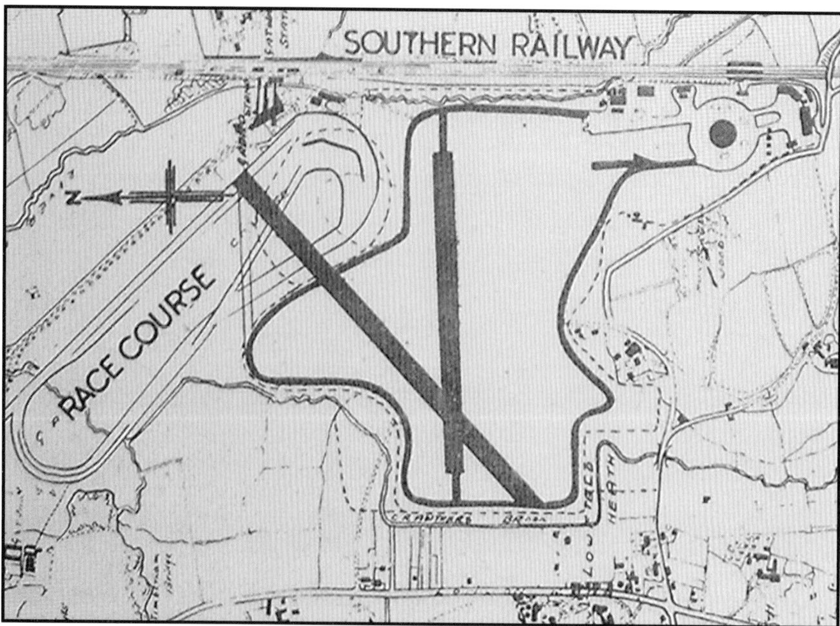

The new airport was officially opened in June 1936 but it was let down by its grass surface which was prone to waterlogging due to poor drainage. It was even being reported that pilots were using the concrete taxiways instead of the turf to take off.

GATWICK

Situated 28 miles south of London on the A23 road and 200 feet above sea level, Gatwick first began life as a civil airport during the 1930s owned by Airports Ltd. The first military use came in 1937 when No. 19 Elementary & Reserve Flying Training School began lessons with Miles Magisters. The outbreak of war saw Gatwick come under military control being designated an operational station in Army Co-operation Command. Grass surface dimensions were then 1,250 yards SE-NW, 1,150 yards E-W and 1,050 yards N-S and NE-SW. A 35-foot perimeter track eventually led to two Army track runways, the longest being 1,400 × 50 yards and shortest being 1,000 × 50 yards. Hangar accommodation was six Blisters and one Bellman together with Drem night landing facility.

A request to the Air Ministry from the Civil Aviation branch that Gatwick should be transferred to them to allow civilian services to continue was granted with the proviso that when needed for military operations, the civil airlines would have to vacate within 24 hours. This situation lasted until May 26, 1940 when the headquarters of No. 70 Wing, Bomber Command arrived together with the Blenheims of No. 18 (Burma) Squadron. They flew in from Wyton on May 26 followed by further Blenheims from No. 57 Squadron two days later. The number of aircraft increased when No. 53 Squadron arrived with more Blenheims on June 13 plus the Fairey Battles of No. 98 Squadron from Château Bougon on June 15. However, by the end of July all the squadrons had left leaving Gatwick without fighter squadrons for the entire duration of the Battle of Britain.

The first of several Army Co-operation squadrons flew in from West Malling on September 3. No. 26 equipped with Lysander IIIs carried out exercises with local army units as well as calibration of anti-aircraft defence.

With the role of the Defiant changing from day fighting to night fighting, detachments from No. 141 Squadron were based at Gatwick during September until the entire squadron arrived on October 22. After a brief stay, they moved to Gravesend on November 3. Further Lysander detachments arrived during September when aircraft from No. 239 Squadron flew in to be followed by the rest of the squadron on January 22, 1941.

Although the airfield was now controlled by the military, the resident civilian companies, Airwork and Southern Aircraft, continued in the modification and repair of Whitleys, Harts and Battles. Working in conjunction with military personnel, this was to continue until the end of the war.

From 1937 there was increasing use of Gatwick by the RAF for training navigators and Volunteer Reserve pilots before formal requisition by the Air Ministry took place in September 1939. This photo is believed to have been taken the previous year.

9th		An anti-gas demonstration took place this morning. A practice gas alarm followed in the afternoon after which a lecture was given by the Commanding Officer and the Medical Officer during which faults were pointed out and questions by personnel were answered.
10th		An enemy aircraft (Dornier) flew low over the aerodrome at 1800 hours. Defence guns opened fire and the machine landed a short distance away. (2 dead, 2 prisoners - 1 wounded).
11th		Group Cypher Officer visited GATWICK to inspect secret documents.
		Group Messing Officer visited GATWICK to inspect airmen's messing.

One of the earliest incidents to occur at Gatwick during the war took place on September 10, 1940 when the station defences opened fire on a Dornier which crashed nearby. However, the machine from 9/KG76 had already been attacked by pilots of Nos. 72 and 92 Squadrons before it came down seven miles away at West Hoathly.

Conversion to the Tomahawk II from the Lysander for all Army Co-op Squadrons began in November 1940, one of the first to do so being No. 26 in February 1941. This aircraft enabled the squadron to carry out several coastal patrols before departing to Weston Zoyland on July 14. No. 239 was to follow a similar conversion but were to leave for Weston Zoyland eight days earlier. Both squadrons would return to Gatwick at varying intervals over the next year, the first being No. 239 which returned seven days after leaving. In addition to calibration work they also carried out offensive operations from Manston during a period of maintenance at Gatwick when the army arrived to lay wire mesh runways. Once completed, August 1941 saw No. 71 Group Army Co-operation Command disband to be replaced by Army Co-op Wings intended to provide closer liaison with local army commands and units.

January 1942 saw Nos. 26 and 239 Squadrons still in residence, the latter converting to Hurricane Is and IICs. Pilots were taken from the former squadron to form No. 171 Squadron on June 15 whilst pilots from No. 239 were posted to form No. 63 Squadron the same day. A further detachment of Tomahawks from No. 400 (City of Toronto) Canadian Squadron came during July as the build-up to Operation 'Jubilee' continued. Having received Hurricanes during January, 239 Squadron did little with them before they further converted to the Mustang I in May. Becoming part of No. 35 Wing together with three other Mustang squadrons, they provided reconnaissance and top cover for the Dieppe landings in August. All the Gatwick squadrons with the exception of No. 171 carried out sorties over the beaches. With 'Jubilee' over, No. 239 left for Twinwood Farm on August 31 leaving a small detachment behind. No. 171 Squadron, having left for Odiham on July 12, came back on August 25 to convert to the Mustang. They left for Weston Zoyland on September 10 only to return on September 20 finally leaving for Hartford Bridge on December 7.

During the latter months of 1942, a number of squadrons and detachments arrived for short periods. These were Nos. 309 (Ziema Czerwienska) Polish, 613 (City of Manchester) and 175, the latter being transferred from Fighter Command to become an Army Co-op Squadron equipped with Hurricane IICs. All carried out offensive sorties before leaving for their home bases.

The Austers of No. 655 (Air Observation Post) Squadron arrived on March 22, 1943 although they left for Detling on April 7.

With the build-up of the Tactical Air Force, No. 123 Airfield arrived on April 7 with the return of Nos. 26 and 239 Squadrons, still with Mustangs. Joined by No. 183 (Gold Coast) a day later, they

For a short period in 1943, No. 183 Squadron were based at Gatwick with Typhoons. The racecourse grandstand can be seen beyond.

Gatwick was decommissioned in 1946 but the Ministry of Transport and Civil Aviation extended its use as a civil airport, initially for a six-month trial. Although PSP steel mesh had been laid down during the war, persistent drainage problems hampered its use which was then mainly by maintenance and cargo businesses. In 1950 it was announced that Gatwick was the government's choice for a second airport for London, mainly for use if flights had to be diverted from Heathrow by bad weather. The development by McAlpines involved closing the airfield from 1956-58 for the construction of a hard runway across the racecourse. The A23 London to Brighton road also had to be diverted as did the River Mole. The racecourse station was rebuilt alongside a new terminal building (now the South Terminal), although the Beehive was retained in the north-eastern corner. The airport was re-opened by Queen Elizabeth on June 9, 1958 becoming the world's first airport having a direct link connecting rail travel and road facilities with an air terminal in one unit. In 1961 its name was changed to London (Gatwick). The original runway of 7,000ft was extended to 8,200ft in 1964, then to 9,075ft in 1970. Three years later a further extension to 10,165ft enabled non-stop operation to the US West Coast to take off with full payloads and a fourth extension in 1998 took place to 10,879ft for long-range operations by wide-bodied aircraft. Although ongoing arguments for the provision of a second runway have yet to be resolved, in 1985 the northern taxiway was converted into a runway but only for use in an emergency.

brought the first Typhoons to operate from the airfield. Classed as mobile units and therefore prone to moving around different bases at short notice, they left for Lasham on May 3 whilst No. 26 left for Detling on June 22 and No. 239 for Fairlop a day earlier.

No. 129 Airfield arrived on July 5 with two Canadian squadrons, No. 414 (Sarnia Imperials) and 430 (City of Sudbury). With brief stays once again, both squadrons were to visit Gatwick at various intervals until early 1944.

Left with no permanent squadrons, the airfield entered a period of care and maintenance until October when the Spitfire IXs of Nos. 19 and 65 (East India) Squadrons arrived. They provided escort to bombers taking the war to Germany before both left for Gravesend in November.

With the wire mesh laid by the army proving unsuitable, it was replaced with the more substantial Sommerfeld Track during the winter of 1943/44. In the run-up to D-Day, No. 130 Airfield, with Nos. 2 and 4 Squadrons, flew in on April 4 the former flying Mustangs and the latter Spitfire Xs. Joined by No. 268 Squadron four days later, all three operated in a photo-reconnaissance role. These sorties continued until June 27 when the entire wing moved to Odiham.

A wing from Fighter Command (now renamed the Air Defence of Great Britain), replaced them over June 27/28 when Nos. 80, 229 and 274 flew in with Spitfire IXs. They began escort duties for a few days before all three squadrons left in early July. A variety of different types arrived with No. 116 Squadron bringing Ansons, Oxfords, Tiger Moths, Hornet Moths and Hurricanes to Gatwick on August 27. Tasked with anti-aircraft co-operation duties, they moved to nearby Redhill on September 7. The station was then left with a number of ground-based units such as No. 1 Aircraft Delivery Unit and No. 49 Maintenance Unit.

Following the end of hostilities the airfield became designated a satellite of Dunsfold. This status lasted until August 31, 1946 when Gatwick was handed back to the Ministry of Civil Aviation eventually to become London's second airport.

This is Gravesend in the 1930s when it was claimed to be London's 'East Airport'. The white landing circle was the usual method of identification for marking aerodromes at that time.

GRAVESEND

Previously a small civil airport, Gravesend was sited just south of Chalk village between the A226 and A2 roads in Kent. A grass airfield, covering 148 acres, it sat 240 feet above sea level overlooking the River Thames and was the starting point for many record-breaking flights prior to the war. When the threat became real, the airport was taken over by the Air Ministry with Airports Ltd, the owners of the site, being awarded a contract to train pilots. No. 20 Elementary and Reserve Flying Training School was formed on September 25, 1937 with a complement of six Tiger Moths and six Hawker Harts.

The Luftwaffe had it listed as Target GB 1089, this picture being taken from an aircraft en route to carry out the first massed attack on London on Saturday, September 7, 1940.

No. 72 Squadron had three postings to Gravesend, the first being from June 1 to July 8, 1940. Squadron members recall that their time there was marred by a notable incident when K9942 landed wheels up on June 2.

No. 20 ERFTS were to remain at Gravesend for two years training Fleet Air Arm pilots as well as those for the RAF but with the outbreak of war the unit closed and Gravesend became a satellite airfield to Biggin Hill. Although only allocated satellite status, unusually it had two decoy sites, one being at Cliffe Marshes and the other at Luddesdown.

It fell to No. 32 Squadron to open the airfield when they arrived with their Hurricanes from Biggin Hill on January 3, 1940. However bad weather ensured that they flew very little before moving to Manston on March 3 to be replaced briefly by No. 56 (Punjab) Squadron. When they left it was No. 610 (County of Chester) Squadron of the Royal Auxiliary Air Force which arrived on May 27 and began operations with their Spitfires over the Dunkirk beaches. Providing top cover, they were to lose two Commanding Officers, Squadron Leaders Alexander Franks and Andrew Smith over the period of the evacuation. With the end of Operation 'Dynamo' they moved back to Biggin Hill.

Another auxiliary squadron arrived on July 3 in the shape of No. 604 (County of Middlesex) flying the Bristol Blenheims. These particular aircraft had been converted from the bomber version to night fighters with a kit manufactured by the Southern Railway Ashford factory. Though they carried out several night patrols, the early airborne radar with which they were fitted constantly failed thus denying the squadron any contacts. Leaving for Middle Wallop on July 26, No. 72 (Basutoland) Squadron had arrived the previous week flying in their Spitfires from Acklington where they had been forced to use Gladiators due to the soft surface at that aerodrome. They left Gravesend a week later, their replacement being No. 501 (County of Gloucester) Auxiliary Squadron equipped with Hurricanes. It was decided that at dawn each day they would fly down to the forward airfield at Hawkinge and it was from there on July 29, during their first engagement, that they claimed six Ju 87s shot down. No. 501 was in daily combat throughout August finally leaving on September 10 for Kenley. As they departed No. 66 Squadron arrived, also flying Spitfires, but after a stay of just under a month they moved out to West Malling.

The formation of No. 421 Flight at Gravesend came at the express wish of Winston Churchill. Formed from personnel of No. 66 Squadron, their role was to patrol high over the Channel and report by radio the number of enemy aircraft forming up over the French coast. Initially equipped with Hurricanes, they converted to Spitfires before moving over to West Malling.

In November the role of the airfield reverted back to that of a night fighter base with the arrival of No. 141 Squadron flying the Defiant. They were joined by No. 85 with Hurricanes, both squadrons remaining at Gravesend over the Christmas and New Year period.

On January 1, 1941, No. 85 moved to Debden. During December another Defiant squadron, No. 264 (Madras Presidency) had joined No. 141 but when they left eleven days later the latter squadron became the sole residents until April 29, 1941.

The squadron came back in 1941 from July 8-26 and again on October 20, this photo being taken eleven days later to mark the occasion when Squadron Leader Desmond Sheen ceremoniously handed over the repaired K9942 to the incoming CO, Squadron Leader Cedric Masterman in the light-coloured overalls ***(above)*** **and in the cockpit of his Spitfire** ***(below).***

With the erection of further buildings and a minor upgrade of the airfield, 1941 saw many Spitfire squadrons rotate through Gravesend. Carrying out 'Ranger' and 'Rodeo' operations, the squadrons were No. 72 (Basutoland) during July, No. 609 (West Riding) July to September and No. 92 (East India) September to October.

In 1942, three Canadian Squadrons of the Commonwealth Air Training Plan arrived in the UK. Using the prefix 400 before their original squadron number, No. 1 became No. 401 (Ram) and it was this unit that came to the airfield on March 19. Other units resident that year included No. 124 (Baroda) May to June and one week in August; Nos. 111 and 71 (Eagle) and 350 (Belgian) June to July; Nos. 65 (East India) and 133 (Eagle) July to August; No. 232 August 14 to 20; No. 165 (Ceylon) August 14 till November 1, and No. 71 back once more from August to September. All the squadrons were equipped with various marks of Spitfires.

This hectic activity called for extensions to the landing area and during 1942 and early 1943, the N-S grass runway was extended to 1,700 yards and the E-W to 1,800 yards. The laying of Sommerfeld Track and Drem airfield lighting gave Gravesend a better all-weather capability. It was also felt that being so close to the sea and in particular the Thames Estuary, an air-sea rescue squadron should be based there so No. 277 Squadron, whose motto was 'We save by Seeking', was posted in with Defiants, Lysanders and the faithful Walrus.

On March 24, 1943, No. 181 Squadron brought the Hawker Typhoon to Gravesend to commence a working up period prior to transferring to the Second Tactical Air Force. More Typhoons arrived on March 30 with No. 245 (Northern Rhodesia) Squadron followed by No. 174 (Mauritius) on May 28. All three squadrons commenced 'Rhubarb' and 'Rodeo' operations with Spitfire VBs replacing the Typhoons in June 1943 when Nos. 19 and 132 (City of Bombay) Squadrons arrived.

Short stays were the order of the day once again as the three squadrons moved to newly-constructed Advanced Landing Grounds nearer the south coast allowing No. 306 (Torun) Polish Squadron to use the facilities for a short period. Further stays came with Nos. 193 (Fellowship of the Bellows), No. 257 (Burma), Nos. 64 and 266 (Rhodesia) Squadrons. Nos. 19, 65 (East India) and 122 (Bombay) Squadrons returned in October 1943 both converting from Spitfires to the Mustang III and becoming part of the Second Tactical Air Force.

The last squadrons to use Gravesend were Nos. 464 (Australian), Nos. 21 and 487 (New Zealand) which, flying Mosquitos, formed No. 140 Wing of the Second Tactical Air Force. By June 13, 1944, they had left and Gravesend was placed under care and maintenance.

The Air Ministry relinquished the airfield in June 1956 and it was sold to become a housing development called Riverview Park. All that remains today is a plaque sited on the wall of the Cascades Leisure Centre commemorating the 14 pilots of Nos. 501 and 66(F) Squadrons who lost their lives whilst flying from Gravesend.

Extensions were made to both runways in 1942-43.

Today, save for a small section of the southern perimeter track, Gravesend has virtually been wiped from the face of the earth.

HAWKINGE

Lying just behind the coast at Folkestone, the Royal Air Force station at Hawkinge (together with Lympne) was one of Fighter Command's most forward bases. After the war it was used as a WAAF Technical Training unit . . .

Aviation came to Hawkinge, a village two miles north of Folkestone in Kent, in 1912 but a permanent airfield was not approved until 1915 when the War Office acquired 166 acres of Lord Radnor's estate. Used by squadrons of the RFC during the war and peacetime by various auxiliary squadrons for summer camps, the RAF expansion plans of 1936 saw Hawkinge designated a forward aerodrome in No. 11 Group and a large building programme began.

Grass surfaced, it measured 1,183 yards E-W, 1,000 yards NE-SW, 800 yards N-S and 700 yards SE-NW. A perimeter track was laid together with the construction of several Belfast hangars. On completion, two of the first squadrons to arrive were Nos. 2 and 25, the latter having been based there in the early 1920s. They flew in with Audax and Gladiators during October 1935 and October 1938 respectively with No. 2 Squadron converting to the Lysander and No. 25 to the Blenheim. The former took their aircraft to France on September 29, 1939 as part of the Advanced Air Striking Force. They were followed by a detachment of Hectors and Lysanders from No. 613 (City of Manchester) Auxiliary Squadron during November 1939 and a detachment of Hurricane Is from No. 3 Squadron during December.

For a brief period Hawkinge was transferred to Training Command, acting as a recruiting centre for candidates for RAF service. The squadrons moved out and the airfield was subjected to intense camouflaging but was returned to Fighter Command in January 1940. However it was an Army Co-operation Squadron, No. 16, which arrived first on February 17. Flying Lysanders, they too were destined for France leaving on April 13 for Amiens. With the impending German assault in the West, No. 17 Squadron brought their Hurricanes down from Debden on May 7 with No. 25 Squadron returning three days later. Further detached Blenheims from No. 604 (County of Middlesex) Auxiliary Squadron arrived to assist in maintaining standing patrols over the Dunkirk beaches during the evacuation. During this period, Hawkinge became one of the busiest aerodromes in Fighter Command as various squadrons used it for refueling and re-arming. Further Hurricane detachments arrived before Operation 'Dynamo' was over.

A detachment of Hurricanes from No. 1 Squadron arrived on June 18 together with No. 245 (Northern Rhodesian) — all using the airfield as a forward base, flying it at dawn and returning to their home aerodromes at sunset.

Friday, July 19 saw No. 141 bring their Defiants in from West Malling but during a patrol later that day they suffered grievously, only two aircraft returning from the seven that took off.

Being the closest airfield to the enemy, it suffered many attacks, one severe raid coming on August 18 causing considerable damage. On the ground, airfield defence consisted of Bofors and Oerlikon guns supplemented by the Parachute and Cable Rocket Defence System.

As autumn approached the Luftwaffe's tactics changed from attacking Fighter Command airfields to bombing major cities. At Hawkinge, enemy raids had resulted in all but one of the Belfast hangars being hit so the aerodrome had to undergo a period of reconstruction when three Extra Over Blister hangars were built, and the damaged buildings repaired.

Only now was a permanent unit based at Hawkinge when No. 421 Flight was formed on November 15 with Spitfires. The duty of the flight was to fly high in order to spot large incoming enemy formations. Reformed as No. 91 (Nigeria) Squadron in January 1941, they were to operate between nearby Lympne and Hawkinge until January 1943.

. . . but all is now just a memory. This was where the main gate lay to the living quarters which were situated on the opposite side of the road to the aerodrome.

A fine summer's day in July 1940 . . . the Battle of Britain is about to begin. These officer and sergeant pilots of No. 610 'County of Chester' Squadron await the call to scramble at A Flight dispersal.

December 1941 saw B Flight of No. 277 (ASR) Squadron arrive. Their Lysanders were supplemented by a Walrus and several Defiants for their task of rescuing downed pilots.

The Spitfire VBs of Nos. 41 and 65 Squadrons, which were posted in at the end of June 1942, stayed but a few days before they were replaced by No. 416 (City of Oshawa) Canadian Squadron and No. 616 (South Yorkshire) Auxiliary Squadron, both participating in Operation 'Jubilee' at Dieppe. The landings over, No. 416 moved to Martlesham Heath and No. 616 to Great Sampford.

Dave Brocklehurst, the curator of the Kent Battle of Britain Museum, pinpointed the same spot for us.

In a memorable sequence of photographs (see also front cover), No. 32 Squadron were also pictured taking a brief respite from action at their dispersal. From L-R: Pilot Officer R. F. Smythe, Pilot Officer K. R. Gillman, Pilot Officer J. E. Proctor, Flight Lieutenant P. M. Brothers, Pilot Officer D. H. Grice, Pilot Officer P. M. Gardner and Pilot Officer A. F. Eckford. All survived the battle and the war except for Keith Gillman who went missing in action on August 25, 1940.

The return of No. 91 (Nigeria) Squadron on May 21, 1943 saw Spitfire XIIs arrive to counter the new FW 190 fighter-bomber but they left on June 28 for Westhampnett. A two-day visit by the Spitfire VCs of No. 501 (County of Gloucester) Auxiliary Squadron during October 1942 saw them return for a longer period in June 1943 when they converted to the Mk IX that extended their range into France.

Further Blister hangars and a runway extension were added during 1943 while more Spitfire squadrons — Nos. 313 (Czech), 322 (Dutch) and 350 (Belgian) — carried out sorties over the Continent. The last to leave, No. 322, departed to Ayr on February 24, 1944 although a month later they returned before moving to Acklington.

Fleet Air Arm units were based at Hawkinge in 1944 when 24 Grumman Avengers of Nos. 854 and 855 Squadron arrived in May. Collectively known as No. 157 (GR) Wing of No. 16 Group, Coastal Command, with its headquarters at Chatham, the squadrons started intensive

Hawkinge remained a grass airfield and never had tarmac runways.

In recent years a housing estate has encroached across the historic landing ground . . .

patrols seeking out U-Boats in the Channel but both returned to Thorney Island in August.

Spitfires returned on August 8 when No. 350 (Belgian) Squadron came back to convert from Spitfire IXs to XIVs. Joined by No. 402 (Winnipeg Bear) Canadian Squadron, both were engaged on ops to counter the flying bombs. The first success came on August 16 when No. 402 shot down three V1s. Moving on by September, the Spitfire VIIs of No. 611 (West Lancashire) Auxiliary Squadron flew in on December 31 followed by the Australian No. 453 on May 2, 1945, to form the Hawkinge Wing. However No. 611 left on March 3 for Hunsdon whilst 453 stayed until it moved to Lasham on June 14.

After the air-sea rescue squadron disbanded, the last units to use Hawkinge were No. 567 from June to August, followed by Nos. 1, 132 and 234 Squadrons which arrived for gunnery courses. With their departure, Hawkinge was reduced to care and maintenance on November 7, 1945.

Used for gliding post-war, it transferred to No. 22 Technical Training Command and re-opened on June 1, 1946 as the WAAF Technical Training Unit. When this was transferred to Jurby, in January 1962 the airfield was once again relegated to care and maintenance although a brief lease of life came the following year when it was used for some scenes in the film *Battle of Britain*.

The Kent Battle of Britain Museum Trust was established on the old technical site and a memorial placed alongside the gymnasium by local aviation historian, Roy Humphreys. A large swathe of the landing ground has now been redeveloped for housing.

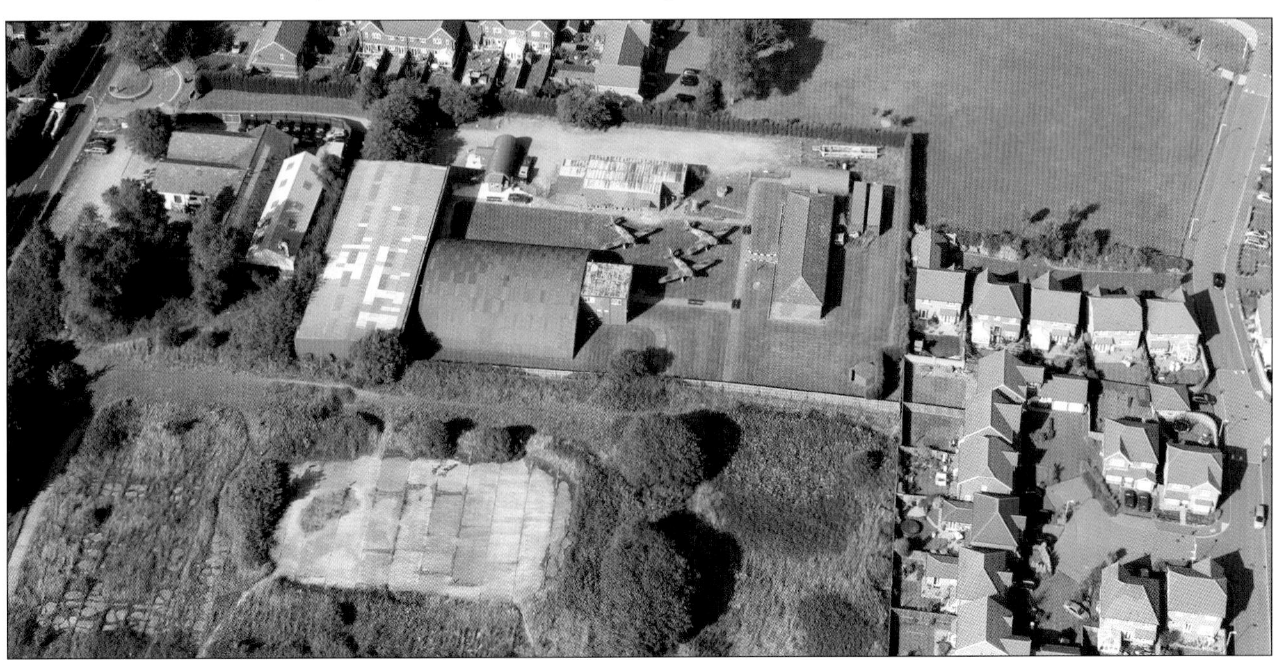

. . . yet fortunately the Kent Battle of Britain Museum keeps the history of this famous aerodrome alive.

HENDON

One cannot talk about Hendon without recalling the thrilling Empire Air Displays, begun in the 1920s, that culminated in June 1937 *(below)*. with a mass flypast of over 250 aircraft *Above:* Here Charles E. Brown pictured the finale of one of the post-war displays.

Sited alongside the south side of the M1 motorway between Edgware and Hendon in north London lies the Royal Air Force Museum. It was established in 1963 in hangarage on the south-eastern side of Hendon aerodrome and was opened by the Queen in 1973.

Hendon was a civil airfield that saw service in both world wars and, lying 230 feet above sea level, it was one of the highest in the south of England. Forever associated with the aviation pioneer, Claude Grahame-White, it became famous during the inter-war years as 'The London Aerodrome', home of the Hendon Air Pageant. After it was sold to the RAF in 1925, it became a training establishment for two auxiliary squadrons, Nos. 600 (City of London) and 601 (County of London), both equipped with the de Havilland DH9A. By 1929 both had converted to Westland Wapitis followed by Hawker Harts and Demons.

From 1937 . . . to 1957 and the final 'At Home' to be held at Hendon, one of over 40 RAF stations holding displays that year.

In November 1957 Hendon closed as a flying station, this picture showing the last aircraft to leave.

No. 24 Communications Squadron arrived on July 10, 1933, and the unit was to remain at Hendon for the duration of the war and into peacetime, their duty being to transport high-ranking officers and ministers of state.

During this period two further auxiliary squadrons arrived, Nos. 604 (County of Middlesex) and 611 (West Lancashire), but they had all left Hendon on the eve of war. No. 248 Squadron reformed at the airfield on October 30, 1939, with the Blenheim IF to work-up on the type before moving to North Coates on February 24, 1940. Dunkirk and the opening phases of the Battle of Britain saw no use for Hendon and it was not until September 6 that No. 504 (County of Nottingham) Auxiliary Squadron brought their Hurricanes south to Hendon. On September 25 a raid on the airfield hit nearby Colindale station killing four airmen and wounding six, but with the focus of enemy attacks now being concentrated on the capital, the squadron left for Exeter the following day. No. 1 Camouflage Unit arrived during November flying a variety of aircraft, their task being to test the effectiveness of airfield camouflage.

The field at the end of Colindale Avenue had first been used by Louis Paulhan to win the *Daily Mail* London to Manchester Air Race in April 1910. Then Claude Grahame-White and Richard Gates acquired the land in December that year for an aerodrome.

The control tower, which dated from 1911, fell into disrepair and was dismantled in 2010 to be moved within the RAF Museum site.

Spitfires arrived in the form of No. 1416 (Army Co-op) Flight to work in liaison with the local searchlight units. Converting to Blenheims, they moved to Benson in the summer of 1941 to be replaced by No. 116 Squadron with Lysanders. Their task was the calibration of predictors and anti-aircraft radar used by the gun batteries around the capital.

The camouflage unit moved to Heston on April 20, 1942 and two weeks later No. 510 Squadron arrived having formed from a nucleus of No. 24 Squadron. Becoming a unit in No. 44 Group of Transport Command, their Dakotas began VIP flights to North Africa and beyond. Re-designated in 1944 as the Metropolitan Communications Squadron, they moved out in the summer leaving No. 24 Squadron as sole residents. When they moved to Bassingbourn on February 25, 1946, No. 601 (County of London) Auxiliary Squadron reformed at Hendon and remained until March 1949. The last unit to leave was the communications squadron in November 1957. Today, although very little remains of the airfield itself, the RAF Museum stands as a fitting and world class reminder of historic Hendon aerodrome.

The airfield was hemmed in by the Midland Railway and the Edgware to Charing Cross Tube line and, as flying speeds increased, Hendon's days were numbered. Fifty years later the aerodrome has been swallowed up by a huge housing estate, leaving the RAF Museum occupying the original hangars in the south-eastern corner.

Opened in July 1929, Heston Air Park soon became a thriving venue for both private pilots and commercial airlines, British Airways Ltd being formed there in 1936. Modern features included customs facilities, floodlights and a night landing system.

HESTON

Lying a mile to the north of Hounslow in Middlesex, at just 100 feet above sea level, Heston might well have become London's main airport with its civil aviation origins dating back to 1928. However, expansion of the site at nearby Heathrow after the war saw the importance of Heston diminish.

Officially opened on July 6, 1929 by Airwork Ltd, it became a hub for private flying as well as a test airfield for Fairey Aviation and the Comper Aircraft Company. When the latter went into receivership, the assets were taken over by the Heston Aircraft Company which designed and built the Heston Racer. The airfield was unique at the time due to the fact that it had a concrete apron and a reinforced concrete hangar.

With the increase in civil aviation, Heston began to operate scheduled services to the Continent as well as becoming a venue for the King's Cup Air Race. It was also the aerodrome from which Prime Minister Neville Chamberlain flew to Germany in September 1938 to seek an accord with Hitler.

The airfield was requisitioned by the Air Ministry in September 1939, becoming an operational satellite to Northolt in No. 11 Group. Small in comparison with others, the grass surfaced landing area measured 1,400 yards SE-NW, 1,200 yards E-W and 800 yards from NE-SW and N-S. A 35-foot tarmac perimeter track together with three aeroplane sheds and one Blister hangar were built with the concrete hangar being used for aircraft storage. The original three-storey control tower was converted to an RAF-type watch office.

It was also the setting for the final act of the Four Power conference in Munich held to decide the fate of Czechoslovakia. On September 30, 1938, Prime Minister Neville Chamberlain flew back to Heston bearing his pact with Hitler which he claimed gave 'peace for our time'. However, Hitler viewed the whole proceedings with contempt and when Germany's Foreign Minister Joachim von Ribbentrop complained to him about signing the document, Hitler scornfully replied: 'Don't take it so seriously. This paper has no importance at all!' Chamberlain's homecoming took place just outside the car park of the M4 services at Heston!

Under the lens of the Luftwaffe in August 1940.

A decision by the Air Ministry to form a photographic reconnaissance flight at Heston led to civilian photographer, Sidney Cotton, being given the rank of Wing Commander and placed in charge. For security reasons this became known as No. 2 Camouflage Unit on November 3, 1939. Renamed the Photographic Reconnaissance Unit, it was equipped with a number of specially modified Spitfires.

Although no squadrons were based at Heston during the Battle of Britain, it saw many movements both civil and military. Despite its lack of squadrons, it was attacked on August 26 leaving the landing area badly cratered. Further attacks during early September caused minor damage and on September 19 a parachute mine wrecked five Spitfires of the PRU and a Wellington bomber. This prompted the Air Ministry to relocate the photo-unit to Benson in December 1940.

Heston was transferred from No. 11 Group to 81 Group (Training) early in the New Year. No. 53 Operational Training Unit (OTU) was formed at the airfield on February 29 with Spitfires and Masters but after having completed several flying courses, it left for Llandow on July 1 to be replaced by No. 61 OTU which remained until April 1942.

A Turbinlite Flight, No. 1422 was stationed at Heston from May 1941 with Bostons, Havocs and Hurricanes, but they achieved little success at night-fighting and were disbanded along with the other Turbinlite units in January 1943.

Transferred back to Fighter Command and No. 11 Group, No. 316 (Warsaw) Polish Squadron brought their Spitfire VBs in from Northolt on April 23, 1942. Joined on May 5 by the Spitfire VBs of another Polish squadron, No. 302 (Poznan), both carried out sorties over the Continent before No. 316 left for Hutton Cranswick and No. 302 for Croydon two months later

No. 116 Radar Calibration Squadron with Lysanders and Hurricanes arrived at Heston on April 20, 1942. With the addition of a Hornet Moth, Tiger Moth, an Oxford and an Anson, the unit carried out the calibration of predictors and anti-aircraft radar used by the gun batteries in the London area. They moved out to Croydon on December 12, 1943.

The return of No. 302 Squadron on July 7, 1942, followed by another Polish squadron, No. 308 (Krakow) on July 30, saw Heston continue its long association with Polish units. Both squadrons moved to Ipswich during September but returned to Heston several times over the next year until No. 302 finally moved to Perranporth on June 20, 1943 and No. 308 to Northolt on November 11,1943.

The Defiants of No. 515 Squadron joined the Polish squadrons when they flew in from Northolt on October 29, 1942. They were used for jamming enemy radar in an operation called 'Moonshine'. Leaving for Hunsdon on June 1, 1943, they converted to Beaufighters and joined No. 100 Group.

A Belgian squadron, No. 350, called for a five-day stay in March 1943, and the next few months saw a detachment of the US 27th Air Transport Group move in from Heathrow on May 7. This was a communications flight used for fast transportation within the UK and it recorded 598 movements between August and December 1943.

When the Second Tactical Air Force was formed in preparation for the invasion of Europe, Heston was classified as No. 133 Airfield and saw the return of Nos. 306 and 308 Polish Squadrons as part of the Northolt Wing with Spitfires. Heston was also chosen as the base for the Allied Expeditionary Communications Flight.

No. 129 (Mysore) Squadron joined the Poles on March 16, 1944. All three

In November 1941, Air Chief Marshal Sir William Sholto Douglas, the C-in-C of Fighter Command visited No. 61 Operational Training Unit at Heston, being pictured here with Flight Lieutenant Brian Kingcome.

The aerodrome is now the Airlinks Golf Course which is due to re-open in 2017.

squadrons were engaged on bomber escort sorties until they moved forward to Advanced Landing Grounds in Kent and Sussex before D-Day.

Heston was now left as a communications base. No. 85 Group Communication Squadron moved in with Oxfords, Proctors, Spitfires and Austers followed later by Dakotas from the American 86th Air Transport Squadron. At the same time Heston was re-designated a satellite of Northolt.

An RAF oblique looking west in June 1941 contrasts with the view today. The M4 motorway cuts a swathe across the former flying field which has now found a new use as a golf course.

Transferred back to civil aviation on January 13, 1945, Fairey Aviation were still busy with Spitfire reconnaissance conversion work and design work on the Sea Hornet. However, with the rapid expansion of Heathrow as the main London airport, Heston was forced to close with Fairey Aviation moving to White Waltham. The final demise came in 1965 when the line of the M4 motorway lay directly across the airfield.

A visible reminder of the airfield are the metal street arches within the local area which incorporate the Heston Napier Racer G-AFOK.

A wonderful line up just in front of the hangars. Nearest the camera are the Spitfires of No. 54 Squadron with four Blenheims of No. 25 Squadron and more Spitfires of No. 74 Squadron beyond. To the right are the machines of No. 65 Squadron.

HORNCHURCH

Originally known as Sutton's Farm, land was first requisitioned at Hornchurch in Essex for an aerodrome in 1915. Situated on the eastern outskirts of London it became an important airfield for the defence of the capital, a role that was to be perpetuated during the second conflict. However by 1919 the airfield had been dismantled and land returned to its owner Tom Crawford. With the decision by the Air Ministry in 1927 to establish 15 new aerodromes for home defence, Sutton's Farm was selected once again, much against the wishes of Mr. Crawford. By April 1, 1928 it was ready for occupation with Squadron Leader Keith Park as the first commanding officer. Twelve years later he would become the Air Officer Commanding No. 11 Group.

Renamed RAF Hornchurch the same year, the next ten years was to see many squadrons pass through the airfield. When war broke out, it became a station in Sector 'D' of No. 11 Group. Grass surfaced, it measured 1,130 yards NE-SW, 1,200 yards N-S, and 800 yards E-W and SE-NW. An 18-foot perimeter track and three 'C' Type hangars together with a Type 3 Watch Office/Flying Control completed the main construction. Being situated in an industrial area there were several high chimneys close to the airfield and, when war came, the London Balloon Barrage provided additional obstructions.

During the inter-war period, No. 54 Squadron reformed at Hornchurch with Siskins, Bulldogs, Gauntlets and Gladiators. In March 1939 they received the Spitfire I and began a period of alternating between Hornchurch and Rochford until the end of the Battle of Britain. Also reforming was No. 74 (Trinidad) Squadron — more commonly known as the 'Tiger' Squadron — on September 1, 1935. They were re-equipped with Spitfire Is during February 1939 and alternated between Hornchurch and Rochford until June 1940. Also present as war broke out were the Blenheim IFs of No. 600 (City of London) Auxiliary Squadron. They left for Rochford on October 16, 1939 returning four days later and converting to the Blenheim IV.

The war began badly for Hornchurch when the 'Battle of Barking Creek' resulted in the first casualties from friendly fire in the Second World War. From Dunkirk throughout the Battle of Britain, the Hornchurch squadrons — Nos. 41, 54, 65 and 74 — came into constant contact with the enemy almost every day. When they were sent for a rest period, their replacements were Nos. 222 (Natal) on May 28; 266 (Rhodesia) on August 14; No. 264 (Madras Presidency) on August 22, and 603 (City of Edinburgh) Auxiliary Squadron on August 29,

November 15, 1962: 'The station is now surplus to Air Ministry requirements and is for sale. Part of the land is to be returned to the original owners, the rest of the station is to be auctioned early next year'. So ran the statement which spelled the death-knell of one of Fighter Command's most illustrious bases. The end came swiftly on Friday, March 1, 1963 in the Sergeants' Mess when, in just 17 minutes of bidding, the aerodrome was knocked down for £517,000.

On June 27, 1940, the C-in-C of Fighter Command, Air Chief Marshal Sir Hugh Dowding, watches as HM King George VI invests pilots with awards. Here, Flight Lieutenant 'Al' Deere of No. 54 Squadron receives the Distinguished Flying Cross and a congratulatory handshake.

Richard Ballard was at the auction: 'Afterwards I walked around the buildings and into the immense empty hangars, scenes of such gallant activities a quarter of a century ago and I surveyed the scene with not a little sadness.' How would Richard have felt if he saw the same location today!

Joe Crawshaw was an airframe mechanic with No. 222 'Natal' Squadron when the airfield was on the receiving end of two heavy attacks in 1940. He took this photo showing the aftermath of the raid on August 31.

The airfield was bombed during the afternoon of August 24 causing disruption to telephone communication and leaving craters in the grass, but one of the worst attacks came on August 31 with the initial attack coming at lunchtime. Five Spitfires were damaged on the ground and the three hangars hit. Once again the grass was pitted with craters. During the afternoon the Luftwaffe returned but this time most of the bombs fell around the perimeter, damaging two Spitfires.

By the end of September it was all change once again as No. 222 Squadron moved to Coltishall on November 11, 266 moved to Wittering on August 21 and 603 moved to Rochford on December 3. By the end of the battle, the Hornchurch-based squadrons claimed to have brought down the most enemy aircraft.

January 1941 saw Nos. 41, 64 and 611 resident with Spitfires. However, No. 41 were only to remain until February 23 when they moved to Catterick whilst No. 64 moved to Rochford on May 9 having converted to the Spitfire IIA. They were to return to Hornchurch on many occasions over the next few years.

As they left No. 611 (West Lancashire) Auxiliary Squadron came in from Rochford on January 27 to convert to the Spitfire IIA before returning there on May 20. Mean-

The aerodrome surface pitted with filled-in craters from the bombing.

while the Hornchurch Wing was established consisting of three squadrons: Nos. 41, 64 (both returning to Hornchurch) and No. 611, with No. 54 coming back to join the wing on May 20. The month also saw the return of No. 603 (City of Edinburgh) Auxiliary Squadron to convert to the Spitfire VA before leaving for Rochford on June 16. Returning on July 9, they further converted to the VB mark. Further Spitfire VBs arrived on August 4 when the Canadian No. 403 (Wolf) Squadron flew in but they moved on to Debden three weeks later.

They were replaced on November 19 by another Canadian unit, No. 411 (Grizzly Bear) from Digby, equipped with Spitfire VBs. The Czech No. 313 Squadron arrived with more Mk VBs on December 15 at which point the Wing consisted of Nos. 411, 313 and 64 Squadrons. At this stage the Hornchurch Wing was carrying out sweeps over France together with long-term resident, No. 54 Squadron, the latter being the aerodrome's longest-serving squadron before it ended its tenure on November 17.

As with 1941, 1942 was to see many squadrons rotate through the station for varying periods. These included Nos. 81, 122 (Bombay), 132 (City of Bombay), 154 (Motor Industries), 340, and 453 Australian. All carried out sweeps over the Continent and acted as escorts for heavy bombers of the USAAF 8th Air Force.

So little remains of the aerodrome that it is fortunate that this solitary E-pen on the northern perimeter survives as a parking area for the nature park which now occupies most of the flying field. On July 1, 1940, Sergeant Pilot John McAdam was posted to No. 41 Squadron — then at Catterick — but pictured here at Hornchurch at the end of the month.

March 1943 saw Nos. 64 and 350 move out with further re-equipping to Spitfire IX and LF IXBs for No. 222 Squadron (which was to spend its last time at Hornchurch

These aerial shots from 1946 and 2010 geographically show the demise of the aerodrome. After it was sold, Hoveringham Gravels (Southern) Ltd began gravel extraction and when that was exhausted the resulting quarry was used as a rubbish tip. By 1979 it was completely full and an earth topping raised the level by several feet.

from December 27 till December 30, 1943 and March 10 till April 4 in 1944). No. 453 (Australian) returned from Rochford on March 27, 1943 and converted from the Spitfire VB to the Mk IXB leaving for Ibsley on June 28. No. 504 (County of Nottingham) Auxiliary Squadron spent two short periods at Hornchurch from January 19 to the 28th and February 4 until March 10. No. 349 (Belgian) Squadron with Spitfire LF IXEs arrived from Friston on March 11 staying until April 6.

Two more raids took place on the airfield on January 21, 1944 and again on February 23, an attack that damaged several Spitfires.

With the advent of the V1 attacks, the balloon barrage which was set up around the area made Hornchurch unsafe for operations. The sector operations room closed down with the aerodrome being controlled by North Weald as the Spitfires moved out.

In January 1945, a detachment from No. 278 (ASR) Squadron arrived, followed by Tempests on May 3 when No. 287 Squadron flew the short distance from Redhill. Sending detachments to Hunsdon and North Weald, they left for Bradwell Bay on June 15.

After the war, Hornchurch was transferred to Technical Training Command but was relegated to care and maintenance in 1947. Reactivated the following year for No. 17 Reserve Flying School, it continued operating until 1953. The Aircrew Selection Centre was based there from 1952 until 1963. The airfield was then put up for auction and. ended up being used for gravel extraction.

HUNSDON

Hunsdon Flugplatz — GB Target 10 366 — as it appeared to the Luftwaffe in October 1941. This was a time when there was great activity at the aerodrome to develop new night-fighting techniques and exercises with anti-aircrafft units protecting London.

In 1938, a site six miles south-west of Bishop's Stortford in Hertfordshire was surveyed by the Directorate of Works for an aerodrome. Hunsdon was selected to become a night-fighter station although only classified as a satellite or RLG. Shortly after acceptance, George Wimpey and Sons arrived to lay down the runways, perimeter track and hardstandings. Work on the dispersed buildings was sub-contracted to H. J. James of Luton and Kent & Co. Officially opening on May 4, 1941, work on building the airfield infrastructure carried on until late 1942.

Situated 254 feet above sea level, the grass landing area measured 1,500 yards NE-SW, 1,300 yards E-W, 1,100 yards SE-NW and 1,000 yards N-S. The perimeter track was 34 feet wide, and a Type 1 Flying Control and several Blister, Over Blisters and Extra Over Blisters plus one Bellman hangar were all constructed in time for the first squadron to arrive: No. 85 from Debden on May 3, 1941 with Defiants and Havocs. They were the first squadron to use Havocs in the night fighter role and they carried out night patrols under the control of a GCI station at Foulness in Essex.

Being the first squadron to use the Havoc in a night-fighting role, some technical problems soon became evident. However, once these had been resolved, the CO, Squadron Leader Peter Townsend, stated that he was pleased with the new aircraft and with the way it performed compared with the Hurricane.

An additional night fighter unit was formed at Hunsdon on June 16. No. 1451 Turbinlite Flight was equipped with Havocs and worked in conjunction with the Havocs of No. 85 Squadron that were employed in the attacking role. However, when No. 3 Squadron arrived on August 9, they took

Probably Hunsdon's main claim to fame came in February 1944 when No. 140 Wing mounted Operation 'Jericho' to breach the walls of the prison at Amiens and release members of the French Resistance. The raid was carried out by six Mosquitoes from two Commonwealth squadrons: No. 487 *(above)* from the Royal New Zealand Air Force and No. 464 *(bottom)* of the Royal Australian Air Force. The RAF's No. 21 Squadron was the back-up in reserve.

over from No. 85 Squadron as their Hurricanes were more suited to flying in company with the Havoc. A second Turbinlite Flight, No. 1459, was also formed at Hunsdon but moved away in September. No. 1451 Flight later became a full squadron, No. 530, but their days were numbered as their lack of success at night saw them disbanded on January 25, 1943 along with the rest of the Turbinlite squadrons.

Operation 'Jubilee' saw No. 85 Squadron operating over Dieppe before they converted to the Mosquito II. With these, night patrols moved up a gear with further conversions to the Mk XV and, by 1943, the Mk XII which they took to West Malling on May 13. They were followed by No. 3 Squadron which also departed to the same Kent airfield a day later having converted to Typhoons. As No. 85 Squadron left, in came No. 157 from Bradwell Bay. Flying the Mosquito II, they converted to the Mk VI before moving to Predannack on November 9.

By now two tarmac runways had been laid. The main on an E-W axis was 1,450 x 50 yards with the secondary 1,250 yards NE-SW. Once completed maintenance of the airfield was taken over by Charles Chaston & Co Ltd.

A fine memorial was dedicated at Hunsdon on May 22, 2005.

This Mosquito, NF XIII, of No. 29 Squadron was pictured at its dispersal in January 1945. This particular aircraft, HK382, was lost on a night flying test on March 16, 1945, killing the pilot and navigator, both Canadians.

With the departure of the Mosquitos, No. 515 Squadron bought their Defiants to Hunsdon on June 1, 1943. A conversion to the Beaufighter IIF saw them depart to Little Snoring on December 15 but before they left, the replacement squadron for 157 arrived. This was the Canadian No. 410 (Couger) Squadron flying Mosquito VIs. Arriving on November 8 they converted to the Mk XIII taking them to Castle Camps on December 30.

With Hunsdon becoming part of No. 85 Group in late December, No. 140 Wing arrived on December 31 comprising Nos. 21, 464 (Australian) and 487 (RNZAF) Squadrons. The Wing had worked up at Sculthorpe under the command of Group Captain Percy Pickard with Mosquito VIs. Having previously been engaged on anti-V1 operations, they had arrived at Hunsdon to perfect their technique for a daring low-level raid on the prison at Amiens in Northern France in order to release French Resistance workers held in the jail. Code-named Operation 'Jericho', all three squadrons left Hunsdon on February 18, 1944 escorted by Typhoons from No. 198 Squadron. Although the attack was successful, Pickard and his navigator, Flight Lieutenant John Broadley were shot down.

For the Wing it was back to attacking V1 launch sites in France. It moved to Gravesend on April 17, 1944 with No. 410 (Cougar) Canadian Squadron returning on April 29 with Mosquito XIIIs. Joined by No. 409 (Nighthawk) Canadian Squadron and No. 29 Squadron on June 19, all three squadrons provided air support on and beyond D-Day. As the Allies advanced into Europe, both Canadian squadrons left for France in late August with No. 29 leaving for Colerne on February 22, 1945.

Another Canadian squadron, No. 418 (City of Edmonton), brought their Mosquito IIs in on August 28, 1944 to convert to the Mk VI before leaving for Blackbushe (Hartford Bridge) on November 21. No. 219 (Mysore) Squadron, which had also arrived with Mosquito XXXs in August, left on October 10, 1944. A five-week stay by No. 488 (RNZAF) Squadron with Mosquito XIIIs allowed them to convert to the Mk XXX before going to France. Further Mk XXXs arrived on November 19 when No. 151 came in from Castle Camps. Carrying out high altitude sorties, they left for Bradwell Bay on March 1, 1945 thus ending Hunsdons long association with the Mosquito.

It was now the turn of the Mustangs of No. 154 (Motor Industries) and 611 (West Lancashire) Auxiliary Squadrons which arrived during March 1945, joined by a Tempest squadron, No. 501 (County of Gloucester) However, Nos.154 and 501 disbanded on March 19 while No. 611 moved to Peterhead on May 7 to disband.

The final units to be based at the airfield were two Canadian squadrons, No. 441 (Silver Fox) and 442 (Caribou). Arriving on April 29, the latter unit quickly converted from the Spitfire IX to the Mustang before leaving for Digby on May 17 together with the Spitfires of No. 441. Two days after they left, the airfield was relegated to care and maintenance, officially closing in July 1947. An airfield memorial was dedicated at Hunsdon on May 22, 2005.

The outer track of the curious double taxiway in the north-western corner of the airfield has been lifted although it can still be discerned on the aerial view opposite. The 17th century Crabapple Cottage still stands although hidden by trees.

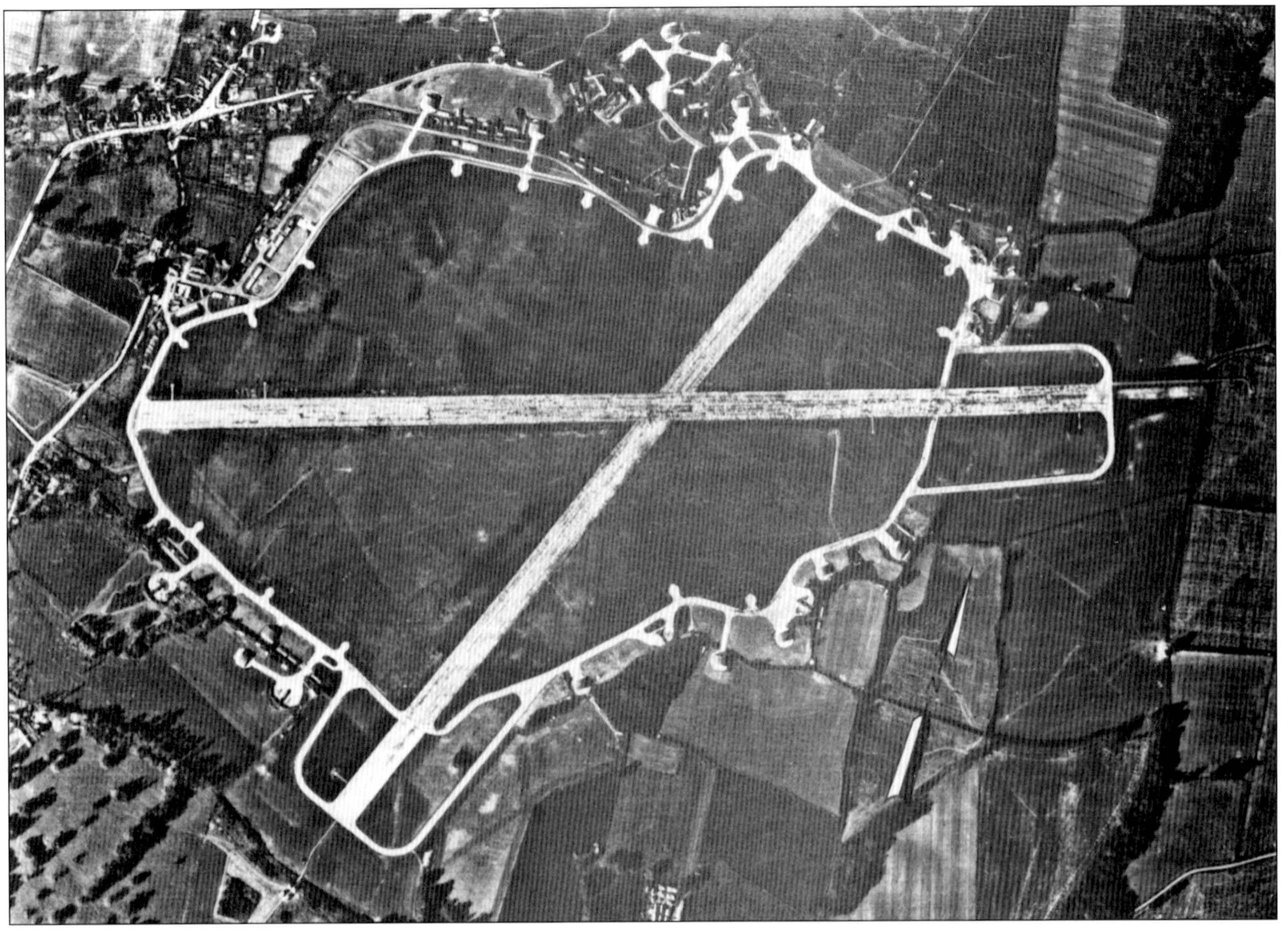

From front-line aerodrome . . . to Hertfordshire farmland . . . how are the mighty fallen!

MOSQUITO HERE

Google

KENLEY

In 1938, one of the largest peacetime exercises took place in Britain with over 900 aircraft battling it out between 'Westland' and 'Eastland'. These Gladiators of No. 3 Squadron were pictured at Kenley on August 4.

Kenley, lying between the A22 and A23 in Surrey, was built primarily for the defence of the capital and was opened in June, 1917 as an Aircraft Acceptance Park. It became a day bomber base after a period of reconstruction in the early 1920s and was further up-graded as war approached.

Previously a grass airfield, from 1936 many squadrons rotated through Kenley necessitating the construction of two concrete runways, the NW-SE measuring 1,000 yards and the NE-SW 1,200 yards. The airfield facilities were also improved including the installation of two fuel dumps, one containing 35,000 gallons of aviation spirit, the other 8,000 gallons of petrol, the work being carried out by Constable, Hart and Company.

Established as the main station in Sector 'B' of No. 11 Group, the first arrival was No. 3 Squadron followed by 'B' Flight of No. 604 (County of Middlesex) Auxiliary Squadron. At this time, squadrons from Kenley were being tasked with helping the British Expeditionary Force stem the German advance, leaving the aerodrome early morning and returning at dusk. Various units passed through the airfield for brief periods including Nos. 17, 229 and 253 (Hyderabad State) Squadrons. The station was attacked many times during the Battle of Britain causing considerable damage and much loss of life.

By autumn two satellite airfields had been allocated to Kenley, Redhill and Shoreham, both operational by the time No. 615 (County of Surrey) Auxiliary Squadron arrived. They were in residence at various times from December 16, 1940, until April 21, 1941, during the course of which they converted from the Hurricane I to the Hurricane IIA.

Joining forces with No. 1 Squadron to form the Kenley Wing, 1941 saw them attacking targets in enemy-occupied Europe.

In June the Hurricane squadrons were replaced by Spitfire units in the form of Nos. 452 (RAAF), 485 (RNZAF) and 602 (City of Glasgow). The wing flew 33 'Circus' operations over Northern France during July and August which saw their first encounters with the new Focke-Wulf 190. Famous names such as Johnnie Johnson, Paddy Finucane

Due to the fact that Kenley was built on common land owned by the City of London, it is protected from development and remains one of the most intact aerodromes of the period still used by the RAF for cadet glider training.

On June 27, 1940, HM King George VI visited Biggin Hill and Kenley, accompanied by the AOC Sir Hugh Dowding, to present awards. Here, at Kenley the King is congratulating Squadron Leader Joseph Kyall who led No. 615 Squadron from March to December 1940, decorating him with the DSO and DFC for his role during the Battle of France. The squadron had returned to Kenley on May 21 but by June 19 was back on operations over France. His Majesty expressed satisfaction on all he had seen on his inspection tour of the station and made special reference to the excellent rifle drill and turn-out of the parade.

Ten years late, John Gossage and Derek Twist chose Kenley as the setting for the first post-war feature film depicting the Battle of Britain. Initially titled *Hawks in the Sun*, when it reached the cinemas in 1951 it had a new title: *Angels One-Five*. Using as many ex-RAF personnel as possible, behind and in front of the camera, the production team were also the first to be given permission to film in the still top secret No. 11 Group Operations Room (see page 118). *Left:* Here, a scene is being filmed on the parade ground. *Right:* We matched the view in 1980 for an article on the film in *After the Battle* No. 30.

Then in 1955 *Reach for the Sky*, the biopic based on the life of Douglas Bader, also featured Kenley where Bader had served before the war. *Left:* With the Station Headquarters block in the background, Kenneth More is on parade with Michael Warre portraying Harry 'Pricky' Day, the C Flight commander of No. 23 Squadron obscuring Lyndon Brook playing the fictitious Johnny Sanderson, with about 20 extras, all dressed in breeches and puttees in the style of the period. *Right:* All the barrack blocks on the south side of the square have been demolished but the empty Station HQ still survives in a fenced-off compound.

On August 18, the aerodrome suffered a devastating attack from nine Dorniers coming in low from the east while another 30 to 50 bombed from high level. One of the attacking aircraft was brought down just outside the boundary of the airfield. Severe damage was wrought to installations and all the hangars were hit plus the sick quarters, Officers' Mess, Sergeants' Mess, Station HQ, and barracks. Ten aircraft were destroyed and six others damaged plus a number of motor vehicles. An officer and seven men were killed and ten other personnel wounded. Twenty-four of the 100 bombs dropped were delayed action.

A prime target, Kenley was again under the eyes of the Luftwaffe at 9.53 a.m. on August 31, 1940 for damage assessment as a further raid by eight dive bombers escorted by 50 fighters took place the following day. However, this time only one bomb fell on RAF property but billets outside the 'drome were seriously damaged. One soldier was killed.

Although 65 years separate these two views, it is remarkable how intact Kenley still appears from the air. However, most of the E-pens of 1940 have gone as has the Operations Room with its blast walls and the barrack blocks seen in the parade photos.

and Al Deere all flew from Kenley during 1941 and in February 1942, Group Captain Victor Beamish assumed command of the station.

The United States Army Air Force 308th Fighter Squadron arrived at Kenley in August. They used Spitfire VBs to gain experience in escort duties for two weeks and were followed by the 4th Fighter Squadron of the 52nd Fighter Group on similar duties. By August 30 they had left and Kenley prepared for Operation 'Jubilee', the ill-fated Dieppe landings. For this the wing operated constantly from dawn to dusk with various other squadrons using the airfield for refuelling and re-arming.

No. 401 (Ram) Canadian Squadron arrived on September 24, 1942, followed by No. 412 (Falcon) to form the Kenley Canadian Wing commanded by Wing Commander 'Johnnie' Johnson in March 1943. No. 401 Squadron moved to Catterick to convert to the Spitfire VB and No. 412 Squadron moved to Angle during January 1943.

It was now the turn of Nos. 66 and 165 (Ceylon) Squadrons to occupy Kenley as part of the Air Defence of Great Britain. Escorting American Marauder bombers, they also flew from the forward base of Friston, high on the South Downs. Now known as No. 127 Airfield of the Second Tactical Air Force, October saw the return of various Canadian squadrons which remained until April 1944. This saw a premature end to operational flying from Kenley as its status was downgraded and it became a disarmament school until 1946 when it went to care and maintenance.

A cameo role came in 1955 when the airfield became the location for the making of the film *Reach for the Sky*, the story of Douglas Bader. Today Kenley remains in the hands of the Ministry of Defence with the army occupying the technical buildings. The RAF presence continues with No. 615 Volunteer Gliding School giving air experience and gliding tuition to Air Cadets with the airfield remaining virtually as it was in wartime.

However, just before it was demolished, we rescued this B Flight readiness board which we found lying on the floor and also one of the Air Ministry Lloyd Loom chairs which were used in large numbers, especially by pilots in the summer of 1940.

When ex-Luftwaffe pilot Leutnant Heinz Möllenbrok of 3./KG2 — who parachuted into a plum tree on August 16, 1940 — saw it displayed in the *After the Battle* office, he immediately ordered: 'You vill take my picture in ze vicker chair'.

LASHAM

Not until September 1941 was authorisation given for land to be requisitioned to build a satellite for the bomber airfield at Aldermaston. Once acquired, McAlpines moved in to clear the site and build runways, dispersal areas, hardstandings, hangars and a technical site. Meantime plans for Aldermaston had changed and in place of the expected RAF Operational Training Unit, it was intended to be handed over to the USAAF, but this did not happen and in another change of plan, Lasham became part of No. 38 Wing of Army Co-operation Command.

Lasham was 618 feet above sea level and situated six miles south-east of Basingstoke in Hampshire. Its three concrete runways, all 50 yards wide, measured 1,900 yards E-W, 1,400 SW-NE and 1,200 yards SE-NW, linked by a perimeter track 50 feet wide. Four T2 hangars were constructed with a Type 2 Flying Control.

Strangely the aerodrome remained unoccupied until March 1943 although it still received attention from the Luftwaffe on January 2, 1943 when it was bombed and machine-gunned by a single aircraft.

No. 175 Squadron brought their Hurricane IIBs in from Stoney Cross on March 11, 1943 as part of No. 124 Airfield. Further units taking part in a large army exercise and using Lasham were No. 412 (Falcon) Canadian Squadron with Spitfire VBs (March 7 to April 8); No. 181 with Typhoons (April 5 to June 2); No. 602 (City of Glasgow) Auxiliary with Spitfire VBs (April 14 to April 29); No. 182 with Typhoons (April 29 to June 2), and finally No. 183 (Gold Coast) Squadron with Typhoons (May 3 to May 20).

Lasham under construction in 1942.

It had been virtually completed by October although still devoid of aircraft. They did not arrive until March 1943.

A fine sequence featuring No. 305 Polish Squadron, technically under RAF Bomber Command, with one of its first Mosquitos.

After this hectic period, No. 124 Airfield moved to the Advanced Landing Ground at Apuldram in Sussex on June 2. The exercise over, No. 10 Group, Fighter Command assumed control of Lasham until August 28 when No. 2 Group of the Second Tactical Air Force took over. In came No. 320 (Netherlands) Squadron flying Mitchell IIs. Arriving on August 30, they saw little action until September when they took part in Operation 'Starkey', a plan conceived to confuse the enemy into believing that a landing by the Allies was imminent in the Pas-de-Calais. Joining them was No. 613 (City of Manchester) Auxiliary Squadron flying the North American Mustang I. They converted to the Mosquito VI to become part of No. 138 Airfield and were joined by No. 305 (Wielpolska) Polish Squadron also flying Mitchell IIs on November 18. They commenced escort and ground-attack missions, the Mitchell proving to be very suitable for this type of operation, later converting to the Mosquito. The squadron remained at Lasham until moving to Blackbushe (Hartford Bridge) on October 30, 1944.

Today it is the sailplanes of the Lasham Gliding Club that have taken over the airfield.

Although closed by the Air Ministry in 1948, fortunately the airfield has survived intact largely due to it becoming the base of the Lasham Gliding Society which was established in 1958, later purchasing the freehold from the Ministry of Defence.

From November onwards the other squadrons concentrated on attacks on enemy transport and airfields. The addition of No. 107 Squadron which came to Lasham on February 1, 1944 with Boston IIIAs and converted to Mosquito VIs saw No. 138 Airfield become an all Mosquito wing.

Attacks commenced on V-weapon sites but as D-Day approached the operations changed to attacking communication in France. In the days following D-Day the Lasham Wing earned a reputation as a precision attack unit, one particular sortie taking place on July 30, 1944. This was an attack on a château used as a rest home for U-boat crews. Six crews from Lasham carried out the attack which was led by Group Captain Leonard Bowser. Whilst the raid was a success, two Mosquitos from No. 107 Squadron were lost. Then in late October 1944, No. 138 Airfield moved over to Blackbushe.

On November 27, No. 84 Group Support Unit arrived from Thruxton as Lasham became designated a satellite of Blackbushe. It remained so until final closure as a military airfield on October 26, 1948. Transferred to the Ministry of Civil Aviation on July 15, 1961, Dan Air Engineering set up their base at Lasham, using it for many years until its demise in 1991. Gliders moved in to keep the airfield open and today Lasham is a busy civil airport still with the Lasham Gliding Society in residence.

This fine memorial beside the entrance records Lasham's wartime past.

LYMPNE

Originally selected for an airfield in 1915 but abandoned due to drainage problems, Lympne became known during the 1930s as the home of civil air races. It again came to the attention of the Air Ministry in 1936 when the Lands Officer visited the airfield with a view to requisitioning it for the RAF. Situated in Kent on a level plain between Ashford and Folkestone, the airfield sat 353 feet above sea level with views out to the coast. The setting up of a Station HQ on November 3, 1936, saw the Hawker Hind bombers of Nos. 21 and 34 Squadrons arrive. It had been intended that Lympne would be allocated to No. 2 (Bomber) Group in December 1937 but this was cancelled; the Hinds left, and the airfield was temporarily placed under care and maintenance.

Although Lympne was ideally situated to become an excellent forward airfield, instead it was allocated to No. 24 Group Training Command to be used for the School of Accounting Clerks! However, seven months later (on May 24, 1939), the station was transferred to Fighter Command with the option of being handed over to the Admiralty. Consequently two months later it was commissioned as HMS *Buzzard* of the Fleet Air Arm. Blackburn Skuas and Rocs disembarked from HMS *Ark Royal* for a short period followed by the arrival of the Naval Air Mechanics School in September 1939. Lympne was then renamed HMS *Daedulus II*.

With the launch of the German offensive in May 1940, it was not long before several units of the Advanced Air Striking Force pushed out of France arrived at Lympne. Space was at a premium as the Lysanders of Nos. 2, 16 and 26 (South African) Squadrons and the Bristol Blenheims of Nos. 18 (Burma), 53 and 59 Squadrons jostled for room before departing for other airfields. Nos. 16 and 26 Squadrons remained on station as, in addition to flying tactical reconnaissance sorties, they were also engaged on supply-dropping operations to British troops trapped at Calais. When these operations ceased, No. 26 moved to West Malling and No. 16 to Redhill.

Lympne was now transferred back to Fighter Command and No. 11 Group. Designated a forward airfield in the Biggin Hill

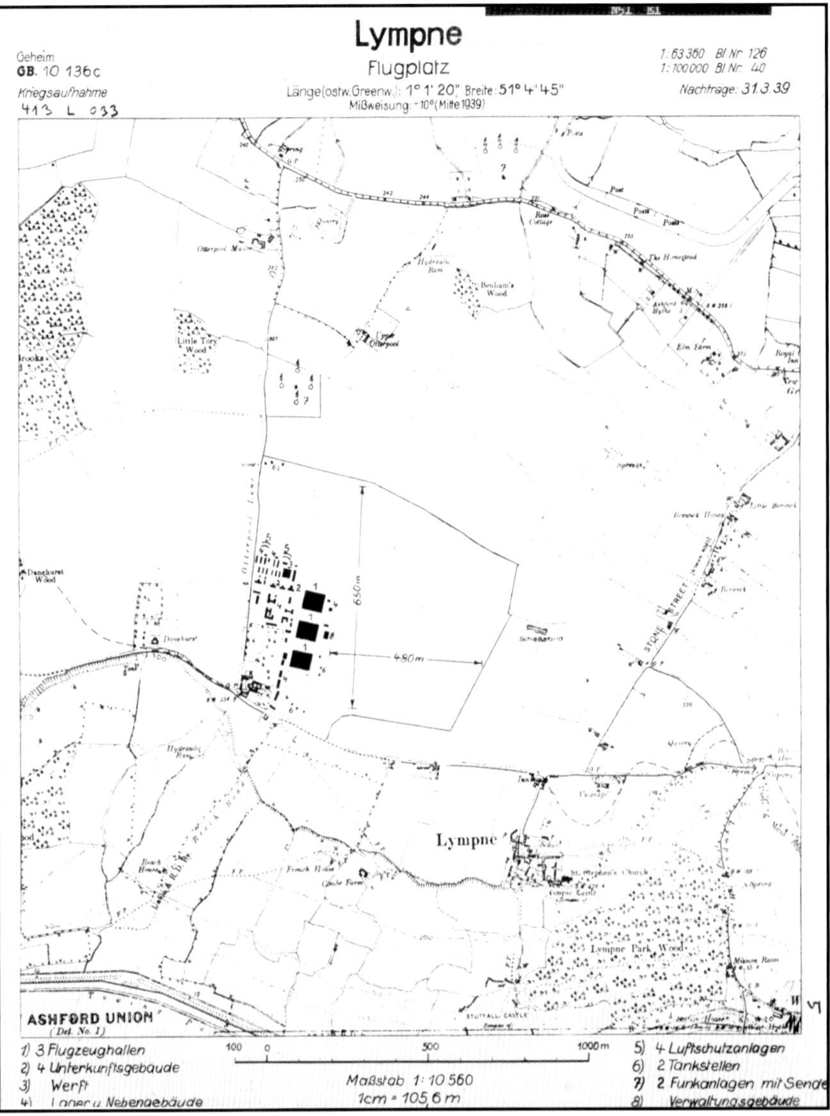

Early in 1939, the Luftwaffe had already listed Lympne aerodrome as a key target, giving it the reference GB 10 136c.

The airfield suffered several attacks, this undated reconnaissance photo showing a great number of hits across the technical site.

Another raid hammers Lympne with sticks of bombs bursting right across the 'drome from south-east to north-west.

sector, the aerodrome first received the attention of the Luftwaffe on July 3 when bombs caused minor damage but it was not until August 12 that a major raid targeted the airfield. By 9 a.m. the Do 17s of the I.Gruppe of KG2 were airborne from Epinoy and 30 minutes later they bombed the airfield from 800 feet causing considerable damage. With repair work still underway, the next major assault was on August 15 when a force of 40 Ju 87 Stukas from II/StG1, escorted by Bf 109s, dive-bombed the airfield in a ferocious attack, destroying most of the remaining buildings. The newly-repaired mains water supply and main electricity cables were severed and Lympne was rendered unserviceable for 48 hours, remaining fit only for emergency use until the spring of 1941.

Having been partially reconstructed, 'A' Flight of No. 91 Squadron arrived in March from nearby Hawkinge. Their task was high altitude coastal patrols to intercept enemy aircraft coming in over the coast. Known as 'Jim Crows', the Spitfire VBs also carried out low-level strike sorties over occupied territory. Their arrival coincided with the decision to bring Lympne up to full satellite status. Construction gangs moved in to build concrete hardstandings and fighter pens together with the erection of three Blister hangars.

In August 1942 came the ill-fated Dieppe operation code-named 'Jubilee'. In support of the operation No. 133 (Eagle) Squadron arrived from Biggin Hill on June 30 and No. 401 (Ram) of the Royal Canadian Air Force, also from Biggin Hill, on August 14. During this period, No. 91 (Nigeria) Squadron was carrying out anti-shipping patrols between Ostend and Le Havre. The operation over, Nos. 133 and 401 Squadrons left Lympne to be replaced by No. 65 (East India) Squadron which flew their Spitfire VBs down from Drem. However, after a stay of just nine days they returned to Drem as further upgrading of the airfield commenced. With its completion, the rest of No. 91 Squadron moved in from Hawkinge.

In March a new sound in the form of the Napier Sabre engine was heard at the airfield when No. 1 Squadron arrived from Biggin Hill with their Hawker Typhoons, immediately commencing operations over the French coast. That month also saw the arrival of a detachment from No. 245 (Northern Rhodesia) Squadron from Gravesend equipped with the bomber version of the Typhoon, universally known as a 'Bombphoon'. With No. 1 acting as escort, both units were now carrying out 'Ramrod' operations: day bomber raids escorted by fighters.

On May 28, 1943, No. 245 moved to Fairlop, being replaced by No. 609 (West Riding) Squadron of the Royal Auxiliary Air Force, also flying Typhoons. Both Nos. 1 and 609 were involved in Operation 'Starkey', an unsuccessful plan intended to tempt the Luftwaffe into large-scale combat. When this was over it was back to 'Ramrods' with No. 609 acting as escort to No. 1 which was now dive-bombing targets of opportunity on the Continent. This pattern continued until mid-December when No. 609 left for Manston to be replaced by the rocket-firing Hurricane IVs of No. 137 Squadron. They carried out anti-shipping strikes before moving to Colerne where they converted to the Typhoon, returning to Lympne on February 4, 1944. One month later they were joined by No. 186 bringing their Spitfire VBs in on March 1.

With the invasion of Europe, Lympne became very busy with the arrival of Nos. 33, 74 'Tiger' and 127 Squadrons for pre-invasion sweeps. Arriving from May 15 to May 17, No. 33 and 74 flew the Spitfire LF IXE whilst No. 127 had the Spitfire HF IX. All three flew fighter-bomber sorties, continuing over the D-Day period before No. 74 was ordered to turn its attention to anti-V1 operations, flying their first sorties shortly after D+3.

All three squadrons left Lympne early in July to be replaced by a Czech wing. Comprising Nos. 310, 312 and 313 Squadrons, they flew bomb-carrying Spitfire LF IXs as part of the Air Defence of Great Britain but after a stay of only a week they were replaced by Nos. 1, 41 and 165 (Ceylon) Squadrons for operations against the flying bombs. A complete re-organisation of the defences resulted in ADGB fighters being given new instructions. Whereas the fighters had previously been allowed to attack the V1s wherever they found them, now batteries of heavy guns had been moved to the Kent and Sussex coastline so that the gunners would get an uninterrupted field of fire at the missiles. The fighters were then given

Now it is industrial buildings and residential housing that straddles the former Fighter Command base.

two patrol lines: one in mid-Channel and the other behind the coastal guns but ahead of the balloon barrage. Using this method, if one form of defence did not get the flying bomb, it was hoped one of the others would.

As the new arrangements began to pay off, in August Nos. 1 and 165 Squadrons left for Detling with No. 41 resuming Channel sweeps. They also converted to the more powerful Griffon-engined Spitfire XIV that could operate at the same altitude as the jet-powered Me 262. They were joined by Nos. 130 (Punjab) and No. 610 (County of Chester) Squadrons but the former unit was replaced by No. 350 (Belgian) Squadron in September.

By December 1944 Lympne was devoid of all squadrons at which point the airfield reverted to an Emergency Landing Ground. In April 1945, Nos. 451 and 453 Squadrons of the Royal Australian Air Force used the airfield as a base for a month but when they left the station was put on care and maintenance, reverting to civilian use after the war. Later renamed Ashford Airport, it had varied success under several operators until it closed in 1974.

The Typhoon was a potent weapon, as was its cousin the bomber version nicknamed the Bomphoon! Here Squadron Leader Tony Zweigbergk hosts a line up with his fellow pilots and mechanics for the 245 Squadron scrapbook.

Now the only reminders of the RAF's former tenure of Lympne are the mouldering remains of barrack huts.

MANSTON

On the outbreak of war Manston was a grass aerodrome, this picture of Avro Ansons and North American Harvard trainers being taken in October 1939. The photographer's vantage point was the watch office on the eastern side, since demolished.

Having been used by both RNAS and RFC units during the First World War, Manston rose to become a major airfield in the second conflict. Lying two miles west of Ramsgate in Kent, on the Thanet coast at a height of 150 feet above sea level, it was classified as a forward aerodrome to the parent station at Hornchurch. The grass landing area dimensions were N-S 1,066 yards, NE-SW 1,330 yards, E-W 1,500 yards and SE-NW 1,170 yards. The facilities included several shed hangars, 44,000 gallons of aviation and 3,600 gallons of MT petrol, the means of refuelling being carried out by bowsers. Night landing equipment included a Drem Type I whilst radio equipment was HF/DF and VHF/DF.

Prior to the outbreak of war Manston was in No. 24 Group, Training Command, but a transfer to No. 11 Group, Fighter Command saw Nos. 235 and 253 (Hyderabad State) Squadrons reform there on October 30, both flying Fairey Battles. Later the former squadron converted to Blenheim IVFs whilst the latter re-equipped with Hurricanes. They were joined by No. 79 (Madras Presidency) on November 12 and by No. 600 (City of London) Auxiliary Squadron on December 27.

The New Year saw Nos. 235 and 253 leave the airfield, the former for North Coates and the latter for Northolt. Several strange looking Wellingtons belonging to No. 3 (General Reconnaissance) Unit arrived in January 1940. Fitted with enormous 48-foot magnetic coils, their duty was to fly at low level over the Channel and East Coast in the hope of setting off magnetic mines.

March 8 saw No. 79 Squadron depart for Biggin Hill leaving behind a small detachment until No. 32 Squadron arrived for a two-week stay. Later Polish airmen from Eastchurch moved in for training. Manston was used as a forward airfield during the evacuation from the Continent by No. 604 (County of Middlesex) Auxiliary Squadron flying Blenheim IFs. By June they had moved to Northolt as No. 600 Squadron came back for a two-month stay.

As the opening phase of the Battle of Britain began, the Luftwaffe carried out several attacks on the airfield, the first being on July 3. A major raid on August 12 caused severe damage yet within 24 hours it was reported operational again. Further attacks followed throughout the month with so much damage and loss of life that at the end of August orders were given to non-essential personnel to abandon Manston. Winston

The aerodrome was soon under the watchful eyes of the Luftwaffe, the original caption to this photograph reading: '(A) Single motor pursuit planes; (B) Hangars; (C) Barracks; (D) Munition Depot, encircled by earth walls; (E) Anti-aircraft guns; (F) Radio station with shadows of high antennas; (G) some painting that attempts to camouflage the landing field.'

Churchill visited the station on the 28th to inspect the damage. He demanded that mobile repair teams be sent to the airfield as soon as possible but Manston was still not ready to accept squadrons until January 1941.

Over the spring period several Hurricane and Spitfire squadrons rotated through, their main task being anti-shipping strikes in the Channel. A later tally for Manston-based squadrons showed that between January and September 1941, 44,600 tons of shipping had been sunk with a further 27,500 tons damaged.

With 'Ranger' operations (deep penetration flights to engage targets of opportunity) and 'Rhubarbs' (low-level strike operations over the Continent) continuing, the airfield was extended by lengthening the E-W and NE-SW grass runways to 1,600 and 1,900 yards respectively.

The end of 1941 saw the arrival of a detachment from No. 825 Squadron of the Fleet Air Arm. Six Swordfish were put on stand-by for a possible break-out by the German battlecruisers *Scharnhorst* and *Gneisenau* and the cruiser *Prinz Eugen* which were lying in Brest harbour. They left on February 12, 1942 to try to reach Germany via the Dover Straits. In the hope of torpedoing the ships, the Swordfish led by Lieutenant-Commander Eugene Esmonde took off but no hits were obtained and all six aircraft were lost. A posthumous Victoria Cross was awarded to Commander Esmonde and five surviving aircrew members were decorated.

German bombing during August 1940 rendered the airfield unusable until the New Year.

Further Hurricane squadrons were joined by Typhoon units with August seeing the North Weald Spitfire Wing using the airfield as a forward base. Consisting of Nos. 242 (Canadian), 331 and 332 (Norwegian) Squadrons, they were supplemented by the Mosquitos of No. 23 Squadron for patrols during Operation 'Jubilee', the Dieppe assault. Frequent rotation of squadrons became familiar during August and September including No. 841 Squadron of the Fleet Air Arm flying their Albacores in for mine-laying and flare-dropping sorties.

Another upsurge in hit and run coastal attacks by the Luftwaffe took place during October resulting in the Typhoons of No. 609 (West Riding) Auxiliary Squadron being based at Manston to combat possible attacks on the airfield. Further Fleet Air Arm aircraft arrived when 'B' Flight of No. 832 Squadron flew in to support the work being done by No. 841 Squadron.

The first months of 1943 saw Nos. 609 and 137 Squadrons continuing the offensive, being joined by No.198 Squadron with Typhoons on March 24. During April an intense security cloak was thrown around the airfield while tests were being carried out at nearby Reculver on Barnes Wallis's 'bouncing bombs' prior to the attack on the German dams.

In addition to the regular squadrons based at Manston, many aircraft used the airfield as an emergency landing ground but with the grass not being ideal for landing heavy bomber aircraft, it was decided to construct a single 'crash' runway on an east-west bearing. The contract for the huge swathe of concrete, 250 yards wide by 3,000 yards long, went to John Laing and Son Ltd with work starting on June 15, 1943.

Many missions now included support and escort for Eighth Air Force operations and preparations for the planned invasion of Europe resulted in Manston becoming No. 123 Airfield in No. 84 Group of the Second Tactical Air Force in March 1944. The new runway was brought into use on April 5, equipped with both Mark II lighting and fuel pipes for the fog dispersal facility code-named FIDO (Fog Investigation and Dispersal Operation).

Situated as it was within a short distance of the coast, it was a life-line to many crews limping back to Britain with damaged aircraft. Crashes were becoming the norm so a decision was made to take advantage of its location to construct a long, wide emergency runway.

It was aligned more or less east-west, five times as wide as a normal runway and over a mile long, with crash bays off to one side and dispersal loops. In the process the old watch office was demolished and a new control tower built north of the runway.

What would the pilots of Fighter Command have thought if they could have known that 25 years after they had fought to save Britain from the Luftwaffe, a full squadron of Messerschmitts would line up on their very own aerodrome!

More Fleet Air Arm squadrons arrived with the formation of No. 155 (General Reconnaissance) Wing of No. 16 Group, Coastal Command. Swordfish from No. 819 Squadron and Avengers from No. 848 Squadron were at Manston for the purpose of seeking out enemy targets with their ASV radar to allow rocket-armed Typhoons to attack. May 23 saw the arrival of the Beaufighters of No. 143 Squadron to begin flying sorties against enemy E-boats while the other resident squadrons turned their attention to anti-V1 patrols. Various Tempest squadrons were posted in for short periods and nearly 100 Horsa gliders towed by Albemarles came in September for the Arnhem operation.

As victory approached, more squadrons arrived for short stays before moving on to the Continent. At this time the tally for Manston was 123 enemy ships sunk, 234 enemy aircraft destroyed and 161 V1s shot down. In peacetime it became a Master Diversion Airfield until the RAF finally left in the 1990s. Today known as Kent International Airport, it is also the main base for the fire-fighting training school for all the three services.

In 1968 Spitfire Productions brought 15 Me 109s and two Heinkels from Spain to film *Battle of Britain*. Together with Spitfires and Hurricanes, it was claimed by the film's publicity team that they posessed the world's 35th largest air force!

And, for the James Bond film *Die Another Day* in 2001, the airfield was transformed into a North Korean airbase.

GB 10 145 b

Nur für den Dienstgebrauch!

Bild Nr. 2711 Z 10

Aufnahme vom 26. 8. 42

Martlesham Heath

Flugplatz

Länge (ostw. Greenw.): 1° 16′ 30″ Nördl. Breite: 52° 03′ 30″

Zielhöhe über NN: 27 m

Maßstab: 1 : 20 000

Lfl. Kdo. 3 Oktober 1942

Karte 1 : 100 000

GB/E 25

MARTLESHAM

Luftwaffe Target GB 10 145 b pictured in October 1942. Martlesham was then undergoing enlargement from the pre-war grass field, the full extent of which can be seen in the photo on page 188 taken a year after the war ended.

Classified as Suffolk's oldest airfield, Martlesham Heath opened in January 1917 as a station for the Royal Flying Corps. It was later the Aeroplane Experimental Unit. Operated by the RFC, its purpose was to test and evaluate not only British aircraft but foreign as well. It was only after a disastrous fire in October 1922 that the unit was enlarged and renamed The Aeroplane and Armament Experimental Establishment. It continued at Martlesham until a move to Boscombe Down in September 1939 saw the airfield become a forward satellite in No. 11 Group with the parent station at Debden.

One and half miles south-west of Woodbridge, and 90 feet above sea level, the landing area was a mixture of grass and heather with dimensions of 1,100 yards N-S, 1,000 yards NE-SW and 800 yards E-W and SE-NW. It had a perimeter track varying in width from 15 to 80 feet made of compacted peat. Five aeroplane sheds and a Type 2 Flying Control, a night landing facility of a MacDonald flarepath, a VHF radio facility and fuel storage of 44,000 gallons on hand to be delivered by tractor-driven bowsers saw Martlesham Heath ready and able to accept a squadron by 1938.

First to arrive on October 22, 1939, were the Hurricane Is of No. 56 Squadron which flew in from North Weald. Leaving a detachment at the latter base, the entire squadron moved back to North Weald on February 28, 1940. Two months later a detachment from No. 29 Squadron with Blenheims arrived. Joined by the Hurricanes of No. 17 Squadron on December 16, 1939 and the Hurricanes of No. 504 (County of Nottingham) Auxiliary Squadron on December 24, the spring of 1940 was to see these two squadrons alternate between Debden and Martlesham Heath until April 1940.

Crews belonging to squadrons of both the Royal Air Force and the United States Army Air Force were based at Martlesham. *Left:* Hurricane of No. 242 Squadron in March 1941 and *(right)* a P-47 Thunderbolt of the 356th Fighter Group in 1944.

A white signals square measuring 42ft was always situated outside the watch office, more commonly known as the control tower. The red square with a yellow diagonal warns pilots approaching the aerodrome that there are temporary obstructions and care must be taken when landing. The white dumb-bell indicates that the surface of the airfield is unserviceable except for the permanent runways, in the case of Martlesham formed from pierced steel planking (PSP). The Landing Direction 'T' displayed during light or variable winds shows the precise direction for landing and taking off, and the '04' board advises pilots on the ground which runway is in use, in this case the NE-SW.

Back in 1979 the control tower was a sorry sight but it has since been beautifully restored by the Martlesham Heath Aviation Society.

The first real resident squadron was No. 264 (Madras Presidency) that had reformed at Sutton Bridge on October 30, 1939 and collected its Defiant Is at Martlesham on December 7, 1940. Sending a detachment to Wittering, the squadron was the first to receive the new Defiant fighter and, after a working up period, they began both day and night patrols before moving to Duxford on May 10. On May 23 No. 85 sent a detachment of Hurricanes to the station from Debden.

The first Spitfires had arrived on March 1, 1940 when No. 266 (Rhodesia) Squadron was posted in after reforming at Sutton Bridge. Moving to Wittering on May 14, Hurricanes returned when No. 257 (Burma) Squadron arrived for the first of two stays. Flying in on September 5 and remaining until October 8, they returned on November 7 until December 16. Led by Squadron Leader Robert Stanford-Tuck, they countered the first Italian raid on Britain. Together with No. 46 Squadron, they claimed three enemy aircraft shot down.

With the move to Coltishall for No. 257 Squadron on December 16, thoughts were turning from daytime defensive measures to night operations. First to use Martlesham as a night fighter base was No. 242 (Canadian) Squadron. They arrived on December 16 with Hurricane Is and quickly converted to the Mk IIB. However their attempts at night-fighting found no success and they moved to Stapleford Tawney on April 9, 1941 to resume offensive operations.

No. 3 Squadron from Castletown had replaced them on April 3. Progressing through the Mk IIB to the IIC, they too found the Hurricane unsuitable for night patrols especially when operating with a Turbinlite squadron. They also moved to Stapleford on June 23.

Being close to the North Sea, a detachment from No. 277 (ASR) Squadron arrived during December 1941. Flying Lysander IIIs and a Walrus, Defiants were added to their complement in May 1942. The unit remained at Martlesham until April 1944.

Here the aerodrome is pictured in July 1946 as Martlesham began a new life as an experimental base.

Flying Hurricanes, No. 71 (Eagle) Squadron crewed by American volunteer pilots touched down at Martlesham on April 5, 1941. Converting to the Mk IIA, they moved to North Weald during June to exchange their Hurricanes for Spitfire IIAs and VBs. The squadron then returned to Martlesham on December 14, staying until May 2, 1942.

Several Spitfire squadrons rotated through Martlesham for very brief periods before No. 182 Squadron formed at the station on August 25. They quickly exchanged their Hurricanes for the Typhoon IA and IB, taking part in various army exercises at Sawbridgeworth before they flew their first operation on January 3, 1943. They moved to Middle Wallop on March 1.

By this time Martlesham had been earmarked to become a USAAF station and contractors moved in to lay two 1,600-yard runways. With just the detachment of No. 277 (ASR) Squadron remaining, the 356th Fighter Group of the Eighth Air Force arrived on October 5, 1943. Now designated Station 369, Martlesham hosted the 359th, 360th and 361st Fighter Squadrons with P-47D Thunderbolts which began working up in preparation for the invasion of Europe. Supporting the landings over D-Day, they went on to give further support during the Arnhem operation in September 1944, earning a Distinguished Unit Citation. Replacing the P-47Ds with P-51 Mustangs in November, they began escort missions as well as attacking ground targets. The group flew its last mission escorting B.17s on May 7, 1945. When they returned to the States in October, Martlesham was returned to the RAF.

Peacetime saw the Bomb Ballistics and Blind Landing Unit resident which was renamed the Armament and Instrument Experimental Unit in 1950. This decade also saw many of the new jet-powered aircraft fly from the airfield but with the disbandment of the experimental unit, Martlesham was downgraded to care and maintenance basis before being finally closed by the Air Ministry on April 25, 1963.

The airfield is now an industrial estate named Adastral Park. The control tower is maintained as a museum by the Martlesham Heath Aviation Society and a memorial to those members of the 356th Fighter Group who lost their lives is situated on the old parade ground.

Sixty years have passed and the airfield is barely recognisable with just a short length of the NE-SW runway remaining.

MERSTON

Merston, a satellite to Tangmere, saw pilots from a variety of nationalities using the aerodrome — American, Canadian, French, New Zealanders and Polish. These are Spitfires of No. 131 Squadron in June 1942.

Situated in Sussex, two and a half miles south-east of Chichester, Merston was to serve as a satellite to Tangmere but, although it was surveyed for requisition in 1939, it was not completed until the spring of 1941. Hangar accommodation consisted of six Blisters with a grass landing area measuring N-S 1,200 yards, NE-SW 1,400 yards, E-W 1,000 yards and SE-NW 1,500 yards.

The airfield was intended to accommodate one squadron as part of No. 11 Group, Fighter Command. However a succession of squadrons, including No. 145 and No. 41, flew low-level sweeps over occupied France from the middle of 1941 until replaced by Nos. 131 (County of Kent) and No. 412 (Falcon) Canadian Squadron.

In August 1942 the Spitfire squadrons moved to nearby Tangmere with Merston then being allocated to the United States Army Air Force. As Station 356 it became the temporary home of the 307th Fighter Squadron, part of the 31st Fighter Group, equipped with Spitfires. Continual waterlogging was partially solved during the summer when Sommerfeld track was laid down together with the construction of 20 hardstandings and extensions to the landing areas, the work continuing until May 1943.

Merston, together with Tangmere's other satellite at Westhampnett, all under the lens of the Luftwaffe's cameras on September 4, 1940.

Once completed, No. 485 (RNZAF) Squadron with Spitfire VBs arrived for bomber escort work to be joined later by No. 184 Squadron with bomb-carrying Hurricanes. No. 174 (Mauritius) Squadron with Typhoons arrived for a working up period before the Canadian Digby Wing, consisting of Nos. 402 (Winnipeg Bear) and 416 (City of Oshawa) Squadron, were attached to No. 11 Group for fighter operations against shipping. These continued until October when the wing split up and Merston became an accommodation airfield for the Second Tactical Air Force in preparation for the invasion of Europe.

Renamed No. 124 Airfield on November 15, 1943, three Typhoon squadrons — Nos. 181, 182 and 247 (China-British) — began attacks on the V1 launch sites. Moving to Hurn in April 1944, No. 145 Airfield (as 'wings' were now called), arrived from Perranporth. This unit consisted of Nos. 329 (GC I/2 'Cigognes), 340 (GC IV/2 'Ile de France') and 341 (GC III/2 'Alsace') – all Free French squadrons flying Spitfire IXs which commenced sweeps over France in preparation for D-Day.

With Operation 'Overlord' a success, the French squadrons left to be replaced by an Air Defence of Great Britain Spitfire IX Wing comprising Nos. 80, 229 and 274 Squadrons. Staying only for a few days, they were replaced by No. 142 Wing with Nos. 303 (Kosciuszko) Polish and 402 (Winnipeg Bear) Canadian Squadron. Remaining until August 1944, they were the last units to occupy Merston which was then reduced to care and maintenance. Shortly thereafter a works flight arrived to remove the Sommerfeld tracking. On March 16, 1945, the airfield was briefly handed over to the Supreme Headquarters Allied Expeditionary Force for use by air disarmament units. This role lasted for two months before the buildings were handed over to the Admiralty for storage of surplus equipment.

The grass surface of Merston now occupied by industrial buildings.

NORTHOLT

Seventy years after Britain was under attack from across the seas, a new threat appeared in 2012 when four Typhoons from the RAF's Quick Reaction Alert Force flew in to Northolt as part of Exercise 'Olympic Guardian' . . .

Lying 14 miles to the west of London, 112 feet above sea level, Northolt made a significant contribution to the defence of London during the First World War when it became a Home Defence night landing ground in 1915. A total of 283 acres were acquired in Middlesex before it was officially opened in March of that year. Between the wars the airfield was used for civilian flying as well as military but with the threat of another war, the station was transferred to No. 11 Group on May 1, 1936.

Northolt became the master station in Sector 'Z' being allocated four satellite airfields: Croughton, Denham, Hendon and Heston. In addition to being a fighter station, a later duty was the assembly of Halifax bombers. It was a grass airfield with the following take off distances: N-S 930 yards, NE-SW 1,100 yards, E-W 1,200 yards and SE-NW 1,330 yards. Two tarmac runways each of 800 yards heading NE-SW and N-S were laid during 1936, Northolt being one of the first airfields to have hard runways. A 50-foot perimeter track was laid together with the construction of five hangars and five H-type barrack blocks. Resident units on the outbreak of war were No. 111 and No. 601 (County of London) Auxiliary Squadron.

The arrival of Group Captain S. Vincent on January 14, 1940 to command Northolt saw the station become an experimental site for airfield camouflage. Not liking what he saw, he implemented his own proposals which allowed the airfield to blend in with its surburban surroundings which may have contributed to the fact that the airfield only received two minor attacks throughout the Battle of Britain period.

. . . but back in October 1940, it was the Hurricanes of No. 615 Squadron that fought off the German raiders.

In August 1939, the Royal Air Force mounted a large air defence exercise . . .

The Dunkirk operation saw No. 609 (West Riding) Auxiliary Squadron with Spitfires providing part of the air cover for the evacuation. Once over, the remains of No. 1 Squadron, sent to France as part of the Air Component of the British Expeditionary Force on the outbreak of war, arrived back at Northolt. Later squadrons based at the airfield included No. 257 (Burma) and a detachment of No. 43 (China-British), both finding little success.

August 2, 1940 saw the formation of No. 303 (Kosciuszko) Polish Squadron which began a four-year association with Polish squadrons and Northolt. During August and September they shared the airfield with the RAF's No. 1 (F) Squadron and also No. 1 Squadron of the Royal Canadian Air Force, all three squadrons often flying together as a wing. With No. 1 Squadron RAF departing to Wittering on September 9, they were replaced by No. 229 Squadron flying Hurricanes.

September saw the Northolt squadrons claim 148 enemy aircraft destroyed with 25 probables and 52 damaged since the battle began. An attack by an enemy aircraft on the 15th did little damage although one month later the airfield received a heavier attack when a lone Ju 88 flew in at 200 feet, dropping two bombs and machine-gunning the buildings. Although attacked by two Hurricanes of No. 229 Squadron who were on base patrol, the raider escaped into cloud.

The Hurricanes of No. 615 (County of Surrey) Auxiliary Squadron arrived on October 10 to replace the Canadians who moved to Prestwick to rest. That month, as they prepared to leave Northolt for Speke, No. 303 Polish Squadron claimed 126 enemy aircraft destroyed during the previous six weeks for the cost of eight pilots killed. This was a tally unmatched by any other squadron.

Replaced by another Polish squadron, No. 302 (Poznan) on October 11, the bad weather and the fact that the enemy were now concentrating on night bombing, was a disappointing time for them and they left for Westhampnett on November 23. However, despite their frustrations, the end of October saw the Northolt score for the month stand at 22½ aircraft destroyed, three probables and 15 damaged.

The New Year brought fresh squadrons as the job of Fighter Command turned from defence to offence. The Polish squadrons, now exchanging their Hurricanes for Spitfires, rotated through Northolt further strengthening their association with the airfield but with Heston gaining station status in 1942, two of the four Polish squadrons moved there. Operation 'Jubilee' saw the squadrons combining to form a wing, the result of which saw them claim 16½ aircraft

. . . the comparison could hardly be greater . . . apart from the difference in speed of the aircraft . . . over 1,000 miles per hour!

GB 10 160 bc
Maßstab etwa 1:13400
500m 0 1km
(1cm : 134 m)

Northolt
Fliegerhorst

GB 10 160 bc
Geheim

Kriegsaufnahme:
0853
Nachträge:
31.8.40

Karte:
1:100 000
Blatt 29

Länge
(östl. Greenw.):
0°25'
Nördl. Breite:
51°33'

Zielhöhe
über N N 37 m

G.B. 10 160 Fliegerhorst
1) Flugzeughallen
2) Werkstätten
3) Unterkunftsgebäude
4) Splittersichere Abstellplätze für Flugzeuge
5) Leichte Flakstellungen ?

LFt. Kdo. 2, Sept. 1940

Luftflotte-Kommando 2 produced their target map of Northolt in September 1940.

The following month a lone Ju88 suddenly appeared overhead and carried out a low-level attack, machine-gunning and dropping two bombs. They exploded between the hangars, blasting the machine of Sergeant Antoni Siudak of No. 303 Squadron as he was taxiing past, killing him and also an airman who was acting as a look-out on the hangar roof.

destroyed for no losses. At around this time a Special Service Flight equipped with a high-altitude conversion of the Spitfire IX was formed to combat high-flying Ju 86 bombers, and flights of up to 42,000 feet were achieved with some success.

With the build-up for the invasion, November 1943 saw Northolt become No. 131 Airfield with Heston becoming No. 133 Airfield. Now known collectively as the 18th Fighter Wing, No. 84 Group, Second Tactical Air Force, both airfields remained at full strength until April 1944 when operations for D-Day saw their squadrons move to Advanced Landing Grounds in the south of England. That month the long association with the Polish squadrons came to an end as the last one, No. 317 (Wilno) Squadron, moved to Deanland ALG in Sussex.

Northolt also lost its sector status as, being close to London, it was constantly in demand for transport purposes. As this role required a longer runway, contractors moved in to extend the NE-SW runway. By 1945 it had become a major transport and civilian base, a role that continues today with both private and military aircraft using the aerodrome.

NORTH WEALD

No. 56 Squadron aloft from North Weald in June 1940 for a sortie to France. One of the dangers of flying from the aerodrome was the proximity on the eastern side of the 600-foot radio masts of the Marconi wireless station.

North Weald has been connected with aviation since 1916, its first claim to fame coming on the night of October 1/2 when 2nd Lieutenant Wulstan Tempest of 'A' Flight of No. 39 Squadron shot down the Zeppelin L31. On December 9, the entire squadron moved in with Bristol F2b fighters and Camels, carrying out many patrols to counter the German air offensive. On November 16, 1918, North Weald was stood down but ten years later was reactivated, being used by various RAF squadrons during the 1920s and early '30s, the main squadrons being No. 29, 56 and 151.

Lying close to Epping in Essex at 283 feet above sea level, the airfield covered an area of some 400 acres. Initially the landing area

In January 2009, a Hurricane once again became resident at North Weald when a MkIIB (BE505) was added to Peter Teichman's warbird collection in Hangar 11.

Left: B Flight of No. 56 Squadron at North Weald on September 3 — the day war was declared. These young Hurricane pilots were no doubt eager to get at the enemy . . . ready prepared to play their parts in any eventuality . . . except that of being targeted by their own side! Within three days two of these men had been shot down by No. 74 'Tiger' Squadron based at Hornchurch, Pilot Officer Hulton-Harrop having the dubious distinction of being Fighter Command's first casualty in the defence of the United Kingdom. From L-R, rear row: Pilot Officer L. Ereminsky, Pilot Officer P. D. M. Down, Flight Lieutenant Ian Soden, Pilot Officers J. H. Coghlan, P. F. Illingworth and F. C. 'Tommy' Rose. Front row: Pilot Officers Montague Hulton-Harrop and E. Holden. John Freeborn was court-martialed along with his Red Section leader, Paddy Byrne, but both were acquitted even though the squadron commanding officer 'Sailor' Malan, who had led them into the attack, appeared for the prosecution denying that he had done so. Instead he claimed that he had ordered Freeborn and Byrne to break off the attack. *Right:* It was not until September 2003 that John Freeborn visited North Weald for the very first time because he said that he didn't think he would be welcome. After inspecting the airfield museum, his host, Bill Aitken, asked if he would like to visit St Andrew's Churchyard where Hulton-Harrop lies buried. To this he readily agreed and Elaine Aitken was on hand to take this memorable photograph. Freeborn said that 'to this day I continue to feel guilt over the needless death of Hulton-Harrop, I blame myself, as I passed around a pilots' order book forbidding us to open fire on single-engine aircraft as they didn't have the range to reach Britain from the airfields in Germany. I felt that I had let my aggressive training and the hypertension at the time get the better of me. However, I shall maintain to my dying day that I followed Malan's order to attack.'

As a prime target, North Weald was on the receiving end of a major raid on August 24, 1940. The station Operations Record Book states that 'eight A/C 151 Squadron left N. Weald to intercept raid approaching aerodrome from East. Enemy consisting of thirty to fifty Do 215s accompanied by up to a hundred He IIIs Me 110s. Bombers were above cloud at 1,500ft in very close formation of sections of three in line astern. Waves of Me 110 were stepped up above bombers which were encircled by other Me 110s at same time. Travelling at almost 200mph, bombers broke cloud and bombed N. Weald from about 15000ft. 150-200 bombs were dropped. Airmen's married quarters and officers' married quarters suffered seriously. Powerhouse badly damaged. Majority of bombs fell along main Epping-Ongar road damaging water supply and gas mains. A number of delayed action bombs dropped; some exploding on following day; remainder dealt with by Demolition Squad. Casualties 9 killed 10 wounded. The killed and majority of wounded were in a shelter which suffered a direct hit.' The air raid shelter that was struck lay beside this oak tree, the force of the explosion also destroying the ends of the nearby barrack blocks. The men were all members of the Essex Regiment on airfield defence duty. John Smith, who was severely wounded in the blast, returned with us to the scene in 1980, recalling how one of the soldiers had been blasted into the branches of the tree.

supported four grass runways but two hard runways, claimed to be the first to be laid at a fighter airfield, were laid down: N-S at 933 yards and E-W slightly longer. Two 'C' type hangars, four Blisters and four Extra Over Blisters were completed by 1938 with the perimeter track half built by 1939.

No. 151, which had reformed at North Weald on August 4, 1936, from a nucleus of No. 56 Squadron, were joined by No. 604 (County of Middlesex) Auxiliary Squadron on September 2, 1939 equipped with Blenheims. With the two former squadrons flying Hurricanes, tragedy came on September 6 when Spitfires from No. 74, 54 and 65 Squadrons based at Hornchurch were scrambled at the same time as Hurricanes from No. 56 and 151 Squadrons to intercept the same suspect attack. The Spitfires mistook the Hurricanes for enemy aircraft and promptly shot two of them down killing Pilot Officer Hulton-Harrop and wounding Pilot Officer Tom Rose who forced-landed badly damaged. Fighter Command thereby lost its first casualties of the war to friendly fire, the episode becoming known as the 'Battle of Barking Creek'.

In the meantime No. 604 Squadron was flying defensive duties by day and by night. In January 1940 they moved over to Northolt, their replacement being the Blenheim IFs equipped with early types of airborne radar belonging to No. 25 Squadron. Arriving on January 16, they sent a detachment to Martlesham Heath before spending a couple of days at Hawkinge on May 10. The squadron took part in covering the evacuation across the Channel as well as patrolling the Dutch and Belgian coasts. Moving to Martlesham Heath they were back on September 2 to convert to the Beaufighter IF finally leaving for Debden on October 8. Unfortunately their time at North Weald saw another friendly fire incident when one of the Blenheims was shot down and another two badly damaged when they were attacked by Hurricanes on September 3. This cost the life of Pilot Officer Douglas Hogg.

North Weald was targeted by the Luftwaffe on August 24 when over 200 bombs were dropped, causing extensive damage to both men and material, a direct hit on a shelter killing nine members of the Essex Regiment manning the ground defences.

With the departure of No. 25 Squadron the Hurricane Is of No. 249 (Gold Coast) Squadron flew in from Boscombe Down on September 1. After they were scrambled from North Weald on September 27, two pilots were lost, one of whom, Pilot Officer Percival Burton, is believed to have died in an act of self-sacrifice when he collided with a Bf 110. The same day the squadron claimed five enemy aircraft destroyed.

A further devastating raid on the airfield came on September 3, direct hits being scored on the hangars and operations block, forcing the ops room and the station headquarters to deploy to a mansion at Blake Hall. Both remained there until the end of the war.

October 8 saw No. 257 (Burma) Squadron bring their Hurricane Is in from Martlesham Heath. Led by Squadron Leader Robert Stanford-Tuck, they returned to Martlesham a month later. Next to arrive was No. 46 from the satellite Stapleford Tawney on November 8. They joined Nos. 249 with December

In 1983 the whole of the domestic site was demolished and redeveloped as a housing estate, yet the oak tree, still bearing its scars from 1940, was spared.

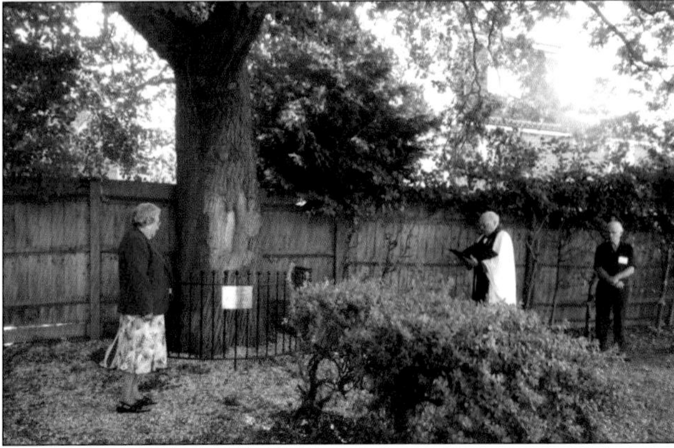

We felt the memory of the soldiers who died should be remembered and on August 24, 2010 — the 70th anniversary of their deaths — we asked John Smith's widow to dedicate a plaque.

Another devastating attack took place on September 3 with both hangars set on fire destroying a Blenheim and two Hurricanes.

Twenty-eight years later the hangars again under attack during the making of the epic film *Battle of Britain*.

seeing No. 56 Squadron return to convert to the Hurricane IIB. The North Weald Wing quickly began patrols over the East Coast with the occasional night sortie for 56 Squadron which moved to Martlesham Heath on June 21, 1941.

Convoy patrols were the remit for No. 71 (Eagle) Squadron that came to North Weald on June 23 with Hurricane IIAs. Manned mainly by American airmen who had volunteered to fight with the RAF, the move saw the squadron begin a busy period of convoy patrols. Having converted to the Spitfire IIA and VB, they moved out to Martlesham on December 14, 1941.

With No. 242 transferring to Manston on July 19, August 18 saw No. 222 (Natal) Squadron arrive with Spitfire IIBs. During the course of the year they converted to the Mk VB and began to carry out sweeps and bomber escorts but moved to Manston on June 30, 1942. During their time at North Weald they were joined briefly by No. 111 Squadron which arrived with Hurricanes from Debden on December 15, 1941.

The last weeks of 1941 also saw a second Eagle Squadron arrive when No. 121 flew in with Spitfire VBs on December 16. In 1942, North Weald was busy with a number of squadrons rotating through for various periods, and by the war's end six nations had joined the RAF there: America, Canada, Czechoslovakia, New Zealand, Poland, and the Norwegians who even looked on North Weald as the birthplace of their air force. Their squadrons were Nos. 331 and 332.

No. 66 Squadron with Spitfire LF IXBs came in from Llanbedr on March 1, 1944. They were part of 132 Wing of the Second Tactical Air Force detailed to carry out pre-invasion sorties, although they moved to Bognor on March 31.

With the Hornchurch sector control closing down in February 1944, North Weald now became responsible for Hornchurch, Southend, Bradwell Bay and Stapleford. A brief visit by No. 127 Squadron with various marks of Spitfires on April 23 saw them move to Lympne on May 16. The Czech squadrons, Nos. 310 and 312, arrived with Spitfire HF IXs on August 28 and 27 respectively, followed by No. 234 on August 28. The latter converted from Spitfire VIs to Mustang IIIs before taking them to Bentwaters on December 17. No. 312 moved to Bradwell Bay on October 3 followed by 310 on December 29.

No. 26 Squadron came with their Mustangs on January 21, 1945 and, sending a detachment to Coltishall, the rest of the squadron moved to Harrowbeer on April 3. A few days stay by No. 130 (Punjab) Squadron on May 10 saw North Weald's long connection with fighters come to an end. The airfield was then transferred to Transport Command which saw No. 301 (Pomeranian) Polish Squadron posted in with Warwick IIIs. Arriving on July 2, 1945 they were joined by No. 304 (Silesian) Squadron with Wellingtons on July 9. They converted to the Warwick I and II with both squadrons moving to Chedburgh in September.

Transferred to Technical Training Command in October, the airfield went to Reserve Command in 1947. Peacetime saw the main runway extended to cater for the fast jets of the auxiliary squadrons until North Weald was put on care and maintenance in October 1953.

Apart from the Royal Air Force, airmen from six nations served at North Weald — America, Canada, New Zealand, Norway, Poland and Czechoslovakia — but it was the arrival of Nos. 331 and 332 Squadrons of the Royal Norwegian Air Force which cemented an enduring relationship with North Weald. In this picture three members of the Norwegian Royal family in exile in London, visit the airfield to decorate three of their pilots with the Norwegian War Cross. L-R: Major Helge Mehre, Crown Princess Astrid, King Olav, Major Wilhelm Mohr, Crown Prince Olav and Major Kaj Birksted.

Led by General Mohr (third from left), the former CO of No. 332 Squadron, Norwegian veterans are pictured in June 2012 on one of their dispersals, specially restored for the 70th anniversary of the formation of the Royal Norwegian Air Force.

Photo taken looking north-west in July 1941 with the aerodrome camouflaged with spoof fields and a meandering stream.

The control tower then stood close to the main N-S runway but when this was extended after the war to cater for fast jets, the original was demolished and a new building was erected on the eastern side.

In 1953 the airfield became the home of the renowned Black Arrows of No. 111 Squadron under Squadron Leader Roger Topp but, when 'Treble One' moved out in 1958, North Weald was relegated to care and maintenance. Then in 1966 it was transferred to the Army before the Ministry of Defence sold it to Epping Forest District Council in 1979. Princess Astrid had returned in 1952 to unveil a monument beside the main gate, dedicated to the people of North Weald, and this was transformed in 2000 into a memorial remembering all those who were stationed and who lost their lives serving at the aerodrome.

REDHILL

Redhill in 1942 with the customary tar lines painted on the surface to try to blend it into the countryside. Today it remains a grass airfield, applications made to lay down a hard runway having been refused.

An area of 100 acres located two miles south-east of Redhill in Surrey, and running parallel with the A23 (now the M23 motorway), was acquired by British Air Transport in 1934 for use as an aerodrome. It was initially home to No. 15 Elementary & Reserve Flying Training School flying Miles Magisters and Hawker Harts, but when the airfield was requisitioned by the RAF in 1939, the school had to move out to Kingstown, near Carlisle.

The first squadron to use the grass airfield (which lay at an altitude of 227 feet above sea level) was No. 16 who flew their Westland Lysanders in from Lympne on June 3, 1940. Departing one month later, Redhill was not used during the early and middle phases of the Battle of Britain. September 12

Redhill began life as a base for flying training as illustrated by this line up of Miles Magisters on the edge of the apron. Four Fairey Battles stand in the distance.

saw No. 600 (City of London) Auxiliary Squadron bring in their Blenheim IVs and a few Beaufighter IFs (the latter equipped with a new mark of airborne radar) for a period of working up. One month later they moved to Catterick to be replaced by the Blenheim IVFs of No. 219 (Mysore) Squadron. They took over the Beaufighters left behind by No. 600 and began a period of conversion as well as flying patrols at night. The squadron suffered several losses before moving on to Tangmere which was far more suitable for heavy aircraft. No further use was made of Redhill until 1941 when Sommerfeld Track was laid together with the erection of eight Blister hangars and further dispersal pens.

For 30 years after the war, Redhill was the home of the Tiger Club after it had to move from Croydon. It was the brainchild of the enigmatic Norman Jones of Rollason Aircraft Ltd who had helped form the club in 1956 with the supply of several Tiger Moths.

Another picture taken from the old control tower, this line of Handley Page Harrows and Bristol Bombays disembarking men and equipment of No. 219 Squadron which was stationed at Redhill with Beaufighters late in 1940.

Now it is 1942 with a Spitfire VB of No. 457 Squadron of the Royal Australian Air Force at readiness with the 'trolley acc' ready to fire up the engine.

No. 1 Squadron now commenced a series of 'Circus' operations escorting bombers or fighter-bombers in the hope of bringing enemy fighters into action. These flights continued until the end of the month when the squadron left Redhill. Spitfires now replaced the Hurricanes of the Kenley Wing with Nos. 452 (RAAF), 485 (RNZAF) and 602 (City of Glasgow) Auxiliary Squadron rotating between Kenley and Redhill for the next eight months. They were joined later by another Australian squadron, No. 457. These squadrons formed the Redhill Wing and when the Australians returned home to fight the Japanese, they were replaced by No. 402 (Winnipeg Bear) Squadron of the RCAF flying the Spitfire VB.

The airfield was now very congested as the Polish Squadron of No. 308 (Krakow) and the Czech squadrons numbered 310 and 312 arrived on July 1. As part of No. 10 Group, they stayed for a few days but then moved to Harrowbeer only to return to Redhill later in the month. In mid-July, No. 602 moved out to be replaced by another auxiliary squadron, No. 611 (West Lancashire) that converted to the Spitfire IX. Carrying out several 'Rhubarb' operations on targets of opportunity, they stayed for one month.

On July 31, No. 350 (Belgian) Squadron flew into Redhill with Spitfire VBs, departing for Martlesham Heath on September 7. During the rest of the year Redhill hosted a Polish squadron — No. 303 (Kosciuszko) — and 310 and 312 (Czech) Squadrons followed by Nos. 412 (Falcon) and 416 (City of Oshawa) of the RCAF. During 1943 No. 401 (Ram) Squadron returned, this time flying the clipped-wing Spitfire V designed for low-level operations.

The three Canadian squadrons, Nos. 401, 411 and 412, became No. 126 Airfield (Biggin Hill) of No. 83 Group, Second Tactical Air Force. They stayed at Redhill until August 5 when they moved to the advanced landing ground at Staplehurst. A brief stay by Nos. 131 (County of Kent) Fighter Squadron and 504 (County of Nottingham) Squadrons forming a Redhill Wing, saw them carrying out escort duties for American bombers but by September Redhill had been reduced to care and maintenance.

The Second Tactical Air Force was formed from Army Co-operation Command in June 1943 to support the invasion of the Continent. The following year additional units were transferred from Bomber Command and Fighter Command, the latter then being renamed Air Defence of Great Britain. Here at Redhill in 1944, fitters service aircraft and armourers prepare belts of 20mm cannon shells.

It remained so for several months until the airfield saw a resurgence of use up to and over the D-Day period. The arrival of the flying bombs in June also saw the airfield host No. 24 Balloon Centre in a defensive role against the V1. Not until January 15, 1945, when it once again became a satellite to Biggin Hill, did aircraft return. Nos. 166 and 287 (Army-Co-operation) Squadrons arrived with Tempests, Oxfords and Spitfires and stayed until May when the airfield became home to No. 36 Maintenance Unit for the clearance and disposal of ordnance.

Redhill reverted to a training station in April 1948 with the arrival of No. 15 Reserve Flying School and finally closed as a military airfield on April 30, 1954. Today is still a very popular light aircraft airfield and also home to Bristow Helicopters.

In a moment of calm, pilots of No. 54 Squadron relax at their dispersal at Rochford aerodrome. One of the squadron's Spitfires can be seen near the railway line to London.

ROCHFORD (SOUTHEND)

First established during the First World War, Rochford — also known as Holt Farm — officially opened as Southend Municipal Airport on September 18, 1935, being requisitioned by the Air Ministry in 1939. Auxiliary squadrons had used Rochford for summer camps together with No. 34 Elementary & Reserve Flying Training School but, on the outbreak of war, the trainers left to be replaced by the Spitfires of Nos. 54 (F) and 74 (Trinidad) Squadron.

Situated two miles north of Southend-on-Sea beside the B1013, the Essex airfield sat just 25 feet above sea level and was deemed a satellite to Hornchurch in Sector 'D' of No. 11 Group.The grass landing area gave take off distances of 880 yards from N-S; 1,245 yards NE-SW; 770 yards from E-W, and 1,025 yards SE-NW with an 18 to 35-foot asphalt perimeter track. Hangar accommodation consisted of two Bellman and three Over Blisters together with four flight dispersals. There were two fuel dumps, one containing 8,900 gallons of aviation spirit and the other 1,280 gallons of petrol.

The early months of the war saw Nos. 54 and 74 Squadrons alternate between Rochford and Hornchurch. The former were to remain until June 1940 with the latter scoring Rochford's first success when an He 111 was damaged over the Thames Estuary on February 13, 1940. The squadron moved out in May.

A brief visit by No. 616 (South Yorkshire) Auxiliary Squadron in May saw them open their scoring when they claimed five enemy aircraft destroyed with another four probables. The return of No. 74 Squadron in June saw Flight Lieutenant 'Sailor' Malan become the first single-seat pilot to destroy an enemy aircraft at night. He followed this an hour later by shooting down a second He 111. When the squadron left Rochford they were replaced by No. 54, which returned for a brief period, and No. 264 (Madras Presidency) which introduced the first Defiants to the airfield.

During August and September various squadrons from Hornchurch and North Weald used Rochford as an advanced base. On October 26, legendary airman Wing Commander Basil Embry took command as Rochford then officially became known as Southend. Upon his arrival he expressed dismay at the state of the airfield and of the Defiants which were, in his view, 'thoroughly bad night fighters'. However, both he and No. 264 Squadron had left Southend by the end of 1940 as the airfield was now scheduled to become a forward offensive fighter base.

After serving for many years as Southend Municipal Airport, it was purchased in 2008 by the Eddie Stobart transport group. In a £100 million investment plan, a new terminal building, control tower, airport hotel, railway station, and runway improvements have now achieved Rochford's formal designation as London Southend Airport.

The war had been fought from Rochford with just a grass landing area, this photo being taken in May 1946.

This still taken from a sequence showing Hurricanes of No. 56 Squadron is believed to show Squadron Leader Edward Knowles landing R4197. He was the CO when the squadron was based at North Weald but they also used Rochford as a forward base.

One of the most bizarre incidents at Rochford took place on August 26, 1940 when a Dornier Do 17Z-3 flopped down in the centre of the airfield! The machine from 2./KG2 had been detailed to bomb Hornchurch but it never got that far, Hurricanes of No. 85 Squadron forcing it down. The four-man crew were quickly taken prisoner.

Early 1941 saw the return of No. 54 (F) Squadron together with Nos. 611 (West Lancashire) — May 20 to June 14 — and No. 603 (City of Edinburgh — June 16 to July 9 — Squadrons, all operating from Southend during the first six months of 1941. An attack on the airfield on May 11 by a force of Bf 109s caused considerable damage but the ground defences managed to shoot down one of the raiders which crashed alongside one of the hangars. In August a Canadian squadron, No. 402 (Winnipeg Bear), arrived flying Hurricane IIs in a fighter-bomber role. Fitted with two 250lb bombs slung beneath each wing, their first mission was to bomb Berck-sur-Mer airfield. Leaving in November, they were replaced by No. 403 (Wolf) Canadian Squadron flying Spitfire VBs.

On May 1, 1942, Southend was transferred to Sector 'E' and a month later No. 121 (Eagle) Squadron, equipped with Spitfires, arrived from North Weald to carry out bomber escort missions. Leaving on September 23, they were re-designated the 335th Squadron of the 4th Fighter Group of the US Eighth Army Air Force. After the Americans left the Belgians arrived in the form of No. 350 Squadron, also flying Spitfire VBs.

October saw the return of the Luftwaffe when a lone Do 17, disabled by anti-aircraft fire, crashed onto one of the dispersals causing some damage and one fatality, a Belgian airman. With the departure of No. 350 to Hornchurch in December, the New Year saw the Spitfires of No. 222 (Natal) Squadron arrive on the first of several visits to Southend. June 1943 saw the station revert back to the Hornchurch sector and short stays by squadrons became the order of the day. With the pace of operations slowing, February 1944, saw the role of the airfield change to that of an Armament Practice Camp equipped with Martinets and Masters. Squadrons arrived for a maximum of one week before returning to their resident bases, one of the last being a detachment from No. 287 Squadron for anti-aircraft duties.

In 1946 the airfield was de-requisitioned, becoming Southend Municipal Airport, now having been renamed London Southend.

Once a front-line base for Fighter Command but now a thriving civil airport under the Eddie Stobart banner.

Pilots of No. 46 Squadron at Stapleford in 1940. Third from the right, not in flying attire, is Pilot Officer Roy McGowan who was shot down over Kent on September 15. Burned on his hands, face and neck, he was admitted to St Bartholomew's Hospital at Rochester.

STAPLEFORD TAWNEY

Designated an operational satellite to North Weald, Stapleford Tawney was situated north-east of London on the A113 between Chigwell and Ongar. The airfield lay on a definite slope, its height above sea level ranging from 300 to 420 feet. Used pre-war by Hillman Airways, expansion saw the arrival of No. 21 Elementary & Reserve Flying Training School operated under contract by Read and Sigrist Ltd. One of the many pilots to pass through the school being 'Johnnie' Johnson.

The grass landing area dimensions were N-S 1,000 yards, NE-SW 1,220 yards, E-W 800 yards and SE-NW 1,150 yards. The surface as well as being rough had a tendency to bog at one end. Hangar accommodation consisted of three civilian types and eight Blisters with six dispersals. Even though classified as a satellite, night landing facilities consisted of floodlights and glim-lamps, something that even some parent airfields did not have.

Early 1940 saw it operating within No. 11 Group when the Hurricanes of Nos. 56 (Punjab) and 151 Squadrons used Stapleford Tawney as a day base returning to North Weald at dusk. It was not until August 29, that No. 151 Squadron became resident. They exchanged bases with No. 46 (Uganda) Squadron on September 1, finally departing to North Weald on November 8 due to the fact that the airfield became waterlogged.

September had also seen the arrival of No. 419 Flight. This was the operational air arm of the Special Operations Executive (SOE) flying Lysanders and Whitleys for covert agent operations, the latter being the largest aircraft to land at Stapleford. They moved to Stradishall on October 9.

With the end of the Battle of Britain no more use was made of the airfield until the arrival of the Hurricane IIAs of No. 242 (Canadian) Squadron on April 9, 1941. Their tenure was marked with tragedy when just 11 days into their stay, three aircraft collided in cloud killing all three pilots including the CO, Squadron Leader Wilfred Treacy. Their main operations were offensive sweeps over France and Belgium. Moving to North Weald on May 22, the next unit to arrive was No. 3 Squadron, also with Hurricanes. Arriving on June 23, their Hurricane IICs carried out similar operations as well as sending detachments to Hunsdon for night-flying practice with Bostons and Havocs of No. 1451 Flight equipped with Turbinlites. The entire squadron moved over on August 8.

Back in 1940, Stapleford Tawney had been the subject of intense camouflage treatment when sooty black lines had been drawn across the landing area to represent hedges. Such was the success of the camouflage at Stapleford that many other East Anglian airfields adopted similar schemes and in June 1941 No. 2 Camouflage Unit arrived with Tiger Moths, Oxfords and Dominies to carry out aerial examination of those sites.

The establishment of a headquarters to consolidate air-sea rescue operations between Northern France and south-east England saw No. 277 (ASR) Squadron established at the airfield with Lysander, Walrus

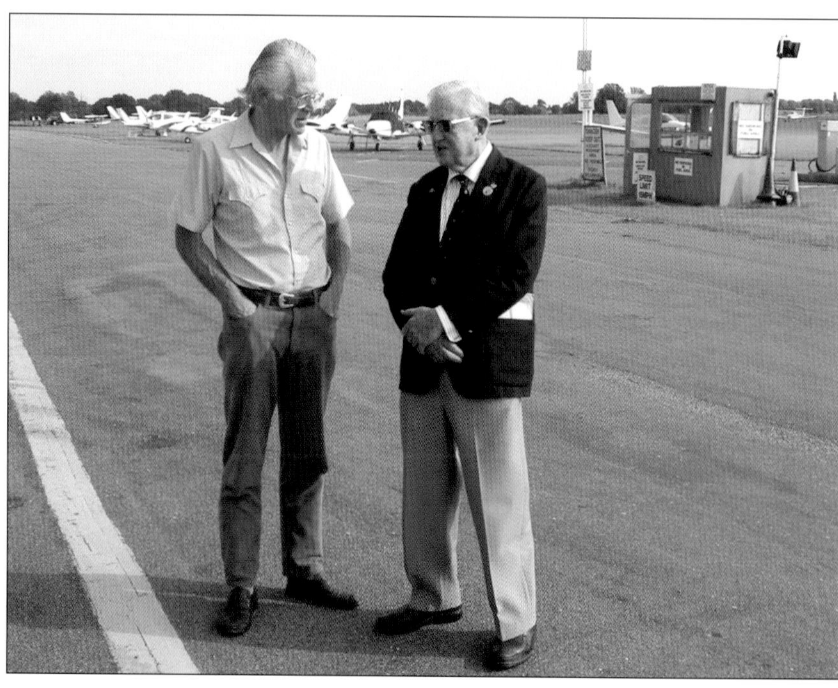

Roy visited the UK from his home in New Zealand in 2006 which gave Winston Ramsey a perfect opportunity to discuss the events of that day at Stapleford.

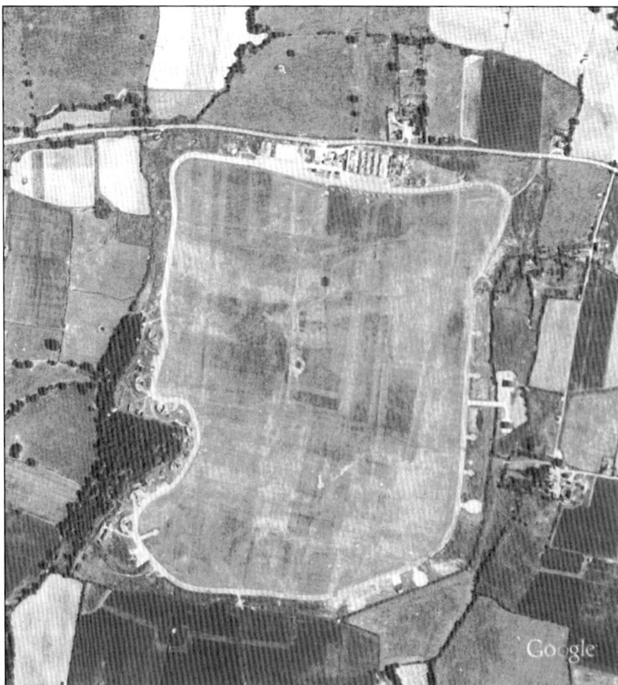

The changing face of Stapleford Tawney . . . from 1940 . . . to 1945 . . . to 2012!

and Defiant aircraft. Sending detachments to Martlesham Heath, Hawkinge and Shoreham, Stapleford became the main base for maintenance and pilot conversion. They stayed until December 7, 1942, when they moved south to Gravesend.

The winter months saw further water logging of the grass and it was not until March 1943 that Stapleford became operational again. At the same time, a change in policy saw the airfield taken from Fighter Command and No. 11 Group and placed under the control of No. 34 Wing of Army Co-Operation Command in No. 12 Group. On March 16, No. 656 (Army Co-Op) Squadron arrived with Tiger Moths and Austers but with the command disbanding in June 1943, the squadron left for Liverpool en route for India.

Stapleford Tawney continued to serve in a minor role with RAF Regiment signals, repair and salvage units using the facilities as part of the Second Tactical Air Force. No. 142 Flight of the London Gliding Command arrived for a brief period in 1944 and, when No. 2 Camouflage Unit moved out in September that year, use of the airfield declined. Two V2 rockets caused damage and deaths but by April 1945, the last of the units had moved and Stapleford Tawney was placed under care and maintenance.

Today it is a thriving aerodrome centered on the Herts & Essex Flying Club which moved in when their pre-war home at Broxbourne was closed down. A hard runway was laid down in the 1990s.

What a sad end to one of the most famous of all the stations of the Royal Air Force. The control tower at Tangmere . . . pictured at the end of the war . . . and in its derelict state in 2013.

TANGMERE

Tangmere, lying 48 feet above sea level alongside the A27 just west of Chichester in Sussex, was founded in 1917 for use by the Royal Flying Corps as a training base. It was transferred to the American Expeditionary Air Force for use in a similar role in 1918. When they left the airfield was mothballed until 1925 when it briefly became a Fleet Air Arm base.

Originally a grass airfield giving take-off distances of 775 yards SE-NW, N-S 800 yards, E-W 1,000 yards and NE-SW 1,500 yards, the expansion period saw two hard runways laid down measuring 1,600 x 50 yards running N-S and NE-SW. These were completed by 1939 allowing Nos. 1 and 43 Squadrons to arrive with Hurricanes, Tangmere being designated a sector station in Sector 'A' with nearby Westhampnett as a satellite. They were joined in August 1939 by No. 605 (County of Warwick) Auxiliary Squadron together with the formation of the Fighter Interception Unit equipped with Blenheims. No. 1 Squadron soon left for France as part of the Advanced Air Striking Force.

The Fighter Command Order of Battle for July 7, 1940, shows Nos. 43, 145 and 601 (County of London) Squadrons in residence. Friday, August 16, saw the first of several crippling raids on Tangmere when the Ju 87 'Stukas' of Stukageschwader 2 dive-bombed the airfield. All the hangars were hit including workshops as well as several accommodation blocks, stores, sick quarters, the Y-service hut. The Officers' Mess was badly damaged. Three Blenheims of the FIU and a Hurricane of No. 43 Squadron were destroyed with three Blenheims, seven Hurricanes and one Magister damaged. Ten service personnel and three civilians were killed with 20 receiving injuries. Airborne before the attack, in retaliation No. 43 Squadron managed to shoot down nine Stukas with damage to three others.

When No. 601 Squadron moved to Exeter, it was replaced by the Hurricanes of No. 17. Saturday, August 31 was also marked by Fighter Command suffering its heaviest losses to date with 39 aircraft shot down and 14 pilots killed. With the FIU moving to nearby Shoreham, several squadrons rotated through including Nos. 213, 607 and 145, back after a rest period at Dyce. The rest of the month saw Nos. 145 and 213 Squadrons fighting side by side until the dark nights and changeable weather forced a change in enemy tactics. By November No. 213 had left for Leconfield as Beaufighters arrived at Tangmere in the form of No. 219 (Mysore) Squadron. They were the first unit to receive the newly-equipped airborne interception mark. Joined by the Spitfire Is of No. 65 (East India) Squadron on November 29, the airfield now went firmly on the offensive.

A night attack on Tangmere on March 13, 1941, saw No. 219 Squadron operating under the control of the Ground Controlled Interception (GCI) at Wartling, near Bexhill, and managing to shoot down two of the bombers. Damage to the airfield was light.

Meanwhile No. 65 Squadron had been replaced by No. 616 (South Yorkshire) Auxiliary Squadron on February 26 which had brought their Spitfires in to join No. 145

And this was the parade when the RAF ensign was lowered for the last time.

recently converted from the Hurricane to Spitfires. Together they formed the 'Tangmere Wing' and carried out many operations over the Continent. Both squadrons moved over to the satellite in May whilst a detachment from No. 23 Squadron flew in from nearby Ford. They were equipped with the American Douglas Havoc, also known as the Boston. Used by the French Air Force, the balance of the French consignment was taken over by the RAF and converted for night fighting. Together with the Beaufighters of No. 219 Squadron, Tangmere now became synonymous with operations by night.

Similar aircraft were used by No. 1455 Flight which formed at the airfield on July 7. These AI-equipped Havocs carried an enormous searchlight in the nose to illuminate the target. Known as 'Turbinlites', the Hurricanes of No. 1 Squadron returned to accompany the Havocs. With very little success, the idea was soon abandoned with the Hurricanes thereafter carrying out independent night sorties. Moving through various marks

RAF Tangmere closed on October 20, 1970 although it had been in its death throes ever since Fighter Command quit the base in June 1958.

The technical site under demolition in October 1983 — the Gas Decontamination Block *(left)* and the Operations Block *(right)*.

The Luftwaffe had done its best to eliminate Tangmere back in 1940 by mounting a dive-bombing attack at lunchtime on August 16. Although many of the Ju 87s were intercepted before reaching the aerodrome, those that got through caused immense damage and destruction in the space of the few minutes that the raid actually lasted. Two hangars were totally destroyed and the other three damaged. The station workshops and the fire-hydrant pump house received direct hits as did a nearby air raid shelter. Stores, sick quarters, the Y-Service hut, Officers' Mess and a Salvation Army hut were also severely damaged. Six Blenheims, seven Hurricanes and a Magister were either destroyed or damaged together with nearly 40 motor vehicles.

of the type, No. 1 Squadron left Tangmere on July 8 for Acklington and conversion to the Typhoon.

The forming of No. 419 Flight saw several black-painted Lysanders arrive at the airfield. These were special duty Lysanders used for carrying agents of the Special Operations Executive to France. Tangmere Cottage opposite the main camp entrance was the holding place for many of the agents.

A further upgrade of the airfield took place during early 1941 including the laying of two asphalt runways. Hangarage now consisted of two Bessonneau, ten Over Blisters and four Extra Over Blisters. With No. 1 Squadron finally leaving Tangmere, it was time for No. 219 Squadron to follow them to Acklington on June 23, 1942. The Dieppe operation the following month saw many squadrons arrive and depart. Now known as the 'Ibsley Wing', Nos. 66, 118 and 501 (County of Gloucester) Squadrons all gave cover for Operation 'Jubilee'. Other units over this period were Nos. 41 and 43, all flying Hurricanes and Spitfires. During this busy period, Merston and Ford were allocated as extra satellites as the squadrons carried out many operations over the Continent. No. 823 Squadron of the Fleet Air Arm arrived in September 1942 for three months anti-shipping patrols over the Channel equipped with the Fairey Albacore biplane.

One squadron that spent its maximum time at Tangmere was No. 486 (RNZAF) which brought their Typhoon IBs in on October 29, 1942, and remained until moving to Beaulieu on January 31, 1944. Their forte was to tackle the Luftwaffe fighter-bombers making low-level attacks on south coast ports, towns and airfields. Further Typhoons flew in on March 28, 1943, when No. 197 Squadron arrived from Drem. Five months later the arrival of No. 183 (Gold Coast) Squadron, also flying Typhoons, saw the formation of the Tangmere Typhoon Wing. When the latter departed, they were replaced by the Spitfire XIIs of Nos. 41 and 91 (Nigeria) Squadrons.

Now it is a housing estate that has transformed the site. The hangars were replaced after the war with three T2s.

With the build up of the Second Tactical Air Force in readiness for D-Day, February 1944 saw the first No. 84 Group Typhoon Wing form up at Tangmere as No. 146 Airfield. No. 197 Squadron was joined by Nos. 183 (Gold Coast) and 257 (Burma) Squadrons who together commenced attacks on V-weapon sites. Further changes resulted in Nos. 183 and 197 Squadrons being replaced by Nos. 198 and 609 (West Riding) Squadrons. No. 266 (Rhodesia) joined one week later before No. 146 Airfield moved to the advanced landing ground at Needs Ore Point.

A very busy Tangmere now saw the six Canadian squadrons of Nos. 126 and 127 Airfields arrive. Nos. 401 (Ram) and 411 (Grizzly Bear) arrived from Fairwood Common with No. 412 (Falcon) Squadron from Biggin Hill in April followed by Nos. 403 (Wolf), 416 (City of Oshawa) and 421 (Red Indian) Squadrons from Kenley a few days later.

V-weapon launch sites were the main targets until D-Day when all the squadrons provided cover for the forward troops. By June 16, the TAF units had moved to airstrips in Normandy, their replacements being No. 132 Wing (Nos. 66, 331 and 332 (Norwegian) Squadrons) and No. 344 (Czech) Wing (Nos. 310, 312 and 313 Squadrons). With brief stays at this period of the war, the latter exchanged places with the Lympne Wing (Nos. 33, 74 'Tiger' and 127 Squadrons) on July 4, before they too became part of the Second Tactical Air Force. Late July saw No. 145 Wing of No. 84 Group comprising Nos. 74 (Trinidad), 329 (GC 1/2 'Cigognes'), 340 (GC IV/2 'Il de France') and 341 (GC III/2 'Alsace') Squadrons arrive for a brief period of escort work until they departed on August 19. They were replaced by No. 135 Wing (Nos. 222 (Natal), 349 (Belgian) and 485 (RNZAF) Squadrons) but they also crossed the Channel at the end of the month.

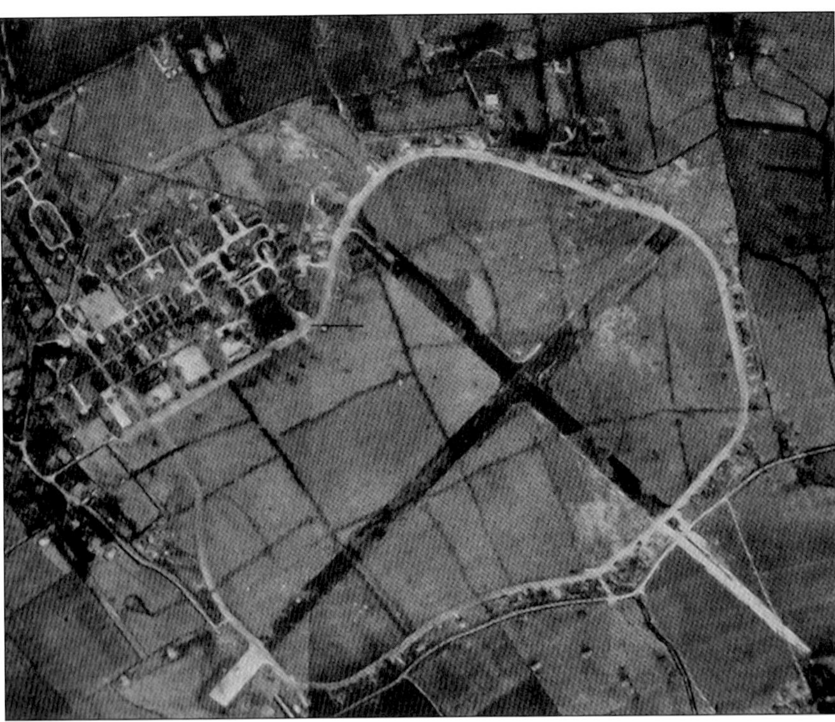

Although an attempt was made to break up the outline of the aerodrome with mock hedge lines, the runways which in this photograph were in the process of being extended, give the game away.

As the end of the war approached, some use was made of the facilities by No. 83 Support Unit flying in the wounded for treatment at nearby Chichester Hospital. The reconstituted Central Fighter Establishment assembled on January 15, 1945 and Tangmere became a major jet aircraft base for the Royal Air Force yet it was not to be and in the end Fighter Command quit the aerodrome in 1958.

The eastern part of the landing ground is now covered with greenhouses for growing tomatoes.

In 1938 the Air Ministry requisitioned land on the Duke of Richmond and Gordon's estate at Goodwood for use as an Emergency Landing Ground for Tangmere, just a couple of miles away to the south-east. The perimeter track was laid later in 1940.

WESTHAMPNETT

Westhampnett was originally an emergency landing ground which was upgraded to satellite status in late 1939. Sited 1½ miles from Chichester in Sussex, four grass runways were laid and strengthened with Sommerfeld tracking, the dimensions being N-S 1,030 yards, NE-SW 1,130 yards, E-W 920-1,000 yards and SE-NW 1,500 yards. A 35-foot tarmac perimeter track was added together with the construction of seven Over Blisters and one Extra Over Blister. Night landing facilities were provided with Glim Lamps, a Chance Light, a flarepath and a Glide Path Indicator, all necessary as the airfield was at risk of fog from the sea during spring and autumn. Encompassed within No. 11 Group, Fighter Command, Westhampnett was deemed a satellite to nearby Tangmere.

The first squadron to arrive on July 23, 1940, was No. 145 equipped with Hurricanes but heavy rain which waterlogged the landing area forced them to leave for Drem after two weeks. Once dried out, the airfield saw No. 602 (City of Glasgow) Auxiliary Squadron arrive on August 13 bringing the first Spitfires to operate from the grass. In action two days later, they shot down two Bf 110s for two Spitfires damaged with the pilots safe. August 18 saw further action when during enemy attacks on Gosport, Tangmere and Ford, 602 were credited with shooting down four Ju 87s for the loss of one Spitfire. The enemy was so badly mauled that this was the last time the Stuka was used in major assaults on Britain. The squadron remained at the satellite until December 17, 1940, when, tired and jaded, they were posted to rest at Prestwick.

The arrival of the Hurricanes of No. 302 (Poznan) Polish Squadron on November 23 found them carrying out coastal patrols with very little contact with the enemy. This changed with the arrival of No. 610 (County of Chester) Auxiliary Squadron also with Spitfires on December 15, whereupon both squadrons carried out escort work for No. 2 Group, mounting daylight raids to Belgium and France. With No. 302 moving to Kenley in April 1941, No. 616 (South Yorkshire) Auxiliary Squadron arrived on May 9 bringing the first Spitfire IIAs to Westhampnett. Together with the Tangmere squadron, No. 145, the Wing was commanded by Douglas Bader. With the increase in operations, a small tin-fronted Watch Office was built together with Nissen huts to replace the tented accommodation.

In July both squadrons converted to the Spitfire VI and it was during an operation on August 9, 1941, that Bader was brought down in a friendly fire incident over northern France. Shortly afterwards No. 610 moved north.

Their replacement was No. 129 (Mysore) Squadron which flew their Spitfire Is in from Leconfield on August 29. Converting through Spitfire IIAs and VBs, they left for Debden on November 1. No. 616 Squadron moved to Kirton-in-Lindsey having converted to Spitfire VIs at Westhampnett and coming from Kirton were No. 65 (East India) Squadron. The return of No. 129 Squadron on December 22 saw the year ending with No. 65 Squadron moving to Debden and No. 41 Squadron bringing their Spitfire VBs from Merston on December 16.

The two squadrons fought side by side during early 1942 as offensive tactics continued. A return to Merston for No. 41 Squadron on April 1 saw No. 340 (Ile-de-France) Free French Squadron use Westhampnett for just two days. Thereafter No. 129 was the sole resident until July 30 when they too departed for Thorney Island.

At this stage Westhampnett entered a new era when it became United States Army Air Force Base No. 352 and the home of the 31st Fighter Group with Spitfires. Originally it had been intended to fly the Bell P-39 Airacobra across the Atlantic to England but the type was deemed unsuitable for operations in the European Theater of Operations so Spitfires were allocated under reverse Lend-Lease conditions.

Operation 'Jubilee' at Dieppe saw the 307th and 309th Fighter Squadrons in daily action. Joined on August 25 by the 308th Fighter Squadron, a visit by the Commanding Officer of the Eighth Air Force, General Carl Spaatz, on September 2, saw the airfield officially assigned to the Americans. On October 9, the 31st Fighter Group handed their Spitfires over to other USAAF units and began to pack their belongings for deployment to North Africa.

Westhampnett as it appeared at the end of the war with a runway extension across the peri-track to the south-east.

Eric Marsden was a mechanic with No. 145 Squadron and in July 1940 his B Flight moved from Tangmere to the satellite at Westhampnett where he took these snapshots. 'Hedges and fences had been ripped out of half a dozen or so fields, a few Nissen huts had been erected on two sides of the field, and we were moved in without beds, lights, or furniture of any kind, not even hooks or nails on which to hang our gear clear of the still wet concrete floors. The dining room was an old open-sided wagon shed. The washing facilities were a cattle trough across which, eventually, someone nailed a couple of pieces of board so that we had somewhere other than the deck on which to put our soap and razors.' *Above left:* An informal group at the dispersal. L-R: Flying Officer Guy Branch, Bill the dog, Adrian Boyd, Pilot Officer James Storrar and Flight Lieutenant Wilhelm Pankratz. *Above right:* Boyd freshens up.

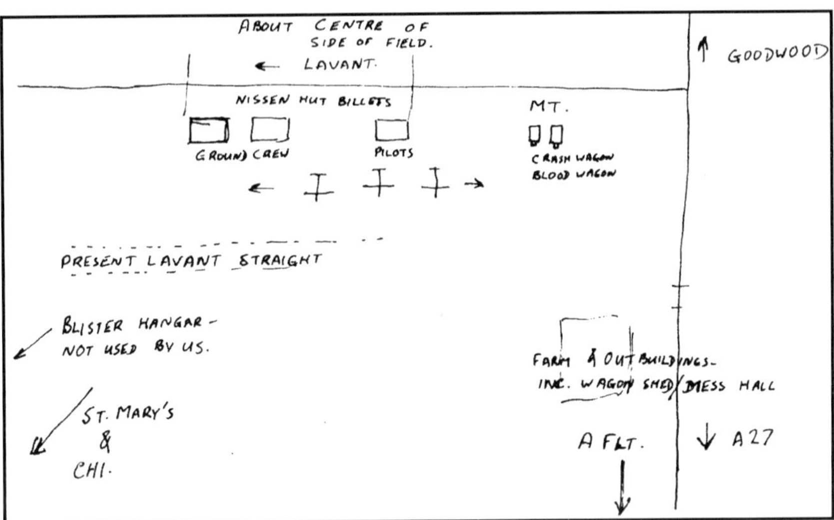

Adrian Boyd makes a low pass over the 'drome. Eric comments that 'we hadn't heard of the "Victory Roll" yet but our blokes had two manoeuvres special to the squadron. If anyone had fired his guns during an operation, he always flew a low pass over his own dispersal point on return — this ensured that the groundcrew had seen the blackened gun-patches on the leading edges, and could have ammo tanks at the ready, to change over as soon as the kite was parked. The other manoeuvre was perhaps an expression of joi d'vivre: a fast low pass over the field, with a vertical pull-up immediately over the hedge, chop throttle, gear and flaps down whilst still climbing vertically; stall-turn on near dead engine, and land from the vertical into a near dead-stick landing and minimum roll — very impressive. I think Boydy did it first, having practised awhile on an Avro Tutor which lived at Tangmere.'

Handed back to the RAF and No. 11 Group, Westhampnett now saw the return of No. 616 Squadron flying the Spitfire VI for high-altitude fighting. Joined by the Spitfire VBs of No. 131 (County of Kent) Squadron on November 7, 1942, both squadrons carried out operations over the Continent. These continued into 1943 until both squadrons left to be replaced by Nos. 485 (RNZAF) and 610 (County of Chester) Auxiliary Squadron. By May, No. 485 had left for Merston whilst No. 610 went to Perranporth on April 30. Brief stays by Nos. 167 (Gold Coast) and 501 (County of Gloucester) Squadrons carrying out escort duties saw No. 41 return on June 21, flying their Spitfire XIIs in from nearby Friston. The same month saw No. 91 (Nigeria) also arrive flying Spitfire XIIs. Both took part in Operation 'Starkey' resulting in the latter squadron becoming the month's top-scoring unit of Fighter Command. With both squadrons moving over to Tangmere in October, the Typhoons of Nos. 174 (Mauritius), 175 and 245 (Northern Rhodesia) Squadrons arrived to form No. 121 Airfield in No. 83 Group. Long-range, low-level sweeps were carried out until No. 121 Airfield moved to the advanced landing ground at Holmsley South.

The 309th of the 31st Fighter Group was the first US squadron to be issued with Spitfires participating in the assault on Dieppe in August 1942 from Westhampnett. ***Left:*** **A group of American and RAF pilots pictured after the raid as Pfc Molar Johnstown** ***(right)*** **reloads the cannons.**

From front-line airfield to motorsport venue — the control tower has seen it all!

This Signal Corps' photograph, taken on September 5, 1942 shows mechanics servicing a Spitfire of the 309th Fighter Squadron.

After the war, motor racing began at Goodwood in 1948 when the 9th Duke of Richmond and Gordon opened the first race on the perimeter track but the circuit was closed in 1966 due to safety concerns from the increasing speed of the cars.

Operation 'Overlord' saw the arrival of the Spitfire IXs of No. 144 Airfield comprising the Canadian squadrons Nos. 441 (Silver Fox), 442 (Caribou) and 443 (Hornet). They completed a training programme at Westhampnett and also managed to carry out several escort duties before leaving for Funtington ALG on April 24. No. 184 Squadron flew in as part of No. 129 Airfield, for 'Overlord'. As June 6 dawned, the Typhoons began attacking gun positions along the Normandy coast with devastating rocket power.

Back at Westhampnett, the arrival of the Communitions Squadron (No. 26) of No. 84 Group indicated that many top brass would be flying from there to the Continent as the Allies pushed inland. Meanwhile, plans were being discussed regarding Mosquitos using Westhampnett, but the idea was abandoned when it was realised that the aircraft was too big and too fast for the grass airfield.

With No. 184 Squadron moving to Holmsley South on June 17, Nos. 41 and 610 Squadrons returned for a few days. It was then the turn of Nos. 130 (Punjab), No 303 (Kosciuszko) Polish and No. 402 (Winnipeg Bear) Squadron of the RCAF to use the airfield for beach-head patrols and bomber escorts. Short stays were also undertaken by Nos. 118 and 124 (Baroda) Squadrons before the airfield was placed under care and maintenance on January 1, 1945. Used for a limited period by the military post-war, Westhampnett became a popular light aircraft venue as well as a racing circuit known as Goodwood.

However, exactly 50 years after opening, the Duke's grandson, the Earl of March, restaged the event with the first Goodwood Revival meeting bringing together historic motor cars, motorcycles, aeroplanes . . . and fashion, in a period setting.

WEST MALLING

Although still under construction for most of the Battle of Britain period, West Malling rose to become the premier night-fighter station in Fighter Command from 1944 onwards. Previously known as Maidstone Airport, the airfield was approved for acquisition as a Fighter Command airfield in June 1939. With George Wimpey being appointed as the main contractor, work began in September that year but it was not until nine months later that a station headquarters was established amid continuing building work.

The airfield lay 280 feet above sea level and four and a half miles from Maidstone in Kent. Due to the over-running building work, it first served as an operational satellite to the parent station of Biggin Hill and a forward landing ground for Biggin and Kenley. Four grass runways were laid out and strengthened with Sommerfeld track. They measured N-S 1,200 yards, NE-SW 1,100 yards, E-W 1,400 yards and SE-NW 1,300 yards, with the N-S being extended to 1,666 yards and the E-W extended to 2,160 yards later in 1940. A 40-foot perimeter track was laid with hangar accommodation consisting of one 'J' type, eight Extra Over Blisters and eight Over Blisters. Night landing facilities consisted of Mk II airfield lighting with two-channel VHF/RT, Bomber and Coastal Darky, VHF/BA and HF/DF.

June 1940 saw the arrival of No. 26 (Army Co-op) Squadron with Lysanders. They were to remain throughout the early phases of the battle, finally leaving on September 3. Although the airfield was far from complete, No. 141 Squadron flying Defiants had arrived on July 12 but in their first operational sortie from the forward airfield at Hawkinge, they lost six machines with one badly damaged. Shortly afterwards they were posted to Prest-

On September 7, 1940, the day when the Luftwaffe launched its full might against London — the day now known as Black Saturday — this shot was taken at 6.52 p.m. as the formations crossed Kent. Then West Malling was still a grass field yet surprisingly not camouflaged with the usual tar lines to break up the outline.

The main runway was concreted and extended at either end. This picture was taken in May 1950.

wick leaving West Malling defenceless when it suffered several heavy attacks which put completion back even further. So much damage was inflicted that the airfield did not become operational until the end of October when No. 66 Squadron brought their Spitfires in from Gravesend. Staying for a month no further squadrons were based at West Malling until April 14, 1941, when No. 264 (Madras Presidency) arrived. Flying the Defiant, this time in the night-fighter role, they stayed until May 1 joining No. 29 Squadron which had brought the first Beaufighters to West Malling at the same time. Included in the aircrew was Flight Lieutenant Guy Gibson who, although a pilot in Bomber Command, had been attached to No. 29 Squadron to gain experience in night operations.

With West Malling gaining a reputation for night-fighting, May 22 saw the formation of a Turbinlite unit — No. 1452 Flight — which was given squadron status becoming No. 531 later in May 1942. The arrival of No. 32 Squadron from Manston the same month saw their Hurricanes flying in conjunction with the Havocs of No. 531. No. 29 Squadron was also joined by No. 1426 (Enemy Aircraft) Flight that had been established to evaluate captured enemy aircraft.

January 1942 saw day fighters return to West Malling. Mainly Spitfires, they came to re-arm and refuel before carrying out bomber escort duties. Operation 'Jubilee' in August brought No. 610 (County of Chester) Auxiliary Squadron to the airfield. Commanded by 'Johnnie' Johnson, they formed part of a No. 12 Group Wing, the other squadrons being Nos. 411 (Grizzly Bear), RCAF, and No. 485, RNZAF. However with the Dieppe operation over, these squadrons departed, together with the Hurricanes of No. 32 Squadron who left for Honiley on September 10. They were replaced by No. 486 (RNZAF) with Typhoons to carry out offensive sweeps over France, Belgium and Holland, the squadron acquiring a reputation for their train-busting activities.

Above: **The technical site showing the three T2 hangars and the J-type hangar with the curved roof facing the control tower, where this parade was held in June 1954 at which the Colours were presented to No. 25 Squadron.**

Flying ceased in 1970 at which point the airfield was sold for the construction of a mixture of commercial and domestic properties. Being Listed Grade II, the control tower has survived midst the new development.

A surprise visitor to the tower in April 1943 was Feldwebel Otto Bechtold in his Focke-Wulf 190A-4 who landed on the aerodrome by mistake! It occurred on the night of April 16/17. **A second FW 190 touched down but Leutnant Fritz Setzer, realising his error, tried to take off but was machine-gunned by ground crews and the aircraft burst into flames.**

January 1943 saw No. 29 Squadron still resident with No. 531 (Turbinlite) Squadron disbanding on the 25th of the month. Then, on the night of April 17/18, some unexpected visitors turned up in the shape of two Focke-Wulfe 190s, one aircraft being destroyed by fire from the guns of the airfield defence crews. The other was captured intact and flown away for evaluation.

After a very successful posting, No. 29 Squadron departed for Bradwell Bay on May 13 being replaced by No. 85 Squadron with Mosquitos. Typhoons also returned for day operations when No. 3 Squadron flew in from Hunsdon to operate in a fighter-bomber role, the aircraft being universally known as 'Bombphoons'. Staying for a month they moved east to Manston leaving No. 85 Squadron as sole residents.

Two Spitfire squadrons were posted in on August 4. They were Nos. 130 (Pubjab) and 234 (Madras Presidency) to escort bombers on day raids. This they carried out for a month until Nos. 64 and 124 (Baroda) Squadrons took over similar duties.

Meanwhile, No. 85 Squadron, now led by John Cunningham, was achieving great success at night. His own personal score had the press dub him 'Cats-Eyes' due to his ability to shoot down aircraft at night. It was a name which he personally hated but which was to stick with him all his life.

No. 96 Squadron, having converted to the newer Mosquito XIII at Drem, flew down on November 8. They joined No. 85 to operate at night while No. 124 Squadron carried out day operations during the last weeks of 1943.

March 18, 1944 saw No. 124 Squadron swap places with No. 616 (South Yorkshire) Auxiliary Squadron at Church Fenton. Both squadrons then became attached to the Second Tactical Air Force in preparation for D-Day.

It was now the turn of No. 85 Squadron to leave, departing to Swannington and No. 100 Group on May 1. No. 29 Squadron returned to their old airfield the same day later joined by No. 409 (Nighthawk) Squadron of the RCAF. As D-Day approached, West Malling hosted Nos. 29, 96 and 409 Squadron flying Mosquitos and No. 91 Squadron flying Spitfires. However the role of West Malling quickly changed when it became one of the main airfields to counter the threat of the flying bomb. The night-fighter squadrons moved out as No. 91 was joined by No. 322 (Dutch) Squadron on June 20. West Malling lay right on the flight path of the V1s to London and, with the launches increasing, Nos. 80 and 274 Squadrons were quickly brought in to help. July saw Nos. 91 and 322 Squadrons leave replaced by No. 157 flying the Mosquito XIX together with No. 85 Squadron. By the end of the month, West Malling squadrons had claimed 278 flying bombs destroyed, to become the top-scoring airfield in Fighter Command.

August saw No. 274 Squadron convert to the Tempest and on the 4th of the month, No. 316 (Warsaw) Polish Squadron arrived with the Mustang III for a short stay. V1 incursions multiplied during August to between 250 and 300 a day but by the end of

With the risk of the unique control tower falling into disrepair, there have been several proposals for its future as a museum, art gallery, restaurant or shop. When this photo was taken in 2013 it was being converted into a Costa coffee house.

'One generation passeth away, and another generation cometh' the words of Ecclesiastes aptly describing the old and the new paraded side by side at West Malling on August 5, 1959. Here the classic outlines of the Spitfire and Hurricane take on a rare delicacy when compared with the Javelin jet fighters of No. 85 Squadron.

the month they began to decline as Allies ground forces began over-running the launch sites in France. By August 31 the airfield was devoid of aircraft having been earmarked for conversion into a major night fighter base. The job of reconstruction fell to No. 5011 Airfield Construction Squadron which supervised local contractors, work taking until June 1945 when it once again became operational.

From April 1941 through to August 1944, the West Malling squadrons claimed to have been responsible for the destruction of 165 enemy aircraft, 34 probables, 59 damaged and over 280 V1s. In 1962 it became a United States Naval Facility base until finally closed and sold for domestic development in 1970. Today only the control tower and a unique flak tower remain to remind us of its wartime history. In 2002 a memorial was unveiled on the site of the old Station Headquarters.

No. 12 GROUP

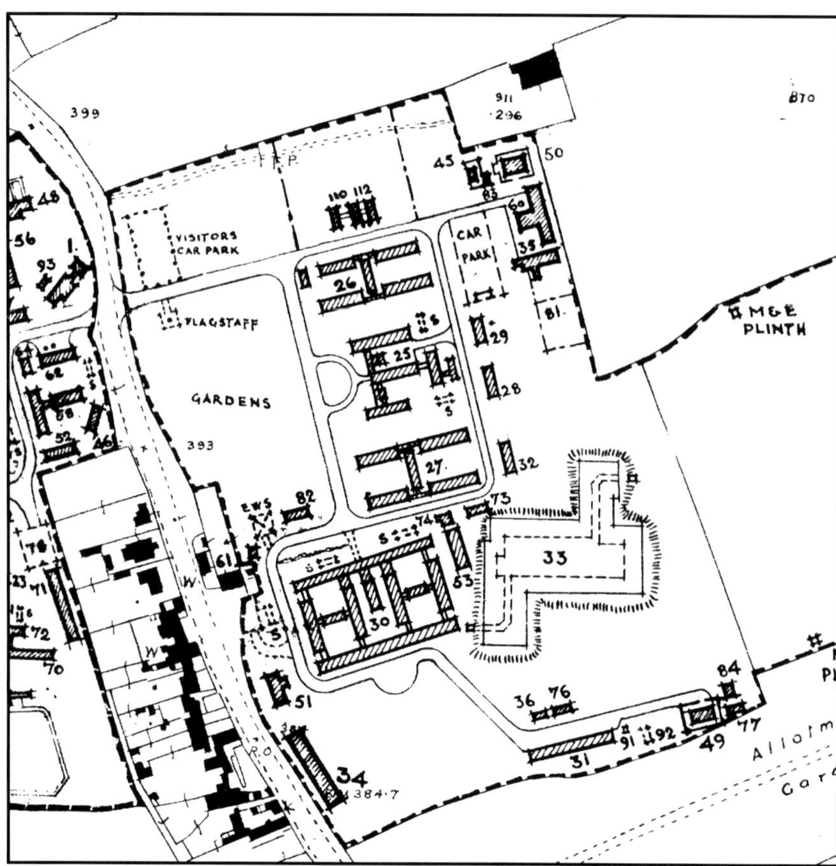

In 1939, No. 12 Group had its headquarters at Hucknall airfield, just north-west of Nottingham, while work was being carried out at nearby Watnall to build an underground Operations Block (No. 33 on plan) with associated domestic sites.

In 1960 there were discussions as to the future use of the site, one proposal being to use the Operations Block for a central headquarters for the Civil Defence. However, there were signs that the ops block was being affected by coal mining subsidence and the whole station was closed in 1961. The underground workings were sealed and the site is now an HGV Test Centre.

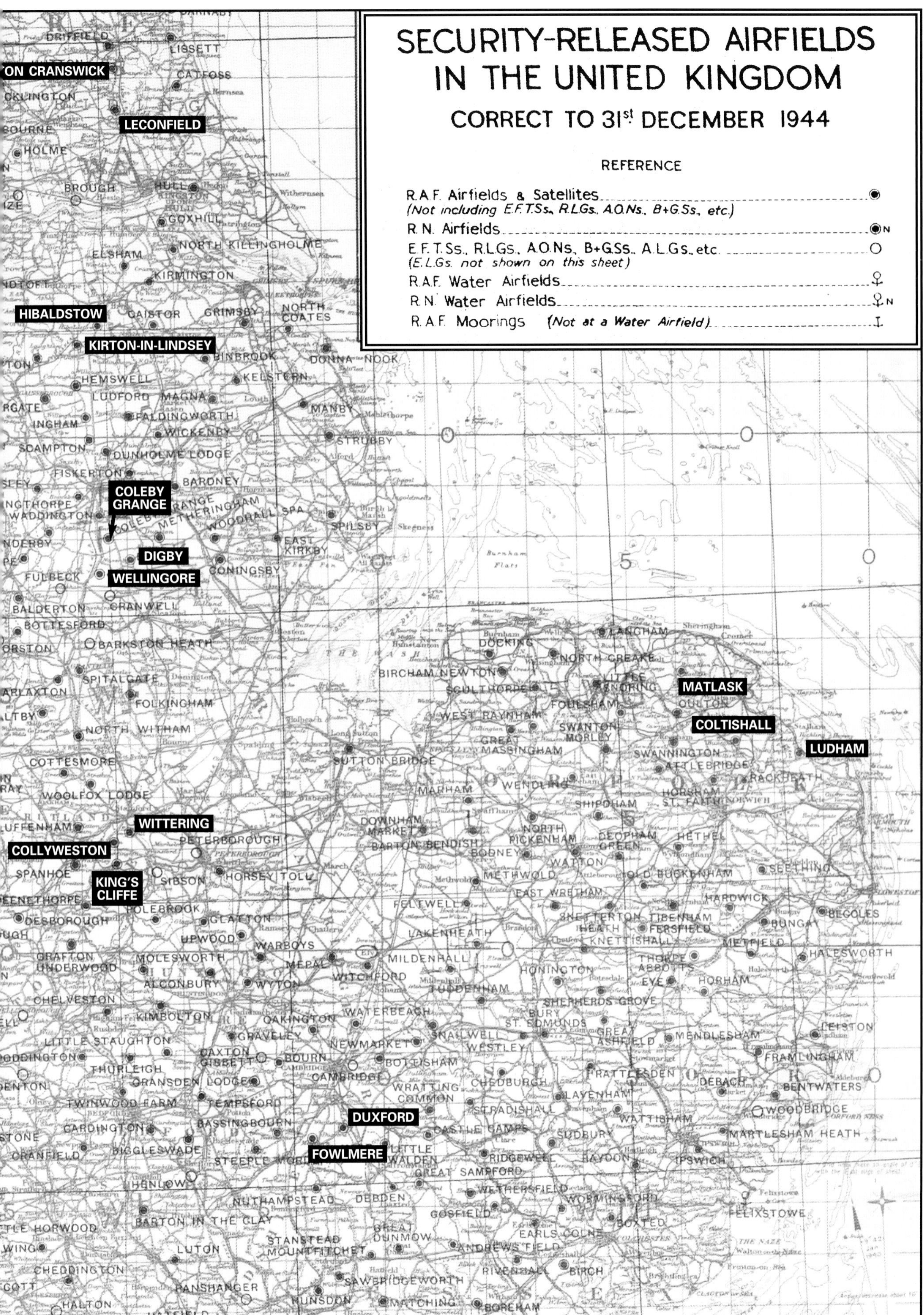
SECURITY-RELEASED AIRFIELDS IN THE UNITED KINGDOM
CORRECT TO 31st DECEMBER 1944
REFERENCE
R.A.F. Airfields & Satellites
(Not including E.F.T.Ss., R.L.Gs., A.O.Ns., B+G.Ss., etc.)
R.N. Airfields
E.F.T.Ss., R.L.Gs., A.O.Ns., B+G.Ss., A.L.Gs., etc.
(E.L.Gs. not shown on this sheet)
R.A.F. Water Airfields
R.N. Water Airfields
R.A.F. Moorings (Not at a Water Airfield)
ON CRANSWICK
LECONFIELD
HIBALDSTOW
KIRTON-IN-LINDSEY
COLEBY GRANGE
DIGBY
WELLINGORE
WITTERING
COLLYWESTON
KING'S CLIFFE
MATLASK
COLTISHALL
LUDHAM
DUXFORD
FOWLMERE

From RAF Baginton and the first American Curtiss Tomahawks to enter service with No. 403 Squadron Royal Canadian Air Force in March 1941 . . . to the airliners of Coventry Airport today. The Tomahawks were soon replaced by Spitfires.

BAGINTON

Land for Baginton was acquired in 1935 for the establishment of a municipal airport for Coventry. The factories of Armstrong Whitworth Aircraft Ltd were close by so there was also a need for an airfield within the vicinity as the company was well advanced on producing the Whitley bomber and Baginton was of sufficient size to allow test flying.

At 270 feet above sea level and three miles south-east of the city, the grass landing area measured 1,500 yards from E-W, 1,260 yards SE-NW and 700 yards N-S and NE-SW. Surrounded by industry, noted obstructions were the Armstrong Whitworth and Alvis Car works and the Coventry and Birmingham balloon barrage and it was prone to fog from October to March. There were four Bellman hangars. No permanent flying control was in operation, rather it was left to the airman of the watch and duty crew for emergency landings or by the duty pilot when a squadron was in residence. Baginton became an operational satellite in Fighter Command, parented by RAF Honiley.

No. 1 Camouflage Unit formed there in September 1939 to carry out experiments in airfield camouflage but no use was made of Baginton during the main part of the battle in 1940. It was not until September 25 that the forming of No. 9 Fighter Group Headquarters at the aerodrome saw No. 308 (Krakow) Polish Squadron arrive from Speke on the same day. Flying Hurricane Is, they were one of a number of squadrons tasked with the protection of the West Midlands. Success came on November 24 when a Ju 88 was shot down during a reconnaissance mission to Coventry. A conversion to Spitfire Is in March 1941 saw them depart to Chilbolton on May 31.

The old control tower with which the wartime crews would have been familiar, was pictured by Paul Francis in 1993.

Three years later it was demolished to be replaced by a much more modern building.

A controversial decision by Warwick District Council to give approval to a large Coventry Gateway project to be built on 740 acres of Green Belt land was announced in 2013. The plan was designed to include a brand new terminal building at the airport in an attempt to promote increased passenger services at Baginton.

Having finished their work, No. 1 Camouflage Unit moved to Hendon on November 8, 1940, replaced by No. 403 (Wolf) Canadian Squadron, an army co-operation squadron, on February 19, 1941. Receiving their Tomahawk I and IIAs in March, they quickly replaced them with Spitfire Is to become a fighter squadron. Working up on the type, they left for Ternhill on May 20.

Armstrong Whitworth was flying test trials with the Albermarle when No. 605 (County of Warwick) Auxiliary Squadron arrived with Hurricane IIAs on May 30. Re-equipping with the Mk IIB, the squadron went on the offensive with sweeps over the Channel and beyond. They took their IIBs to Honiley on September 4 and a month later left for the Far East.

No. 457 Squadron was established at the airfield on June 16 with Australian aircrew and RAF ground crews. Flying Spitfire Is, they carried out several unsuccessful scrambles before leaving for the Isle of Man on August 7.

The station was quickly becoming a kitting-out centre for squadrons moving overseas and another squadron to reform that month was No. 135. Taking over the Hurricanes left behind by No. 605 Squadron, they left for Honiley on September 4 en route to the Far East. Then in December, No. 79 (Madras Presidency) Squadron brought their Hurricane IIBs in from Fairwood Common and left for India on March 4, 1942. Next was No. 134 Squadron with Spitfire VBs which arrived on March 26 and left for Egypt on April 10. A brief visit by No. 32 Squadron Hurricane Is to prepare for an overseas posting to North Africa saw them become the last fighter unit to use Baginton.

Meanwhile the aerodrome was kept busy with the test flying of Armstrong Whitworth's Whitleys destined for Coastal Command. Trials were also conducted with a conversion to be used for towing gliders for paratroop operations.Between March 1937 andl June 1943, the company had built 1,182 Whitleys and test flown most of them from Bagington. Later years saw Lancaster and Lincoln conversions taking place.

Peacetime saw Meteors leaving the factory, some being flown from the grass, but later developments demanded a hard runway and in 1960 one a mile long was laid down. When the Armstrong Whitworth factory closed in July 1965, Jersey Airlines moved in to begin scheduled services to the Channel Islands. Now known as Coventry Airport, the airfield is operated by Coventry City Council.

CHURCH FENTON

One of the RAF's premier stations in Yorkshire for over 75 years is now sadly scheduled to close. The famous fighter base saw its operational use come to an end in 2003 but all is not lost as moves are afoot to preserve it as a base for historic aircraft.

Church Fenton was one of those small airfields that the Directorate of Works at the Air Ministry decided was worthy of expansion. There was much local opposition to these plans but nevertheless work went ahead on establishing a large airfield during 1936 on 260 acres of land, some privately owned and some belonging to West Riding County Council.

Some ten miles south-west of York, and just 27 feet above sea level, the airfield was categorised as a night fighter sector station with satellites or relief landing grounds at Hutton Cranswick, Sherburn, Acaster Malbis and Wombleton. The grass surface measured 1,400 yards NE-SW and E-W, 1,200 yards SE-NW and just 800 yards N-S. Two concrete runways were added, the longest being 1,600 yards and the secondary 1,400 yards, both 50 yards wide. A large 105 feet concrete perimeter track led to two 'C' Type hangars, two Bellman and eight Over Blisters. A Type II Flying Control gave night landing facilities of Drem lighting on the E-W runway only together with numerous radio facilities consisting of VHF/DF Homer, Mobile VHF/DF Tender for ZZ Homing, a HF/DF Homer and three VHF/DF Fixers.

Several squadrons used the facilities prior to and during the opening phases of the war, namely No. 72 (Basutoland) with Gladiators and later Spitfires; No. 213 (Ceylon) with Gauntlets, and No. 64 with Demons and Blenheims. A detachment of Battles and Blenheims from No. 245 (Northern Rhodesia) Squadron came in during February and stayed until May 12, 1940.

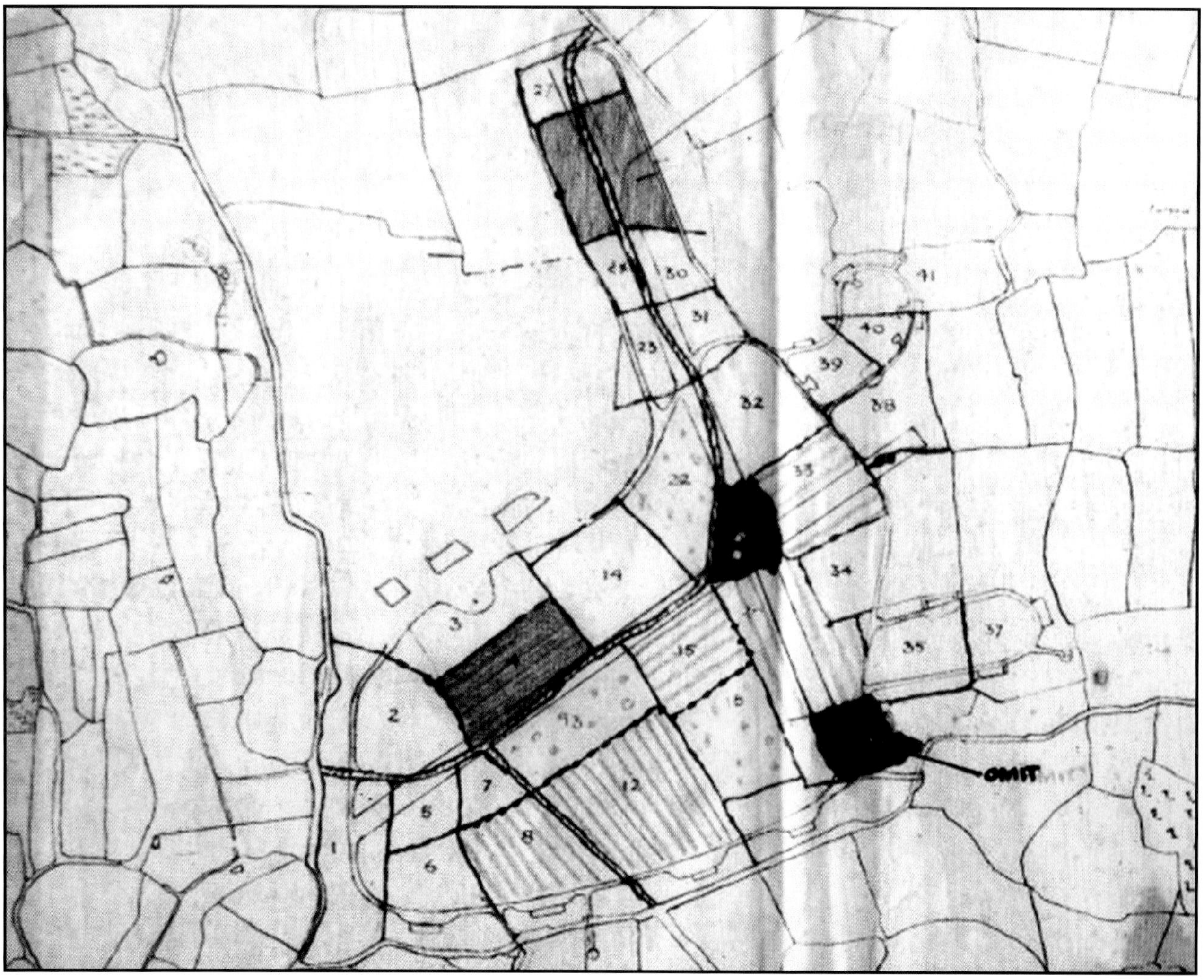

This was the camouflage pattern drawn up by the Air Ministry Directorate of Works for Church Fenton.

Left: **Writing in 1999 with this photo from his scrap-book, Aircraftman Graeme Gillard commented that 'my Gladiator, K6139 is not shown. It was SOC [struck off charge] after a mid-air collision over Selby in '38, crashing on a railway line'.** *Right:* **The hangar is currently used by the Yorkshire University Air Squadron, due to move out to Linton-on-Ouse.**

No. 242 (Canadian) Squadron formed up at Church Fenton with Blenheims, Battles and Hurricanes on October 30, 1939 moving to Biggin Hill on May 21, 1940. Five days earlier No. 249 (Gold Coast) Squadron had also arrived to collect its Hurricanes before moving to Leconfield the next day. Flying both Hurricanes and Spitfires, it returned to Church Fenton on July 8 remaining until August 14 when they moved to Boscombe Down.

With the battle raging in the south of the country, No. 71 (Eagle) Squadron consisting of volunteer airmen from the USA, reformed at the airfield in September, 1940. First equipped with Brewster Buffalos, these were exchanged for Hurricane Is in November. Working up on the type, they moved to Kirton-in-Lindsey on November 23.

Brief visits by No. 234 Squadron with Spitfire Is on May 22, and No. 87 with Hurricanes two days later, saw the former become the highest scoring squadron in No. 10 Group during the battle. They left for St. Eval on June 18 with No. 87 moving to Exeter on July 5.

After seeing heavy fighting on the Continent, No. 73 Squadron flew in from France on June 16 to re-group and begin night fighter training. Sending a detachment to Sherburn, the rest of the squadron moved to Castle Camps on September 5. The third Polish squadron to be created was born at Church Fenton when No. 306 (Torun) received their Hurricanes. Commanded by a British CO, they worked up on their aircraft before taking them to operational status at Tern Hill on November 7.

With No. 73 Squadron having departed, their replacement was No. 85 Squadron which arrived from Castle Camps with Hurricane Is on September 5. Although the Hurricane was not suited to night fighting, the squadron practiced their art before becoming operational on their move to Kirton-in-Lindsey on October 23. With more night-fighting in mind, December 1940 saw the formation of the first night fighter training

The aerodrome in reality pictured in June 1942 complete with the disruptive field pattern.

Eight-gun fighters like Spitfires and Hurricanes needed their wing-mounted armament harmonised so that all guns converged in a cone of fire at whatever the preferred range was required by the pilot. This was usually 100 yards. Here the mechanics support the tail of the Spitfire on a trestle while the armourer fires the guns.

unit when No. 4 Operational Training Unit formed here. Later re-numbered No. 54 OTU, it had a mixture of aircraft including Defiants, Hurricanes and Blenheims.

The aerodrome was attacked by the Luftwaffe during the night of April 26/27, 1941. With aircraft landing after a night practice, a Ju 88 infiltrated the circuit just as two aircraft were landing. Managing to shoot them down before bombing the airfield, a third Blenheim was destroyed on the ground. Minutes later a Defiant entering the circuit was also shot down. Despite these incidents, the OTU remained at the station until May 1942 when it moved to Charterhall.

It was a detachment from No. 288 Squadron of the Army Co-operation Command that arrived on November 18, 1941 with a selection of aircraft — Hurricanes, Spitfires, Blenheims, Lysanders, Hudsons and Defiants — to provide practice for anti-aircraft units in Lincolnshire and Yorkshire.

The arrival of No. 25 Squadron on May 17, 1942 saw Church Fenton return to offensive operations. When the unit arrived it was equipped with the Douglas Havoc but, after sending a detachment to Predannack, the rest converted to the Mosquito II in October and the Mk VI in August 1943, commencing night sweeps over the Continent. No. 488 (RNZAF) Squadron, having been disbanded n the Far East in March 1942, was reformed here on June 25 with Beaufighter IIFs before being posted to Ayr on September 1.

Meanwhile, No. 25 Squadron were installing a new mark of airborne interception radar in their aircraft to enable them to carry out bomber support operations before transferring to Acklington on December 19, 1943. Prior to them leaving, No. 26 (South African) Squadron with Mustang Is arrived from Ballyhalbert on July 21. Leaving a detachment at Church Fenton, the rest of that squadron moved to Hutton Cranswick on December 28.

August had seen further Beaufighters arrive when the Mk VIFs of No. 96 Squadron came in on August 6, 1943 for a brief period, while June 6 had seen the Spitfire VIs of No. 234 (Madras Presidency) Squadron arrive for the first of two stays. Leaving on July 8 for Honiley, they returned on December 31 leaving for Coltishall on January 28, 1944.

That year saw several operational changes with No. 124 (Baroda) flying Spitfire VIIs in on March 18 and out on April 23. They were replaced by the Mosquito XIIs of No. 604 (County of Middlesex) Auxiliary Squadron for one week only. The Polish No. 307 (Lwow) Squadron, also equipped with the Mk XII, flew in from Coleby Grange on May 6. With a detachment to Coltishall, they converted to the Mosquito Mk XXX, remaining at Church Fenton until January 27, 1945.

The last day of 1944 saw No. 456 (Australian) Squadron bring in their Mosquito XVIIs. Converting to the Mk XXX, they commenced high-altitude bomber escort duties, but their departure on March 16, 1945 was virtually the last wartime use of the airfield.

After the war, Church Fenton was retained as a fighter base and was one of the first to receive a squadron of Meteors followed by Hunters. Flying training dominated the post-fighter era with No. 7 FTS with Jet Provosts and No. 2 FTS and the Royal Navy Elementary Flying Training School with Bulldogs. The station was also the first to receive the Short Tucano basic jet trainer.

The operational use of Church Fenton remained until 2003 when it became the home of the Yorkshire University Air Squadron and also No. 2434 Squadron of the Air Training Corps. However, its days were numbered and the university aircraft were scheduled to move to Linton-on-Ouse by 2014.

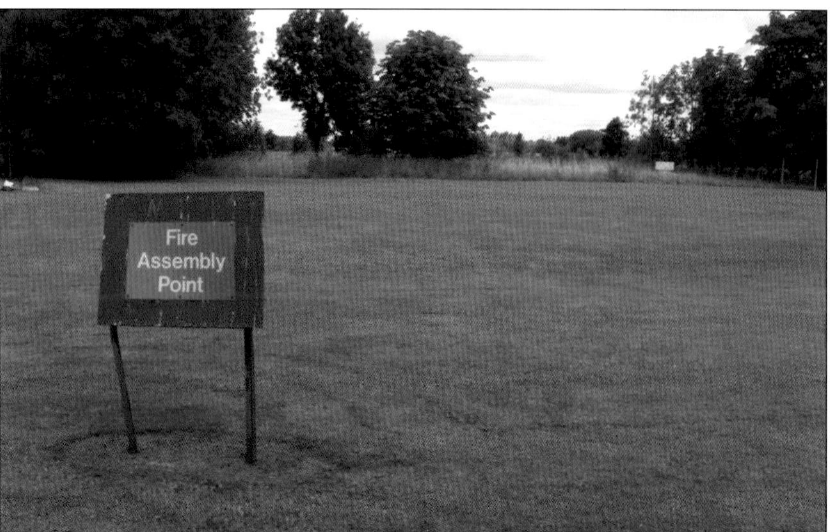

Unfortunately the stop-butt at Church Fenton has gone but the notice is appropriate!

The custom of parking a Spitfire beside the main entrance of an RAF station began in the late 1940s, particularly at those aerodromes which had seen service during the Battle of Britain. In its time Church Fenton had two: RW382, an L.F.XVIE which never saw wartime service, and BM597. She was taken on charge by the RAF in April 1942 and flew with two Polish squadrons — Nos. 315 (Deblin) and 317 (Wilno) — before suffering a flying accident. After repair by Vickers-Armstrong, she was reissued in April 1945 to No. 58 Operational Training Unit but retired later that year. After then being displayed at Hednesford and Bridgnorth, BM597 arrived at Church Fenton in 1964, being sent to Pinewood for making the moulds for the replicas required for the film *Battle of Britain.* She returned in 1969 but in February 1988 the Air Force Board of the Ministry of Defence deemed that historic aircraft were now too valuable to be left outside to deteriorate, so they were removed to be replaced with glass-fibre replicas.

Coleby Grange photographed on April 16, 1947 by No. 58 Squadron. Disbanded at the end of the war, it was reformed in October 1946 as a photo-reconnaissance unit equipped with Mosquitos.

COLEBY GRANGE

Categorised as an operational satellite to Digby, the other function of Coleby Grange was as a night fighter base. Located on open heathland six miles south of Lincoln, it lay close to the satellite airfield at Wellingore. Bordering the A15 trunk road, the aerodrome lay 200 feet above sea level with grass dimensions of 1,670 yards NE-SW, 1,300 yards E-W, 1,235 yards SE-NW and 800 yards N-S. A 35-foot peri-track gave access to one Bellman hangar and eight Over Blisters. Drem runway lighting was installed together with a VHF transmitter and Homing Aid. A blind approach facility could be activated if required.

Work on laying out the airfield began in 1939. Once ready, it was used initially as a relief landing ground for Cranwell before being allocated to No. 12 Group. First aircraft to arrive was a detachment of Hurricanes from No. 253 (Hyderabad State) Squadron during May 1940. They were joined by a Defiant detachment from No. 264 (Madras Presidency) Squadron during July, but both stays were very brief. Having left by August, no further units used the station for the rest of the year.

Not until July 26, 1941, did a permanent squadron arrive in the shape of No. 409 (Nighthawk) Canadian Squadron again with Defiant Is. With these aircraft proving inadequate for the purpose, conversions went ahead to Beaufighter IIFs although the CO, Squadron Leader Norman Petersen, was killed on August 2. Further conversions to the Mk VIFs saw detachments operating at Kirton-in-Lindsey and Hibaldstow. The squadron claimed success on the night of November 1 when the new CO, Wing Commander Paul Davoud, claimed a Do 217.

This severely charred Mosquito was pictured at Coleby Grange on September 27, 1943. Flight Lieutenant M. Cybulski and Flying Officer H. Ladbrook of No. 410 Squadron had attacked a Do217 over Holland, closing to within 100 feet before opening fire. The Dornier exploded with such a force that the Mossie was enveloped in burning fuel.

Always an all-grass airfield, it has now returned to agriculture under the auspices of J. H. Baxter & Sons.

July 1942 proved a good month when five aircraft were claimed destroyed and one damaged. A move to Acklington on February 23, 1943, saw a detachment remaining at Coleby Grange until the entire squadron returned on December 19.

Their replacement during the break was another Canadian squadron, No. 410 (Cougar). With Mosquito IIs, they arrived on February 21, 1943, converted to the Mk VI and departed for West Malling on October 20. Further Mk VIs arrived on November 7 when No. 264 (Madras Presidency) flew in. Moving to Church Fenton on December 18 saw them convert to Mark XIIIs.

Prior to their departure, the arrival of No. 288 Squadron on November 9, 1943, saw Spitfires, Oxfords and Martinets at Coleby, a detachment being left behind when the squadron moved to Digby on November 25.

Beaufighters returned on February 5, 1944 with No. 68 Squadron though this was a short visit before it was back to the Mosquito XIIs of No. 307 (Lwow) Polish Squadron. They arrived on March 2, 1944 and left for Church Fenton on May 6.

By the autumn, Coleby Grange was left with no permanent squadrons, and, after it was transferred to No. 27 Group, it relinquished its fighter status and once more became a satellite to Cranwell and No. 17 Service Flying Training School. Joined by No. 1515 Blind Approach Training Flight in February 1945, then later in the year by No. 107 Elementary Glider School giving glider instruction to Air Cadets, all these units had left by 1954 when the station was relegated to care and maintenance. It was re-activated in 1959 for No. 142 Squadron armed with Thor ballistic missiles. When they were phased out, the aerodrome was returned to agriculture.

The Canadian squadron, No. 409 (Nighthawk), exchanged their Defiants (T3937 pictured *above* in July 1941) for Beaufighters. *Below:* This is T3145 later the same year.

In 1959 under Project 'Emily', Intermediate Range Ballistic Missiles (IRBM) were deployed in the United Kingdom to counter the perceived threat from the Soviet Union. With a range of 1,500 miles and carrying a 1.44 megaton thermonuclear warhead, 60 missiles were split between 20 squadrons of Bomber Command. No. 142 Squadron was based at Coleby Grange from July 22, 1959 until May 24, 1963. The rockets were to be launched from transporter-erector trailers which were stored in shelters mounted on rails which could be rolled away ready for lifting to an upright position. This launch procedure took 15 minutes, time to target being approximately 18 minutes.

COLLYWESTON

In November 1941 a dedicated unit to maintain and fly captured German aircraft was set up at Duxford but when the US 78th Fighter Group were given the airfield in April 1943, the Luftwaffe aircraft were moved north to Collyweston.

The site of Collyweston aerodrome in Northamptonshire was originally the First World War training airfield known as Easton-on-the-Hill. Closed in 1919, the Directorate of Works looked at the site during the expansion period and decided that it would be an ideal relief landing ground for nearby Wittering airfield.

Located three and a half miles south-west of Stamford, and 282 feet above sea level, the grass landing area, increased since the days of the Royal Flying Corps, measured 1,500 yards N-S, 1,460 yards NE-SW, 1,260 yards SE-NW and 1,000 yards E-W. Very basic in its facilities, the grass perimeter track was only 18 feet wide and initially there was no hangar accommodation. No formal airfield control was available, this being carried out by any personnel present at the time working from an airfield caravan. Fuel storage was limited to 24,000 gallons of aviation spirit and 1,000 gallons of MT petrol. No night landing or radio facilities were available.

Designated a satellite or relief landing ground in No. 12 Group, it was the Blenheim IFs of No. 23 Squadron that first touched down on May 31, 1940. They commenced night patrols although their aircraft had not yet been fitted with airborne radar. Despite this, the night of June 18/19 saw Flight Lieutenant Raymond Duke-Woolley shoot down a He III H-4 that ditched off shore at The Hood, Cley-next-the-Sea. Night operations continued until August 16 when the squadron moved back to nearby Wittering.

In July a detachment of Spitfire Is from No. 266 (Rhodesia) Squadron arrived to provide defence for Coventry but they left when the remainder of the squadron was posted from Wittering to Eastchurch on August 12.

The airfield played no positive part in the 1940 battle although fighter squadrons operating from Wittering used the 'drome from time to time. No. 266 Squadron did not return until October 3, 1941, having converted to Spitfire VBs at Martlesham Heath. Remaining for just under three weeks, they left for King's Cliffe on October 24. Their replacement was No. 133 (Eagle) Squadron with Hurricane IIBs. Arriving on September 18, they left for Fowlmere a month later.

The winter of 1941-42 saw very little activity due to the waterlogged surface but by April it had dried out sufficiently to allow No. 1529 Beam Approach Training Flight bring in their Miles Masters. However bad weather and servicing problems forced the flight to disband in November, once again leaving the airfield with no permanent unit.

Inevitably enemy aircraft force-landed in the UK during the war and in 1941 an enemy aircraft flight had been established at Duxford. By 1943 the RAF had quite a collection and No. 1426 (Enemy Aircraft Flight) moved to Collyweston on April 12 at which time it consisted of He IIIs, Ju 88s, Me 110s and Me 109s. The flight was to remain at the station for almost two years during which time further types arrived to be evaluated and demonstrated at other airfields. The CO was Flight Lieutenant Ernest Richard Lewendon who lost his life in October 1944 when the FW 190 he was test flying from another airfield burst into flames. The flight finally left Collyweston on May 8, 1944.

During February 1943, a detachment of Spitfire VBs and IXs came in from No. 288 (Army Co-operation) Squadron. Converting through various types of aircraft including Oxfords, Martinets and Beaufighters, they remained until August 1945, when the entire squadron moved to Hutton Cranswick.

No further use was made of Collyweston although American servicemen of the 57th Fighter Control Station moved in as the war ended with a vast array of radar and radio equipment. When they left after several months, the airfield became fully integrated with RAF Wittering and thus lost its identity.

No. 1426 (Enemy Aircraft) Flight possessed a wide variety of machines. ***Top:*** **FW 190 A5/US (Werk Nummer 2596) was landed by Unteroffizer Werner Orne of I./SKG10 at Manston on June 20, 1943 and the Ju 88 (140604) was captured at Vélizy-Villacoublay in September 1944.** ***Above:*** **This A-5 (3457) model, formerly of 3./KG30 landed in error at Lulsgate Bottom after a raid on Birkenhead in July 1941. It was later featured in the 1943 film** ***The Adventures of Tartu.***

Being situated barely a mile west of Wittering airfield, when the latter airfield was extended in August 1945 (see page 283), Collyweston was swallowed up at the western end of the long runway creating a safety overshoot zone.

COLTISHALL

One of the saddest days in the history of RAF Fighter Command came on July 21, 2004 when the Ministry of Defence announced that the Norfolk base of Coltishall would close on November 30, 2006.

Reputed to be the most active airfield in East Anglia, Coltishall is perhaps better known for its part as the main Battle of Britain base tasked with protecting that area and the North Sea. Just 50 feet above sea level and eight miles north-east of Norwich in Norfolk, it was originally called Scottow Aerodrome. However, with its expansion during 1939, it was renamed after the local village of Coltishall.

Initially the landing area was just grass with take-off distances of 1,600 yards NE-SW, 1,300 yards E-W and N-S and 930 yards SE-NW, but three Sommerfeld Track runways were laid down to give better all-weather serviceability. Four large 'C' type hangars were built with Blisters added later. A Type 2328/39 concrete watch office controlled airfield movements and the operation of the Drem runway lighting and radio facilities consisting of VHF/DF homing and ZZ homing. A massive 144,000 gallons of aviation fuel was indicative of the usage envisaged for Coltishall.

When completed the aerodrome was destined to become a bomber station but by May 1940 these intentions had changed and it became a sector station in No. 12 Group with accommodation suitable for two fighter squadrons. No. 66 Squadron flew the short

Although many other wartime airfields have come and gone, Coltishall was special as it had remained a fighter station throughout its life. The final ignomy pictured by Stuart Thurtle — the removal of the Jaguar gate guardian.

The Hurricane of Squadron Leader Robert Stanford-Tuck who led No. 257 Squadron at Coltishall from October 1940 to July 1941.

distance from Horsham St Faith with their Spitfire Is to become the first residents. Arriving on May 29, they flew North Sea patrols in addition to air cover over Dunkirk. Moving to Kenley on September 3, they had witnessed the return of the remnants of No. 242 (Canadian) Squadron to Coltishall after heavy fighting in France. The decision to place Squadron Leader Douglas Bader in command saw the unit rise from its low morale state to become one of Fighter Command's most famous squadrons. They left on October 26 returning briefly to Coltishall for a two-week stay on November 30.

The airfield was attacked by the Luftwaffe on August 19 causing damage to one of the hangars. With the battle being fought down south, No. 12 Group put forward the theory that two or more squadrons flying together as a wing would achieve more than a single squadron and the theory was put into practice during September. Units participating in the big wings over this period were the Coltishall squadrons, Nos. 66 and 242, together with No. 616 (South Yorkshire) Auxiliary Squadron with Spitfire Is (September 3-9); No. 74 'Tiger' with Spitfire IIAs (September 9-October 15); No. 72 (Basutoland) with Spitfire Is (October 20-30), and No. 64 with Spitfire Is (October 15-November 11).

On November 7, 1941, No. 257 Squadron departed, never to return.

The Luftwaffe attacked the airfield again on November 8 and a few days later No. 222 (Natal) Squadron arrived from Hornchurch on November 11. Flying Spitfire Is, they converted to the Mk IIAs and IIBs during their stay. Their main duty was 'Kipper' patrols, so named because they protected the North Sea fishing fleets from enemy attacks.

No. 257 (Burma) Squadron brought the first Hurricanes to Coltishall on December 16. Flying the Mk I, they swiftly converted to the Mk IIC and IIB. In March 1941 they began to take the offensive with fighter sweeps over the Continent, claiming several victories before leaving for Honiley on November 7, 1941.

Over 70 squadrons have served at Coltishall since it first opened in 1940; now, 65 years later, it fell to No. 6 Squadron to perform the final salute as the RAF Ensign was lowered for the last time.

With No. 222 Squadron having left for Matlask on June 6, a detachment from No. 151 Squadron arrived for night-fighting duties. Equipped with Defiants and some Hurricanes, they remained until April 30, 1943 when they converted to Mosquitos at Colerne.

The third Eagle squadron — No. 133 — reformed at Coltishall on July 31, 1941, with Hurricane IIBs but they moved to Duxford on August 15 around the same time that an air-sea rescue flight arrived with Lysanders and Walrus aircraft. On October 1, the flight was re-designated No. 278 Squadron and operated between Matlask and Coltishall until April 1944.

A detachment of Havocs from No. 93 Squadron moved in during December. Joined by Beaufighter IFs from No. 604 (County of Middlesex) Auxiliary Squadron, the former also flew Wellingtons and Bostons before disbanding on November 18, 1941 and being renamed No. 1458 (Turbinlite) Flight. The 604 Squadron detachment remained until August 12, 1942 when the entire squadron moved to Warmwell.

July 1941 also saw Beaufighter IIFs fly in when a section from No. 255 Squadron was posted to Coltishall. With the arrival of the rest of the squadron on September 20, a working up period began although bad weather restricted activities. The squadron departed for High Ercall on March 2, 1942.

With No. 257 Squadron leaving in November, 1941, their place was taken by the Whirlwinds of No.137 Squadron. They commenced sweeps and coastal patrols but left after just two weeks for Matlask. At the end of the year Spitfires returned when No. 152 (Hyderabad) Squadron came in from nearby Swanton Morley on December 17. Remaining over the Christmas period, they left for Eglinton on January 17, 1942.

With the New Year, several Beauforts from No. 42 Squadron were ordered down from Leuchars in an attempt to intercept three German capital ships which were about to leave Brest and travel by the quickest route to reach Germany. On February 12 the warships were detected entering the English Channel whereupon nine Beauforts loaded

Coltishall as it appeared at the end of the war, still a grass airfield but with extensions.

with torpedoes took off from Coltishall. However no hits were achieved and, despite attacks by other squadrons, the ships made it through the Channel practically unscathed.

The operation over, the Beauforts returned to Leuchars and Beaufighter IFs of No. 68 Squadron came in from High Ercall on March 8. They began a very hectic period flying 83 patrols over the East Coast in April alone. Sending a detachment to Peterhead, the squadron converted to the Mk VIF in February 1943. They finally left in February 1944.

Spitfire VBs came in when No. 154 Squadron arrived on March 12. Having reformed at Fowlmere, they moved back there on April 5 but Spitfires returned on January 17, 1943 with No. 118 Squadron. Tasked with escorting Beaufighters of Coastal Command, they moved to Westhampnett on August 15.

That month also saw a detachment from 151 Squadron return, this time with Mosquito VIs and, together with the rest of the squadron at Wittering, they began to maintain standing patrols over the North Sea. Typhoon IBs of No. 195 Squadron were also present at Coltishall that August, using the 'drome for just under a month. Their arrival had been preceded on August 4 by No. 611 (West Lancashire) Auxiliary Squadron. Flying Spitfire LF VBs, they were to alternate between Coltishall, Southend, Manston, Ford and Ayr, returning to Coltishall for the last time on February 19, 1944.

With so many movements, the contractors moved in during 1943 to lengthen the runways and strengthen them with additional Sommerfeld Track.

Polish squadrons dominated 1944 with the first arriving on April 28. No. 316 (Warsaw) Squadron flying Mustang IIIs carried out East Coast convoy flights, high-altitude patrols, and Coastal Command escort duties. Moving to West Malling on July 4, they returned to Coltishall on August 27 until October 24 and from May 16, 1945, till August 10. Other Polish squadrons at the airfield during the last two years of war were Nos. 315 (Deblin) from October-November 1944 and August-November 1945; No. 303 (Kosciuszko) from September 1944 to

Flying operations were suspended from October 1956 until May 1957 for the construction of the 2,500-yard runway.

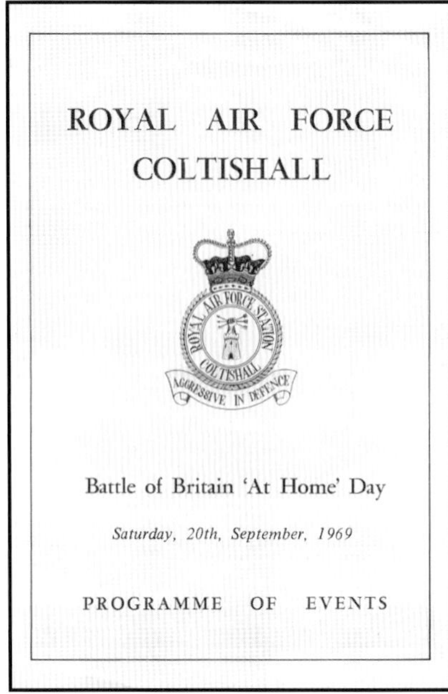

ROYAL AIR FORCE
COLTISHALL

ROYAL AIR FORCE STATION
COLTISHALL
AGGRESSIVE IN DEFENCE

Battle of Britain 'At Home' Day

Saturday, 20th, September, 1969

PROGRAMME OF EVENTS

RAF stations traditionally opened their doors in September each year for a Battle of Britain 'At Home' with a flying show and static displays. In the early years after the war, up to 80 bases would hold events but, as the years passed, this dwindled, although Coltishall was proud to have maintained the tradition throughout. The programme for 1969 lists a three-hour flying programme which included Lightnings, Hunters, Phantoms, Varsitys, a Hercules, Chipmunk, Andover, Sea Vixen, Buccaneer, Auster, Belfast, Argosy, VC10, Jet Provost, Victor, Sioux, Vulcan plus contributions from Belgium, Denmark and France. The jewel in the crown was that Coltishall had hosted the RAF's Historic Aircraft Flight. This is Spitfire (PM631) photographed in 1969, the year the name was changed to The Battle of Britain Memorial Flight. The unit was based at Coltishall from 1963 to 1973.

After the Ministry of Defence closed Coltishall in 2006, the facilities were offered to other government departments and in January 2007 the Home Office expressed interest in using the station for a new immigrant detention facility. In the end it was announced that part of the domestic site containing the H-Blocks, including the Airmen's Mess and Social Club, were to be converted into a Category C prison (one level above an open prison), primarily to hold sex offenders. HMP Bure opened in November 2009.

August 1945; No. 307 (Lwow) May-August 1945; No. 309 (Ziemia Czerwienska) August-October 1945); No. 306 (Torun) August-October 1945, and No. 318 (Danzig) in August 1946.

Further Spitfire VIs from No. 234 (Madras Presidency) Squadron arrived on January 28, 1944, to carry out sweeps over the Continent. They joined No. 85 Group of the Second Tactical Air Force and left for Bolt Head on March 18. A Czech squadron, No. 312, with Spitfire HF IXs, flew in from Lympne on July 11, leaving for North Weald on August 27.

Despite being too far away to play a significant part in the D-Day landings, the pace of movements at Coltishall continued. No. 229 Squadron arrived on July 1 with Spitfire IXs undertaking armed reconnaissance missions as well as providing cover for No. 100 Group operations before moving to Manston on September 25. That same month the sound of the Tempest Vs of No. 274 Squadron was heard briefly although they moved to France after a week or so. Nos. 602 (City of Glasgow) and 603 (City of Edinburgh) Auxiliary Squadrons came in with various marks of Spitfires in April 1945.

The airfield became a major peacetime base in Fighter Command, hosting the Battle of Britain Memorial Flight for a time and becoming the main Jaguar base until being handed over to Defence Estates for disposal in November 2009. The 600-acre airfield and all the buildings were passed to the Ministry of Justice which then sold it on to Norfolk District Council for £4 million while North Norfolk District Council gave approval for the

Coltishall in 2013. Out of bounds — the Officers' Mess built in the traditional style of the 'Expansion Period' aerodromes.

Quarters still bearing the wartime dark earth and olive drab make-up.

The heart of the camp — now sealed off with a Home Office mesh fence.

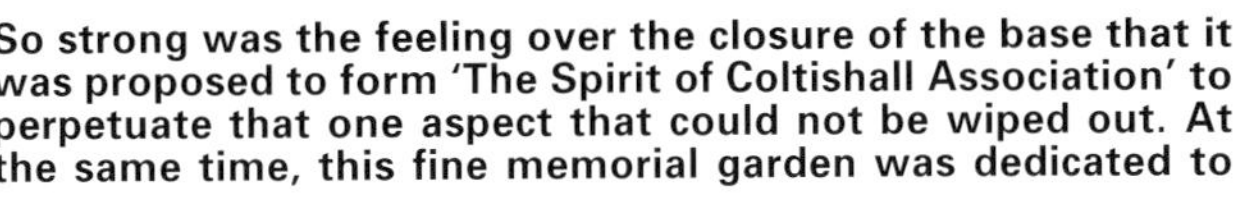

So strong was the feeling over the closure of the base that it was proposed to form 'The Spirit of Coltishall Association' to perpetuate that one aspect that could not be wiped out. At the same time, this fine memorial garden was dedicated to commemorate 'the only Battle of Britain station to have remained a fighter station throughout its 66-year history and the personnel who served here, many of whom made the ultimate sacrifice'.

DIGBY

RAF Digby became a major Canadian fighter base which began with the arrival of the Winnipeg Bears of No. 402 Squadron in December 1940. With aircrews at the ready, these two pilots were pictured scrambling to their machines on April 21, 1941.

Dating back to when the Royal Naval Air Service was based there during the First World War, a site near the village of Scopwick in Lincolnshire was used between the wars by various flying schools until it was earmarked in 1935 for expansion. The aerodrome was situated six miles north of Sleaford and 115 feet above sea level and it was allocated satellites at Wellingore and Coleby Grange.

Its grass landing area measured 1,750 yards NE-SW; 1,350 yards SE-NW; 1,200 yards N-S, and 1,050 from E-W. The perimeter track 18 feet wide led to two 'C' type and six Over Blister hangars. An RAF Type 2 Flying Control, a Macdonald night landing system, VHF homing and a ZZ approach aid were in use by the time No. 46 Squadron brought their Gauntlets in on November 15, 1937. By March 1939 they had converted to Hurricane Is and moved to Acklington but January 1940 saw them back at Digby until they moved to Scapa Flow in May for embarkation for Norway on HMS *Glorious*.

No. 504 (County of Nottingham) Auxiliary Squadron were another unit to be based at Digby just prior to the war. Equipped with Hinds, Gauntlets and Hurricane Is, they flew in on August 27, 1939, and began a working up period prior to taking their Hurricanes to Debden on October 9. No. 73 Squadron came in from Debden with Gladiators on November 1937 and, after re-equipping with Hurricane Is, they flew to Le Havre-Octeville on September 9, 1939.

No. 229 Squadron reformed at Digby on October 6, 1939, equipped with Blenheim IFs with detachments at Biggin Hill and Kenley, until they exchanged their aircraft for Hurricanes and moved to Wittering on June 26, 1940. No. 611 (West Lancashire) Auxiliary Squadron had also arrived that October with Spitfires but moved to Southend in December.

No. 222 (Natal) Squadron, another Spitfire unit, arrived on May 10 from Duxford but they only stayed for 13 days. Two days before they left, No. 111 Squadron came from Northolt with Hurricanes. They, too, only remained for nine days until returning to North Weald on May 30.

More short stays followed with No. 79 (Madras Presidency) in from Biggin Hill on May 27 and out on June 5. No. 56 (Punjab) Squadron with Hurricane Is came on May 31 and left on June 5 for North Weald. They were followed by No. 29 Squadron. Arriving on June 27 with Blenheim IFs, they commenced night patrols without the aid of airborne radar, moving to Wellingore a month later.

After the bitter fighting over France and at Dunkirk, No. 151 Squadron moved to Digby for a rest period on September 1. Flying Hurricane Is, they sent a detachment to Wittering before leaving for Bramcote on November 28.

The second Canadian squadron to form in Britain did so at Digby on December 11, 1940. With personnel drawn from Nos. 110 and 112 Squadrons, RCAF, the new unit became No. 2 Squadron, RCAF. A day later it was renumbered No. 402 (Winnipeg Bear) Squadron and equipped with Hurricane Is which arrived on March 1, 1941. They began an intensive working up period, progressing through the Mk IIA and IIB, they left for Martlesham Heath on June 23.

Digby soon became a major base for the creation of more Canadian squadrons. Nos. 409 (Nighthawk) and 411 (Grizzly Bear) formed on June 16, 1941, the former with Defiant Is and the latter with Spitfire Is, followed at the end of the month by No. 412 (Falcon) with Spitfire IIAs. All the squadrons began a working up period before No. 409 moved out to Coleby Grange on July 26; No. 412 for Wellingore on October 20, and No. 411, having converted to Spitfire IIAs and VBs, for Hornchurch on November 19.

As the Canadians left, the Americans of No. 121 (Eagle) Squadron brought their Hurricane Is and IIBs in from Kirton-in-Lindsey on September 28, returning there five days later.

It was now the turn of No. 92 (East India) Squadron to be posted in with their Spitfire VBs on October 20. They left on February 12, 1942, en route for the Middle East. Before they left, No. 288 Squadron was

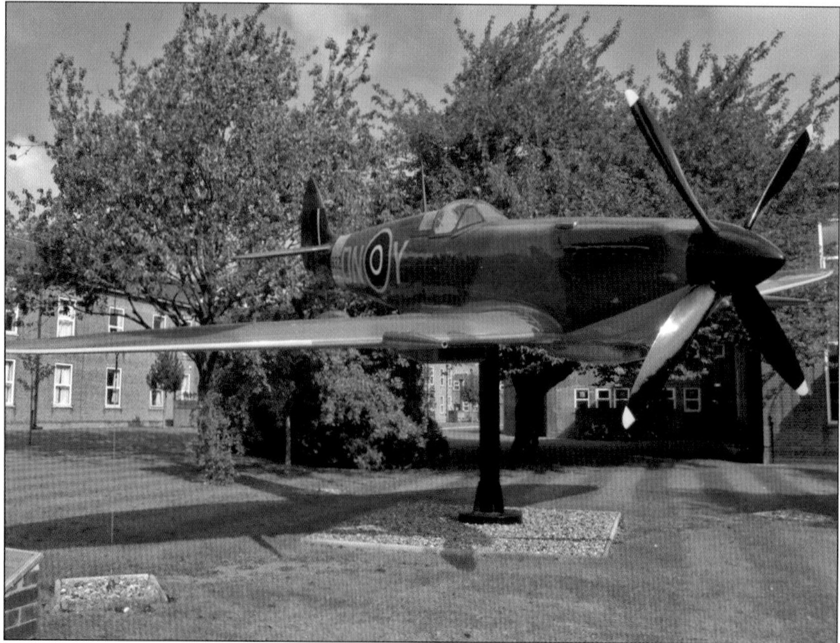

Then it was Hurricanes . . . now it is a replica Spitfire which stands guardian to the station.

Duxford, Coltishall, Wittering, Church Fenton, Kirton-in-Lindsey and Digby were all sector stations in No. 12 Group. It is therefore very fitting that its wartime Sector Operations Block has been restored as a museum 'to pay tribute to all those who served and fought during the Second World War'. The idea for the project began in April 1995 and a dedicated team of volunteers worked for two years to restore the block to its former glory. Contemporary furniture and communications equipment was 'liberated' from other RAF bases. On September 3, 1939, AC2 Charles Mayhew was on duty in the Traffic and Receiving Room of the Operations Room at Digby. Shortly after 1100 hours, he received a signal over the No. 12 Group teleprinter circuit and brought it to the attention of the Duty Fighter Controller. He, in turn, briefed the operations staff and broadcast the information to the station. 'War has broken out with Germany'. The signal was returned to Charles who was then expected to file the signal or destroy it. Instead, he took one of the copies and held onto it for the next 58 years. When the RAF Digby Operations Room was opened in May 1997, Charles returned to present the museum with the unique document.

formed at Digby on November 18, 1941 from a No. 12 Group Anti-Aircraft Co-Operation Flight. Equipped with a Blenheim IV, Lysander II and III, Hudson III, Hurricane I and a Defiant I with detachments at Church Fenton and Duxford, they remained until moving to Wellingore on December 6, 1942.

Spitfire VBs returned when No. 609 (West Riding) Auxiliary Squadron arrived on November 19, 1941 to carry out intensive fighter sweeps and bomber escorts. They moved to Duxford on March 30, 1942. Their replacement, No. 601 (County of London) Auxiliary Squadron, arrived on March 25 also with Spitfire VBs, before leaving on April 10 en route to Egypt. December saw No. 198 Squadron formed at Digby with Typhoons but they moved out to Ouston in January 1943.

More brief movements followed. No. 167 (Gold Coast) Squadron flying Spitfire VCs came in on May 13 and departed on May 18, and No. 350 (Belgian) Squadron arrived on August 25 with Spitfire VCs until going to

In March 2005 Digby was handed over to Defence Intelligence and it now forms part of the Joint Service Signals Organisation. Its current role is described as 'supporting both strategic decision makers at the highest level and front line on a 24-hour basis'.

Between the wars, both civil and military aerodromes had a circle marked out in chalk. Measuring from 100-150ft in diameter, landing circles were the symbol used to indicate the landing area on grass airfields before the advent of runways.

West Malling on September 7. They returned to Digby on September 19 before moving south again to Hawkinge on October 1.

With the forming of the Digby Canadian Wing, the squadrons involved were No. 416 (City of Oshawa) from June to August 1943 and October 1943 to February 1944; No. 438 (Wild Cat) November-December 1943; and No. 402 (Winnipeg Bear) March-August 1943 and January-February 1944.

January 1943 also saw the return of No. 288 Squadron having added a Spitfire VB and IX to their complement. Leaving for Coleby Grange on November 9, they returned on the 25th remaining until January 12, 1944, now also with an Oxford and Martinet.

Three more Canadian squadrons formed at Digby in February 1944: No. 441 (Silver Fox), No. 442 (Caribou), and No. 443 (Hornet). April saw No. 527 arrive from Snailwell. They carried out radar calibration duties before leaving for Watton in November 1945. Another radar calibration unit — No. 528 Squadron — joined them in May although they disbanded at Digby in September.

With the end of the war in sight Digby was prepared for its peacetime role. It became a training unit with Nos. 1 and 2 Initial Training Schools and No. 19 Flying Training School as part of the RAF College at Cranwell. This carried on until 1953 when the base became a major signals station.

We have seen a harmonisation stop-butt earlier at Church Fenton. Unfortunately most have now been removed, the one at Digby being located on the north-eastern perimeter.

Google

DUXFORD

Duxford . . . from 1939 . . . to 1954. In May 1939 it was the destination of the world's fastest fighter; in October 1954 Air Marshal Sir Dermot Boyle, the AOC of Fighter Command, escorts Emperor Haile Selassie on an inspection of No. 64 Squadron's Meteors.

Dating back to March 1918, Duxford was built by P & W Anderson Ltd of Aberdeen with a labour force including German prisoners of war. Used for training and also host to various United States Air Service units, it was situated eight miles south of Cambridge and 124 feet above sea level, the dimensions of the grass landing area were N-S 1,000 yards, NE-SW 1,500 yards, E-W 1,400 yards and SE-NW 1,500 yards. This was encompassed by an 18-foot asphalt and concrete perimeter track. The hangar accommodation stood at three sheds, four Over Blister and four Extra Over Blister. Night landing facilities were a McDonald Flare Path supplemented by goose flares and floodlights with radio facilities of DF (Direction Finding) and ZZ Homing. Two satellites or Relief Landing Grounds were allocated at Fowlmere and Snailwell.

During the inter-war period the airfield was home to many fighter squadrons and in

And in 1968 it enjoyed a brief interlude when the pseudo German Air Force moved in for the filming of *Battle of Britain*.

The first squadron to be equipped with the new Supermarine fighter was No. 19. The Vickers-Supermarine test pilot Jeffrey Quill flew in the first Spitfire I (K9789) to Duxford on August 4, 1938.

Today Duxford provides pleasure flights in veteran aircraft and gives air experience to young tyros.

1938 No. 19 made history when they became the first squadron to convert to the Spitfire. Along with Nos. 66 and 611 (West Lancashire) Auxiliary Squadrons, Duxford became operational as a sector station in Sector 'G' of No. 12 Group.

With the departure of the auxiliaries on October 4, 1939, No. 222 (Natal) Squadron reformed at the airfield flying Blenheim IFs but by March 1940 they had converted to Spitfires and left for Digby. No. 19 Squadron moved to Hornchurch to help provide air cover for the Dunkirk evacuation and was to alternate between Duxford, Fowlmere and Hornchurch during the Battle of Britain.

The first Czech squadron was formed up at Duxford on July 10 with Hurricanes. No. 310 (Czech) Squadron was led by a British commanding officer, Squadron Leader George Blackwood who regarded his pilots as 'very keen and eager to have a crack'. They were to remain at the airfield until June 26, 1941.

Another Hurricane squadron, No. 242 (Canadian) led by Douglas Bader, came to Duxford from Coltishall on October 26, 1940. Manned by Canadians, Bader's job at Coltishall had been to raise the morale of the squadron as it had suffered severe losses whilst in France. It was during a previous sortie in September when his squadron claimed 12 victories that he became convinced that the theory of operating a 'Big Wing' comprising several squadrons should be put into practice. He suggested to Air Chief-Marshal Leigh-Mallory that had he more aircraft,

Another first at Duxford was the formation there of the first squadron made up of refugee pilots from Czechoslovakia. The date was July 10, 1940 — the day when the Battle of Britain was officially deemed to have begun.

And in came the Canadians! No. 242 was led by Squadron Leader Douglas Bader, seen here outside the Officers' Mess with Pilot Officer William McKnight, left, and Flight Lieutenant George Bale.

Time marches on. Today, although the old mess is part of the Imperial War Museum site, the building is fenced off on the north side of the A505. Sean Rehling kindly unlocked the gate for us.

more of the enemy would have been shot down. An exaggerated claim later added further impetus to the idea. However the wing was later expanded to five squadrons with the addition of No. 302 (Poznan) Polish Squadron and the return of No. 611 (West Lancashire) Auxiliary Squadron. By the end of the battle the wing claimed to have shot down 152 enemy aircraft at a cost of 30 pilots and aircraft.

Being that much further north, Duxford escaped serious enemy attacks though the odd isolated raider did drop bombs on the satellite at Fowlmere. November 1940 saw Bader take No. 242 Squadron back to Coltishall whilst the following month saw the Air Fighting Development Unit move in from Northolt, this being an experimental unit testing captured enemy aircraft against RAF machines.

No. 19 Squadron ended its long stay by moving to Matlask on August 16, 1941 with No. 310 having moved to Martlesham Heath on July 20. Six days later No. 56 (Punjab) Squadron brought their Hurricane IIBs in from the same airfield. They converted to the Typhoon IA before leaving for Snailwell six months later.

No. 601 (County of London) Auxiliary Squadron arrived on August 16 bringing the

From 1942 to 1945 Duxford became Station 357 of the USAAF. This early post-war shot shows the Pierced Steel Planking runway which was laid down to support heavier aircraft when the 78th Fighter Group moved in with P-47 Thunderbolts.

The aerodrome was closed to flying between October 1949 and July 1951 for the construction of a 6,000 ft concrete runway to cater for the jet era — Meteors, Javelins and Hunters — but by 1960 Duxford became surplus to requirements . . . and to Fighter Command.

Never targeted by the Luftwaffe, it was left to Spitfire Productions to cause the greatest damage when one of the hangars dating from the First World War was blown up. Then the building of the M11 motorway removed the southern end of the airfield.

unfamiliar sound of the American Airacobra to Duxford. They were the only RAF squadron to be equipped with the type which, in the event, proved troublesome and not easy to fly. However they persevered until moving to Acaster Malbis on January 6, 1942, and re-equipping with the Spitfire VB.

In 1942, Duxford was allocated to the United States Army Air Force becoming Station 357 and home to the 78th Fighter Group, the first personnel arriving on April 13, 1943. Equipped with the P-47 Thunderbolt, they exchanged them for the P-51 Merlin-powered Mustang later in 1944. Due to the size and weight of the P-47, the grass landing area was extended and reinforced with Pierced Steel Planking on the NE-SW axis. Remaining at Duxford until the end of the war, the unit was unique in that it won two Distinguished Unit Citations for operations other than bomber escort. This was in addition to claiming nearly 1,400 enemy aircraft destroyed in the air and on the ground for the loss of 264 of their own.

Officially handed back to the RAF on December 1, 1945, it became a major peacetime base finally closing on August 1, 1961. It was used for flying and ground sequences in the film *Battle of Britain* and is now one of Europe's foremost aviation museums housing part of the collection of the Imperial War Museum.

FOWLMERE

One could say that Fowlmere has had four lives: first as a training base in the First World War (of which nothing remains); then as a Fighter Command satellite, followed by a period under the United States Army Air Force, and now as a private airfield.

Fowlmere, three and a half miles north-east of Royston in Cambridgeshire, was established along with Duxford as a First World War training station for the rapidly expanding air force. It was opened as No. 31 Depot Training Station in 1918 but, whereas Duxford was retained after the war, the extensive facilities built at Fowlmere were deemed surplus to requirements. The large Belfast hangars that had only just been erected were pulled down and the site returned to agriculture.

When the second conflict approached, a new site, close to the original, was requisitioned on land belonging to Manor Farm. It was a large grass airfield and just 100 feet above sea level. The contractors cleared hedges and trees, a T2 and seven Blister hangars being erected with basic Nissen hut accommodation for personnel.

Categorised as a satellite to nearby Duxford, VHF radio gave daylight control but no night landing facilities were available.

The first unit to arrive was No. 19 Squadron that brought their Spitfire IBs in from the parent airfield on June 25, 1940. Eight days later they returned to Duxford before coming back to Fowlmere on July 24. Sending a detachment to Eastchurch, they converted to the Spitfire IIA before returning to the parent station on November 1 and becoming part of the Duxford Spitfire Wing.

A brief visit by the Defiants of No. 264 (Madras Presidency) Squadron on July 3 for a working up period saw them depart to Kirton-in-Lindsey on July 23, no permanent

The large First World War technical site lay here but all was swept away without a trace in the 1920s.

Treble One Squadron with Spitfire VBs arrived on September 27 as they prepared to go overseas, leaving for North Africa on October 20. This period also saw the airfield enter a period of reconstruction.

During this time No. 167 Squadron Spitfire VCs arrived on March 5, 1943 together with No. 411 (Grizzly Bear) Canadian Squadron, staying for eight and seven days respectively. The last RAF squadron to use Fowlmere was No. 2 with Mustangs, arriving on March 19 and leaving on April 27 for Sawbridgeworth.

In April the airfield was handed over to the United States Army Air force which quickly laid down two runways of 1,400 and 1,600 yards, surfaced with Pierced Steel Planking. Station 378 then came under command of the 66th Fighter Wing of the Eighth Air Force, and the P-51B Mustangs of the 339th Fighter Group were operational by May. They remained at Fowlmere for just over a year during which time they claimed over 100 enemy aircraft destroyed on the ground together with the award of a Distinguished Unit Citation for the destruction of 58 enemy aircraft during escort missions. After they left Fowlmere in October 1945, the airfield saw no further flying units before it was sold in 1957 and returned to agriculture.

Duxford having been retained after 1918, with the storm clouds brewing of a new war, Fowlmere was revived as its satellite. The rather primitive facilities were centred around Manor Farm. Here, the farm buildings with Dutch barn on the left forms a backdrop to the classic shot of a No. 19 Squadron machine.

squadrons being based at Fowlmere during August and September. A raid that month on the 22nd saw the landing area cratered but this was the only time the airfield was attacked. Repairs were soon in hand and by early 1941 the airfield was operational again.

No. 154 reformed at Fowlmere on November 17, 1941. They were equipped with Spitfire IIAs a week later and were operational by February 1942. Converting through the Mk IIBs, VAs and VCs, they carried out East Coast patrols before moving to Coltishall on March 12, 1942. Leaving a detachment at Fowlmere, the squadron returned on April 5 for a month before moving to Church Stanton.

February 24, 1943, saw Austers of No. 655 (Army Co-Op) Squadron arrive to carry out local exercises with army units for two weeks and later in July No. 174 (Mauritius) Squadron Hurricane IIBs spent three days at Fowlmere.

In 1979 when we took this comparison the scene had changed little over the previous 40 years . . . but now look at the difference another 30 years makes!

Pilot Officer Wallace Cunningham, Sub Lieutenant Arthur Blake and Flying Officer Francis Brinsden relax outside the crew rooms.

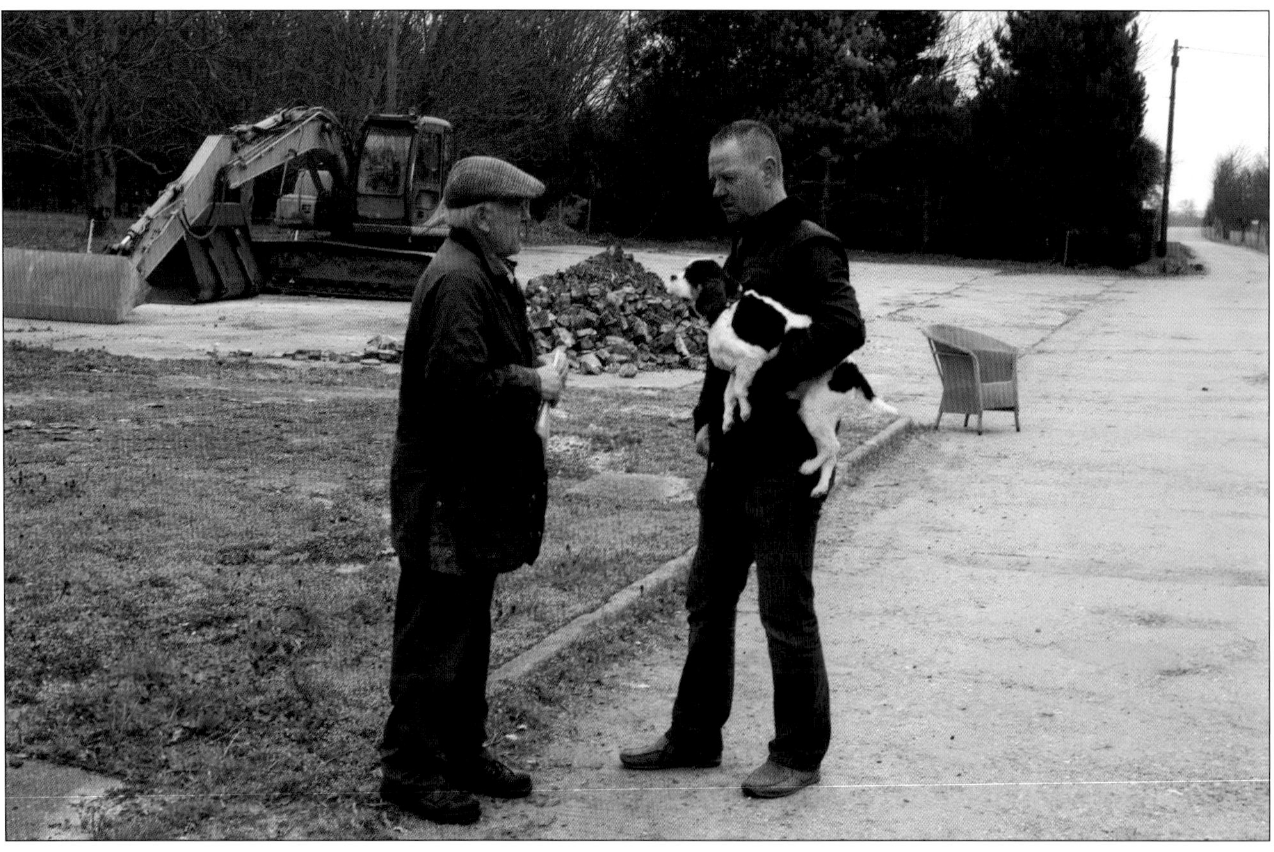

The Nissen huts disappeared in the 1960s and the Dutch barn, which served the station as a motor transport garage, was unfortunately blown down in the storm of 1991. However, we could not resist returning again to Fowlmere with our genuine Air Ministry Lloyd-Loom chair (ex-Kenley, see page 175) to complete the comparison. Martin Sheldrick, who is steeped in the wartime history of his farm, takes time out to reminisce on past events with Rob Green and Oliver.

No. 19 Squadron dated back to the First World War and, although disbanded in 1919, it was reformed in 1923 at Duxford. It was stationed there throughout the inter-war years until moving to Horsham St Faith in April 1940 but it was returned to Duxford the following month, alternating between there and Fowlmere. *Left:* Here the CO, Squadron Leader Brian Lane, is pictured third from left with his pilots in the crew room. *Right:* The squadron dining room was in the second Nissen hut.

The brick barn opposite the Dutch barn was used as the mess hall and it was there that one of the aircraftmen, Robert Hoften, painted this mural on the end wall using aircraft dope. As it was fading, Martin had it photographed for posterity in 1979. Then, in July 1988, an elderly gentleman drove up and walked into the barn where Martin was working. He said: 'I've come to see if my painting is still on the wall', and Robert was only too pleased to accept Martin's request to restore the painting.

The Spitfires of No. 19 Squadron (P7420 seen here being refuelled) used the grass to take off but when the heavier American fighters arrived in April 1943, two runways reinforced with PSP matting were laid down. The photo below dating from 1947.

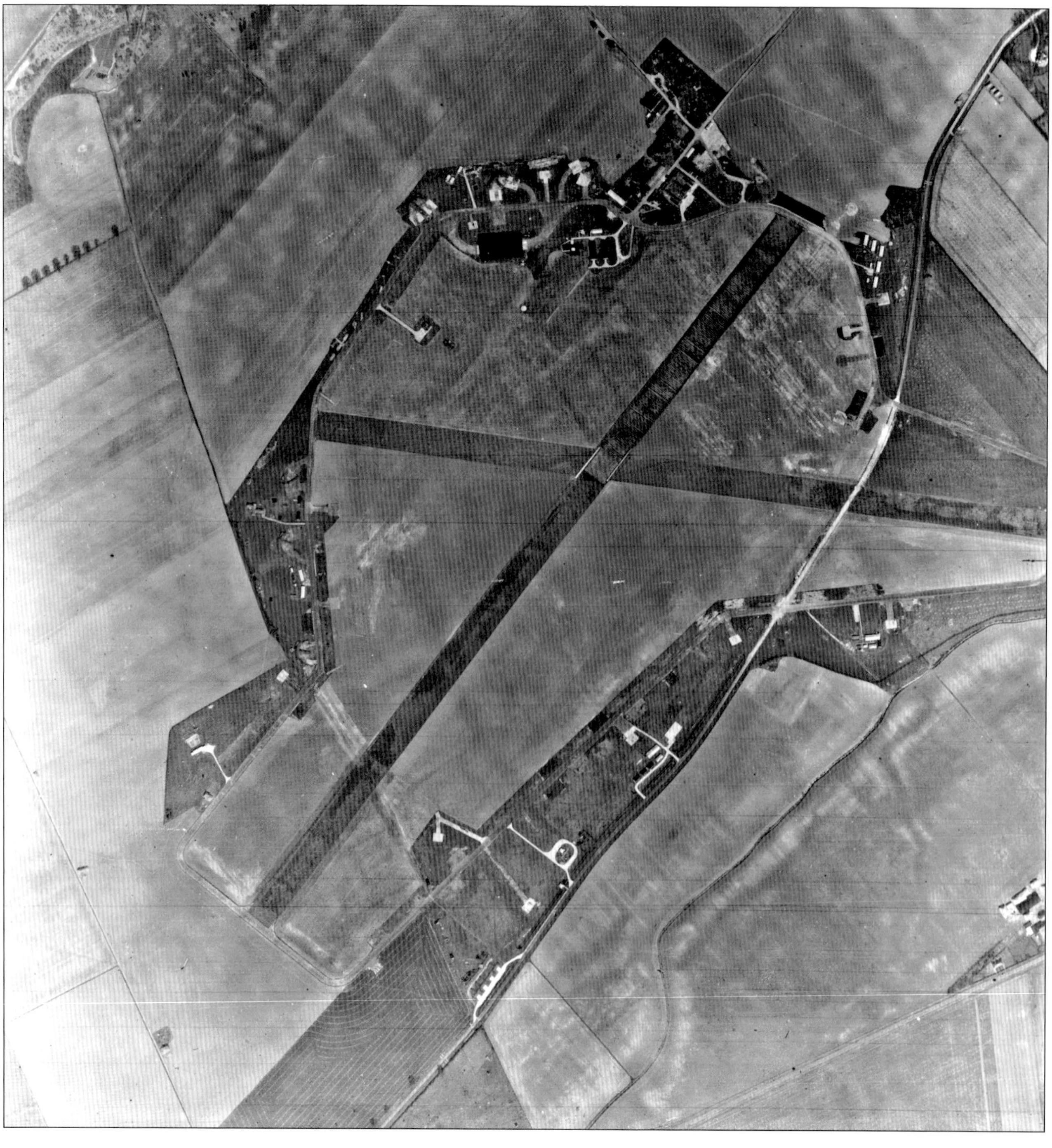

And the fourth phase in the aviation history of Fowlmere began in 1987 when Martin had the idea of preparing two grass strips (not on the US alignment) to create a private airfield for light aircraft, using the re-clad wartime hangar.

This memorial remembers the tenure of the fighter units of the US Eighth Air Force yet nothing marks the use of Fowlmere by the RAF.

HIBALDSTOW

Hibaldstow had a relatively short life as a Fighter Command base, the first unit to be posted there being No. 253 Squadron with Hurricane Mk IIB night fighters. The nearest aircraft is SW-S, a presentation aircraft named Samasthans II.

As an operational satellite to Kirton-in-Lindsey, Hibaldstow was first intended to become a bomber base. It was located three miles south-west of Brigg in Lincolnshire and lay just 25 feet above sea level. The grass landing area permitted take-off distances of 1,540 yards from E-W, 1,316 yards from SE-NW and 1,260 yards N-S, but when the runways were laid they measured respectively 1,575 yards, 1,165 yards and 1,200 yards, all the standard 50 yards wide. The 50-foot perimeter track linked 12 Blister hangars and a Type 2 Flying Control. Drem runway lighting was installed plus VHF radio communications. Completed in 1941, it received a change of role when it was assigned to No. 12 Group, Fighter Command.

No. 255 was the first squadron to use Hibaldstow when its Defiant Is and Hurricane Is came in from the parent station on May 15, but serviceability problems saw the Defiants exchanged for Beaufighter IIFs during July. Sending a detachment to Coltishall, the entire squadron moved there on September 20.

The next day saw the arrival of No. 253 Squadron with Hurricane IIBs. Working through the IIA and IIC marks, their first night success came on April 29-30 when Warrant Officer Y. Mahe shot down a Ju88D-1. In June the squadron was joined in the night-fighting role by No. 1459 (Turbinlite) Flight which was commanded for six months by Squadron Leader James Nicolson, the only pilot to be awarded the Victoria Cross during the Battle of Britain. Flying Havocs and Bostons in the searchlight role, they were joined by another Turbinlite unit, No. 1453, on September 11, 1942. Both gained squadron status, No. 1459 becoming No. 538 Squadron and No. 1453 becoming No. 532, but both were disbanded along with all the other Turbinlite units on January 25, 1943.

Meanwhile, No. 253 Squadron alternated between Hibaldstow and Friston until November 13, 1942, when they left for Maison Blanche in North Africa. When they departed the airfield was allocated to No. 53 OTU based at Kirton. Spitfires, Miles Masters and Magisters were frequent visitors but no further use was made of Hibaldstow for fighter operations.

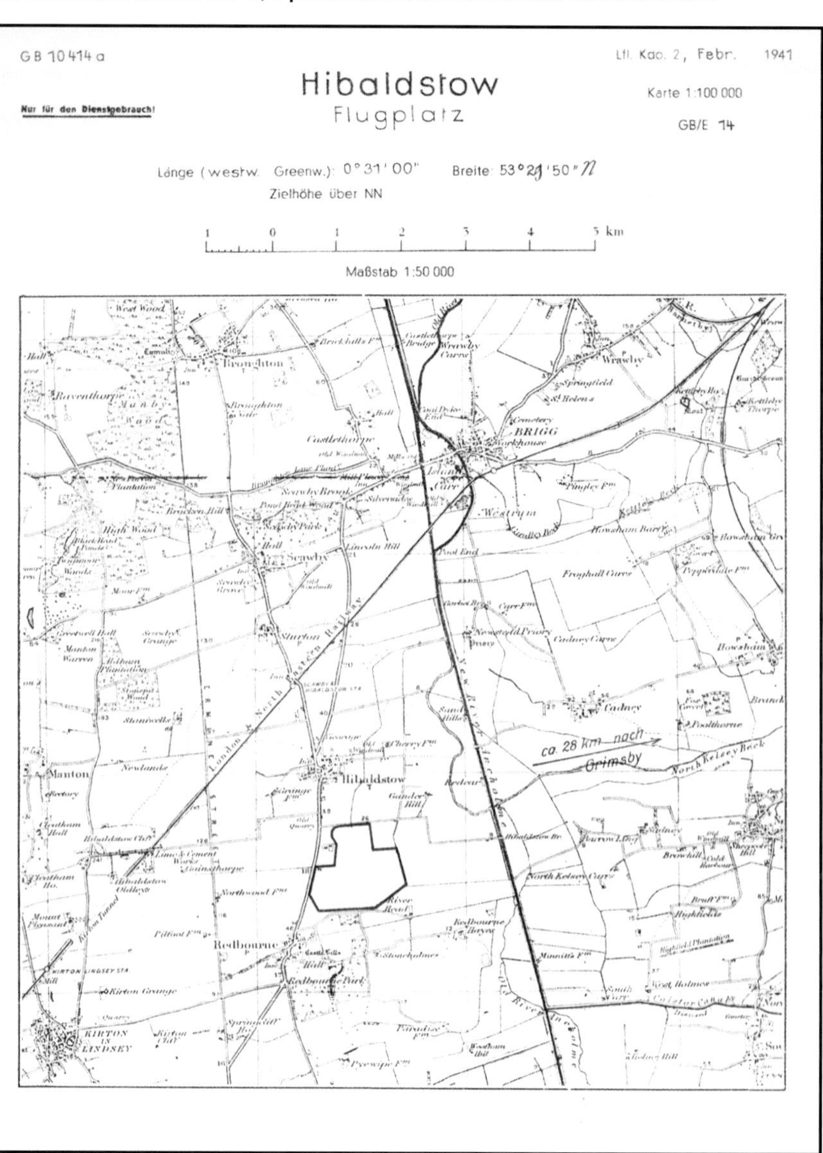

The most bizarre incident to occur at Hibaldstow — and unique throughout all the stations of Fighter Command — was when Flight Lieutenant Neill Cox *(left)* took a WAAF for a joy ride . . . sitting on the tail of his Spitfire! LACW Margaret Horton (pictured *right* after the flight) was a member of B Flight of No. 53 Operational Training Unit. On February 14, 1945 there was a gusty wind so the call went out for 'Tails', meaning that a mechanic was required to sit on the tail of the Spitfire while it taxied out to take off to stop the risk of the wind flipping it onto its nose. Reaching the end of the runway, the pilot would normally waggle the elevator as a signal to the mechanic to get off but Margaret misread Cox's hand-signal and stayed put. With the weight on his tail, Cox had great difficulty getting the Spitfire airborne but the WAAF had been spotted and he was was immediately ordered to land. Margaret held on for dear life throughout the short flight and unbelievably survived the ordeal with just a bruised arm.

Back on the ground, the pilot was still completely unaware of what had caused his aircraft to misbehave! When questioned, Margaret protested that she had only been following orders but she was later fined for the loss of her beret! She died in 1982. Cox had seen earlier service in the Mediterranean and ended the war with two DFCs. He died in July 2011. Amazingly the actual aircraft he had used that day still survives. Spitfire AB910 flew 143 operational missions, destroying a Dornier 217 and supporting operations over Normandy before being sent to Hibaldstow. After the war, she was used for air racing and was displayed by the Supermarine test pilot Jeffrey Quill before being donated by Vickers-Armstrong to the Battle of Britain Memorial Flight in 1965.

So, bearing in mind Margaret's solo flight without a parachute, it is fitting that Hibaldstow now hosts the Skydivers of Target Skysports!

By 1947 Hibaldstow had reverted to private ownership. Most of the buildings were demolished and the land used for farming.

The parachuting centre dates back to the 1960s when several skydiving clubs came together, moving to Hibaldsow in 1992.

HUTTON CRANSWICK

Hutton Cranswick could almost be considered an all-Polish aerodrome for, of their 15 squadrons formed in Britain, six of their fighter units were based there although all had departed by the time the squadrons came under Polish command in April 1944.

Lying at 107 feet above sea level, alongside the A164 Watton Road to the south of Driffield in Yorkshire, Hutton Cranswick opened in January 1942 as part of No. 12 Group. Three concrete runways were laid down with the main E-W being 1,650 yards and the two intersecting 1,320 yards and 1,110 respectively. A 50-foot perimeter track and two T2 hangars were built with accommodation for both airmen and airwomen together with a Type 2 watch office for airfield control.

The first unit to arrive was No. 610 (County of Chester) Auxiliary Squadron on January 14, 1942. Bringing their Spitfire VBs in from Leconfield, they commenced shipping patrols before moving to Ludham on August 21. Meanwhile, No. 19 Squadron, also equipped with Spitfire VBs, arrived on April 4 leaving for Perranporth a month later.

On May 7, No. 308 (Krakow) Polish Squadron arrived to begin the first of several postings. Bringing their Spitfire IIAs up from Exeter, they left for Redhill on July 1, returning six days later until July 30. The same day another Polish squadron, No. 316 (Warsaw), arrived from Heston with Spitfire VBs. Convoy patrols were carried out but with very little action the squadron moved south to Northolt on March 12, 1943.

On November 19, 1942, the Poles were joined by the Typhoon IBs of No. 195 Squadron. Having been formed at Duxford four days earlier, they began a lengthy working-up period before moving to Woodvale on February 12, 1943.

Another Polish squadron came in with Spitfire IXs on March 12, 1943. No. 306 (Torun) Squadron, although sent to Hutton Cranswick to rest, flew the occasional operation until it moved to Catterick on May 30. They had been joined by another Polish squadron, No. 302 (Poznan), on April 17. Flying Spitfire VBs, they moved to Heston on June 1 to be replaced by yet another Polish unit, No. 315 (Deblin). They flew up from Northolt on June 2 for a month before leaving for Ballyhalbert on July 6.

The last of the Polish squadrons to be based at Hutton Cranswick was No. 308 (Krakow) which returned on July 5, 1943. Moving to Friston on September 7, they came back on the 13th until transferring to Heston on September 21. Converting to the Spitfire IX, they returned again from December 2-18 when they flew south to Northolt.

Two Mustang squadrons now took up station when Nos. 168 and 170 arrived on September 20, 1943. Part of Army Co-operation Command, No. 168 commenced attacks on shipping and coastal targets whilst No. 170 was a tactical reconnaissance unit. Both squadrons moved to Huggate over October 10-11.

The formation of No. 291 Squadron at the airfield on December 1, 1943, saw Hutton take on an additional role to that of offensive operations. Formed from Nos. 1613, 1629 and 1634 Flights with Henleys, Martinets, Hurricanes and Vengeance aircraft, its main task was to provide target-towing facilities for anti-aircraft units situated along the East Coast. Sending detachments to Southend, Eastchurch, Ouston, Acklington and Eshott, they remained at Hutton Cranswick until June 26, 1945. Another specialised unit to arrive was a detachment of No. 278 (ASR) Squadron with Lysanders, Walrus and Ansons. It remained until April 1944 when it moved to Bradwell Bay.

The Spitfire VIs of No. 234 (Madras Presidency) Squadron were posted in on October 15, 1943. Remaining until December 31, they exchanged places with No. 26 Squadron that had arrived two days earlier with Mustang Is. Sending a detachment to Ballyhalbert, they carried out fighter reconnaissance duties leaving for Scorton on February 12, 1944.

The New Year brought a change in direction for the airfield as it became No. 16 Armament Practice Camp with squadrons arriving to perfect their gunnery techniques: No. 91 (Nigeria) with Spitfire XIIs (February 8-20); No. 26 with Spitfire VAs (April 26-29); No. 310 (Czech) with Spitfire LF IXs (February 21-25); No.403 (Wolf) Canadian with Spitfire IXBs (February 24-29); No. 443 (Hornet) Canadian with Spitfire IXBs (March 27-April 8); No. 441 (Silver Fox) Canadian with Spitfire IXBs (March 18-April 1); No. 442 (Caribou) Canadian with Spitfire IXBs (April 25-May 1), and No. 439 (Westmount) Canadian with Typhoon IAs (May 11-20).

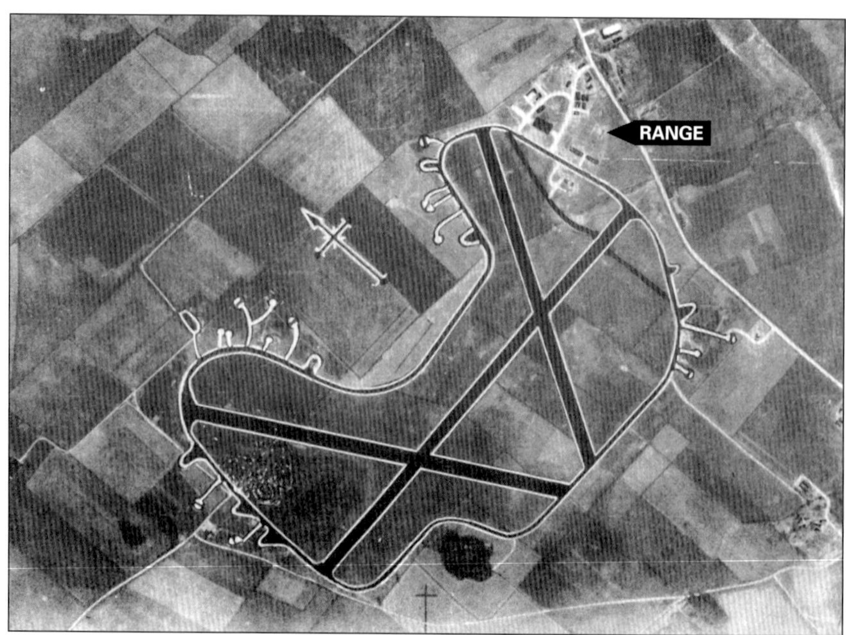

The huge mound of earth forming the stop-butt to the machine gun range was located on the eastern side although no trace of it remains today as the former technical site has since expanded with new industrial units.

No. 315 Squadron 'City of Deblin' had been formed at Acklington in January 1941 — this is a nice shot of their mascots during their brief stay at the airfield.

On January 8, 1943, Sergeant Stefan Sztuka was on the point of taking off when the undercarriage of his Spitfire (R6960) caught a pile of snow and the port leg was torn away. When Sztuka returned he managed to touch down on one wheel, the aircraft sustaining minor damage.

February 1944 also saw a detachment of Hurricane IVs fly in when B Flight of No. 309 (Ziema Czerwienska) Polish Squadron arrived for a brief stay. In July a detachment of No. 310 (Czech) Squadron came back with Spitfire VBs departing to North Weald on August 28.

As the war drew to a close, the last wartime unit, No. 124 (Baroda) arrived on April 10, 1945 with Spitfire HF IXEs. Moving to Bradwell Bay on July 15, they returned on August 10. When the Armament Practice Camp closed in mid-1946, no further use was made of the airfield. Much of it is now an industrial estate with the watch office surviving as a private residence with small areas of runway still visible. The original Battle Headquarters is still in situ and in good condition but visitors must obtain prior permission to see it from the residents of the old control tower.

KING'S CLIFFE

This Northamptonshire airfield, situated 12 miles west of Peterborough at 250 feet above sea level, was previously known as Wansford as well as 'K2' and used as a night landing ground from December 1916. Requisitioned for development to a fighter satellite in 1939, Wimpey became the main contractor and moved in to remove hedges, trees, and fill in ditches before consolidating the grass landing area.

Completed by 1941, the Spitfire VBs of No. 266 (Rhodesia) Squadron arrived on October 24. They carried out shipping strikes before moving to Duxford on January 29, 1942. A day later their place was taken by No. 616 (South Yorkshire) Auxiliary Squadron flying Spitfire IIBs. A conversion to the Mk VI saw them carrying out East Coast patrols before moving to West Malling on July 3. Returning to King's Cliffe four days later, they stayed for only a day before moving to Kenley.

The first of three postings by No. 485 (RNZAF) Squadron saw their Spitfire VBs fly in from Kenley on July 8. Departing to West Malling on August 16, they returned on August 22 until going to Kirkistown on October 24. They came back on November 13 but moved away again on January 2, 1943 to Westhampnett.

The Spitfire VBs of No. 93 Squadron were the next residents, coming in on September 8, 1942 prior to going overseas. They were followed by a detachment of No. 349 (Belgian) Squadron during June 1943 with Spitfire VAs. With the rest of the squadron arriving on June 29, 1943, a stay of six days saw them depart to Wellingore.

Since December 1942, a few P-39 Bell Airacobras of the 347th Squadron had flown in heralding the start of a long association with the USAAF. Prior to their arrival, hard runways had been laid down by W & C French Ltd. These measured 1,100 yards and 1,325 yards, with the main on an E-W axis at 1,700 yards. A 50-foot perimeter track, 12

King's Cliffe (sometimes seen as Kingscliffe) dated back to the First World War and saw service with both the RAF and USAAF. This Spitfire was the mount of Squadron Leader Colin Gray who led No. 616 Squadron from September to February 1942.

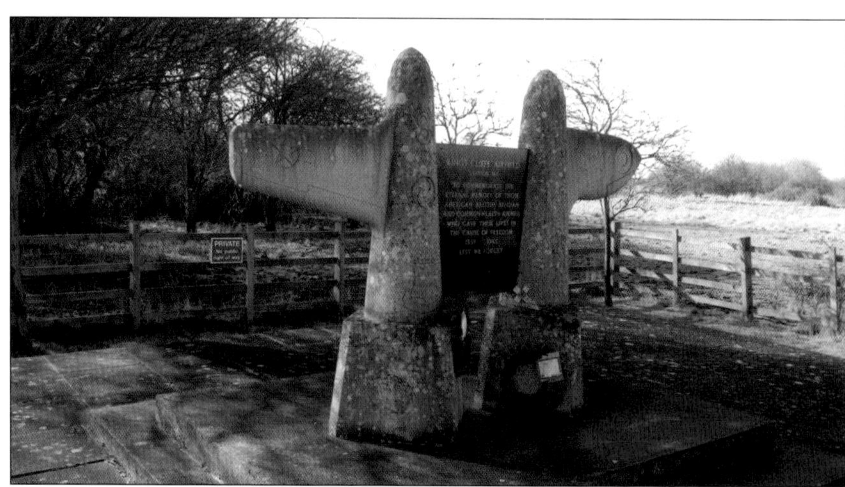

Returning to agriculture, a memorial was later dedicated beside the old Roman road commemorating the British, American and Commonwealth airmen who served at the airfield.

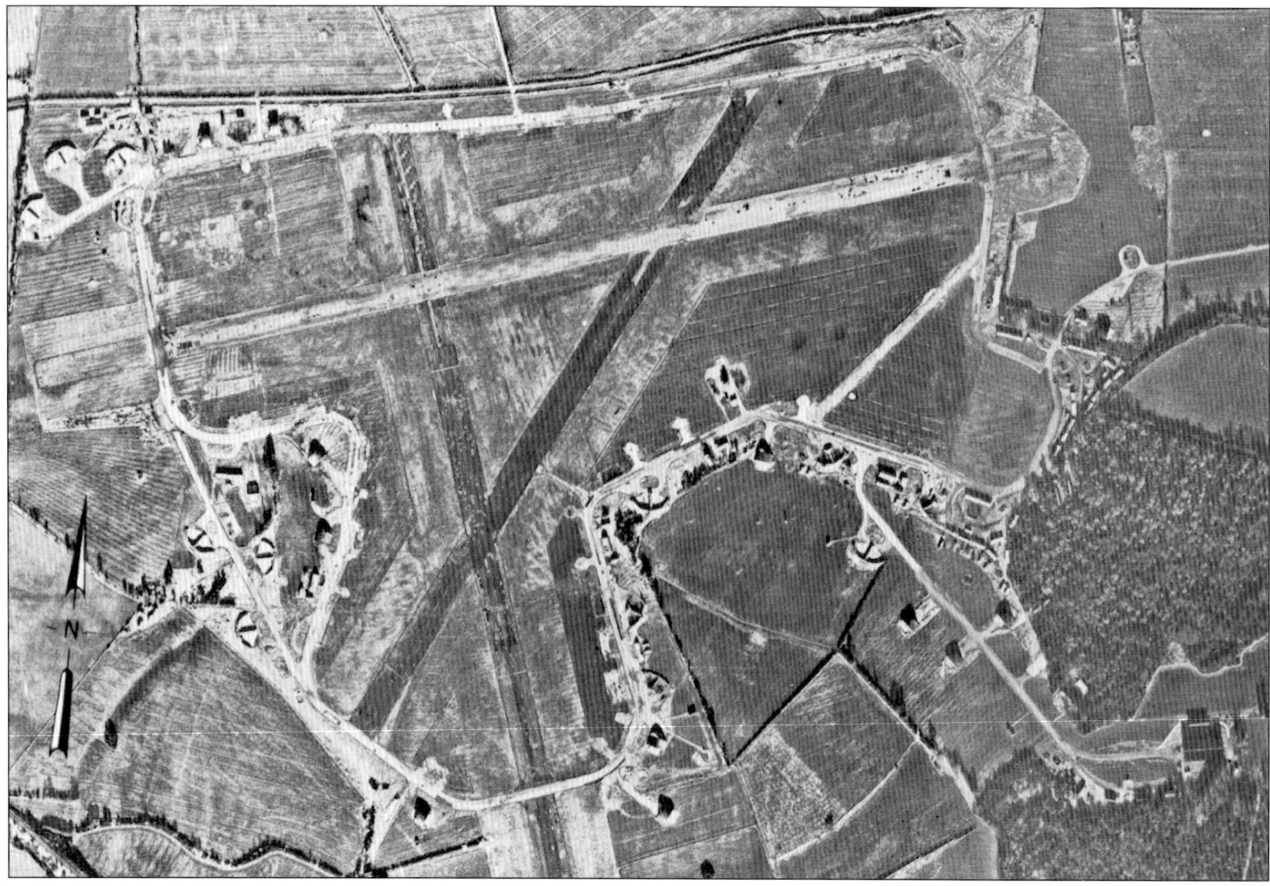

On March 29, 1943, the Duke and Duchess of Gloucester visited the 56th Fighter Group which had taken over the aerodrome in January that year.

Blister hangars, two T2 hangars and a control tower were built at the same time.

Designated Station 367, the 56th Fighter Group arrived in January 1943 whilst the 347th Squadron returned to Duxford. Equipped with P-47 Thunderbolts, the new arrivals were to learn RAF fighter control procedures plus flight training. Moving to Horsham St Faith in April, the RAF returned briefly in May in the shape of a detachment of No. 91 (Nigeria) Squadron flying Spitfire XIIs.

The US 20th Fighter Group flew in on August 26. They entered combat with P-38 Lightnings during December, flying bomber escorts and fighter-bomber missions. Receiving a Distinguished Unit Citation on April 8, 1944, they converted to the P-51 Mustang in July and by the war's end had flown 312 missions.

With their departure, King's Cliffe became a holding centre for German prisoners of war returning home until the RAF relinquished the airfield in 1947. Returning to agriculture, a memorial was later dedicated beside the old Roman road commemorating the British, American and Commonwealth airmen who served at the airfield.

Fortunately the control tower still stands, albeit in a derelict condition.

KIRTON-IN-LINDSEY

Kirton Lindsey (Manton) was first used as a landing ground during the First World War by ' B' Flight of No. 33 Squadron, but after the unit disbanded in 1919 this site quickly returned to agriculture.

A different site nearby was earmarked during the inter-war expansion period for a grass airfield with a take-off distance of 1,100 yards SE-NW and 1,000 yards in other directions. A 39-foot perimeter track led to three 'C' Type hangars and four Over Blisters. A watch office with a meteorological section controlled the night landing facilities consisting of a modified MacDonald flare path and Aldis lamps. Radio facilities were VHF/DF with a blind approach ZZ system. With the intended accommodation being three fighter squadrons, Kirton as a sector station in No. 12 Group was allocated three satellites at Caistor, Hibaldstow and Goxhill.

Opened in May 1940, No. 222 (Natal) Squadron flew in on the 23rd with Spitfire Is followed the next day by No. 253 (Hyderbad State) with Hurricane Is. Five days later No. 65 Squadron with Spitfire Is arrived from Hornchurch. After only five days No. 222 left for Hornchurch, returning on June 4. No. 253 moved to Turnhouse on July 21 whilst No. 65 Squadron left for Hornchurch on June 5. No. 264 (Madras Presidency) arrived with Defiant Is on July 23 and No. 74 with Spitfire IIAs on August 21. With No. 264 sending detachments to Coleby Grange and Ringway, they departed for Hornchurch on August 22. Back again at the end of the month, they finally left for Southend on October 29. Meanwhile, No. 74 Squadron was posted to Coltishall on September 9.

Replacing them was No. 85 with Hurricane Is which came in from Church Fenton to rest on October 23. Detachments were later sent to Caistor, Debden and Gravesend before the whole squadron moved to the latter airfield on November 23.

A wartime schematic plan of Kirton-in-Lindsey reproduced from the secret Air Ministry directory of *Airfields and Flying Boat Bases in the United Kingdom*.

The Polish squadron, No. 307 (Lwow), formed up at Kirton on September 5. Receiving Defiant Is, they moved to Jurby on November 7. Before they left No. 616 (South Yorkshire) Auxiliary Squadron had arrived with their Spitfire Is from Coltishall on September 9. After heavy fighting during the Battle of Britain, they carried out convoy patrols from Kirton, returning south to Tangmere on February 26, 1941.

Another squadron to form up at the airfield on November 23, 1940, was No. 255

The Boulton Paul Defiants of No. 264 Squadron pictured at the aerodrome in the summer of 1940 before departing for Hornchurch on August 22. Although the Defiant had achieved initial success with its four-gun turret armament, German pilots soon had the measure of the machine and during three separate actions in four days No. 264 lost ten Defiants with five pilots and nine gunners killed. Their losses were far too great and the Defiant was thereafter confined to the role of a night fighter.

Kirton-in-Lindsey was finally closed in March 2012. North Lincolnshire Council hope to be able to preserve the Operations Room as a museum-cum-memorial; meanwhile the Trent Valley Gliding Club continue to enjoy this beautiful grass airfield.

with Defiant Is. Acquiring Hurricane Is in March 1941, they moved to Hibaldstow on May 15. They had been joined by No. 71 (Eagle) Squadron on November 23, also equipped with Hurricane Is. Carrying out their first operational patrol on February 5, they moved to Martlesham Heath on April 5, 1941.

No. 65 Squadron returned to Kirton on February 26 flying Spitfire IIAs. A conversion to the Mk IIB saw them depart to Oulton on September 28. No. 452 Squadron was formed on April 8, 1941 with Spitfire Is and IIAs as the first of the Australian squadrons. They moved down to Kenley on July 21.

Also reforming at Kirton on May 5 was No. 121 (Eagle) Squadron with Hurricane Is and IIBs, moving to Digby on September 28. Another squadron to reform was No. 136 on August 20, 1941. Equipped with the Hurricane IIA and IIB, they began a working up period before leaving for the Far East. The return of the auxiliary squadron, No. 616 (South Yorkshire), on October 6, 1941 with Spitfire VBs, saw them exchange them for the Mk IIB before departing for King's Cliffe on January 30, 1942. Two months later No. 486 (RNZAF) Squadron formed at Kirton with Hurricane IIBs but quickly moved to Wittering on April 9. Replaced by the Polish No. 306 (Torun) Squadron on May 3, 1942, they left for Northolt on June 6 with further Spitfire VBs arriving from Redhill when No. 457 (Australian) Squadron came to prepare for service in Australia. Arriving on May 31, they left on June 18.

A further Polish squadron came for the first of two stays on June 16, 1942. This was No. 303 (Kosciuszko) Squadron with Spitfire VBs which began to carry out East Coast patrols. They claimed three Ju 88s destroyed before leaving for Redhill on August 15 to take part in Operation 'Jubilee'. Arriving back five days later, they left for Northolt on February 2, 1943.

During their stay, No. 303 Squadron witnessed the arrival on June 10 of the American 94th Squadron of the 1st Fighter Group equipped with P-38 Lightnings. After a brief stay to gain operational experience, they left on August 24. The Hurricane IICs of No. 43 Squadron arrived on September 1 before leaving for North Africa on October 28. Before they departed another American unit, the 91st Squadron of the 81st Fighter Group arrived with P-39s on October 9 but they had moved away by the end of 1942.

The last two squadrons to fly from Kirton were Polish. No. 302 (Poznan) flew in with Spitfire VBs on February 1, 1943 and No. 317 (Wilno) Squadron which joined them on the 13th. They commenced bomber escort duties with both squadrons leaving Kirton during April. With their departure the role of the airfield changed to that of a fighter OTU.

On June 6, 1944, it became the home of No. 53 OTU with Masters and Spitfires. Taking on Hibaldstow as its satellite, the training continued until May 1945 when the unit disbanded. Continuing its training role in peacetime, Kirton was put on care and maintenance in 1957 but was re-opened three years later as a gliding school and also the home of No. 7 School of Technical Training. Closing again in December 1965, it was transferred to the army and was renamed Rapier Barracks.

LECONFIELD

Opening as a No. 3 Group airfield for Bomber Command, Leconfield was allocated to Fighter Command for the first two years of the war. One of the first expansion airfields to be built during 1936, it was situated three miles north-west of Beverley in Yorkshire at a height of 25 feet above sea level. Laid out in the usual three- runway bomber airfield configuration, the main runway measured 2,000 yards with the secondaries 1,400 and 1,100 yards. Four 'C' Type hangars and a Type II Watch Office were built, the latter controlling the McDonald runway lighting and the high frequency direction-finding equipment. Indicative of the intended high usage of Leconfield, storage of aviation spirit stood at 140,000 gallons with 5,000 gallons of motor transport fuel.

These are the Hurricanes of No. 245 Squadron pictured in February 1940 when they were converting to the type from Blenheims and Battles.

No. 616 was formed in November 1938 as a squadron in RAF Bomber Command but eight months later was transferred to Fighter Command, initially with Gloster Gauntlets and Fairey Battles. These were exchanged for Spitfires in October 1939.

Completed by 1939, it passed to No. 12 Group of Fighter Command which posted in the Spitfire Is of No. 72 (Basutoland) Squadron from Church Fenton on October 17. With a detachment at Drem, they returned to Church Fenton on November 1 returning to Leconfield on January 12, 1940. The following day they moved back to Church Fenton and acquired Gladiator I and IIs, finally returning to Leconfield on October 13 for just six days.

Two squadrons reformed at Leconfield on October 30, 1939: No. 234 (Madras Presidency) with Battles, Blenheims and Gauntlets, and No. 245 (Northern Rhodesian) with Blenheims and Battles. The former unit converted to Spitfire Is in March 1940 and moved out to Church Fenton on May 22, while No. 245 converted to Hurricanes at the same time and took them to Drem on May 12.

On June 6, No. 616 (South Yorkshire) Auxiliary Squadron brought their Spitfire Is in from Rochford having fought over Dunkirk, adding eight enemy aircraft to their tally on August 15. Five weeks later the squadron moved to Kenley but not before they had witnessed the creation of the first of the Polish squadrons led by a British CO. No. 302 (Poznan) Polish Squadron formed

Before the Second World War there was no co-ordinated air-sea rescue organisation for recovering aircrew from the sea, the organisation then relying on high-speed launches stationed at flying boat bases. Then on January 14, 1941, the Directorate of Air Sea Rescue Services was set up using Lysanders and Walrus aircraft. The first peacetime air-sea rescue squadron, exclusively using helicopters, was No. 275 Squadron in 1953 when the unit painted their aircraft all yellow. Over the years several different helicopters have been used, particularly the Westland Whirlwind and Sea King, seen here on the tarmac at Leconfield.

Air Chief Marshal Sir Hugh Dowding was replaced as AOC-in-C of Fighter Command on November 25, 1940 by Air Marshal Sir Sholto Douglas, seen here decorating Polish pilots the following month at Leconfield when Nos. 302 and 303 were in residence.

This is Pilot Officer Marian Pisarek receiving his DFC. He went on to become the CO of No. 308 (City of Krakow) Squadron before promotion to Wing Commander in charge of the 1st Polish Fighter Wing. He went missing over France on April 29, 1942.

up on July 13, receiving Hurricane Is shortly thereafter. By August it was operational over the North Sea with the first kill coming on August 20 when Squadron Leader Jack Satchell, the CO, shot down a Ju88A-1. Sending a detachment to Duxford, the squadron moved to Northolt on October 11. In return, another Polish squadron, No. 303 (Kosciuszko), came in from Northolt the same day. Having achieved success on August 30 when Flying Officer Ludwik Paszkiewicz attacked and shot down a Bf 110, they found little action at Leconfield and returned to Northolt on January 3, 1941.

No. 129 (Mysore) Squadron reformed at the airfield on June 16 that year with Spitfire Is and, after a working-up period, they became operational in July, moving south to Westhampnett on August 29. A Czech squadron, No. 313, arrived on July 1 again with Spitfire Is but after converting to the Mk IIA they moved to Portreath on August 26. Three days later it was the turn of No. 610 (County of Chester) Auxiliary Squadron to bring in their Spitfire IIAs. Changing to the cannon-armed Spitfire VBs, they carried out bomber escort work before leaving for Hutton Cranswick on January 14, 1942. They were the last fighter squadron to be based at Leconfield as the airfield was then returned to Bomber Command for the remainder of the war.

Today it is the home of the Defence School of Transport, part of the Defence College of Logistics and Personnel Administration. In addition, two Sea King helicopters of 'E' Flight, 202 Squadron, are based at the airfield in the search and rescue role.

Sir Trafford Leigh-Mallory replaced Sir Sholto on November 28, 1942 until November 15, 1943. Sir Roderic Hill then became the Fighter Command C-in-C until May 14, 1945.

The RAF's photographic reconnaissance squadron, No. 541, took this shot of Leconfield on August 25, 1945.

Today, the airfield has been adapted to its current role as a base for the British Army.

Armourers set the tail fuzes on 500lb bombs destined for V2 launch sites in Holland. This is Ludham in March 1945, the Spitfire XVI fighter-bomber being on the strength of No. 603 Squadron which was based there from January to April 1945.

LUDHAM

Twelve and a half miles north-east of Norwich lay Norfolk's most easterly airfield. At a height of just 50 feet above sea level, it lay between Hickling and Barton Broads, so being close to water, it was prone to ground mist. Thus a MacDonald runway lighting system was installed from the beginning, controlled by a Watch Office Type 3156/41, later upgraded by the addition of a switch room to a Type 1536/42.

Originally a large grass airfield, the addition of three runways, 1,400 x 50 yards and two 1,100 x 50 yards gave the satellite all weather serviceability. With the addition of four Extra Over Blisters and a 50-foot perimeter track, Ludham was ready for occupation by October 1941.

Categorised as a fighter operational satellite to the parent station of Coltishall, the first unit to arrive was No. 19 Squadron with Spitfire VBs. Arriving from Matlask on December 1 they gave fighter support to bomber squadrons attacking targets in France and Holland, remaining until April 4, 1942.

Replaced by No. 610 (County of Chester) Auxiliary Squadron on the same day, their Spitfire VBs were soon in action managing to shoot down a Ju88 on April 27 over Lowestoft. Commanded by Squadron Leader

The two blister hangars which once stood behind the watch office have long gone and the hedges grubbed out.

When pictured by Edward Lowdell, the control tower was the venue for the airfield museum which has since closed down.

'Johnnie' Johnson, they found further success when a Do 217E-4 was shot down in the sea. Detached to West Malling to provide cover for the Dieppe landings, they returned to Ludham on August 21 and converted to the Spitfire VC before moving to Castletown on October 15.

The previous day had seen No. 167 (Gold Coast) Squadron bring their Spitfire VBs to the airfield. They were tasked with attacks on the Continent, one particular sortie resulting in the destruction of several gas-

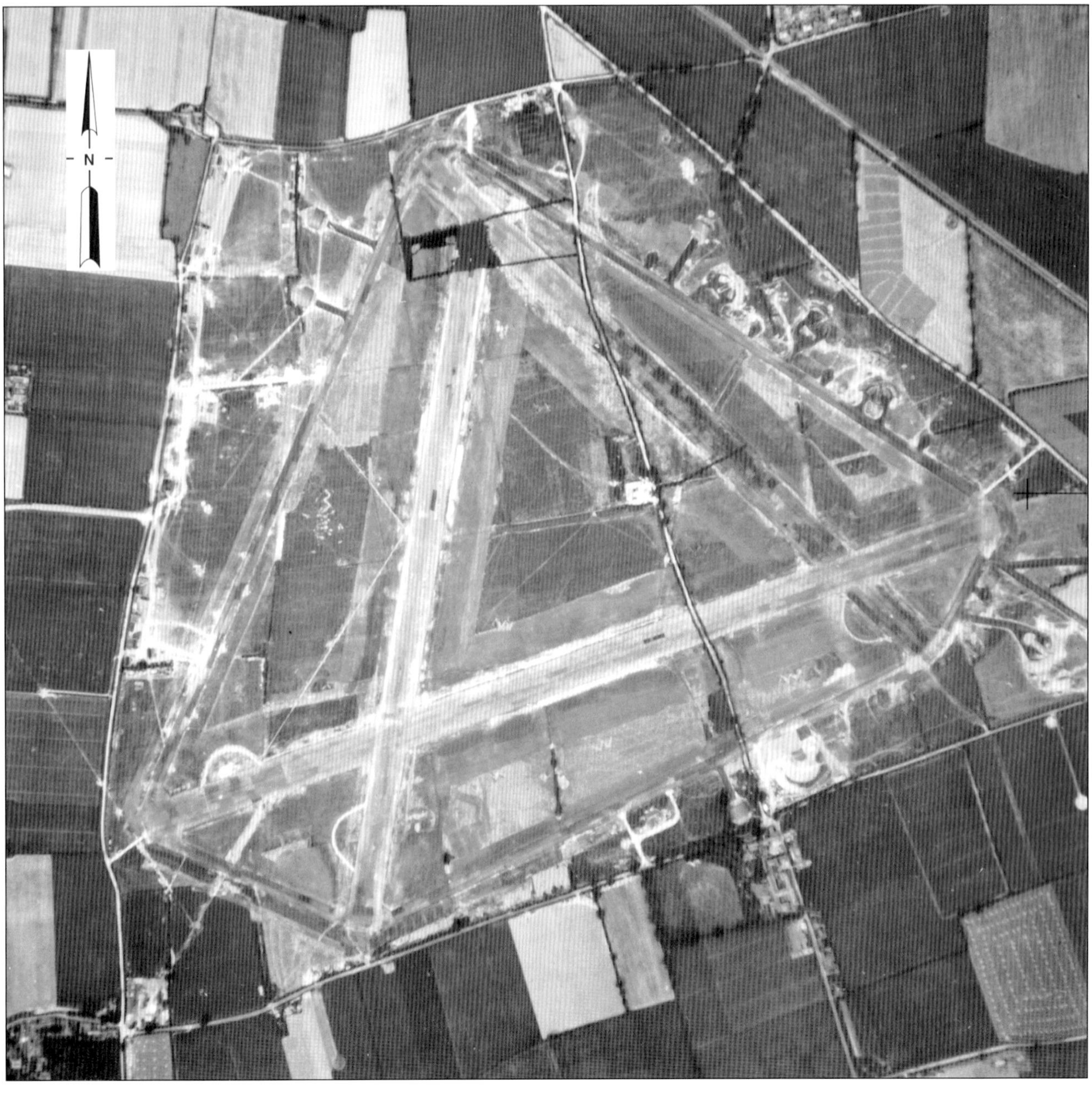

Ludham photographed on July 2, 1942. The two blister hangars are in the top north-western corner.

holders in Holland. A conversion to the Spitfire VC saw them depart to Kidlington on March 1, 1943.

The Typhoon IBs of No. 195 Squadron came in from Woodvale on May 13, 1943, to carry out coastal patrols before moving to Matlask on July 31. Replaced by No. 611 (West Lancashire) Auxiliary Squadron the same day, their Spitfire LF VBs worked up for low-level operations before moving to Coltishall on August 4.

This exodus left Ludham in the hands of the Air Ministry Works Department before it was due to be handed over to the USAAF. However this never took place and the airfield languished empty until August 1944 when the Royal Navy took over, renaming it HMS *Flycatcher*. Later it was handed back to the Air Ministry with fighters returning in the form of No. 91 Squadron equipped with Spitfire XXIs. Arriving on April 8, 1945, they moved to Fairwood Common on July 14. They had been joined by the Spitfire IXBs of No. 1 Squadron on May 14 who converted to the new Spitfire F.21 before departing to Hutton Cranswick on July 23, 1945.

With their departure no further use was made of Ludham and it was returned to agriculture.

One of the hangars was dismantled and re-erected by a crop-dusting firm on the end of the E-W runway, a section of which is used today by light aircraft.

CONTROL TOWER

Apart from the tower, no memorial exists at Ludham to record its illustrious history.

MATLASKE

A fine study of a Typhoon IB of No. 56 Squadron. They were based at Matlaske for nearly a year before moving south to Manston. In the background one of six double blast pens that lay around the perimeter.

Located five and a half miles from the village of Holt in Norfolk, and at a height of 176 feet above sea level, the relief landing ground at Matlaske (sometimes spelt without the 'e') possessed three grass runways of 1,500, 1,430 and 1,230 yards surrounded by a 35-foot perimeter track. A single-storey Watch Office was provided with four Extra Over Blister hangars. There were Glim Lamps and Goose Neck flares for night operations. Intended to accommodate one fighter squadron and a flight of air-sea rescue aircraft, the airfield came into use during October 1940.

Initially it was used as a dispersal for Spitfires of No. 72 (Basutoland) Squadron based at Coltishall, attracting a Luftwaffe attack on October 29. Five Do17s strafed the airfield damaging some of the aircraft and buildings. Personnel were quickly moved to a nearby mansion, Matlaske Hall, for safety and it was not until May 1941 that the airfield was back in use. Again, two days before the arrival of No. 222 (Natal) Squadron, another attack caused more damage and cratered the grass.

Coming in from the parent station on June 6, the Spitfire IIAs and IIBs of the squadron were soon dispersed around the outside of the landing area before commencing patrols over the North Sea fishing fleets. A move to Manston on July 1 saw No. 601 (County of London) Auxiliary Squadron replace them. Initially flying Hurricanes, they were re-equipped with the Airacobra but after suffering several mishaps with this new American aircraft, the squadron reverted back to the Hurricane which they took to Duxford on August 16. Their replacement was No. 19 Squadron, their Spitfire IIAs posted in from Fowlmere the same day. Changing to the Spitfire VB, they left for Ludham on December 1, 1941.

The forming of No. 278 (ASR) Squadron from a nucleus of No. 3 (ASR) Squadron on October 1 saw a Lysander and Walrus based at the aerodrome, Matlaske being an ideal base for rescue missions over the North Sea.

Now, sadly, all has been swept away, save for odd lengths of peri-track but thankfully the Airfields of Britain Conservation Trust erected this memorial on February 27, 2011. At the time of writing (October 2013) the trust have erected memorials at seven airfields in England and three in Scotland, although Matlaske is the first which served under Fighter Command.

One of the RAF's most illustrious squadrons, No. 56 had two stints at Matlaske: from August 1942 to July 1943, and again for a brief period in September 1944. This picture of Typhoon DN374 is dated March 2, 1943.

Whirlwinds of No. 137 Squadron arrived from Coltishall in November. With a detachment at Snailwell, they commenced East Coast convoy escorts. Carrying on similar duties into 1942, on February 12 they were escorting destroyers in the Channel area when they came upon the German capital ships making a dash through the Dover Straits. Coming into contact with the Luftwaffe fighter escort, they lost four pilots. Continuing the escort work the squadron moved to Drem on August 2, returning briefly for 14 days on August 11 before moving on to Snailwell.

A brief stay by the Typhoon IBs of No. 266 Squadron from August 2 until August 11 saw them replaced by those of No. 56 (Punjab) Squadron. They stayed for nearly a year — from August 24, 1942 to July 22, 1943 — when they moved to Manston.

During May that year, several enemy attacks were carried out on Lowestoft with one spilling over to Matlaske. Further Typhoon squadrons came in to combat the FW 190s causing the problem. A detachment from No. 245 (Northern Rhodesia) Squadron arrived late May, being joined by No. 195 Squadron on July 31. Meanwhile, Spitfire IXs of No. 611 (West Lancashire) Auxiliary Squadron had flown in on July 1 but after a quick conversion to the Spitfire LF VB, they left for Ludham on the 31st. With the enemy attacks on coastal towns petering out, No. 195 Squadron left for Coltishall on August 21 with the detachment from No. 245 having joined the rest of the squadron at Fairlop on May 28.

June 4, 1943, saw the return of No. 19 Squadron with their Spitfire VCs for a brief stay, moving to Gravesend two weeks later. Shortly after they left, Matlaske was placed under care and maintenance. Whilst this appeared premature at this stage of the war, most of the action was further south, plus the fact that consideration was being given to offer the USAAF the use of Matlaske. In preparation for this, the Watch Office was upgraded but the Americans never moved in apart from the 2nd Engineer Battalion which used the airfield for training. Not until September 19, 1944, were any flying units based at Matlaske. On that day the Tempest Vs of No. 486 (RNZAF) Squadron arrived followed two days later by the Tempest Vs of No. 3 Squadron and No. 56 Squadron. Together they formed No. 150 Wing but all of them left the airfield after only one week.

Their place was taken by a Mustang wing comprising Nos. 19 (East India), 65 and 122 (Bombay) Squadrons. With Nos. 19 and 122 arriving on September 28 and No. 65 following a day later, all three units commenced bomber escorts until mid-October when they left. With their departure a Spitfire wing flew in. Nos 229, 453 (Australian) and 602 (City of Glasgow) Auxiliary Squadron arrived for similar escort duties as well as attacking V2 launch sites. All three squadrons transferred to Swannington on November 20 with No. 453 returning briefly from March 15 to April 6, 1945.

Just before D-Day, the US 7th Photographic Group based at Mount Farm took this shot.

Whirlwind squadron, No. 137, was a resident at Matlaske from November 1941 to August 1942.

Today virtually nothing remains — this is the base of the large T2 hangar on the northern side.

Another Australian squadron, No. 451, brought their Spitfire XVIs in on February 23, 1945 departing to Swannington the next day only to return on March 22. When they left for Lympne on April 6, once again the airfield was put on a care and maintenance basis until the RAF finally left in October 1945. Handed back to the landowners, it has now reverted to agriculture.

MEMORIAL

SITE OF CONTROL TOWER

The position of the control tower and the present day memorial are indicated.

WELLINGORE

In August 1941 the Motor Industry announced that its Fighter Fund had topped £190,000 enabling it to equip a complete squadron with 20 Spitfires. The lucky unit was No. 154 which became the Motor Industries Fighter Squadron.

Wellingore in Lincolnshire became the location of an airfield during the First World War, it being expanded over the winter of 1939-40 to become an operational satellite and Relief Landing Ground for Digby. Lying 250 feet above sea level and ten and a half miles south of Lincoln, the grass airfield measured 1,200 yards NE-SW, 1,100 yards SE-NW, 1,060 yards E-W and 1,030 yards N-S. A 35-foot concrete perimeter track, eight Blister hangars and several hutted buildings were in place when No. 29 Squadron arrived on July 27, 1940, with their Blenheim IFs. Flying with the squadron at this time was Flight Lieutenant Guy Gibson, later to achieve fame as the leader of the 617 Squadron operation against the German dams. The squadron commenced North Sea patrols before converting to the Beaufighter IF in September and moving south to West Malling on April 27, 1941.

There now began an association with Canadian squadrons in line with the parent station Digby. The Hurricanes of No. 402 (Winnipeg Bear) Squadron were the first to arrive during May 1941. Carrying out East Coast patrols, they moved to Martlesham Heath in June. Next to arrive were the Spitfires of No. 412 (Falcon) Squadron who moved in on October 20, 1941. Flying the Mk IIA, they began operating over Northern France but having converted to the Spitfire VB, they too moved to Martlesham on May 1, 1942.

No. 54 Squadron stayed from June 2-18, 1942 after which they moved to Australia. Another squadron to arrive briefly was No. 154 (Motor Industries). Arriving with Spitfire VBs on September 1, they left a month later en route for North Africa. With Wellingore becoming more of a transit airfield, No. 81 with Spitfire VBs also arrived on September 1 with orders for North Africa.

Normal operations returned on December 6 when a variety of aircraft from No. 288 Squadron flew in from Duxford. An army co-operation squadron, their equipment consisted of a Defiant, Blenheim, Hudson, Lysander and Hurricane. Tasked with providing anti-aircraft duties in Yorkshire and Lincolnshire, they left for Digby on January 18, 1943.

Mustangs flew in on March 30 when No. 613 (City of Manchester) Auxiliary Squadron brought them in from Ringway. With escort duties for Coastal Command and anti-submarine strikes their main duty, they moved to Clifton on May 28.

With rapid changes being the order of the day, No. 416 (City of Oshawa) Canadian Squadron arrived with Spitfire IXs on May 29, leaving for Digby on June 7 before returning on September 19 only to return to the parent station on October 2. August 5

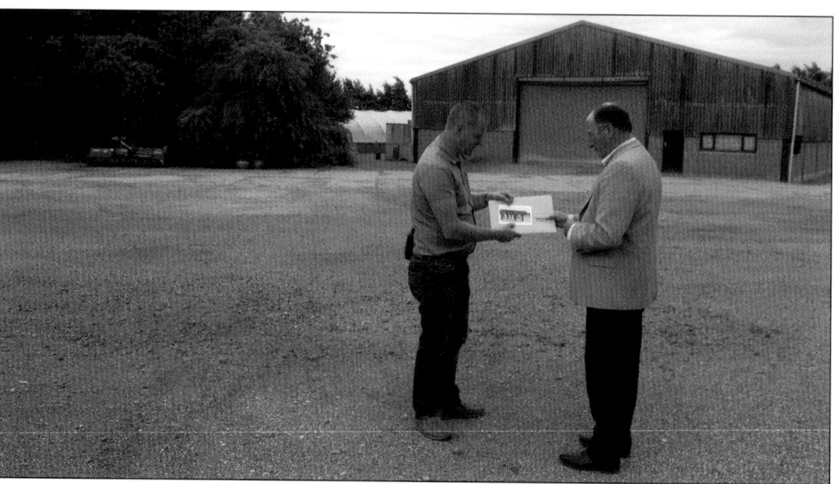

In heraldry terms the crest was unique as it included the unrestricted sign from the Highway Code. Presenting the crest at Wellingore was the AOC-in-C of No. 12 Group, Air Vice-Marshal Richard Saul. Unfortunately the long low building which once housed the station headquarters was demolished many years ago although the concrete base can still be seen. Richard Overton *(right)*, who now owns the airfield, kindly stood in with Rob Green for our comparison.

A photo of a young American pilot in front of the same building in 1941. His aspirations to join the RAF were thwarted by the US State Department so he crossed the border into Canada and in December 1940 enlisted as an Aircraftman 2nd Class in the RCAF. By June 1941 he had completed his course with No. 2 Service Flying Training School, graduating as a Sergeant Pilot. Being commissioned soon after arriving in Britain, on September 23 he was posted to No. 412 Squadron, RCAF, then based at Wellingore. His name: Pilot Officer John Magee.

had seen a Belgian Squadron, No. 349, come in from King's Cliffe for just 11 days. Then on January 1, 1944, No. 439 (Westmount) Canadian Squadron formed at Wellingore from No. 123 Squadron of the RCAF. Receiving Hurricane IVs, they left for Ayr seven days later.

When No. 402 (Winnipeg Bear) returned on February 12 for a two-month stint carrying out anti-V1 patrols, they were to be the last fighter unit to be based at the airfield. In April 1944 Wellingore became a RLG for nearby Cranwell and at the cessation of hostilities a temporary home for German POWs awaiting repatriation. Once this was completed, the airfield was returned to the original owners of the land, the Overton family.

STATION HQ

Wartime Britain was covered with over 800 aerodromes so the risk of collisions was always a real danger. Just three miles due south from Wellingore was the busy Service Flying Training School at RAF Cranwell. Thursday, December 11, 1941 dawned a misty, overcast, yet mild winter's day, and despite a ten-tenths cloud base of 1,200 feet, the weather was deemed fit for flying and the aircraft of No. 412 Squadron at Wellingore readied for a squadron formation flight. The Spitfires took off at 10.40 a.m. Pilot Officer Magee, (in A Flight), flew Spitfire VZ-H, AD291. For almost an hour the flight was uneventful until just before the squadron turned for home. As they let down through cloud to the south-east of their airfield they encountered an Airspeed Oxford carrying out a training exercise from Cranwell. As Magee emerged from the cloud a collision was inevitable. His Spitfire struck the Oxford and both aircraft immediately fell out of control.

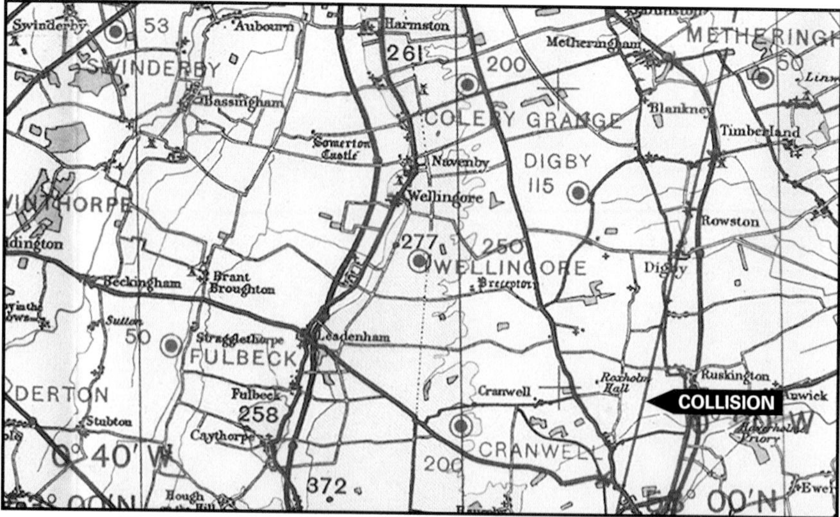

Meteorological data for that day indicates a mid-morning cloud base of 2,500 feet, but the official accident report states that the collision occurred at 1,400 feet so it may be assumed that the accident took place somewhere around these altitudes. Given that both aircraft then entered a rapid rate of descent and that a certain period had to be allowed for 'thinking time' and time taken in releasing harness straps, R/T and oxygen connections and then in actually abandoning the aircraft, precious little margin for safety would be available from an aircraft stricken at such a low altitude. It would have been very difficult for the pilot-under training and sole occupant of the Oxford, LAC Ernest Griffin, to abandon his aircraft as the escape hatch on the Oxford was some feet to the rear on the port side. As the rest of the pilots landed back at Wellingore, Pilot Officer Rod Smith of B Flight was sent aloft to locate the crash. When he returned he, together with Squadron Leader Jack Morrison, Flight Lieutenant Hart Massey, the intelligence officer, and Pilot Officer 'Dusty' Davidson raced to the crash site of Magee's Spitfire in Hart's sports car. The aircraft was burning fiercely and ammunition was exploding so the wreck could not be approached. An eyewitness hearing a bang overhead said she saw the pilot falling from the sky without an open parachute and Magee's body was discovered some distance away in the same field. The Lincolnshire Police report states that 'At 11.30 hours on 11th December, 1941, an Airspeed Oxford aircraft from RAF Cranwell and a Spitfire attached to RAF Digby came into collision in mid-air and crashed, both pilots being killed and their machines completely destroyed. The Airspeed Oxford fell near Roxholm Hall [1] and the Spitfire into a field [2] about half a mile to the north-east of the Hall.' The police officer attending the incident was Sergeant H. Challand, stationed at nearby Sleaford. Writing in March 1988, Mr Challand described how 'I attended the incident about half an hour after it had happened, by which time Magee's body had been removed, but I remember seeing the impression in the soil where he had fallen. This was about two or three hundred yards to the north of Roxholm Hall. The Oxford had fallen into a paddock just in front of the Hall. It was completely smashed up and the body of the unfortunate pilot was still inside.

Aircraft Type	No.	Pilot, or 1st Pilot	2nd Pilot, Pupil or Passenger	Duty (Including Results and Remarks)	Single-Engine Aircraft Day Dual (1)	Day Pilot (2)	Night Dual (3)	Night Pilot (4)	Multi-Engine Aircraft Day Dual (5)	Day 1st Pilot (6)	Day 2nd Pilot (7)	Night Dual (8)	Night 1st Pilot (9)	Night 2nd Pilot (10)	Passenger (11)	Instr/Cloud Flying [Incl. in cols. (1) to (10)] Dual (12)	Pilot (13)
—	—	—	—	— Totals Brought Forward													
IRE V	H	SELF		CONVOY PATROL		1:35											
	F	SELF		W.C.2 TO DUXFORD		0:45			50 FT. CEILING!								
	F	SELF		DUXFORD TO W.C.2		0:55											
LEY	SG-T	S/L	SELF	LOCAL FLYING		[illegible]									0:10		
STER		SELF	F/L MASSEY	LOCAL FLYING		0:20											
STER		SELF		TO COLBY		0:10											
IRE V	H	SELF		SQUADRON FORMATION (PRACTISE SWEEP)		1:00											
	D	SELF		'PIPSQUEAK' INTERCEPTION AND HIGH ALTITUDE DOGFIGHT		1:20			LEARNED EFFECT OF NO OXYGEN								
	D	SELF		NIGHT FLYING		1:00			AIRSPEED INDICATOR U/S — BROUGHT IN (FORMATION) BY P/O SMITH				1:00				
	E	SELF		SEARCHLIGHT EXPERIMENT + CO-OP.		1:40											
	A	SELF		A/C TEST (FORMATION — BEAUFIGHTER + HUDSON)		1:15											
	H	P/O MAGEE		PRACTICE WING FORM.		:50	Collided With Oxford					[signature] S/Ldr Comm. Officer — 412 Squadron					
		GRAND TOTAL [Cols. (1) to (10)] 245 Hrs. 40 Mins.		Totals Carried Forward	10	50											

If a pilot is killed or fails to return, it is the sad duty of the commanding officer to write to the next of kin and compile the last entry in the dead pilots' log book. Here Squadron Leader Morrison has added John Magee's fatal 50-minute flight.

ORDERS: 'No. 412 Squadron — Funeral of Pilot Officer J. G. Magee. The funeral will take place at 14.30 hours on Saturday 13th December 1941, at Scopwick Parish Church. Personnel of the Escort and Bearer parties, and Squadron representatives are to assemble at 12.45 hours at Wellingore Hall. Personnel of the firing party and the trumpeters, and personnel of the attending party from Station Headquarters, and 609 and 92 Squadrons will assemble at the Main Guard Room, Digby, at 13.30 hours. Transport will be available to carry personnel to Scopwick where they will form up at the crossroads at 14.15 hours. The tender carrying the coffin will leave the mortuary, Station Sick Quarters, at 14.00 hours, preceded by the Padre'. John once wrote to his mother that 'I am convinced that my place is in England' — now his place is forever in England as he was laid to rest in Grave 33 of Row 3 of Scopwick Burial Ground.

High Flight

Oh! I have slipped the surly bonds of Earth
And danced the skies on laughter-silvered wings;
Sunward I've climbed, and joined the tumbling mirth
of sun-split clouds, — and done a hundred things
You have not dreamed of — wheeled and soared and swung
High in the sunlit silence. Hov'ring there,
I've chased the shouting wind along, and flung
My eager craft through footless halls of air....

Up, up the long, delirious, burning blue
I've topped the wind-swept heights with easy grace
Where never lark, or even eagle flew —
And, while with silent, lifting mind I've trod
The high untrespassed sanctity of space,
Put out my hand, and touched the face of God.

From the day that John Magee first enlisted in the Royal Canadian Air Force until the day he died, he never let on to anyone in the Service that he loved and wrote poetry. It was on the evening of September 3, 1941, in a room he shared with another officer, that he wrote on an ordinary sheet of notepaper his memorable sonnet which will forever be his legacy. Three days later he turned the paper over and wrote a letter on it to his parents — the Reverend John Magee and his British-born wife Faith. In April 1943 they donated the original to the Library of Congress in Washington but unfortunately the manuscript has been disfigured by a crude accession stamp and inscription, surely a travesty by such an august body. The Reverend Magee published the poem in his magazine of St John's Church, Lafayette Square, Washington (just opposite the White House) on December 21. It caught the attention of a reporter with a Washington newspaper which subsequently published it, thereby setting off a train of events which were to secure its immortality. Within a short space of time, *High Flight* had appeared in newspapers in Britain, and was included in the *Daily Telegraph Third Miscellany* (August 1942), *More Poems for The Forces* (1943) and *Twentieth Century Verse* (Clarke, Irwin and Co. Ltd, Toronto, 1945) amongst others. In Dallas, Texas, Dr Lloyd Pfautsch, an eminent composer and conductor of chorale music of the period, even set *High Flight* to a musical accompaniment.

When Magee's verse was first published in Great Britain, it caught the attention of the parents of LAC Griffin, at their home in Headington, Oxford. A footnote to the verse described how Magee had been killed on active service in Britain on December 11, 1941. Ernest and Mary immediately recognised that this was the same date of death as their son's and although the exact circumstances of the accident were never communicated to the parents, they had learnt that their son had been killed in a mid-air collision with another pilot who had also died. The Air Ministry refused to confirm to Mr and Mrs Griffin that Magee had been involved in the collision with their son, but undeterred, they managed to make contact with the Reverend and Mrs Magee, with whom they entered into a friendly and lengthy correspondence. Eventually, in April 1942, at the suggestion of Faith Magee, Mr Griffin wrote to the CO of No. 412 Squadron at Wellingore seeking confirmation of the facts. On April 8, the squadron adjutant replied to the Griffins confirming that indeed both men had died in the same accident. Ernest Aubrey Griffin was cremated at Oxford Crematorium, his name appearing on the left-hand column of the Commonwealth War Graves Commission Memorial.

When John Magee arrived in the United Kingdom he was first posted to No. 53 Operational Training Unit at Llandow in South Wales. There, on August 7, he made his first flight in a Spitfire and it was most probably then that he composed *High Flight*. As he explained in his letter home, 'it started at 30,000 feet and was finished soon after I landed'. Nevertheless it is Wellingore in the Lincolnshire countryside that has claim to John's legacy. On January 14, 1942 the Royal Canadian Air Force issued an official press release which announced that 'Pilot Officer John Gillespie Magee, Jr., an American citizen born of missionary parents in Shanghai and educated at Britain's famed Rugby School, was killed on active service in Britain last December 11th. He was 19 years old and had the cause of freedom in his heart. Pilot Officer Magee had poetry in his heart, too, and in the form of a sonnet he left a message to youth which his parents consider may be greater than anything he had done in the way of fighting.'

WITTERING

Early beginnings at Wittering during the pre-war years when the aerodrome was the home of No. 11 Flying Training School. The Luftwaffe had the airfield earmarked as target GB 10247 early in 1939.

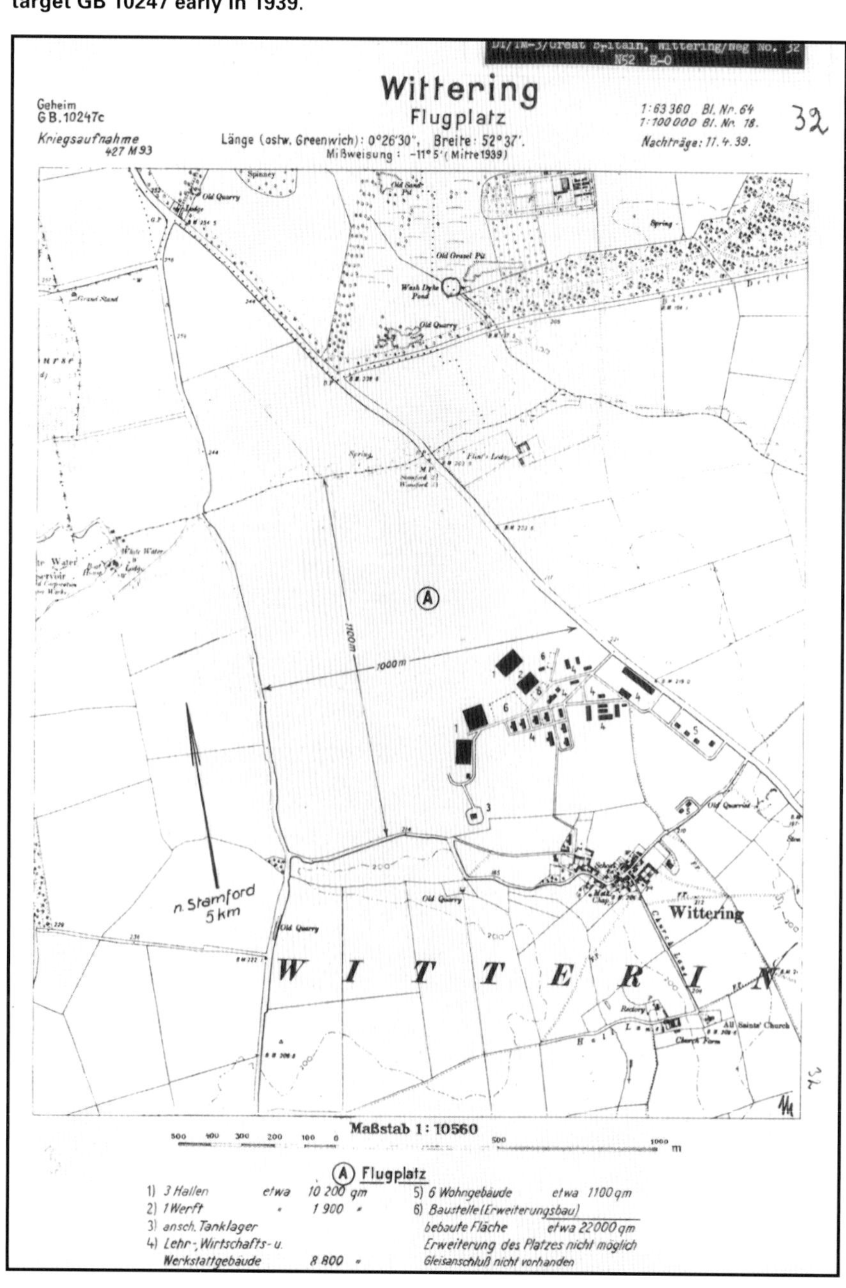

Three miles south of Stamford in Northamptonshire, and lying 250 feet above sea level, the airfield went by the name of Stamford when first established in 1916. As a Royal Flying Corps base for the FE2Bs of No. 38 Home Defence Squadron and the Camels and Pups of No. 90 Squadron, it later became the home of No. 1 Training Depot. No. 5 Training Depot was established at Easton-on-the-Hill which was situated at the western end of Stamford and was independent from No. 1. However with the formation of the RAF in 1918, the Stamford depot was re-named RAF Wittering whilst the Easton depot became RAF Collyweston. Both were placed into care and maintenance in 1920.

Construction began to enlarge the site in 1924 when it was decided to base the Central Flying School at Wittering. Replaced by No. 11 Flying Training School in 1935, another period of expansion saw the airfield become a base within No. 12 Group, Fighter Command. At this time the grass landing area measured 4,800 yards E-W, 1,900 yards NE-SW and 980 yards N-S. A tarmac perimeter track was laid but with instructions to be used by cars only! A Type I Flying Control and two double aircraft sheds were in situ by the time the station re-opened as a night fighter parent station on April 11, 1938. Aviation fuel capacity was 49,000 gallons with 4,000 gallons of MT petrol. With satellites at King's Cliffe and Collyweston, the other stated functions were that of a Blind Approach Training and Turbinlite airfield.

In May 1938 the resident units were No. 23 with Demons and No. 213 (Ceylon) Squadron with Gauntlets. With the former converting to the Blenheim IF and the latter to Hurricane Is, No. 610 (City of Chester) Auxiliary Squadron brought their Spitfire Is in on October 10, 1939, the squadron being tasked with East Coast patrols. In December, a detachment of Defiant Is from No. 264 (Madras Presidency) Squadron arrived to complement the Blenheims in night fighting. No. 213 Squadron sent detachments to Manston, Biggin Hill and Merville in France before moving to Biggin on June 9, 1940. No. 23 Squadron meanwhile moved to nearby Collyweston on May 31, returning on August 16. They finally moved to Ford on September 12.

A detachment of Spitfire Is from No. 266 (Rhodesia) Squadron, which had arrived on March 1, was joined by the rest of the

No. 25 Squadron spent over a year at Wittering as a night fighter unit. It switched from the Blenheim to the Beaufighter in September 1940. R2069 pictured crashed on March 24, 1944, when it lost control while making a dummy attack on a B-17.

Flying Officer Arthur 'Taffy' Clowes of No. 1 Squadron with his Hurricane pictured in its blast pen in October 1940. Having survived the Battle of Britain, this particular aircraft was lost when it crashed on landing at Ternhill on March 25, 1942.

squadron on May 14. With a detachment at Collyweston, the remainder moved to Eastchurch and Hornchurch for nine days, returning to Wittering on August 21. They were to remain for a year and a quarter during which time the squadron scored its first kill when Pilot Officer Frederick Ferris and Sergeant van Schaick shot down a Ju 88A-5 on March 8, 1941 although Ferris was killed during the combat.

No. 74 'Tiger' Squadron with Spitfire IIAs spent seven days at Wittering from August 14, resting from heavy fighting down south. They were followed by the Hurricane Is of No.1 Squadron which came in from Northolt on September 9. They returned on December 15.

Another resident night fighter squadron in January 1940 was No. 23, also equipped with Blenheim IFs.

With heavy night bombing now taking place over the Midlands, No. 25 Squadron with Beaufighters arrived on December 27. They had achieved success whilst flying from North Weald and Debden and during their stay they also flew Havocs, taking those and the Beaufighters to Ballyhalbert on January 16, 1942.

No. 25 Squadron had been joined by No. 151 on December 23. Flying Defiant Is and Hurricanes, they arrived from Bramcote to join the detachment that had been at Wittering since September. Sending a flight to Coltishall, they converted through the Hurricane IIC, Defiant IIs onto Mosquito IIs before finally leaving on April 30, 1943.

The New Year of 1941 saw Wittering come to the attention of the Luftwaffe when a small force of enemy aircraft cratered the grass. Another raid occurred on March 14 resulting in the deaths of five airmen. These raids came at a time when thought was being given to linking Wittering and Collyweston together to provide a longer main runway. Work was completed on the project within a month thanks to the tremendous efforts of the station's commanding officer, Group Captain Basil Embry.

No. 486 (RNZAF) Squadron arrived on April 9, 1942 to work in conjunction with No. 1453 (Turbinlite) Flight. They were operational on September 2 with Bostons and Havocs. Flying the Hurricane IIB, the New Zealand squadron carried out several operations with the Turbinlite aircraft before converting to the Typhoon IB and moving to North Weald on September 27. The end of the month also saw No. 152 Squadron bring their Spitfire VBs in from Angle prior to going overseas to North Africa in November.

In September 1942 it was decided that Wittering was to become a joint RAF/USAAF base. No. 151 Mosquitos were still operating from the grass when the P-47s of the 63rd Fighter Squadron of the 56th Fighter Group flew in. They stayed until March 1943 when the arrival of the Air Fighting Development Unit and No. 787 Naval Air Fighting Development Unit saw the aerodrome back in RAF hands.

A later arrival was No. 151 which had been in the forefront of the combats further south. Now in the night fighter role, they were equipped at Wittering with the Defiant.

The end of an era. In December 2010 the Harrier force, which had made Wittering its home since 1968, was summarily executed.

No. 82 Squadron photographed Wittering in May 1947 but from 1952 until 1954 the airfield was closed for the construction of a 9,000ft concrete runway, 200ft wide, to become a base for Britain's nuclear deterrent force. It was on the disbandment of the V-bomber force in 1968 that Wittering then became known as 'the home of the Harrier' when No. 1 Squadron returned to be equipped with the world's first vertical take-off and landing aeroplane. This unique aircraft was axed in the Strategic Defence and Security Review in 2010. (For the present-day comparison of the airfield, see page 233.)

The Americans came back in August 1943 with the P-38s of the 55th Squadron of the 20th Fighter Group, remaining until April 1944. Meanwhile, the Canadians of No. 438 (Wild Cat) Squadron had arrived with their Hurricane IVs on December 19, 1943, jostling for space with the Americans. They moved to Ayr on January 10, 1944. Another unit stationed at Wittering at this time was the Fighter Interception Unit which moved in from Ford. Experimenting with equipment and techniques for aerial fighting, they remained until mid-1944.

The last wartime unit to use the airfield was No. 68 Squadron with the Mosquito XIX. Arriving on February 8, 1945, a conversion to the Mosquito XXX saw them move back to Coltishall on the 27th. By the end of the war, Wittering squadrons lay claim to over 150 enemy aircraft destroyed, 50 probables and 61 damaged. With a change to Flying Training Command on March 31, 1945, the airfield would later become the future home of the RAF's Harrier force.

Through its close association with Spitfire LA255 which had been issued to it in 1945, No. 1 Squadron were permitted to retain their gate guardian long after all other stations had been made to surrender theirs under the Ministry of Defence ruling of 1988. On the decommissioning of the Harriers, LA255 underwent restoration and is now on charge with No. 1 Squadron Association at Leuchars.

When No. 151 Squadron departed, another Beaufighter unit, No. 141 took their place equipped with the Beaufighter IFs and led by Wing Commander 'Bob' Braham. Arriving on April 30, 1942, they conducted sorties against both trains and ships in addition to flying escort duties to Coastal Command aircraft. With a detachment at Drem, the squadron converted to the Beaufighter VIF during May with a final conversion to the Mosquito II before moving to West Raynham on December 4.

No. 13 GROUP

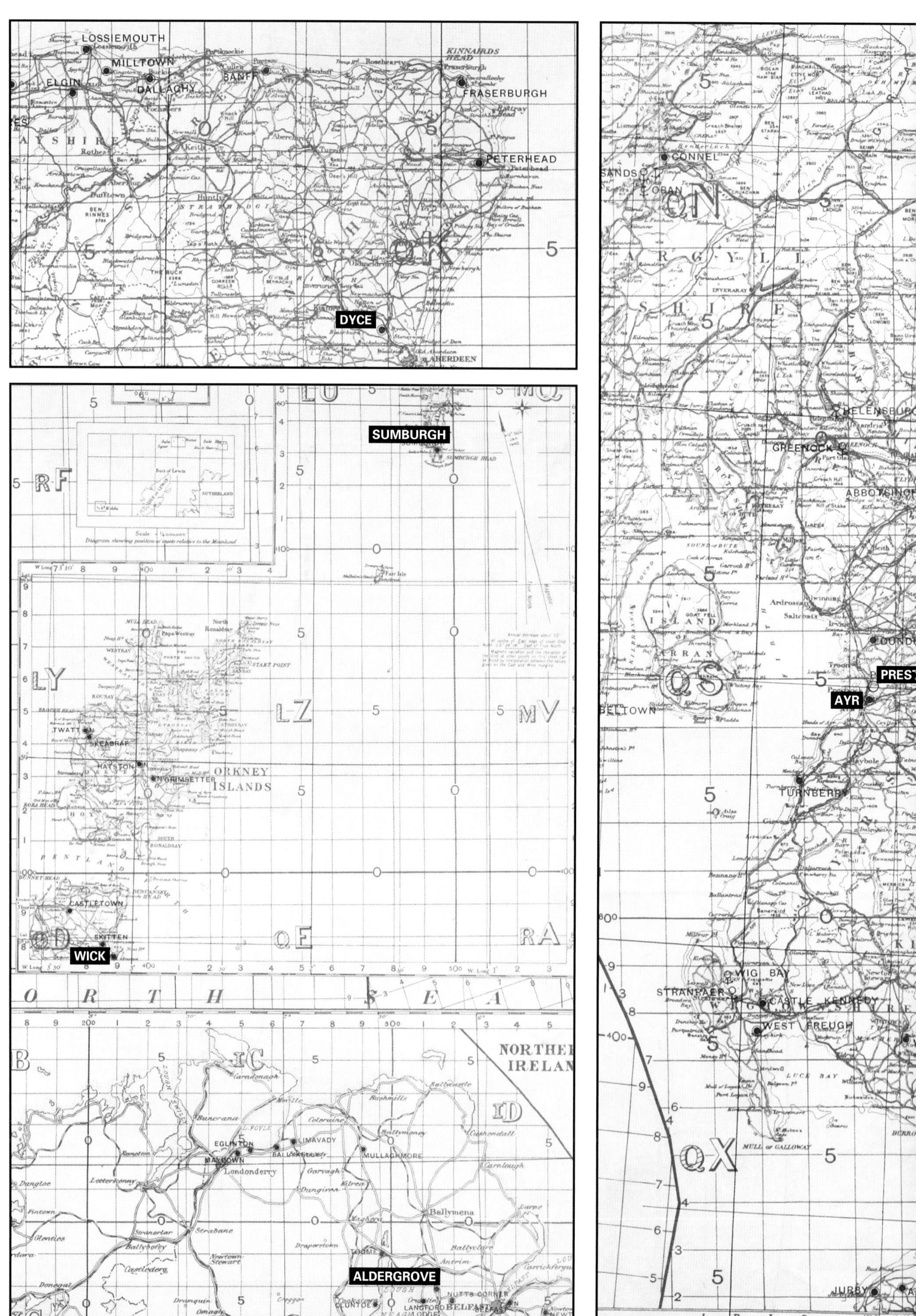
LOSSIEMOUTH
MILLTOWN
ELGIN
DALLACHY
BANFF
FRASERBURGH
PETERHEAD
DYCE
ABERDEEN
SUMBURGH
ORKNEY ISLANDS
TWATT
SKEABRAE
HATSTON
GRIMSETTER
CASTLETOWN
SKITTEN
WICK
EGLINTON
MAYDOWN
BALLYKELLY
LIMAVADY
MULLAGHMORE
ALDERGROVE
NUTTS CORNER
LANGFORD LODGE
CONNEL
OBAN
HELENSBURGH
GREENOCK
ABBOTSINCH
ARRAN
AYR
PREST
TURNBERRY
WIG BAY
STRANRAER
CASTLE KENNEDY
WEST FREUGH
JURBY

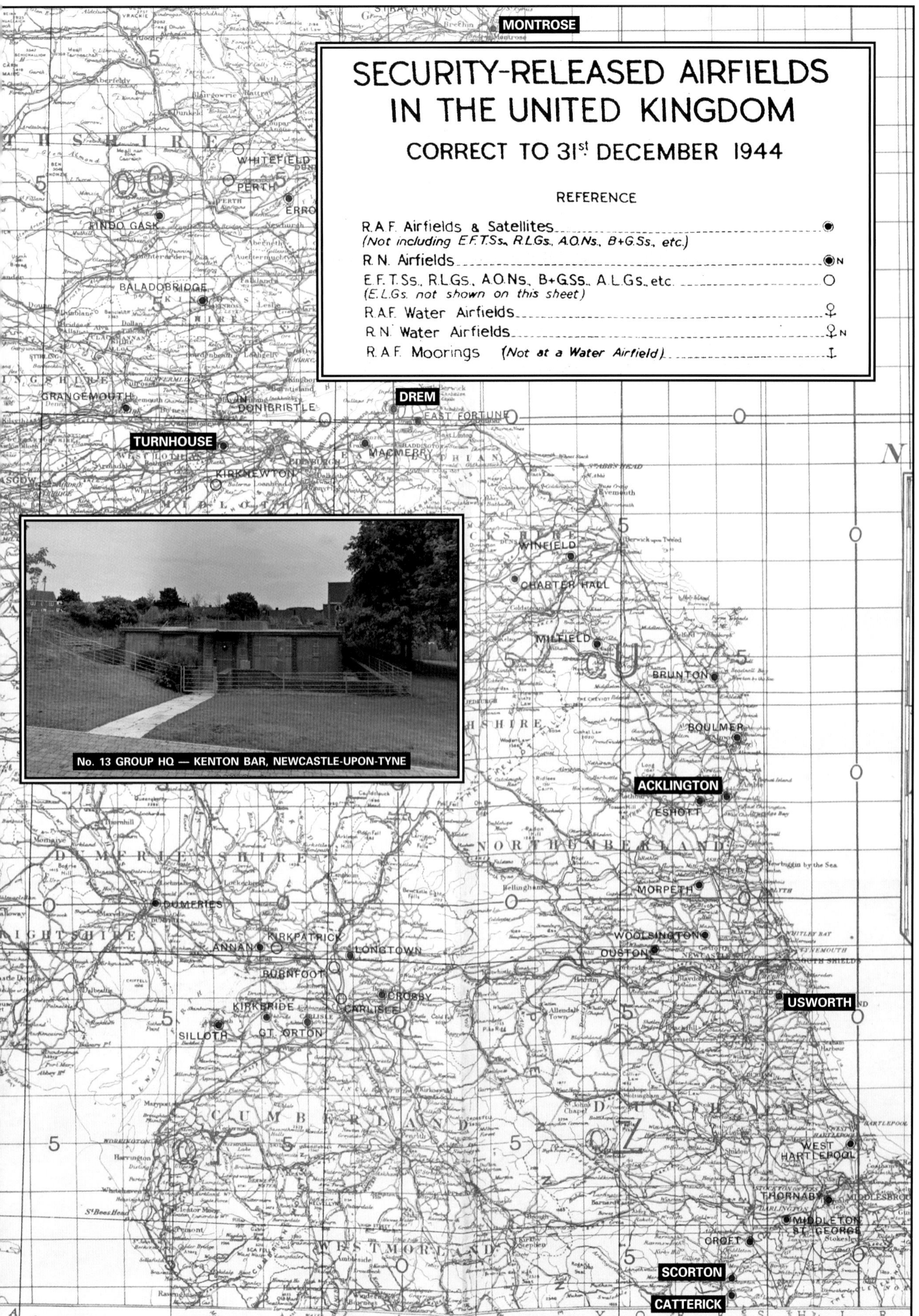

No. 13 GROUP HQ — KENTON BAR, NEWCASTLE-UPON-TYNE

Living up to the squadron motto 'Swift', this Spitfire from No. 72 was pictured over the Northumbrian coast sometime in 1941. At the time the unit was based at Acklington carring out convoy patrols

ACKLINGTON

This aerodrome was originally known as Southfields during the First World War and had been laid out within the vicinity of a coal field. The official, then secret, description of the airfield states that the permanent landmarks within the area of the base were 'Coquet Island five miles NE, Coquet River two miles N and NW. Broomhill Slagheap one mile E and by night, Broomhill Slagheap on a moonlit night'.

Grass surfaced, the dimensions were 1,400 yards N-S, 1,350 yards NE-SW, 1,250 yards SE-NW and 1,200 yards E-W. At 120 feet above sea level, the surface condition after precipitation was stated to be 'satisfactory except after abnormal rainfall'. In order to rectify this, three tarmac runways were constructed, the main being 1,600 yards and the secondaries 1,330 and 1,100 yards, all 50 yards wide. An abnormally large perimeter track measuring 16,500 x 50 feet gave access to one Bellman hangar, two 'F' type hangars and ten Over Blisters. A Type 1 Flying Control controlled the full Drem night landing facility together with VHF radio on two channels and a high frequency Darkie system for coastal and bomber emergencies. The accommodation scale was for three squadrons of day and night fighters with the airfield category and function being an operational satellite or RLG in No. 13 Group, Fighter Command with the parent stations at Ouston and Usworth.

Acklington first opened in 1938 as an Armament Training School which later became No. 2 Air Observers School. With the outbreak of war the school moved out to allow No. 607 (County of Durham) Auxiliary Squadron to bring in their Gladiator Is in from Usworth on October 10, 1939. Moving to Croydon a month later they were posted to France as part of the Air Component of the British Expeditionary Force. November saw a four-week stay by the Hurricane Is of No. 111 Squadron before they moved over to Drem.

The first of several squadrons to reform at the airfield did so on October 1 when No. 152 received their Gladiator I and IIs, later replaced by Spitfire Is in December. With detachments at Leconfield and Sumburgh, the rest of the squadron moved down to Warmwell on July 12, 1940.

It was the Hurricane Is of No. 43 Squadron that next flew in on November 18, 1939. Their first victory came on January 30 when Flight Lieutenant Caeser Hull and Sergeant F R Carey shot down an He 111. Three weeks later the squadron moved north to Wick.

March 2 saw No. 72 (Basutoland) Squadron arrive from Church Fenton with Spitfire Is for the first of two postings. Moving to Gravesend on June 1 to cover the Dunkirk evacuation with Spitfires and Gladiators, they came back to Acklington after five days remaining until August 31. On August 15 they took part in thwarting an attack by the Luftwaffe against Driffield airfield.

No. 72 was the first squadron to be equipped with the Gloster Gladiator in February 1937, their first Spitfires arriving two years later. However, when they were posted to Acklington the aerodrome being then only grass was unserviceable for the heavier monoplane, so for the first two weeks in March 1940 the squadron had to revert to the Gladiators. This picture taken during that period shows one of their machines but, in this case, a very special one as RN-D was being flown here by Flight Lieutenant James Nicolson *(right)* who would become the only pilot in Fighter Command to be awarded the Victorial Cross.

Arriving from heavy fighting down south, No. 32 Squadron came to Acklington on August 27. Flying Hurricane Is, they had been based at Biggin Hill during June, July and August but now, apart from a few standing patrols, they were rested until December 15 when they moved to Middle Wallop.

To provide defence for the North-East, the Hurricane Is of No. 258 Squadron flew in from Drem on December 17 but with little action they were moved to Jurby on February 1, 1941.

Acklington now began a period of Polish occupation when on January 8 No. 315 (Deblin) Polish Squadron formed at the airfield. Another Polish squadron, No. 317 (Wilno) was established just over a month later. Both were equipped with Hurricane Is and after a working up period, carried out a few North Sea patrols before 315 left for Speke on March 13 and 317 for Ouston on April 29.

A detachment of Defiants from No. 141 Squadron arrived during April to counter the heavy night attacks that were being meted out to towns and cities in the North-East. After the rest of the squadron had converted to the Beaufighter IF whilst at Drem, they joined the detatchment at Acklington on January 29, 1942, the whole squadron moving to Tangmere on June 23.

Another squadron to form up at the airfield was No. 406 (Lynx) Canadian Squadron on May 5, 1941. They were equipped with several marks of Blenheims but quickly received Beaufighter IIs with Merlin engines. After a working up period, Flying Officer Robert Fumerton and Sergeant Leslie Bing claimed the first victory on the night of September 1 when they shot down a Ju 88. The unit moved north to Ayr on February 1, 1942.

A detachment of Spitfire Vs from No. 167 Squadron came in during April 1942, followed by the Hurricane IIBs of No. 1 Squadron on July 8. The latter quickly converted to the Typhoon IB and began an intense period of working up before moving to Biggin Hill on February 9, 1943. Two months after the arrival of No. 1 Squadron, No. 219 (Mysore) arrived with their Beaufighter IFs from Tangmere. By the time they departed on October 21, 1942, they had claimed 44 enemy aircraft destroyed.

Nicolson failed to come through, being lost just days before the war ended when a Liberator in which he was a passenger in a raid on Rangoon crashed in the Bay of Bengal on May 2, 1945.

The Acklington airfield memorial to all those who served at the station was dedicated in Chevington Cemetery (on a minor road between South Broomhill and the airfield) on March 28, 2010.

Replaced by a Canadian squadron, No. 410 (Cougar), they exchanged their Beaufighter IIFs for Mosquito IIs managing to shoot down a Ju 88 on January 21 before moving to Coleby Grange on February 21, 1943.

No. 539 Squadron formed at Acklington from the nucleus of No. 1460 (Turbinlite) Flight on September 2, 1942 but, like all the Turbinlite squadrons, they were disbanded on January 25, 1943.

Another Canadian squadron, No. 409 (Nighthawk) arrived on February 23 with Beaufighter VIFs. Sending detachments to Drem, Coleby Grange, Peterhead and Coltishall, they spent an indifferent period at Acklington before departing to Coleby Grange on December 19, 1943. The year also saw further movements with No. 198 with Typhoon IBs (February 9-March 24); No. 350 (Belgian) with Spitfires (March 23-June 8, July 20-August 25); No. 349 (Belgian) with Spitfires (August 25-October 22), and No. 130 (Punjab) with Spitfires (December 21-January 4, 1944).

The New Year was to see more squadrons rotating through the airfield: No. 56 (Punjab) with Typhoon IBs (February 23-March 7); No. 266 (Rhodesia) with Typhoon IBs (March 15-23); No. 164 (Argentine-British) with Typhoon IBs (March 8-16); No. 222 (Natal) with Spitfires (February 25-March 10); No. 322 (Dutch) with Spitfire VC and XIV (March 10-April 24).

A short period of reconstruction during late 1944 saw Acklington designated a forward airfield as No. 19 Squadron with Mustang IVs flew in from Peterhead on May 23, 1945. They moved to Bradwell Bay on August 13. The next day the Mosquito XXXs of No. 219 (Mysore) Squadron arrived to become the last piston-engined unit to use Acklington. From May 1946 until 1972 the airfield was used as an armament practice camp and, after a period of care and maintenance, the technical site was redeveloped as a prison whilst the flying field was subjected to open-cast mining.

Having been an armament camp in the immediate post-war years, the Home Office took over a portion of the airfield for Acklington Prison which opened in 1972, the most northerly adult prison in England, with just under 1,000 male prisoners. The landing ground itself was at one stage subjected to open-cast mining operations.

As we have seen at other bases, a Spitfire was an essential requirement as a gate guardian at RAF stations after the war. No one knows more about the history of Spitfires which survive today than Gordon Riley, having recently completed a definitive two-volume history titled *Spitfire Survivors*: 'TB252 was ordered as part of the seventeenth order placed with the Castle Bromwich Aeroplane Factory for 1,884 Mk IX Spitfires dated April 19, 1944, and delivered to No. 9 MU at Cosford on January 6, 1945. After preparation for service at Cosford, TB252 was passed on to No. 84 Group Support Unit on March 1 at Thruxton for final preparation and issue to No. 329 (Cigognes) Squadron, a Free French unit operating with the RAF. Within a week of joining its unit the aircraft sustained damage, being re-issued after repair to No. 341 (Alsace) Squadron on March 15. When the unit gave up its aircraft on November 7, TB252 was transferred to No. 135 Wing on January 15, 1946. It then moved on to No. 350 (Belgian) Squadron of No. 146 Wing based at Fassberg, Belgium. TB252 continued to serve with the Belgians until further damage was sustained later that year. The Spitfire was returned to the UK, being issued after repair to No. 61 OTU at RAF Keevil in Wiltshire on May 29, 1947. No. 61 OTU was renamed No. 203 Advanced Flying School moving to Chivenor in October. It survived a mid-air collision with SL577 on November 30, 1948 which resulted in a forced landing near Braunton, Devon. It was then transferred to the School of Land Air Warfare at Old Sarum on January 18, 1949 before moving to No. 33 MU at Lyneham on February 27, 1953 for storage. After more than two years in store, TB252 was allocated to RAF Odiham, as a ground instructional airframe on September 12, 1955. It had arrived at Odiham still wearing its RAF serial and with a black top cowling but was repainted and placed on display in an all-silver scheme. On August 21, 1959 it appeared on the gate at RAF Acklington *(above)*, still in its all silver scheme but by September 1960 it was camouflaged and wearing the yellow codes "RR-M", said to be the initials of the CO. It avoided being used in the *Battle of Britain* film and on July 14, 1969 it arrived on the gate of RAF Boulmer, moving on to RAF Leuchars on December 5 that year, being displayed in the wartime markings of No. 340 Squadron until the spring of 1986, when it moved south to Bentley Priory as a replacement for SL574, which had been donated to the American Eagle Squadron at San Diego, California. When repainted in 1987 the codes had been corrupted to read "G-WH" on the starboard side. Following the RAF's decision to remove genuine Spitfires from outside display, TB252 was acquired by Tim Routsis in mid-1988 and was moved to the Essex workshops of Vintage Fabrics on November 16 that year. Here it was inspected and found to be in remarkably complete condition and in September 1990 it was moved to Historic Flying Ltd's new premises at Audley End, Essex. Registered as G-XVIE, restoration work started late in 1997 on behalf of new owner Nicholas Springer of Germany but this was halted when the aircraft was sold. In May 2002 it was reportedly purchased by American collector Tony Banta of Livermore, California.

Without its gate guardian, the prison had an inauspicious start with a number of high profile escapes!

ALDERGROVE

RAF Aldergrove was opened in May 1918 but it was not until July 1940 that air defence was provided by the Hurricanes of No. 245 Squadron, this picture being taken in the winter of 1940-41.

By this time, Aldergrove's grass permitted four take-off directions — north, north-east, south and south-east.

This aerodrome, at a height of 260 feet above sea level lay 13 miles north-west of Belfast in Antrim, Northern Ireland. It was used as an airfield by manufacturers Harland & Wolff. Opened in 1918 as an Aircraft Acceptance Park, it closed a year later but was retained by the RAF to be used for summer camps and air exercises. With the outbreak of war, No. 2 Armament Training Station became No. 3 Air Observers School. It later became No. 3 Bombing and Gunnery School until this disbanded on July 11, 1940.

As the grass surface became unfit for landing after heavy rain, by the summer of 1940, three tarmac runways were under construction, two being 1,200 x 50 yards and the third 980 x 50 yards. A Type II flying control, later upgraded to a Type 343/43, several Blister hangars and large aeroplane sheds were constructed together with Drem runway lighting. There were limited radio facilities.

No. 502 (Ulster) Auxiliary Squadron which had been established at Aldergrove as a special reserve squadron in May 1925, was now transferred to the auxiliary air force with the outbreak of hostilities. Flying Ansons, Bothas and Whitleys, they were to remain at Aldergrove until January 27, 1941.

Although designated a sector station in No. 13 Group of Fighter Command, it was

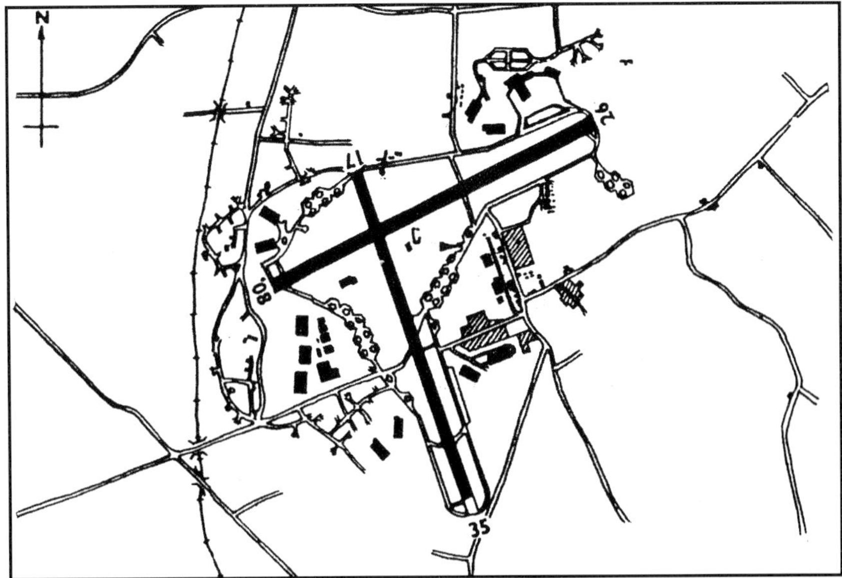

Three tarmac runways were then laid down on the bearings of 070, 130 and 165 degrees but by the 1960s the NW-SE (130) runway had been eliminated.

Fast forward 50 years and we can see that the main 08-26 (now 07/25) has been lengthened to just over 3,000 yards.

Flashback to 1941 with DX-K of No. 245 Squadron taxiing back to its dispersal following a shipping patrol.

In recent years Aldergrove has seen an increased helicopter presence with the Chinooks of No. 18 Squadron; the Wessex of No. 72 and Pumas of No. 230. The Army Air Corps also joined in with their Lynx and Gazelles.

the Royal Navy that occupied the airfield once war broke out when No. 774 Squadron of the Fleet Air Arm arrived on December 25, 1939. Flying Rocs, Skuas, Swordfish and Sharks, they were attached to No. 3 Bombing and Gunnery School. A move to Evanton on July 3 saw No. 231 Squadron, RAF, reform at Aldergrove from No. 416 Flight. Equipped with the Lysander III, the squadron moved on to Newtownwards 12 days later.

In addition to the RAF, the airfield was shared by No. 23 Maintenance Unit with the first aircraft arriving in November 1939. By 1940, Wellingtons, Hampdens and Blenheims were being prepared for squadron service.

On July 20 the Hurricane Is of No. 245 (Northern Rhodesia) Squadron were posted in for air defence. With detachments at Limavady and Ballyhalbert, the squadron saw action over Belfast with the commanding officer shooting down a Do 17 over the Irish Sea on May 13, 1941. They moved to Ballyhalbert on July 14.

During 1939 and 1940 several detachments from Coastal Command came to Aldergrove: Blenheim IVFs of No. 254 Squadron (August 1940 to January 1941 and May 29 to December 10); No. 224 with Hudsons (May 1939-April 15, 1940); No. 233 with Blenheim IVs (August 3-September 14, 1940 and Hudsons from December 8, 1940 to August 16, 1941), and No. 102 Squadron with Whitleys during September and October 1940.

It was back to Fighter Command when No. 272 Squadron reformed at Aldergrove on November 18, 1940 from flights of Nos. 235 and 236 Squadrons. Flying Blenheim IVFs, they carried out shipping escort duties before moving to Chivenor on April 3, 1941.

Convoy patrols became the remit of No. 252 Squadron when they arrived on April 6, 1941 flying Beaufighter ICs but by May most of the aircraft had been sent to Malta, their place being taken by the Blenheim IVFs of No. 254 Squadron which arrived on May 29. They carried out several anti-shipping strikes before leaving for Dyce on December 10. Five days later No. 143 Squadron arrived with Blenheim IVs, remaining until April 23, 1942.

By this time Aldergrove had transferred from Fighter Command to Coastal Command and the base was left to Liberators, Fortresses and Wellingtons. No. 23 Maintenance Unit continued serving at the airfield until 1978 when it disbanded. Aldergrove officially closed as an RAF airfield in September 2009 and is now better known as Belfast International Airport.

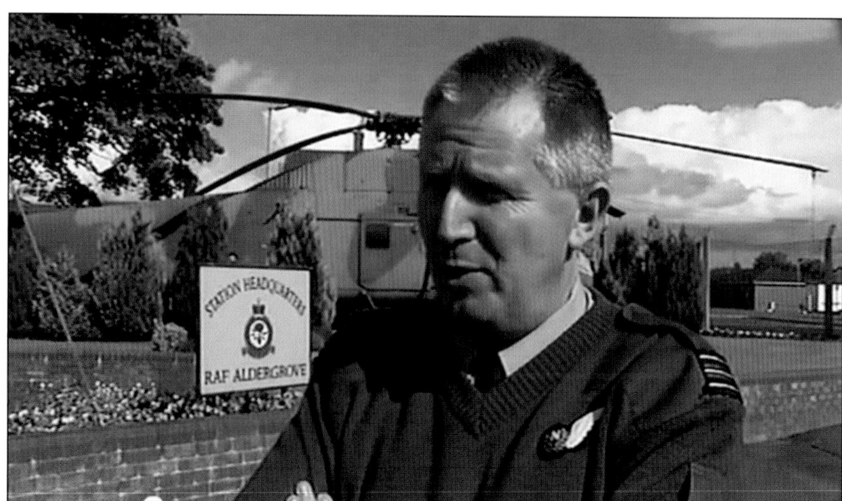

However, in April 2008, the Armed Forces Minister announced that No. 230 Squadron was to be relocated to Benson in England, and that Aldergrove would close, effectively ending 91 years of RAF history in Northern Ireland. The RAF facility on the south side of the airfield would then become the joint Helicopter Command Flying Station Aldergrove. Squadron Leader Jim Maginnis *(above)*, the Chief-of-Staff at Aldergrove, announced that the final parade would take place on September 20, 2009.

In May 2006 the northern civilian side of the airfield was named after Belfast's soccer legend, George Best.

AYR

Originally called Heathfield, Ayr was one of the main airfields for the defence of Scotland. Situated two miles north east of Ayr town and just 50 feet above sea level, the grass surface after precipitation was described as 'very soft. Never been serviceable for landing'. Consequently three concrete runways in the standard triangular pattern were under construction by the autumn of 1940. With the longest being 1,600 x 50 yds, next 1,360 x 50 yds and the shortest 1,200 x 50 yds, a 50 foot perimeter track was laid at the same time. Three Bellman hangars and a Type II Regional watch office plus the VHF/DF trailer provided control of the Drem night landing facility. Designated a sector station in No. 13 Group, Fighter Command, Ayr had satellites at Turnberry, West Freugh and Machrihanish.

Construction of the airfield began in October 1940 and was officially opened on April 7, 1941. Such speed in building was not common at that time but many surrounding buildings were requisitioned. With accommodation listed as two fighter squadrons, first to arrive were the Spitfire Is of No. 602 (City of Glasgow) Auxiliary Squadron on April 15. A detachment was sent to Montrose whilst the rest of the squadron converted to the Spitfire IIA and left for Kenley on July 10. The Defiant Is of No. 141 Squadron flew in to convert to the Beaufighter IF on April 29. They carried out night patrols claiming eight enemy aircraft destroyed in May before a move to Acklington on January 29, 1942.

The first Canadian squadron at Ayr, No. 410 (Cougar) formed at the airfield on June 30, 1941. Receiving Defiant Is, working up on them took until August 6 when they moved to Drem. Whilst there a conversion to the Beaufighter IIF saw them back at Ayr on June 15, 1942, to commence night patrols over Scotland and the north. With no enemy aircraft seen, they moved to Scorton on September 1.

February 1, 1942, saw another Canadian squadron fly in. No. 406 (Lynx) were the first Canadian nightfighter squadron to form. Their Beaufighter IIFs were tasked with defending the Clyde and its associated industry. Sending a detachment to Scorton the rest of the squadron moved there on June 16.

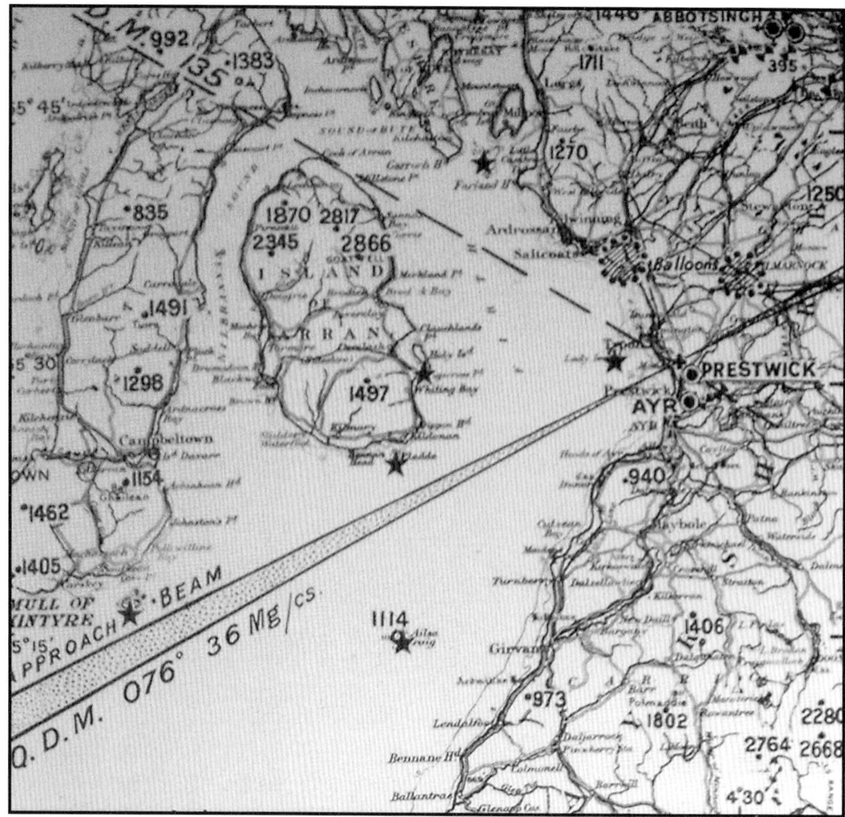

The aerodrome at Ayr on the western coast of Scotland lay barely a couple of miles south of the International Airlines Terminal at Prestwick, a staging post used to bring aircraft in from the United States.

The beginning of 1942 also saw the Spitfire IIAs of the first Free French Squadron arrive, No. 340 (GC IV/2 'Ile de France'). Several abortive scrambles were flown before they converted to the Spitfire VB and moved to Redhill on April 1, 1942.

The Hurricane IIBs of No. 312 (Czech) Squadron came in on August 19, 1941. A detachment to Turnhouse saw the rest of the squadron change to Spitfire IIAs, IIBs and VBs with which they carried out convoy patrols managing to accumulate 231 operational hours. They moved to Fairwood Common on January 1, 1942.

Another squadron to form at Ayr was No. 165 (Ceylon) on April 6, 1942. Equipped with Spitfire VAs and VBs, detachments went to Drem and Turnhouse before the squadron moved to Eastchurch on August 15, 1942. Other Spitfire squadrons based at Ayr over this period were Nos. 72 (Basutoland) (August12-September 26), 232 detachment (May-August), 222 (Natal) (October 22-March 27, 1943).

The Mustang Is of No. 241 (Army Co-Op) Squadron arrived on May 2, 1942. Carrying out several army exercises they left on November 12 en route for North Africa.

Because Prestwick was still grass, it was convenient that the newly-completed hard runways at nearby Ayr were available for use when necessary by heavier aircraft. This B-17C Flying Fortress (AN529), pictured on the aerodrome, was one of a batch of 20 flown to Britain and issued to No. 90 Squadron which had been specially reformed in May 1941 to operate the American aircraft. This particular machine was written off in Libya later that year.

So close were the two airfields that Ayr was literally swallowed up by the huge expansion of Prestwick after the war. The extensions to its runways can be seen on the right with only the end section of the NE-SW runway at Ayr remaining.

The overhead view graphically shows the change . . . from 1943 to 2013.

FAIRWAY VIEW

This is Fairway View pictured by Chris Cooper — just a normal suburban street — but once the main NW-SE runway at Ayr.

Partnering them at Ayr were the Beaufighter IIFs of No. 488 (RNZAF) Squadron which arrived on September 1, 1942. Conversion to the VIF mark saw detachments at Drem and Coltishall before they left for Drem on August 3, 1943.

In contrast the Auster IIIs of No. 652 (Army Co-Op) Squadron flew in from Methven on July 2, 1943 to carry out local army exercises before moving to Ipswich on December 7 prior to going to Normandy in June, 1944. Other units coming and going during 1943 were No. 835 Fleet Air Arm Squadron with Swordfish and Sea Hurricanes (July 30-September 20), the USAAF 415th Night Fighter Squadron with Beaufighters (April-June), No. 278 (ASR) Squadron with Walrus and Ansons. No. 169 Squadron reformed at Ayr on October 1, 1943, equipping with Mosquito IIs when they moved to Little Snoring on December 8.

With Ayr now supporting an armament practice camp, No. 1490 Flight arrived to provide target towing aircraft. Numerous squadrons attended the camp on a weekly basis with No. 439 (Westmount) Canadian Squadron with Hurricane IVs arriving on January 8, 1944 for a two month stay. They converted to the Typhoon IB and had left by the time of the arrival once again of the Fleet Air Arm which prompted Ayr to be transferred to the Admiralty on September 16, 1944.

With the closure of the armament practice camp, the station became HMS Wagtail, a shore facility to house squadrons from carriers based in Scotland. This usage continued until 1946 when Ayr was put to care and maintenance. Re-activated for USAF units based at nearby Prestwick from 1951 till 1957, the site was returned to its owners shortly after with most of the buildings being pulled down.

In May 1942, Spitfire AD540 was on the strength of No. 242 Squadron, newly-reformed and based at Turnhouse although B Flight was currently detached to Ayr. But this was no ordinary Spitfire — it was a presentation aircraft which had been donated by the people of Newmarket. Presentation aircraft were sponsored by individuals or organisations, the Minister of Aircraft Production having set a figure of £5,000 for a single-engined fighter. (The real cost was much higher, the engine alone costing £2,000, fuselage £2,500, wings £1,800, guns £800, propellor £350 right down to sparking plugs at eight shillings and rivets at sixpence!) AD540 had been named *Blue Peter* after the chestnut colt born in Lord Rosebery's stables at Newmarket and winner of the Derby in May 1939. On May 23, 1942, Pilot Officer David Blair, who had only recently completed his flying training, took off from Ayr in *Blue Peter* to escort the *Queen Mary* on her approach to the Clyde carrying one of the first contingents of American troops to arrive in mainland Britain. At 20,000 feet, the aircraft was seen to suddenly disappear into a storm cloud. Baling out too low, the pilot's body was discovered half a mile from where *Blue Peter* crashed. Exactly 50 years later, the site was investigated by members of the Scottish Region of the Spitfire Society led by Ralph Davidson and a huge amount of wreckage was uncovered from a bleak mountainside north of Carsphairn. (The full story is recounted in *After the Battle* No. 85.)

CATTERICK

The Way to the Stars — **the title adopted from the Latin motto of the RAF 'Per Ardua ad Astra' — was released in 1945. The opening shots show a derelict airfield 'Half-penny Field' recently abandoned with sheep grazing and empty hangars . . .**

One of the first military airfields, Catterick opened in November 1915 for training pilots for the defence of the north of England. With the formation of the RAF in 1918, it became No. 49 Training Depot and served as such throughout the inter-war years.

At 175 feet above sea level, the airfield was grass measuring 1,020 yard from E-W, 933 yards N-S, 857 yards SE-NW and 716 yards NE-SW. A single tarmac 1,020-yard runway and a 50 foot perimeter track were added, the latter leading to 12 double and four single dispersal pens for the accommodation of 28 fighter aircraft. These were situated south-east and north-east of the airfield. A fuel dump containing 81,000 gallons of aviation spirit and 5,800 gallons of MT fuel was dispensed by means of a tanker. Prone to fog morning and evening when a westerly wind was blowing, the nearby River Swale could also cause misty conditions. The usual facilities of a Type II flying control, Drem runway lighting and VHF and HF radio communications were provided.

The first resident was No. 26 Squadron which reformed at Catterick in Army Co-op Command on October 11,1927. In 1935 the airfield was visited by the Directorate of Works as it was considered worthy of expansion. Two 'C' type hangars and a large domestic and work site were constructed at the end of which Catterick was transferred from Army Co-op Command to become a sector station in No. 13 Group, Fighter Command with a satellite at Scorton.

Resident squadrons as war broke out were Nos. 41, 609 (West Riding) Auxiliary, 219 (Mysore) and a detachment from 64 Squadron, all flying Spitfire Is. With No. 609 moving to Acklington on October 6, 1939, and No. 41 to Wick on October 19, the opening phases of the war saw No. 219 and the No. 64 detachment ready for action. No. 41 Squadron were to alternate between Catterick and Hornchurch until February making its first kill on April 3, 1940 when Flight Lieutenant Ryder shot down a He 111 earning a DFC in the process.

Another squadron that was to alternate between Catterick and Hornchurch was No. 54 who first arrived at Catterick on May 28 with Spitfire Is. Just before they arrived the detachment from No. 64 Squadron had taken their Spitfires to Kenley on May 16 to cover Operation 'Dynamo'.

. . . but this is actually Catterick, today the British Army's Marne Barracks. The scene looks almost unchanged over six decades later.

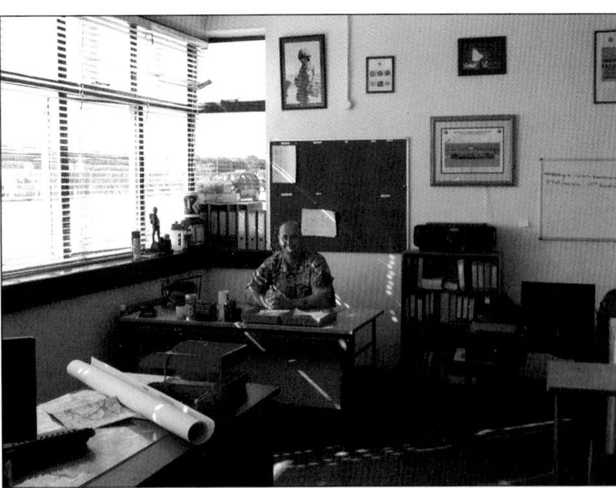

Dating from 1935, the control, or watch tower was built during the period between the wars when the RAF's facilities were being expanded. The squadron featured in the film is a fictitious one, No. 720, commanded by Squadron Leader Carter played by Trevor Howard. As there is now very little flying at Catterick, the ground floor of the tower has been modified and converted into an office. Sergeant John Devlin enjoyed standing in for the actors.

With the air battle raging down south, No. 600 (City of London) Auxiliary Squadron was posted in from Redhill on October 12 with the Beaufighter IF. They had arrived to continue working up on the type, managing to send detachments to Drem, Acklington and Prestwick. September saw the arrival of No. 504 (County of Nottingham) Auxiliary Squadron equipped with Hurricane Is although they left for Hendon after only four days. No. 219 Squadron departed for Redhill on October 12..

The first squadron to reform at Catterick was No. 256 on November 23. Flying Defiant Is in the night fighter role, the squadron began an intense working up period before moving to Pembrey on January 4, 1941. Three days later another squadron reformed at the airfield; this was No. 68 Squadron with Blenheim IFs. They too commenced working up before taking the aircraft to High Ercall on April 23.

Carrying on this tradition, No. 313 (Czech) Squadron next formed at Catterick on May 10. This was the third Czech squadron to be established and, receiving Spitfire Is, it became operational within the month, moving to Leconfield on July 31.

A few weeks earlier No. 1472 Flight flying Masters had also formed up to give air support training to the nearby Home Forces Battle School. The County of Kent Fighter Squadron, No. 131, arrived on July 10 equipped with Spitfires purchased by public subscription in Kent. After a brief stay, they moved to Ternhill on August 6 after witnessing the arrival of the Hurricane I and IIBs of No. 331 (Norwegian) Squadron, another unit that had formed up at the airfield on July 21 — the first of the Norwegian squadrons in the RAF. They were joined by the Spitfire IIBs of No. 145 Squadron, which had flown in to rest on July 28. Conversion to the Mk VB saw them carry out North Sea patrols before leaving on February 11, 1942, en route for the Middle East.

Once the film flashes back to the war years, the timeline is May 1942 when the squadron is seen equipped with the Douglas DB-7 Havoc (known also by the RAF as the Boston).

The fire tender shed with the crew ready for action. Save for the vehicle, time has virtually stood still.

When No. 720 Squadron is posted to the Middle East, the transport is filmed exiting the main gate.

Further Spitfire Is came in when No. 122 (Bombay) Squadron arrived from Ouston on August 31. Converting to the Mk IIA in September, they moved to Scorton on October 6, 1941. Replacing them were the Hurricanes of No. 134 Squadron on their return from a three-month detachment to Russia on December 7, 1941. They converted to the Spitfire VA before moving to Eglinton.

The second Norwegian squadron to become part of the RAF, No. 332, formed at Catterick on January 15, 1942. Initially given Spitfire VAs they switched to the Mk VBs in April, sending a detachment to Thornaby at the same time. After flying several convoy patrols the squadron moved to North Weald to join its sister squadron.

On July 16, 1942, the Mustang Is of No. 63 Squadron flew in, departing to Weston Zoyland on November 6, returning to Catterick on November 13 for a further eight-day stay.

The Canadians of No. 403 (Wolf) Squadron were posted in from Martlesham Heath on June 19, 1942. Sending a detachment to West Hartlepool, they moved to Manston on July 1, returning a week later to carry out a few interception patrols and enjoying a rest period. They returned south on January 23, 1943 with a move to Kenley.

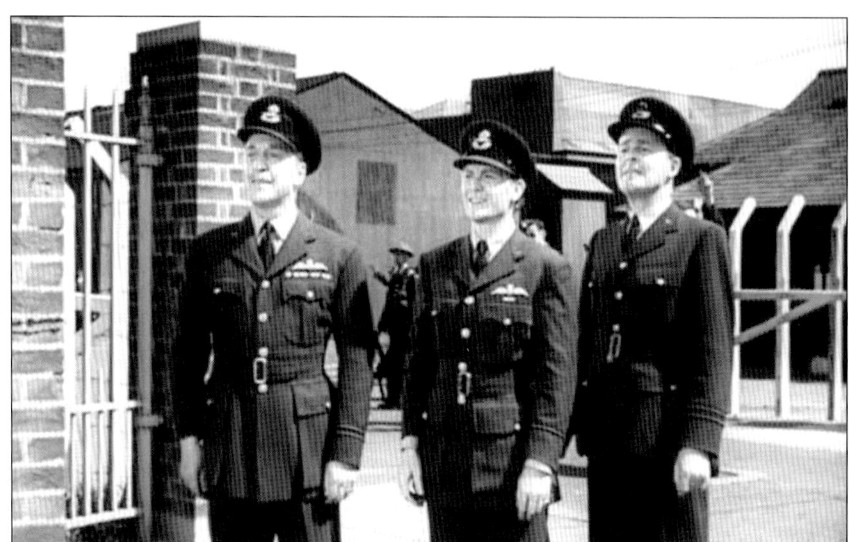

Basil Radford (as Tiny Williams), John Mills (Peter Penrose) and Hugh Dempster (playing 'Tinker' Bell) see them off as they are to remain behind at the station to welcome the new arrivals from the USA.

The guardroom in the right background remains unchanged although the entrance gates have been relocated further up the road.

In come the Americans with B-17 Flying Fortresses. The first raid by the US Eighth Air Force on August 17, 1942 to Rouen is featured in the film although this was actually carried out by the 97th Bomb Group based at Grafton Underwood. The Eighth's commander, General Ira Eaker, rode aboard *Yankee Doodle* of the 414th Bomb Squadron for this operation which inaugurated participation by the United States in the air war in Europe. To give the film an American flavour, the title was changed for the US release to *Johnny in the Clouds* derived from a poem recited in the film as a tribute to a dead American airman. *For Johnny* was composed by John Pudney, one of the writers: 'Do not despair . . . For Johnny-head-in-air; He sleeps as sound . . . As Johnny underground. Fetch out no shroud . . . For Johnny-in-the-cloud; And keep your tears . . . For him in after years. Better by far . . . For Johnny-the-bright-star, To keep your head . . . And see his children fed.'

When No. 403 Canadian Squadron left they were immediately replaced by another Canadian unit, No. 401 (Ram) on January 23, 1943. Converting from the Spitfire VB to the Mk IX variant, they carried out a period of intensive training. Sending a detachment to Thornaby, the squadron became part of No. 83 Group in the Second Tactical Air Force, moving to Redhill as part of the Kenley Wing on May 29.

Catterick now saw a period with fewer changes in squadron movements. No. 130 Squadron's Spitfire VBs came in from West Malling on September 18, 1943 for a brief posting, departing to Scorton on November 10.The disbandment of the Air Support Unit, No. 1472 Flight five days later saw the airfield strangely quiet, and the end of operational flying at Catterick was marked early in 1944 with an 11-day stay by the Spitfire LF IXBs of No. 222 (Natal) Squadron. The airfield was used as an aircrew allocation centre in 1945 before becoming the main depot for the RAF Regiment. When this unit moved to Honington in 1994, Catterick was handed over to the army and is now named the 'Marne Barracks'.

This is where the film parade was held alongside the control tower.

So now back to reality. The first of the Norwegian squadrons to be formed in the Royal Air Force was No. 331 established at Catterick on July 21, 1941. Cato Guhnfeldt, the squadron historian, explains that this picture was taken on May 4, 1942 during a stop-over while en route from Skeabrae in the Orkney Islands (see page 348) to their new base down south at North Weald. The second squadron of the Royal Norwegian Air Force, No. 332, had been established earlier that January and both squadrons then made North Weald their permanent station for the next two years. The affinity that these two units have for the Essex airfield has lasted right up to the present day with frequent visitors from Norway (see page 198). *Below:* This is A Flight of No. 219 which had been reformed at Catterick as a night-fighter squadron with Bristol Blenheims.

Early in 1914, Lord Baden Powell proposed to Field-Marshal Horatio Kitchener, the Secretary of State for War, that an 'Aldershot of the North' should be established in north Yorkshire where the countryside would provide excellent training grounds. A camp initially for two divisions (i.e. 40,000 men) was established four miles west of the Great North Road at Catterick complete with its own road and rail facilities. During the last year of the First World War the Catterick garrison was divided into two with the infantry at Scotton and the artillery and tanks at Hipswell. There was also a POW camp. In the 1920s the War Office decided to make the facilities permanent and brick buildings began to replace the wartime huts, eventually comprising more than a dozen separate barracks. The aerodrome just to the east of the Great North Road was taken over by the RAF Regiment in 1950 but it was later given to the Army. So where the Spitfires lined up in front of the hangars, now lies a huge vehicle park.

Squashed in between the Great North Road and the River Swale, originally grass, a single runway was added later on a NW-SE axis.

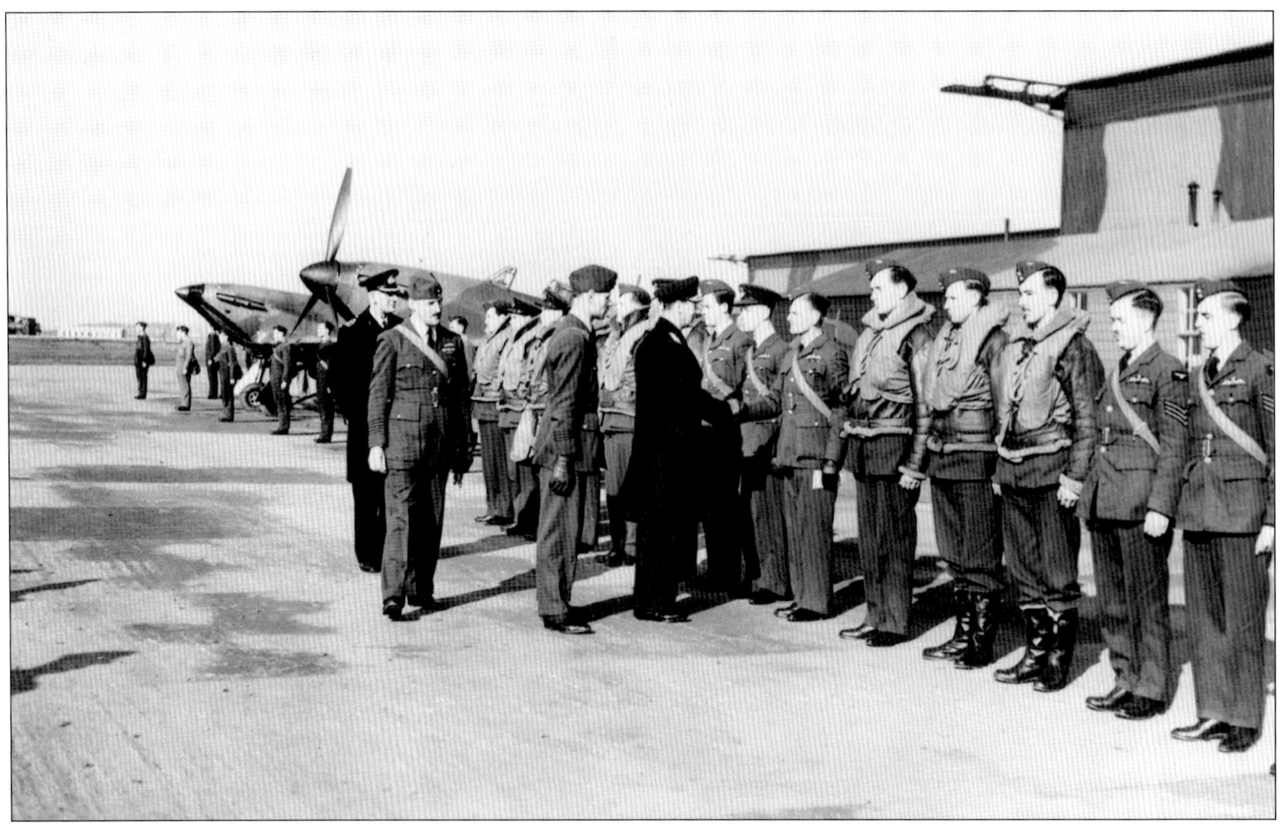

When HM King George VI visited Drem during his Scottish tour in February 1940, the aerodrome had already been party to the demise of early raiders including the first German bought down on the British mainland — a Heinkel from Stab/KG26 on October 28.

DREM

Initially called West Fenton as an airfield had existed on the site since 1916 when it was used by No. 77 Home Defence Squadron, this became No. 2 Training Depot with Avro 504, SE5A and Pup and Camel biplanes. It also housed the American 41st Aero Squadron. Re-named Gullane at the end of the First World War, it remained empty until 1933 at which point the grass was re-sown and it became RAF Drem in 1938.

Three grass runways were marked out, the main being 1,600 x 100 yards and the other two 1,406 x 100 yards. A concrete perimeter track 35-feet wide led to three Bellman hangars and 14 Blisters. A Type II flying control controlled landing facility and the VHF. DF/Homer, VHF ZZ and Darkey Homer. With the parent station at Turnhouse, Drem was designated a forward aerodrome in No. 13 Group, Fighter Command.

With the advent of war, Spitfire Is of No. 609 (West Riding) Auxiliary Squadron were posted in from Acklington on October 17, 1939, tasked with the defence of the Scottish Lowlands. They moved south to Northolt on May 19, 1940 having shot down an He 111 on February 27 off St Abb's Head, Berwickshire.

No. 609 had been joined by No. 72 (Basutoland) Squadron on December 1, 1939, also with Spitfire Is. Carrying out coastal and convoy patrols, they left for Leconfield on January 12, 1940. Further Spitfire Is arrived when No. 602 (City of Glasgow) Auxiliary Squadron flew in from Grangemouth on October 13, 1939. Leaving for Dyce on April 14, 1940, they came back on May 28 finally moving to Westhampnett on August 14.

No. 111 Squadron had a brief stay with their Hurricane Is when they came in on December 7, 1939 but they moved out to Wick on February 27, 1940. On April 4 the Blenheim IFs of No. 29 Squadron arrived for night defence duties although their posting was only for just over a month as they departed to Debden on May 10.

Five more Hurricane squadrons rotated through Drem during 1940: No. 145 (August 14-31); No. 232 (October 24-November 11); No. 245 (Northern Rhodesia) (May 12-June 5); No. 263 (Argentina) (June 12-28 and September 2-November 28), and No. 605 (County of Warwick) Auxiliary (May 28-September 7). October 15 saw the arrival of No. 141 Squadron with Defiant Is for one week.

The year of 1940 also saw a development of some significance when the Drem runway lighting system was invented at the airfield. Night landings by Spitfires and Hurricanes were made difficult due to the fact that the pilot could not see ahead due to the Merlin engine in front of him and also the glare of the exhaust. Experiments were carried out placing a circle of glim lamps positioned on the normal curving approach that a Spitfire or Hurricane pilot had to adopt. Once developed it enabled aircraft to land at night and eventually it became standard on all airfields. One of the first squadrons to use the facility was No. 600 (City of London) Auxiliary Squadron when a detachment of Beaufighter IFs arrived on October 12, 1940, with the entire squadron following on March 14, 1941. With a detachment at Prestwick, they left for Colerne on April 28.

Hurricanes returned to Drem on December 12, 1940, when No. 43 Squadron flew in. Tasked with the defence of Scapa Flow, they left on February 22, 1941 for Crail, returning

Keith Davies was disappointed to find that the wooden crew room, seen behind the airmen on parade, had only recently been demolished, the hangar having been extended and reclad.

One of the photographers covering the Royal visit on February 28 would appear to have taken this shot of his colleagues for fun but fortunately for us it shows two of No. 609 Squadron's Spitfires in the distance.

on March 1. Now classified as a day and night fighter squadron, conversions to the Hurricane IIA and IIB saw them destroy several enemy aircraft before moving to Acklington on October 4, 1941.

By the spring of 1941 it was the Spitfire squadrons that were to swiftly rotate through the base. No. 611 (West Lancashire) Auxiliary were there from November 13 to June 3, 1942; No. 64 from May 20 to August 6 and again from October 4 to November 17, 1941; No.123 (East India) between August 6 and September 22, and No. 340 (Ile de France) December 20-January 1, 1942.

No. 410 (Cougar) Canadian Squadron was the third Canadian night fighter squadron to form in the UK. Bringing their Defiant Is to Drem on August 6, 1941, they swiftly converted to the Beaufighter IIF but, leaving a detachment behind, they moved to Ayr on June 15, 1942. August 10 saw No. 222 (Natal) Squadron arrive with Spitfire VBs for a six-day posting. Two days after the Canadian squadron had left, No. 453 (Australian) Squadron reformed at Drem with Spitfire VBs. They witnessed an attack on the airfield on August 12 that caused damage to the operations room and four of their Spitfires. They left for Hornchurch on September 25 but not before their replacement, No. 222 (Natal) Squadron had arrived back on August 21. Carrying out the usual convoy patrols, they moved to Ayr on October 27, 1942.

The Whirlwinds of No. 137 Squadron were based at Drem for nine days from August 2, 1942, with a new squadron, No. 197 that had formed up at Turnhouse, moving to Drem on November 25. After one week they received the Typhoon IA but once the working-up

Spitfires, hangar, photographers . . . all have passed into the pages of history.

The first air attack upon British territory during the Second World War took place on October 16, 1939 against shipping in the Firth of Forth, seen in the distance on this shot of Drem looking westwards. Two of the Junkers Ju 88s were shot down, one by No. 602 from Drem, the other by No. 603 based at Turnhouse (page 326).

The sleek machines of the Australians in No. 453 Squadron have long departed from Drem but all is not lost . . .

period had been completed, they moved on to the Mk IB and commenced East Coast patrols. They moved south to Tangmere on March 28, 1943.

A flying visit by No. 65 Squadron Spitfire VBs from September 20, 1942 until January 3, 1943 saw them back at Drem on January 10 to carry out bomber escorts. They finally departed to Perranporth on March 29.

No. 488 (RNZAF) Squadron with the Beaufighter IIF sent a detachment from Ayr to Drem on September 1, 1942. Converting to the Mk VIF variant, the entire squadron arrived on August 3, 1943 tasked with the night defence of the Clyde area. A further conversion to the Mosquito XII saw them move to Bradwell Bay on September 3. In their place came No. 96 Squadron. Arriving the next day they converted from Beaufighters to Mosquito XIIIs taking them to West Malling on November 8.

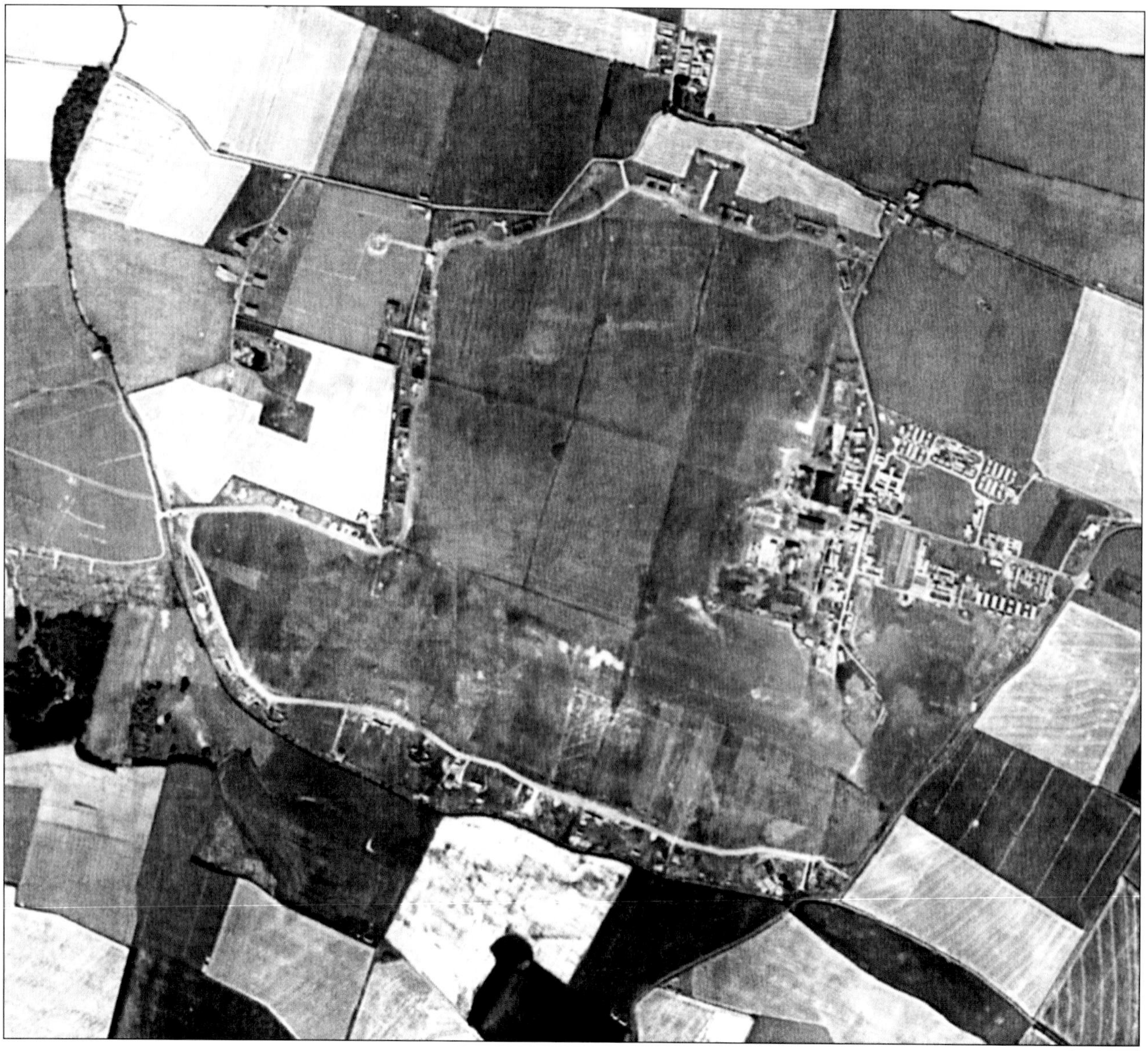

No. 186 Squadron was established at Drem on April 27, 1943, but moved to Ayr on August 3 to re-equip with Hurricanes. October 9 saw No. 281 (ASR) Squadron arrive with Defiant, Walrus and Anson types before disbanding on November 22.

The Poles arrived on November 9 when No. 307 (Lwow) Squadron flew their Mosquito VIs in from Predannack. Sending a detachment to Sumburgh, they converted to the Mk XII in January 1944 before moving to Coleby Grange on March 2.

Since 1942 a Royal Navy squadron detachment had been stationed at Drem. No. 784 Squadron was a night fighter training school equipped with Fulmars, Fireflies, Hellcats and Harvards. The entire squadron arrived on July 21, 1944 but left on August 3 when it embarked aboard HMS *Campania*. It returned to Drem on August 18 until September 6.

During 1944, Drem returned to hosting units on air defence duties with both a Spitfire and Hurricane squadron. Nos. 91 (Nigeria) came with Spitfires (March 17-April 23), and No. 309 Polish (Ziema Czerwienska) with Hurricane IV, IIC and Mustang I and III (April 23-November 14). No. 340 (GC IV/2 'Ile de France') with Spitfire IXBs was the last wartime fighter squadron at the station. Arriving on December 17, 1944 they stayed until January 30, 1945, and as they left Drem was transferred to the Admiralty and commissioned as HMS *Nighthawk* on June 21, 1945.

. . . as Rolls-Royce engines can still be heard on the old technical site, courtesy of Keith Cornwell and Tony Brown of A1 Classic Cars.

Reverting back to RAF control in March 1946, it was put on a care and maintenance basis and later became a government civil engineering department with the majority of the surviving buildings becoming occupied by small businesses as part of the Fenton Barns Retail Village. A small historical collection and exhibition is on show in the Arts and Crafts Gallery in the village which records the duties of RAF Drem during wartime.

The 'City of Glasgow' squadron, No. 602, were transferred to Fighter Command's No. 13 Group in January 1939, the CO then being Squadron Leader Andrew Farquhar, this photograph being taken at Dyce.

DYCE

Despite being one of the sites suggested by Sir Alan Cobham and his National Flying Services Ltd to become a municipal airport, a 130-acre site at Dyce in Aberdeenshire, was rejected by the local council. In the end it was Mr. E.L. Gandar-Dower who established the airport that opened on July 4, 1934, and brought civil air travel to that part of Scotland. With the prospect of war, RAF squadrons began to use the airfield which by 1938 had been taken over by the military.

Six and a quarter miles north-west of Aberdeen and 237 feet above sea level, the grass surface measured 1,400 yards NE-SW, 1,360 yards N-S, 1,350 yards SE-NW and 1,200 yards E-W. A 50-foot concrete perimeter track, four Bellman hangars and one Bessonneau hangar together with several domestic blocks were ready for occupation by 1940. Hard runways were still under construction at this time due to the fact that the surface condition of the grass after heavy rainfall was fairly soft. Fog prevalence was rated at 14.7 days per year. A Type II flying control, Drem night landing and radio facilities of HF/DF, two long range HF/DF and a fighter sector homer were established with Dyce initially becoming a Coastal Command parent station in No. 13 Group with the additional function as a Fighter Command satellite to Peterhead.

With Dyce officially becoming an RAF station on October 16, 1939, No. 612 (County of Aberdeen) Auxiliary Squadron, which had been formed at the airfield on June 1, 1937, began to fly convoy escorts with their aged Avro Ansons. Accompanied by a unit known as No. 1 Coastal Patrol Flight flying unarmed Tiger Moths, they carried out the first wartime patrols from Dyce.

Spitfires came to the airfield on January 17, 1940, when No. 603 (City of Edinburgh) Auxiliary Squadron arrived at a time when the runways were being laid down. With a detachment at Montrose, they moved to Drem on April 14, having shot down an He 111 off Aberdeen during their stay. The same day another auxiliary squadron, No. 602 (City of Glasgow) arrived with Spitfire Is, staying just over a month before moving to Drem.

Hurricane Is were the next to fly in when a detachment from No. 145 Squadron arrived in early August. By the 31st the entire squadron had arrived for a rest period before moving south to Tangmere on October 9. An eight-day stay by the Defiant Is of No. 141 Squadron saw them transfer to Turnhouse before the Hurricane Is of No. 111 Squadron came in from Drem on October 12. Sending a detachment to Montrose, they converted to the Spitfire I and IA. After a working up period they moved to North Weald on July 20, 1941.

Hurricanes returned the following day when No. 310 (Czech) Squadron arrived. This was the first unit to form from Czech personnel in the UK and their first duty was the defence of Aberdeen. A change to Spitfire IIAs in October and the Mk VB in November brought the squadron down south to Perranporth on December 24, 1941.

January 1941 had also seen the Blenheim IVFs of No. 248 Squadron based at the airfield. Recently transferred from Coastal to Fighter Command, the Blenheims patrolled the coastal waters around Scotland. With a detachment at Wick, they moved to Bircham Newton on June 15. Further Blenheim and Beaufighter squadrons over the year were No. 254 with Blenheim IVFs (December 10-February 11, 1942 and June 1-October 10, 1942); No. 235 with the Blenheim IF and

Although cameras were frowned on in the air force, Eric Marsden, a mechanic serving with No. 145 Squadron, took a chance and snapped these pictures when B Flight was detached to Dyce in September 1940. This former civil aerodrome had been taken over for the duration by the Air Ministry in October 1939 . . .

. . . but just look at it now! The discovery of oil in the North Sea transformed Aberdeen airport into the busiest heliport in Europe.

In February 1942, Swedish Airlines began to carry out diplomatic flights from Dyce using DC-3s painted orange to aid identification. On May 9, 1943, the crew of a Ju 88 from 10./Nachtjagdgeschwader 3 were detailed to attack one of the Swedish machines but it appears that they instead decided to defect. Signalling to their base at Kristiansand that they were going down with engine failure, they headed for Aberdeen, being intercepted and escorted to Dyce by Spitfires from No. 145 Squadron. It was a unique prize as the aircraft was equipped with the latest Lichtenstein night-fighter radar. The three-man crew were taken prisoner while the aircraft was flown to Farnborough for detailed examination. Today it is displayed in the Battle of Britain Museum at Hendon.

Beaufighter IC (June 4, 1941-March 25, 1942); No. 143 with Beaufighter ICs and Blenheim IV (July20-September 27 and December 5-December 16, 1941); No. 410 (Cougar) Canadian detachment with Defiant I and Beaufighter IIF (August 1941-June 1942); No. 404 (Buffalo) Canadian with the Blenheim IVF and Beaufighter IIF (October 9-December 3, 1941 and September 24, 1942 to January 22, 1943).

With Dyce now earmarked to become a training station, the penultimate unit stationed there was a detachment of No. 416 (City of Oshawa) Canadian Squadron Spitfire VBs which arrived during April 1942. They left as the squadron moved to Westhampnett but the detachment returned during July, leaving after nine days to join the squadron at Martlesham Heath. The last wartime unit to use Dyce was a Fleet Air Arm squadron, No. 887, with Fulmars. A suggestion that the aerodrome could be used by Bomber Command Lancasters did not come to fruition and from March 1, 1945 it became home to a number of OTUs.

With the end of the war in sight, Spitfires returned when Nos. 331 and 332 (Norwegian) Squadron came in on April 22 for a month. Spitfire IXEs of No. 129 (Mysore) Squadron were at Dyce from May 26 till June 10. Further units were No. 165 which exchanged their Mustang IIIs for Spitfire IXEs between May 29 and June 15; No. 130 (Punjab) with Spitfires (May 24-June 20); No. 234 (Madras Presidency) with Mustang IVs (July 3-July 27), and No. 122 (Bombay) with Mustang IV and Spitfire IX (July 3-August 29).

After the war, Dyce was used by the Aberdeen University Air Squadron and No. 612 (County of Aberdeen) Auxiliary Squadron but the RAF presence ceased with the disbandment of the auxiliaries in March 1957. Today the airport is the busiest heliport in the country due to its strategic position near the North Sea oil rigs.

As these two verticals show, the new post-war main has been driven right across the wartime runways laid down in 1940.

This early post-war shot shows the flying control and the Bellman hangars on the south-western corner facing the NE-SW runway.

In spite of modern developments, the same area can just be made out, the crowning glory being that the outline of the windsock circle is still visible in the grass. This runway has since been relegated to a taxiway.

MONTROSE

The Montrose Air Station Heritage Centre now maintains the spirit of aviation at one of Scotland's oldest aerodromes dating back to before the First World War. They are fortunate to have retained the Second World War headquarters building.

Classified as the oldest military airfield in Scotland, Montrose dates back to 1913. It was used as a training and fighter station by the Royal Flying Corps during the First World War but put under care and maintenance in March 1920. Re-activated under the 1935 expansion scheme, it once again became a training station.

The aerodrome was located one mile north of Montrose in the county of Angus at just 30 feet above sea level. Grass-surfaced with good drainage qualities, it measured 1,700 yards NE-SW, 1,600 yards SE-NW, 1,450 yards N-S and 800 yards E-W. The perimeter track was still under construction in 1939, but two runways were marked out and strengthened with Sommerfeld Track. Obstructions were noted as a large chimney 150 feet above sea level just off the south-west corner. Facilities consisted of 128,000 gallons of aviation fuel and 4,500 gallons of MT spirit with refuelling by bowser. Three snow-ploughs and one power-driven roller were available in preparation for adverse weather conditions. Hangar accommodation was three aircraft sheds, four Bellman, four Bessonneau and six Blisters. Airfield control was by a watch office with night landing facilities of Chance Floodlight and flare path. Radio facilities were VHF and Darky (Bomber and Coastal) Direction Finding. Accommodation was provided for a 1,500-strong flying instructors school.

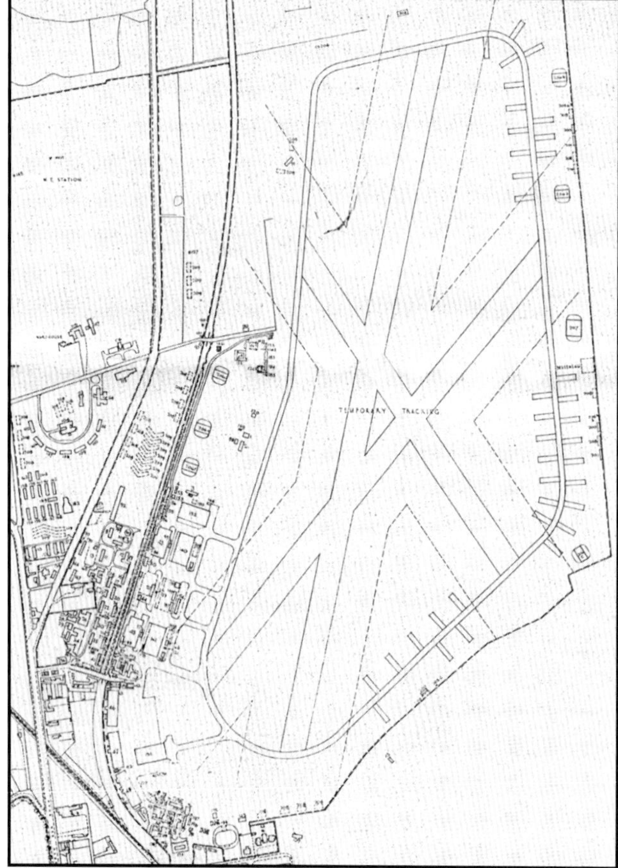

By 1945 three Sommerfeld Track runways had been laid down but have since been lifted.

Two of the original Bellman hangars still stand midst the modern industrial site.

Although Montrose was primarily a training station, its inclusion is warranted as there were Fighter Command deployments to the airfield. ***Above left:*** **This Hawker Fury was delivered to No. 8 Flying Training School direct from the manufacturer, General Aircraft Ltd. The commanding officer at the time was Flying Officer Bob Ker-Ramsay, who had as one of his students, a certain Pilot Officer Brendan Finucane, whose flying ability was rated as 'below average'. Fortunately he took to the Fury at Montrose — possibly this very machine — to develop his ability so that later 'Paddy' Finucane became a Wing Commander and one of the RAF's most decorated and top-scoring fighter pilots before he was posted missing in July 1942.**

Because of new industrial buildings intruding into the former technical site on the western side of the airfield, this is the view today looking across to where the Gauntlet was parked.

Allocated to Flying Training Command with a satellite or RLG at Stracathro, Montrose was opened on January 1, 1936 with No. 8 Flying Training School in residence. Initially using Hart and Audax aircraft, these lasted until replaced by Masters in May 1940. No. 269 Squadron came in with Ansons on August 25, 1939, leaving for Wick on October 10. At the same time No. 13 Flying Training School that had been based at Drem joined No. 8 at Montrose.

During 1940, fighter protection of the area was given over to a detachment of No. 603 (City of Edinburgh) Auxiliary Squadron flying Spitfire Is. Arriving during January 1940, a move to Hornchurch on August 27 saw a detachment of Hurricanes from No. 111 Squadron replace them. The Luftwaffe raided Montrose on October 25 when He111s dropped several bombs and strafed the airfield, killing six men and wounding 18. Two of the hangars were destroyed together with the Officers' Mess.

With the Hurricanes of No. 111 leaving on July 5, 1941, No. 232 arrived from Elgin on April 29. Again with Hurricane Is and IIBs, they became non-operational at Montrose prior to moving overseas which they did on May 10.

With the disbandment of No. 8 FTS on March 25, 1942, No. 2 Flying Instructors School took their place. From this time on Montrose was devoted to flying training with no further fighter units based there. When the instructors school closed during 1944 the aerodrome was put on care and maintenance and quickly fell into disrepair. Although it remained an airfield, and was used occasionally by helicopters, no further use was made of the facilities.

Despite the exposed site beside the North Sea, Montrose is fortunate to still have two of the wartime hangars in good condition.

PRESTWICK

In December 1940, No. 602 Squadron was ordered to Prestwick for a rest period after serving since August at Westhampnett under Squadron Leader A. V. R. Johnstone and it was during this posting that it was featured in the wartime movie *A Yank in the RAF*.

Prestwick in Ayrshire opened on February 17, 1936, the first resident being No. 12 Elementary and Reserve Flying Training School with Tiger Moths and Hawker Harts, renamed No. 12 Elementary Flying Training School when Ansons and Battles were added in September 1939.

Lying three miles north-east of Ayr and just 35 feet above sea level, the original grass surface measured 1,500 yards NE-SW, 1,300 yards N-S, 1,200 yards E-W and 1,050 yards SE-NW. However, as ground conditions after rain were unreliable, two concrete runways were constructed, the main 2,200 yards long and the other 1,500 × 100 yards. A 100-foot perimeter track led to hangar accommodation of five Bellman and five factory sheds. A 1938 art deco style headquarters and clubhouse were built together with an airport hotel with roof-top air traffic control, this being quite unique. With Mk II airfield lighting available at 30 minutes notice and numerous radio facilities installed, Prestwick was to become a transatlantic control and reception airfield in Ferry Command operating both civilian and military aircraft.

Then Prestwick was still a grass airfield, the first runway of 2,200 yards not being completed until March 1941. A cross-wind runway (08-26) of 1,500 yards came into service in March 1942.

In October 1940, the approach control was set up in Powbank Mill *(left)* just off the south-western corner, and from January 1941 the attic became the Fighter Command Ops Room. The mill was linked to the airfield by a small stone bridge across the Pow Burn. *Above:* Although the mill has since been demolished, Chris Cooper was thrilled to find the long-disused bridge which originally accessed the airfield.

DISPERSAL

The 602 dispersal was located just beyond the bridge and the 'scramble' sequence filmed there is a joy to watch.

SITE OF POWBANK MILL

No. 603 (City of Edinburgh) Auxiliary Squadron with Spitfire Is was the first fighter unit to arrive on December 16, 1939. They were awaiting the completion of RAF Dyce and they moved there on January 17, 1940. Another auxiliary squadron, No. 610 (County of Chester), arrived with Spitfire Is on April 4 but they stayed for just a month. On July 25 the remnants of No. 141 from West Malling arrived with Defiant Is. They had received a bad mauling at the hands of the Luftwaffe on July 19 when six aircraft had been shot down with a severe loss of aircrew. The remaining aircraft and crews were quickly posted to Scotland to rest and regroup before moving on to Dyce a month later.

A stay of five days from August 23 by the Hurricanes of No. 253 (Hyderabad State) saw them replaced by more Hurricanes of No. 615 (County of Surrey) Auxiliary Squadron who had been sent north to rest. Having fought in the Battle of Britain during July, they returned to Northolt on October 10.

As the pilots cross the bridge from the Mill they run towards their dispersal at which point . . .

Although re-enacted for a wartime Hollywood film, this sequence is still valuable to history as it shows one of the RAF Fighter Command's most famous auxiliary squadrons in action and Chris visited Prestwick specially to match it up.

Although he found that the 1941 scene had been transformed out of all recognition, he was pleased that the long, low building seen in the background of the next comparison, now painted white, was still standing as a common reference point.

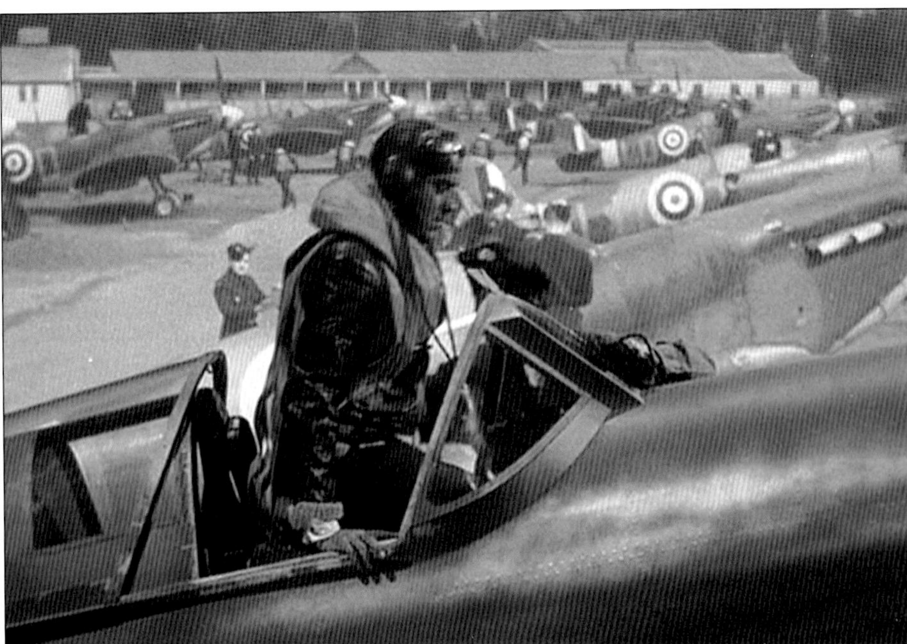

When Prestwick was loaned to Coastal Command, the Whitley Vs of No. 102 Squadron arrived on September 1 for convoy escort duties. With a detachment at Aldergrove, the rest of the squadron moved to Linton-on-Ouse on October 10.

Fighters returned on December 17 when No. 602 (City of Glasgow) Auxiliary Squadron arrived with Spitfire Is. They, too, had been fighting in the south of the country and had come to rest. They moved to Ayr on April 15, 1941. Later that year, No. 1 Canadian Squadron was based at Prestwick with Hurricanes for a few weeks prior to Christmas 1941 before moving to Castletown.

Prestwick now took on a new role — that of an Atlantic ferry organisation — as thousands of American and Canadian-built aircraft passed through the airfield. In July 1941 this ferry bridge was taken over by RAF Ferry Command which remained at Prestwick for the rest of the war. Today it is a main transatlantic airport operated by Prestwick Airport Limited.

. . . the camera pans round to show the aircraft parked in front of the long crew-room.

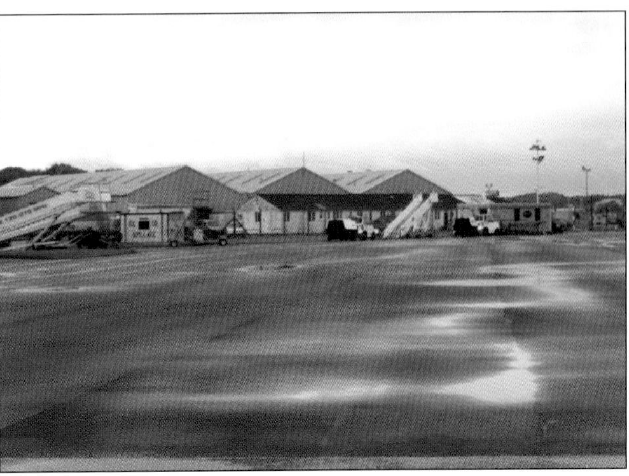

There were three casualties during the filming of an air-to-air combat sequence over Norfolk on May 26. The camera ship was an Anson of No. 500 Squadron piloted by Sergeant Edward Polden but as the Hurricanes of No. 257 Squadron came in to attack, there was a mid-air collision with one of the machines. Although Pilot Officer Hone managed to bale out, Polden and the two cameramen, Otto Kanturek and John Parry, in the Anson were killed.

SCORTON

Pilots of No. 122 Squadron enjoy a spot of trap-shooting, always promoted to improve a fighter pilot's aim. On the left is the acting CO, Squadron Leader Herbert Hallowes. The unit was at Scorton between October 1941 and April 1942.

Deemed an operational satellite or relief landing ground to Catterick in Yorkshire, Scorton lying a mile to the north also functioned as a night fighter station. It opened in October 1939 as a large grass airfield some 200 feet above sea level.

First to use the sparse facilities was a detachment of No. 219 (Mysore) Squadron which arrived from the parent station during late 1939 with Blenheim IFs. Beginning shipping patrol duties, they moved to Redhill with the rest of the squadron on October 12, 1940.

During 1941 three runways were laid down, the main being 1,400 x 50 yards and the other two 1,100 x 50 yards. A watch office was added together with the erection of 12 Blister hangars.

Operating as an airfield within No. 13 Group, the first permanent squadron to arrive was No. 122 (Bombay) with Spitfire IIAs. Posted in on October 6, 1941, a conversion to the Mk IIB in October and the Mk VB in November saw them carrying out convoy patrols over the Firth of Forth before moving to Hornchurch on April 1, 1942.

On April 6 No. 167 (Gold Coast) Squadron reformed at Scorton. Receiving Spitfire VBs, they sent a detachment to Acklington before moving to Castletown on June 1. They were replaced by a Canadian squadron detachment, No. 406 (Lynx). Flying Beaufighter IIFs, the rest of the squadron arrived on June 16. They had previously found success flying from Ayr and this was to continue at Scorton when on July 7, 1942, the squadron claimed four enemy aircraft destroyed with one probable. Conversion to the Beaufighter VIF saw them move to Predannack on September 4.

Another unit moving in from Ayr was No. 410 (Cougar) Canadian Squadron. Arriving on September 1, with Beaufighter IIFs, it was a brief stay as they moved to Acklington on October 20. The following day No. 219 (Mysore) Squadron returned with their Beaufighter IFs. Since the detachment was based at Scorton during 1940, their tally had steadily risen resulting in a score of 44 victories by the end of August 1942. It was a quiet period over the winter months and the squadron moved to Catterick on April 24, 1943.

No other units were stationed at the airfield until November 10 that year when No. 130 (Punjab) Squadron arrived with Spitfire VBs. A brief move to Ayr on the 16th saw them back on the 30th before going on to Acklington on December 21. The squadron came back to Scorton to disband on February 13, 1944.

A rapid series of conversions befell No. 604 (County of Middlesex) Auxiliary Squadron when they brought their Beaufighter IFs in on April 24, 1943: first to the Beaufighter VIF, then to the Mosquito XII in February 1944 and finally to the Mk XIII in March. They then moved to Church Fenton on April 25 to become part of the Second Tactical Air Force.

The Typhoon IBs of No. 56 (Punjab) Squadron brought a new sound to Scorton. Arriving on February 15, 1944 and leaving on the 23rd, it was the first of three visits, the others being March 7 to 30 and April 7 to 28, 1944. During the latter posting they converted to Spitfire IXs before moving to Newchurch in Kent. The last wartime RAF unit to fly from Scorton was No. 26 with Mustang Is. They arrived on February 12 and departed for Hutton Cranswick on the 28th.

During May 1944, the 422nd and 458th Night Fighter Squadrons of the USAAF Ninth Air Force arrived from Charmy Down. Later that month they received their Northrop P-61 Black Widow fighters and commenced training at night under RAF instructors. When they left in July 1944, Scorton reverted to being a satellite airfield and a storage facility for RAF Balloon Command. Finally closing in 1945, most of the buildings were demolished including the watch office.

Today the aerodrome has virtually ceased to exist having been subjected to intensive quarrying which has removed most of the airfield surface. This fine memorial was set up in August 2013 overlooking the site.

Scorton aerodrome was slotted in between the River Swale and the York & Newcastle Railway, the Richmond branch line on the northern side being closed in March 1969 after which the track was lifted.

SUMBURGH

Of the two aerodromes on the Shetland Isles — Scatsta in the north and Sumburgh at the southern tip, it was the latter that was taken over by Fighter Command's No. 13 Group. These are the pilots and ground crew of No. 602 Squadron in 1942.

Located on the southern tip of the Shetland Isles just below sea level, Sumburgh was surrounded by several high hills. With obstructions such as Fitful Head at 927 feet, Ward Hill at 250 feet and Compass Hill at 350 feet, flying in and out of the aerodrome could be a dangerous business.

An airfield had been established on the site in 1933 when Captain E.E. Fresson of Highland Airways began a series of scheduled services. This large area of grass came to the notice of the Works Directorate of the Air Ministry and was requisitioned for the RAF. By 1939 it supported a flight of aged Gloster Gladiators, the only fighter aircraft at the time capable of using the field. It was soon realised that considerable improvement would be needed if Sumburgh was to play a part in defending Scotland and its islands. Consequently upgrading began with the construction of three runways together with the construction of a Type 1 Flying Control and several aircraft sheds. With sea fog being prevalent in spring, summer and autumn, night landing facilities included Drem, Planet and Chance Light. An angle of glide indicator was also installed due to the difficult approach together with six W/T transmitters and receivers and a Darky Watch being made available for direction finding.

Sumburgh first opened as an operational station in Coastal Command with a satellite or Relief Landing Ground at Scatsta. The other functions of the base were as a fighter sector and civil air station. Initially opening on May 13, 1940, two Blenheim squadrons arrived: Nos. 254 (May 16-August 2, January 7-May 29, 1941) and No. 248 (July 14, 1940-January 6, 1941). They carried out reconnaissance sorties over the North Sea and the Atlantic. Meanwhile the Gladiator flight — known as the 'Sumburgh Fighter Flight' — moved to Roborough for the defence of Plymouth, becoming No. 247 (China-British) Squadron in the process.

Further defence for the Highlands arrived when a detachment of Hurricane Is from 'B' Flight of No. 3 Squadron came in from Skeabrae during July 1940. They reformed as No. 232 Squadron and moved to Castletown on September 18. Another Hurricane detachment from No. 3 Squadron arrived during January 1941, leaving for Martlesham Heath on April 3. As they left No. 17 Squadron sent a further Hurricane detachment to Sumburgh to carry out convoy patrols. They remained until June 1941.

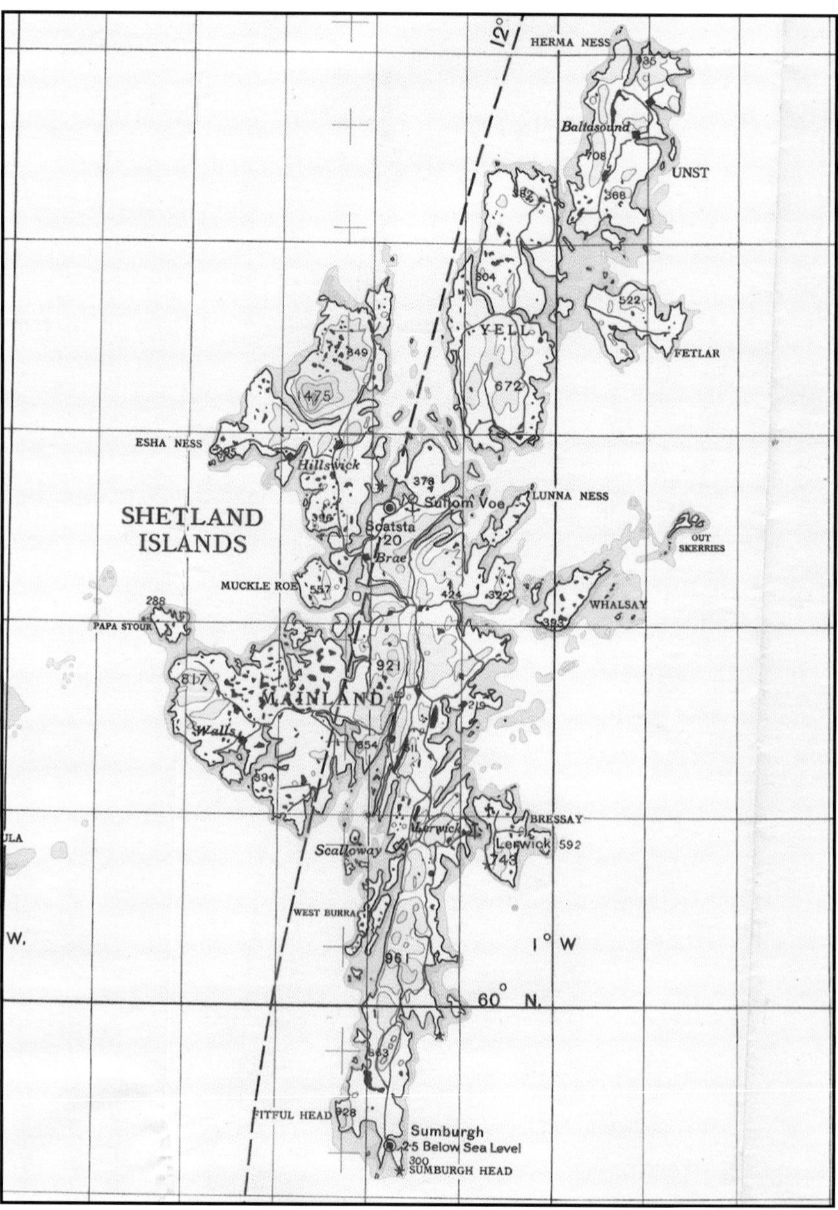

This is from the Orkneys and Shetlands sheet of RAF War Edition, GSGS 4369 of 1944.

The aerodrome at Sumburgh came into its own after the passing of the UK Continental Shelf Act in 1964, becoming in the 1970s the fastest growing airport in the United Kingdom. The discovery of the huge Brent oilfield east of Shetland greatly added to the airfield's traffic and this new terminal building was opened in 1979.

By June 1940 when the Luftwaffe took this photo, three runways were under construction.

No. 42 Squadron sent several Beaufort Is to the airfield on March 1 prior to leaving for the Middle East in June. Next to visit were two naval squadrons: No. 880 Squadron with Sea Hurricanes on September 15 for three weeks and No. 821 with Swordfish on November 5 for a five-day stay.

Fighters had returned to Sumburgh on September 27 when No. 143 Beaufighter ICs arrived from Dyce. A Coastal Command strike squadron, they moved back to Dyce on December 5 having claimed a Ju 88 on October 19.

No. 404 (Buffalo) Canadian Squadron with Blenheim IVFs flew in on December 3 to join the detachment that had been at Sumburgh since October. They left for Dyce on March 26, 1942, returning to Sumburgh on August 5 to convert to the Beaufighter IIF which they took back to Dyce on September 24. Further Coastal Command squadrons came during 1942. No. 248 returned on May 30 with the Beaufighter VIC and left for Dyce on August 5. July 29 saw the Hudson IIIs from No. 608 (North Riding) Auxiliary Squadron come in. Exchanging them for the Mk IIIA variant, they went to Gosport on August 27. Further Hudsons arrived on September 23 with No. 48 Squadron. They carried out anti-submarine patrols before leaving for Gosport on November 30.

As Coastal Command had a flying boat base at Sullom Voe (see map), at first Sumburgh was also part of that command. This picture shows the station buildings surrounding the watch office.

The first Fighter Command unit to be stationed on the island were the Gladiator pilots of the Sumburgh — or Shetland — Fighter Flight.

Although a digression, we ought to include mention that the first casualty of the war occurred on the Shetlands on November 13, 1939. At 1 p.m. four bombs were dropped on Sullom (the mainland of Shetland), the only victim being the poor celebrated rabbit! The photographer, most probably a Mr R. Williamson, was driven to the scene by John Halcrow, seen standing in the crater holding up the unfortunate bunny. However, it is common knowledge on the islands that it was in fact a gutted specimen obtained from the local butcher and taken to the crater for effect!

A detachment of No. 125 (Newfoundland) Squadron equipped with Beaufighter VIFs spent several months at Sumburgh. Arriving in September 1942, they stayed until April 15, 1943 carrying out anti-submarine duties. Detachments became ever frequent with No. 602 (City of Glasgow) Auxiliary arriving with Spitfire VBs in September 1942 until January 1943; No. 234 (Madras Presidency) with Spitfire VIs from January till April 1943; No. 313 (Czech) with Spitfire VCs, June till August 1943; No. 310 (Czech) with Spitfire VIs, July to September 1943, and No. 453 (Australian) with Spitfire VCs from October 1943 till January 1944.

Continuing the detachments, by late 1943 it was the turn of Mosquitos to be based at Sumburgh. No. 307 (Lwow) Polish Squadron sent several Mosquito VIs north during November 1943, but conversion to the Mk XII in January 1944 saw the entire squadron move to Coleby Grange on March 2.

June 14, 1944 saw the Avro Ansons of No. 1693 (GR) Flight begin anti-submarine patrols. They remained at Sumburgh until May 1945. Yet again several fighter detachments were resident as the end of the war approached. No. 118 flying Spitfire VIIs came in during March and left in July 1944; No.611 (West Lancashire) Auxiliary Squadron from October to December 1944 with Spitfire IXs whilst No. 598 had a target towing detachment of Lysanders and Martinets.

With the closing down of the Coastal Command operations room at the end of the war, on August 29, 1945 Sumburgh was put on care and maintenance. Later the start of civilian scheduled services from the Scottish mainland, and the discovery of oil under the North Sea, saw Sumburgh once again become an important airfield. It is currently Shetlands main airport and is operated by Highlands and Islands Airports Ltd.

The main runway (09/27) was extended in 2005-6 to cater for larger aircraft which meant that the A970 which crossed the runway had to be controlled by traffic lights. Then, a £12 million contract was begun in 2013 to extend the ends in the sea.

TURNHOUSE

The RAF basically quit Turnhouse in 1957 since when it has been developed into Edinburgh's Airport yet not all has been swept away. This is the old entrance, complete with RAF crests on the gateposts, the building on the left being the station headquarters.

As the most northerly flying base during the First World War, this Midlothian aerodrome was established in 1915 as part of the Royal Flying Corps. It became home to No. 603 (City of Edinburgh) Auxiliary Squadron in 1916 flying Wapitis, Harts and Hinds, and with the amalgamation of the RFC with the Royal Naval Air Service, the station became RAF Turnhouse.

Situated 16 miles west of Edinburgh, it was a large grass airfield with a 50-foot perimeter track leading to the SE-NW runway of 1,300 x 50 yards, the E-W being 1,100 x 50 yards and the N-S just 900 x 50 yards. A Type 2 flying control controlled the night landing facility of Glims and McDonald lighting together with strip-lighting and radio links of R/T, H/F and VHF radio. With accommodation provided for three squadrons of day fighters, Turnhouse opened as a sector station in No. 13 Group with satellites at Kirkwenton and Drem.

One of the first squadrons to reform there was No. 141 with the Gloster Gladiator on October 4, 1939. A transfer to Grangemouth two weeks later saw them return with Defiants on June 28, 1940. A move to West Malling on July 11 saw them operating from the forward airfield at Hawkinge. On July 19 the squadron scrambled seven aircraft but only one returned. Consequently, the remainder of the squadron was sent to Prestwick to rest and regroup. Arriving on July 21 they moved back to Turnhouse on October 30.

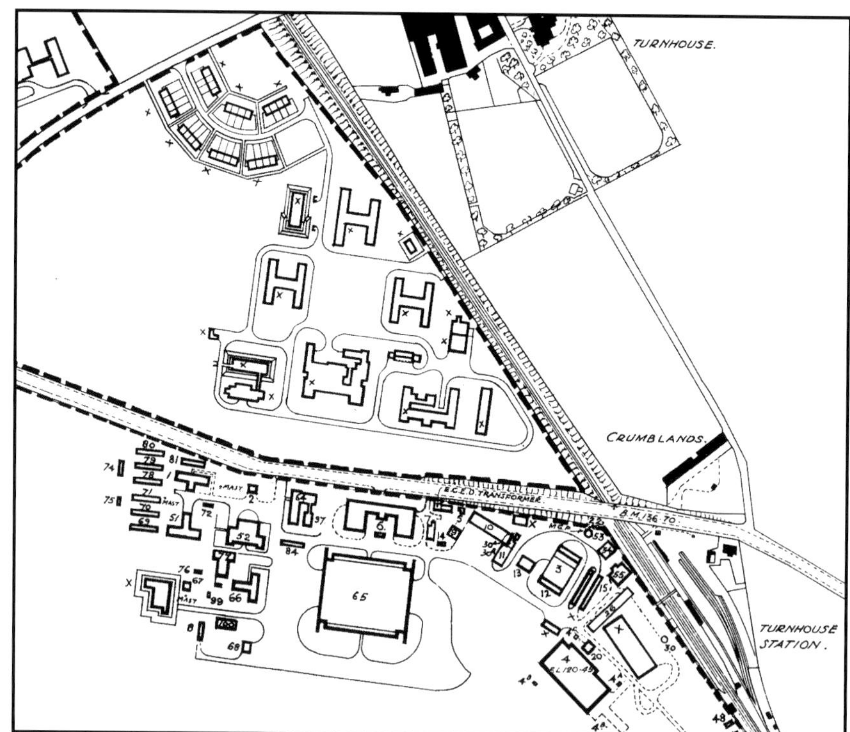

September 1939 — Gladiator K7936 of No. 603 Squadron with the Pipe Band.

The 'C' type hangar (65 on the plan) still stands in the old RAF camp on the north side.

The original grass airfield had three take-off and landing directions: 1,300 yards SE-NW, 1,100 yards E-W, and 900 yards N-S. Tarmac was laid down on the SE-NW direction runway with co-ordinates of 13/31, magnetic variation making it now 12/30.

When the Vampires of No. 603 Squadron arrived in 1952, the runway was extended to 2,000 yards and an aircraft carrier style of catcher net installed at the southern end to protect the A8 from overruns. The Ministry of Defence transferred ownership of the airfield to the Ministry of Aviation in 1960 in recognition of the expanding civilian passenger services which BEA had begun in 1947. However, as the runway was subject to severe cross winds, a completely new one was laid down on an east-west axis (06-24) to take advantage of the prevailing westerly wind. This was 3,000 yards and able to accommodate all modern large airliners.

Chocks away! WAAF flight mechanics ready a Miles Martinet target tug of No. 290 Squadron for its next flight.

No. 603 (City of Edinburgh) Auxiliary Squadron had brought its Spitfire Is in from Drem on May 5. With detachments at Montrose and Dyce, they moved to Hornchurch on August 28. No. 245 (Northern Rhodesia) took their place on June 5 with Hurricane Is. With an interim detachment to Hawkinge, they left for Aldergrove on July 20. The next day No. 253 (Hyderabad State) Squadron replaced them, again with Hurricane Is. Departing to Prestwick on August 23, it was the Spitfire Is of No. 65 (East India) Squadron that were next in. Arriving on August 27 a short stay saw them depart to Tangmere on November 29.

Turnhouse now saw a period of squadrons reforming. No. 122 (Bombay) did so on May 5, 1941 with Spitfire Is before moving to Ouston on June 26 whilst No. 123 (East India) Squadron reformed on May 10 also with Spitfire Is. They moved to Drem on August 6. The establishment of a Free French Squadron, No. 340 (GC IV/2 'Ile de France') took place on November 7. Equipped with Spitfire Is, they sent a detachment to Drem before the entire squadron moved there on December 20. They were to return to Turnhouse for a few days on March 21, 1943.

When No. 81 Squadron returned to the UK after serving in Russia, they were re-equipped with the Spitfire VA and became operational again on February 1, 1942 at Ouston, returning to Turnhouse on February 14. Returning to Ouston on March 15, it was back to Turnhouse on March 29 with detachments at Drem, Ouston and Ayr. Conversion to the Spitfire VB saw them once again depart to Ouston on April 13.

Another squadron to reform at Turnhouse was No. 242 (Canadian) on April 10, 1942. After receiving Spitfire VBs they moved to Ouston on May 15. Three days later No. 13 Group Anti-Aircraft Co-operation Flight moved in with Oxfords and Defiants. Re-equipping with Martinets in June 1943, they remained at Turnhouse right up until1945.

Several Fleet Air Arm squadrons spent time at the airfield. No. 882 with Martlets arrived on February 13 and left on March 17, 1942 followed by No. 801 with Sea Hurricanes from April 29 to May 27, 1942. The Fairey Fulmars of No. 884 Squadron spent two periods at Turnhouse from March 22 to July 6 and July 11 to July 21, 1942. Finally No. 808 with Seafires came in on June 14 leaving on July 20, 1943.

A return to RAF units saw No. 232 Squadron fly in with Spitfire VBs on August 3, 1942 prior to moving to North Africa. The forming of No. 341 (GC III/2 'Alsace') Squadron of the Free French on January 18, 1943 saw Spitfire VBs return. After a working up period they moved south to Biggin Hill on March 21. Mustang Is flew in on July 27, 1943, when No. 63 Squadron arrived from Macmerry. Carrying out exercises with local army units, they moved to Thruxton on November 8 but returned to Turnhouse on January 22, 1944, sending detachments to Tealing, Peterhead and Dundonald. The squadron finally moved to Woodvale on April 27. They had been joined at Turnhouse by another Mustang unit, No. 268, on November 8, 1943. Flying the Mk IA variant, they also carried out local exercises before moving to North Weald on January 17, 1944.

No. 290 Squadron arrived to carry out target towing duties on August 25, 1944. Equipped with Martinets, Oxfords and Hurricanes, detachments were sent to West Freugh, Farnborough and Long Kesh. A conversion to the Spitfire VB in December saw them depart to the Continent in February 1945.

March that year saw further Spitfire units arrive with No. 329 (GC 1/2 'Cigognes') Free French Squadron on March 9 although their stay was brief as they moved to Skeabrae less than a month later. No. 164 (Argentine-British) with Spitfires arrived on June 17, leaving for Fairwood Common on November 20. No. 303 (Kosciuszko) Polish with Mustangs were based at the airfield from December 1, 1945 till January 5, 1946 and No. 603 (City of Edinburgh) Auxiliaries from April 28 to May 7, 1945, only returning to Turnhouse on July 28, 1945 to disband.

In 1961 the runway was lengthened to allow large civilian aircraft to use the airfield and, when the Air Ministry relinquished control, the British Airports Authority took over, Turnhouse becoming Edinburgh Airport.

Then . . . and now . . . the contrast could not be more bizarre!

The gate guardian at RAF Turnhouse was a Spitfire RW393 which had originally done the rounds of a number of units — No. 6 MU, Fighter Command Communications Squadron, Reserve Command Communication Squadron, No. 31 (Metropolitan Communication Squadron), until it was issued to No. 602 Squadron in 1956 as an instructional aircraft. The following year it was displayed at Turnhouse (bearing the codes XT-A of No. 603 City of Edinburgh Squadron) where it remained on guard duty until 1989.

Thanks to the efforts of Tim Routsis and friends, RW393 was replaced with a fibreglass replica but displayed with the original plaque although at a different location on Jubilee Road. It bears the markings of Squadron Leader George Denholm's aircraft (L1067 coded XT-D) when he was commanding officer of No. 603 Squadron in 1940-41. (Although the replica is named 'Blue Peter' , it must not be confused with the one of the same name mentioned on page 299.)

USWORTH

'Inspecting the course' at Usworth. The AF code on the Hurricane denoting No. 607 Squadron dates the photo to the rather boggy conditions which were experienced on the aerodrome in the summer of 1940.

Prone to industrial haze and ground mist, Usworth lay four miles east of Gateshead in County Durham. The aerodrome had been used during the First World War, when facilities were very basic, by No. 36 Squadron flying Bristol Fighters but when the unit was disbanded in June 1919 the airfield became disused.

Usworth was reactivated when No. 607 (County of Durham) Auxiliary Squadron formed there. Work soon got underway to bring the airfield up to a reasonable standard and by September 1932, the squadron was able to move in with Wapitis. Joined by No. 103 Squadron with Battles on February 26, 1937, before they moved to Abingdon in September 1939, Usworth became a fighter satellite in No. 13 Group, Fighter Command with the parent base at Ouston.

At 120 feet above sea level, the aerodrome measured 1,170 yards from E-W, 1,310 yards NE-SW, 1,080 yards N-S and 1,000 yards SE-NW but in 1939 work commenced on laying two runways both 800 x 50 yards.. There was

When Chris Cooper arrived at Usworth in 2013 he found that someone had moved the goal posts!

a 50-foot tarmac perimeter track leading to eight dispersal pens and 34 hardstandings. Hangarage was one Lamella, one Bellman and 10 Blisters. Additional buildings were constructed especially on the north side where new accommodation blocks had been built for the WAAFS.

With No. 607 Squadron moving to Acklington on October 10, 1939, No. 43 Squadron had brought their Hurricane Is in from Tangmere on September 8, 1940. They had seen heavy fighting during the Battle of Britain and had been sent north to rest. They moved to Drem on December 12. The return of 607 on June 4, 1940, this time with Hurricane Is, saw them depart to Tangmere on September 1 and return to Usworth on December 12 for a month stay. They left for the last time for Macmerry on January 16, 1941.

Usworth now began a long period as a training station when No. 55 OTU with Hurricanes arrived on March 14, 1941. Moving to Annan on April 25, 1942, Usworth was relegated to care and maintenance until the

GB 10 235 bc

Maßstab etwa 1:18 000

500 0 500 1000 m

(1cm : 180 m)

Usworth

Fliegerhorst

ca. 4 km Usworth

650 m

900 m

650 m

ca. 5 km Sunderland

River Wea →

GB 10 235 bc

Geheim

Kriegsaufnahme: 087

Nachträge: 24. 9. 40

Karte: 1:100 000 Blatt 3

Länge (westl. Greenw.): 1° 28'

Nördl. Breite: 54° 55'

Zielhöhe über NN 37 m

G.B. 10 235 Fliegerhorst.

1.) 2 Flugzeughallen
2.) 2 kl. Hallen
3.) Tankstelle
4.) Flughafengebäude u. Werkstätten
5.) Unterkünfte
6.) 2 Munitionsbunker
7.) Splittersichere Abstellplätze für Flugzeuge
8.) Peilstation
9.) Landehindernisse

Usworth was targeted by the Luftwaffe on August 15, 1940 but the attack was beaten off by the combined efforts of guns and fighters.

The RAF presence at Usworth continued after the war with glider training of air cadets until July 1962 when the Air Ministry sold it to Sunderland Corporation for £27,000. The corporation re-surfaced the two runways, and opened Usworth as Sunderland Airport, but it was to last less than 25 years, although there was one last significant event, as historian Dave Charles explains: 'It was on Friday, January 21, 1983 that Avro Vulcan B2 XL319 was to touch down at Usworth. RAF Waddington gave the airport authorities 48 hours notice to organise fire-cover, the local brigade providing 4 appliances to supplement the 2 airport tenders, plus an ambulance to comply with the RAF's conditions for landing. On the Friday morning, at 11.00, a call went up "It's coming!" as the shape of the large delta came into view from the south. XL319 made a large circuit followed by a low flypast. Squadron Leader MacDougall radioed to say he would make one overshoot and then land. He came in low over the hill and the housing estate at the east end of the runway, the undercarriage gently touched until the throttles were opened and the Vulcan accelerated away making a noise that only a Vulcan can, turning tightly back into the circuit. MacDougall touched her down on the end of the runway and deployed the brake 'chute. Later he said he could have stopped halfway down the runway. However, he taxied on to the end for the benefit of the Press and, after releasing the 'chute, he taxi-ied along the perimeter track to a disused dispersal which would be a temporary home until the grass near the North East Aircraft Museum dried out. As the aircraft was turned around to facilitate towing later, a BBC cameraman who did not move when he was told was blown back across the field for about ten feet as the jet blast swept around. However, the only damage suffered was to his pride.'

The North East Aircraft Museum keeps the spirit of Usworth alive with over 30 aircraft including their star exhibit, Vulcan XL319.

English Electric Lightning F.53 (ZF594)

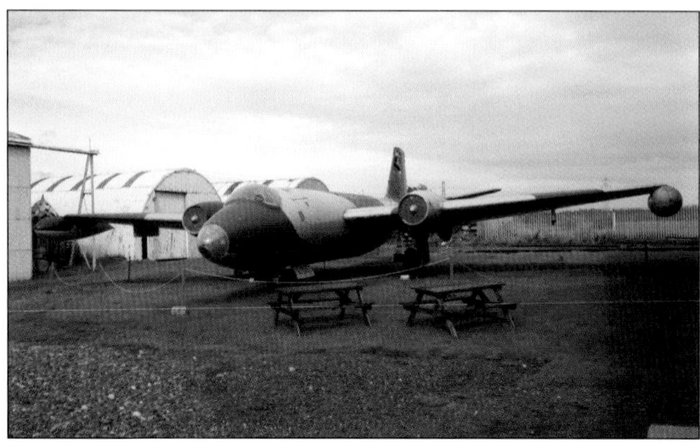

English Electric Canberra TT.18 (WJ639).

forming of No. 62 OTU on June 23, 1942. This unit was used in the radar training role and had 12 Avro Ansons on strength for the purpose. However, with the unit moving to Ouston during June 1943, Usworth returned again to care and maintenance.

April 1944 saw it used as a base for an Air-crew Disposal unit, responsible for finding posts for tour-expired aircrew, which came in during June and remained until January 1945. In 1963 Usworth became Sunderland Airport which flourished for many years until it closed in 1984. The site is now the home of the Nissan car manufacturing plant.

Dave Charles explains that sadly the high spot of a Vulcan landing at Usworth was to prove to be almost the last significant event for the airfield, for shortly afterwards the local council announced that the airfield was to be closed as it had made a loss and was the preferred site for the Nissan car factory. Fortunately Sunderland Council offered an adjacent site for the museum so its survival was guaranteed. Nissan decided to retain the large Lamell hangar erected in 1929 for storage and garage facilities. However, the runways would be lost under the factory's vast expanse. Usworth closed at 1500 GMT on May 31, 1984, most of the departing aircraft making low passes and generally beating up the field. The RAF sent a Jet Provost to pay their last respects and the airport manager, Bob Henderson, fired off a few shots from a Very pistol as the flag was lowered. As the airfield fell silent the bulldozers moved in and so vanished another British airfield. The first phase of the Nissan Motor Company's UK factory was completed by August 1986 when the target was 24,000 cars per year. This was planned to increase to 100,000 cars per year by 1990 being constructed by a workforce of 2,700.

WICK

Then . . . and now in the far north of Scotland. The landscape has barely changed in over 70 years apart from the main NW-SE runway having been doubled in length to 2,000 yards.

Sometimes known as Hillhead Farm, scheduled airline services were established at Wick by Highland Airways during the early 1930s. The aerodrome was a large expanse of grass, but the wet conditions which prevailed after constant rain required that for wartime service Wick had three tarmac runways laid down in 1939, all three being 1,000 x 50 yards. Lying 119 feet above sea level, the airfield had good visibility but persistent sea fog sometimes occurred during spring and summer. Four C-type hangars were built and a Type 1 regional watch office which controlled the Drem runway lighting and VHF radio. Allocated a satellite at Skitten, it initially came under the umbrella of No. 18 Group, Coastal Command.

With the station headquarters opening on September 15, 1939, No. 803 Fleet Air Arm squadron arrived with Blackburn Skuas to carry out fighter patrols. They were partnered by the Ansons of No. 269 Squadron that were posted in on October 10 to carry out coastal patrols. A brief appearance by Spitfires of No. 41 Squadron on October 19 saw them depart to Catterick after only six days. By November 1939 detachments of Hampdens from Nos. 50 and 61 Squadron came to carry out raids over Germany with No. 803 Squadron moving to Hatston on February 10, 1940.

A sad photo believed to have been taken at Wick. Maureen Shaw sent us this photo of her brother, Flight Lieutenant Henry Ferriss, with two pilots of No. 111 Squadron at the aerodrome early in 1940. The unit was there from February to May that year. Flying Officer David Bury with the squadron's mascot Gangster was killed in France on May 19, Henry on August 16 and Flight Lieutenant Stan Connors two days later. Maureen thinks that Gangster was killed when Croydon was bombed on August 15.

Servicing 1940's style. The RAF bowsers could refuel three aircraft at once, this picture being taken during No. 111's tenure.

By now Wick had become a sector station for the protection of the Highlands. With this role, Nos. 43 and 111 Squadrons arrived with Hurricanes in February, 1940. Carrying out defensive patrols they had a miserable time before flying south to fight in the Battle of Britain. Further Hurricane Is had arrived on February 28 when No. 605 (County of Warwick) Auxiliary Squadron flew in from Leuchars. Moving to Hawkinge on May 21, they were replaced by another auxiliary squadron, No. 504 (County of Nottingham), with Hurricane Is on May 22. After a month stay they moved to Castletown.

May 30 saw No.3 Squadron arrive, also with Hurricane Is. Having fought during the Battle of France, they were sent to Wick to rest and regroup before moving to Castletown on September 3. A decision by the Air Ministry at this time saw the fighter sector headquarters move to Kirkwall with Wick becoming a Coastal Command station for the rest of the war. Not until November 28, 1945, did fighters return in the shape of Mustang IIIs when No. 316 (Warsaw) Polish Squadron arrived from Andrewsfield. They carried out numerous exercises with the army until they moved to Hethel on March 15, 1946. They were joined by another Polish squadron, No. 303 (Kosciuszko), with the Mustang IV variant on January 5, moving to Charterhall on March 6.

As a civil airport Wick's John O'Groats airport runs regular flights to Aberdeen with a new terminal building on the site of one of the wartime hangars.

Although no longer used for air traffic control, Chris Cooper found that the original watch office still stands overlooking the Jetstreams of Eastern Airways although where the Hurricanes would take on 97 gallons, the jet requires 874!

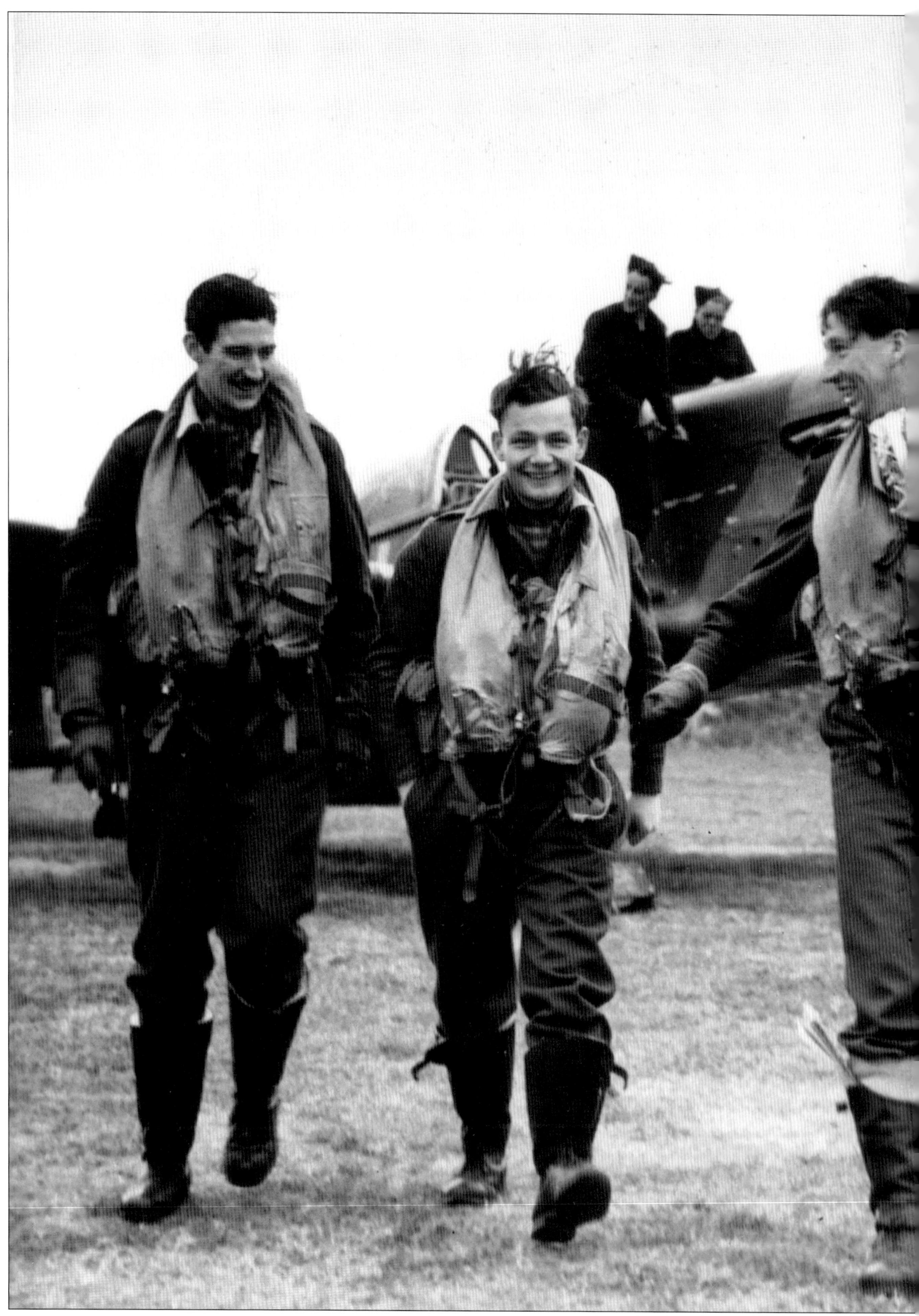

No. 14 GROUP

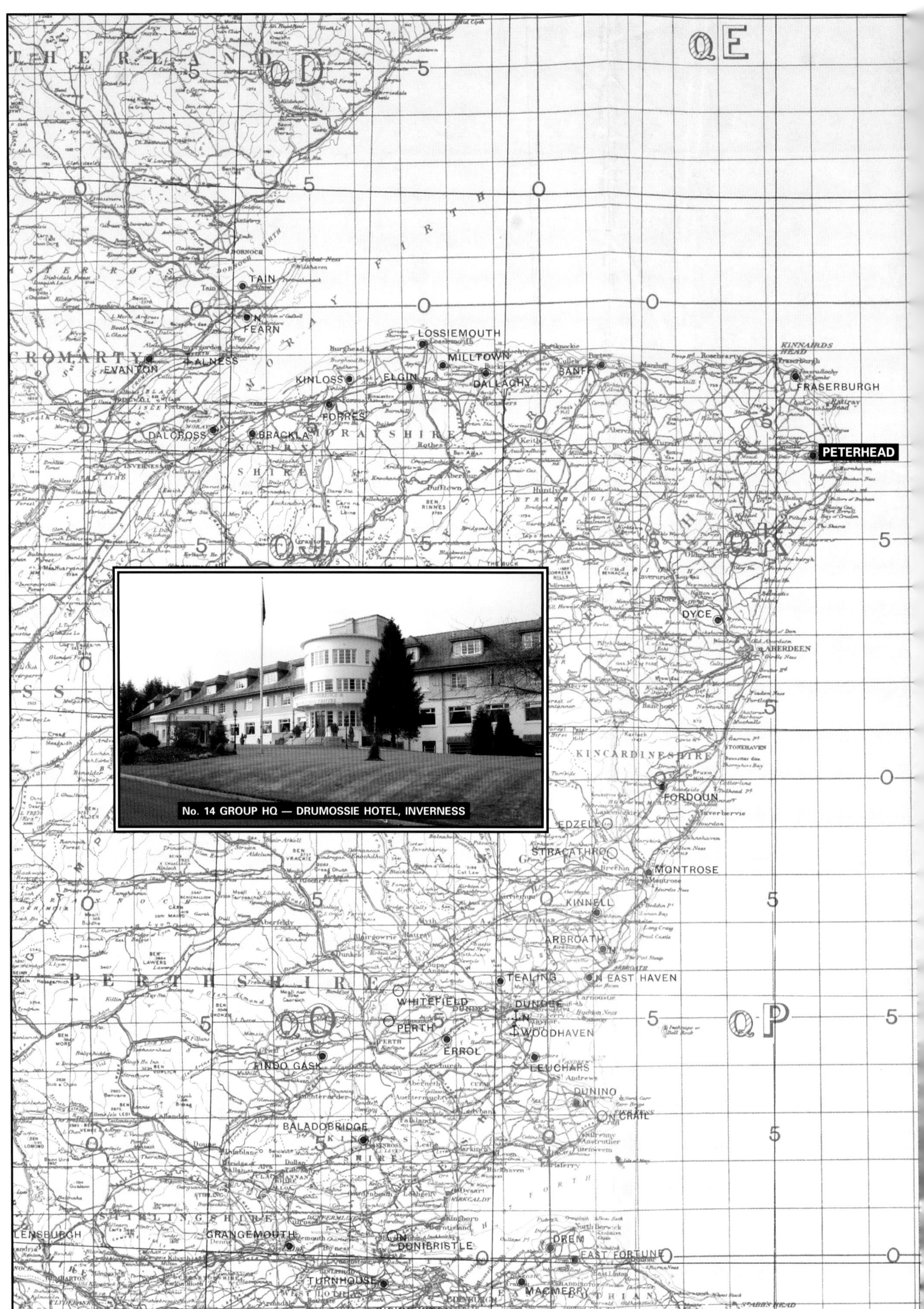

No. 14 GROUP HQ — DRUMOSSIE HOTEL, INVERNESS

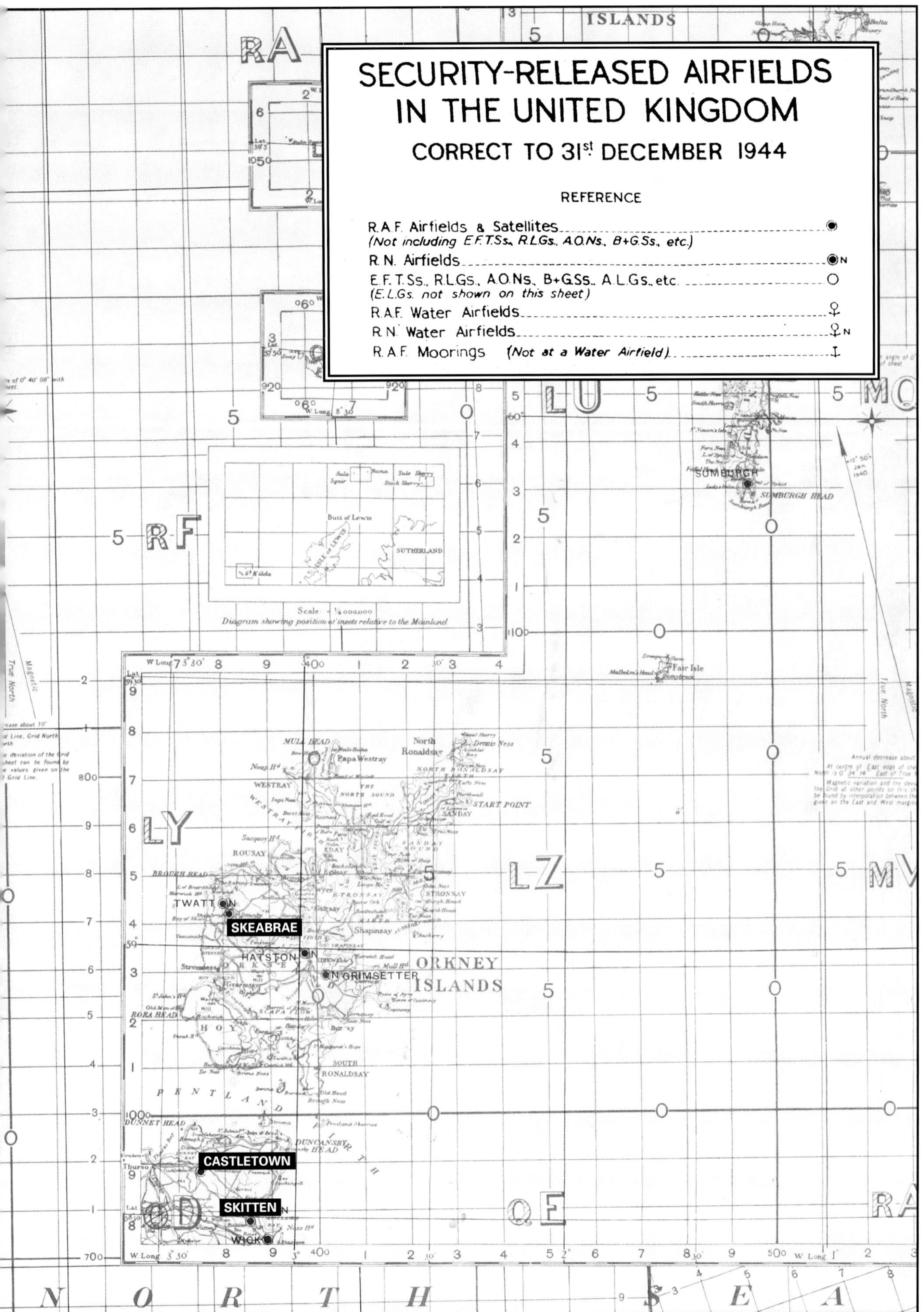
SECURITY-RELEASED AIRFIELDS
IN THE UNITED KINGDOM
CORRECT TO 31st DECEMBER 1944
REFERENCE
R.A.F. Airfields & Satellites
(Not including E.F.T.Ss., R.L.Gs., A.O.Ns., B+G.Ss., etc.)
R.N. Airfields
E.F.T.Ss., R.L.Gs., A.O.Ns., B+G.Ss., A.L.Gs., etc.
(E.L.Gs. not shown on this sheet)
R.A.F. Water Airfields
R.N. Water Airfields
R.A.F. Moorings (Not at a Water Airfield)
SUMBURGH
SUMBURGH HEAD
Fair Isle
TWATT
SKEABRAE
HATSTON
GRIMSETTER
ORKNEY
ISLANDS
CASTLETOWN
SKITTEN
WICK
PENTLAND
NORTH SEA

CASTLETOWN

With permanent landmarks in the vicinity of the airfield being Dunnet Head and Bay and by night Dunnet Bay and a flashing beacon, Castletown in the Highlands was one of the remotest airfields in Scotland. Given the harsh winters, the grass surface was poor and usually unusable although fortunately fog prevalence was nil.

The large landing area measured 1,300 yards N-S, with the E-W 1,200 yards, NE-SW 1,100 yards and SE-NW 1,050 yards. A 45-foot perimeter track gave access to one Bellman hangar. Three hard runways were laid, each being 1,000 x 50 yards. Due to its anticipated low usage, just 12,000 gallons of aviation spirit was available on site and 1,400 gallons of MT fuel.

Due to its northerly latitude there were fewer daylight hours so night landing facilities were essential. These consisted of a flarepath comprising of a double path of Glim lamps with two leading lights 30 yards outside the runway and one light each side 50 yards from the windward end of a floodlight. Radio facilities were by way of a mobile tender with VHF/DF. A Type 2 flying control gave airfield surveillance.

Encompassed within No. 14 Group, Fighter Command, and classed as an operational satellite of Wick, it opened in May 1940 when Hurricane Is from No. 504 (County of Nottingham) Auxiliary Squadron came in from the parent station on June 21, 1940. They had just returned from France and were at Castletown to rest and regroup before moving on to Catterick on September 2. Replaced the same day by No. 3 Squadron Hurricane Is, they only stayed for eleven days to then be replaced by the Hurricane Is of No. 232 Squadron on September 18. They moved to Skitten on October 13.

One of Fighter Command's most northerly aerodromes, Castletown in Caithness lay just a few hundred yards from the foreshore of the Pentland Firth.

No. 3 Squadron had moved to Turnhouse but were back at Castletown on October 13. They then moved to Skeabrae on January 7, 1941, returning to Castletown on February 10 for the last time. Fleet Air Arm Fulmars of No. 808 Squadron came in on September 5, 1940. They arrived for a working-up period moving to Donibristle on October 2 before embarking on HMS *Ark Royal*.

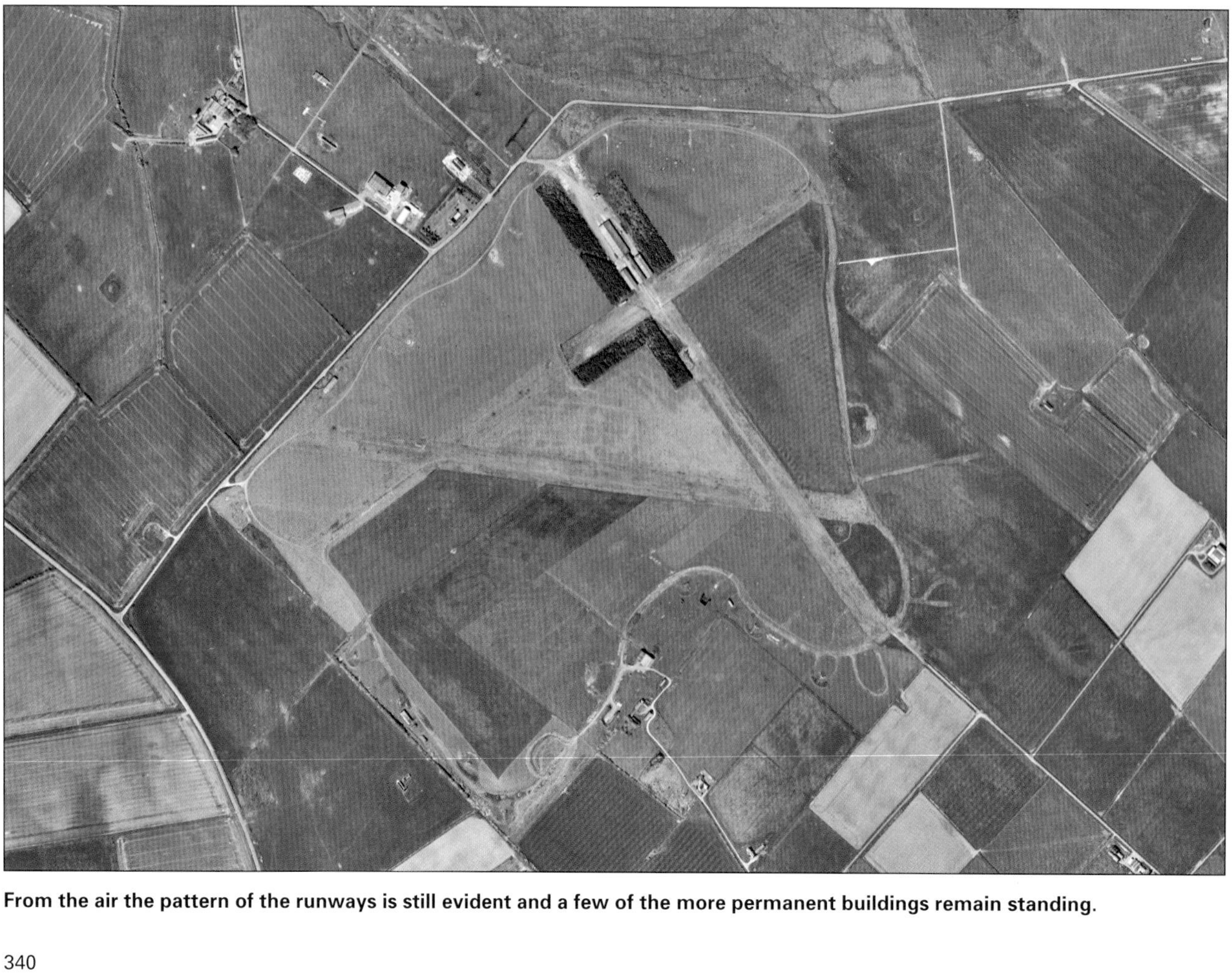

From the air the pattern of the runways is still evident and a few of the more permanent buildings remain standing.

No. 123 Squadron had its early beginnings in the First World War although it was not reformed until May 1941 in Scotland, where it served time at Turnhouse, Drem and Castletown. This picture was taken at the latter station just before the pilots took off for a shipping patrol over the vital anchorages in the Firth of Forth.

No. 1 Canadian Squadron formed up at Castletown during December 1940. This was one of the Canadian squadrons serving with the RAF under the British Commonwealth Air Training Plan. In 1941 it became No. 401 (Ram) Canadian Squadron under British operational control.

The Hurricane Is of No. 260 Squadron arrived for the defence of the Scapa Flow naval base on January 7, 1941. A move to Skitten on February 10 saw further Hurricane Is fly in when No. 213 (Ceylon) Squadron moved from Driffield on February 18. They were preparing to embark on HMS *Furious* for Egypt and left Castletown on May 11.

Next in was No. 17 Squadron whose Hurricane Is and IIAs arrived on April 5. Detachments were sent to Elgin and Sumburgh before they left for Elgin on June 16. The reforming of No. 124 (Baroda) Squadron on May 10, 1941 saw the first Spitfires at the airfield. Receiving the Mk I in May, they converted to the IIB in October and VA and VB in November. Becoming operational in June, they commenced coastal patrols as well as acting in the role of an Operational Training Unit to bring pilots up to operational standard before posting them to squadrons. The squadron flew south on November 17 to Biggin Hill to join the Biggin Hill wing.

The stop-butt for harmonising the guns in the Spitfires.

Another squadron to bring Spitfires to Castletown was No. 123 (East India). Their Mark IIAs arrived on September 22, 1941. Sending a detachment to Tain, they converted to the Spitfire VB in January 1942 and remained until April 11 when they prepared to leave Castletown and move to Egypt.

Further Spitfire IIAs arrived when No. 54 Squadron came north from Hornchurch on November 17, 1941. Shortly after arrival they converted to the IIB and in March 1942 to the Spitfire VB. Remaining at Castletown until June 2, 1942 when they took the VBs to Wellingore.

Shortly after the first Spitfire squadron arrived in 1941, the Blenheim IVFs of No. 404 (Buffalo) Canadian Squadron came in from Thorney Island on June 20, 1941. Moving around the Scottish airfields they left for Skitten on July 27. Hurricane IIAs and IIBs of No. 607 (County of Durham) Auxiliary Squadron arrived the same day. Staying just under a month they moved to Martlesham Heath on August 20.

The Norwegian Squadron, No. 331, brought further Hurricanes to Castletown on August 21. Staying for a month, they left for Skeabrae. After a quiet period No. 167 (Gold Coast) Squadron flew in on June 1, 1942. Flying Spitfire VBs, they sent a detachment to Peterhead and left Castletown on October 14.

It was now the turn of No. 610 (County of Chester) Auxiliary Squadron to defend the Highlands. Bringing their Spitfire VCs in on October 15, 1942, they were tasked — like most of the Castletown squadrons — with the defence of Scapa Flow. However after an uneventful few months they moved south to Westhampnett on January 20, 1943.

Further Spitfire VCs arrived when No. 131 (County of Kent) Fighter Squadron flew up from Westhampnett. They came in on January 22, 1943 for a period of training carrying out coastal patrols as part of that exercise. Leaving for Exeter on June 26, they had witnessed the forming of No. 282 (ASR) on January 1, 1943, with Walrus and Anson aircraft.

No. 54 Squadron was posted to Castletown in November 1941, one of its leading pilots being Sergeant Desmond Ibbotson who had built up a score of 11 enemy aircraft destroyed.

Detachments were sent to Peterhead, Drem and Ayr, the squadron remaining at Castletown until disbanding on January 12, 1944 when it was absorbed into No. 278 Squadron.

As No. 131 Squadron left for Exeter, No. 310 (Czech) Squadron left Exeter for Castletown. Conversion from the Spitfire VC to the VI saw the squadron send a detachment to Sumburgh before they left for Ibsley on September 19, 1943. The Spitfire VCs of No. 504 (County of Nottingham) Auxiliary Squadron were the next to arrive just as No. 310 departed. They also converted to the Spitfire VI variant and after a brief stay, departed to Peterhead a month later. Returning on March 10, 1944, and having converted to the Spitfire IXB, they promptly reverted to the VB variant and left for Digby on April 30. This was the last fighter squadron to leave Castletown, the airfield being placed on care and maintenance shortly thereafter. Gradually falling into disrepair, its final demise came when RAF Lossiemouth was selected as the base for further squadrons.

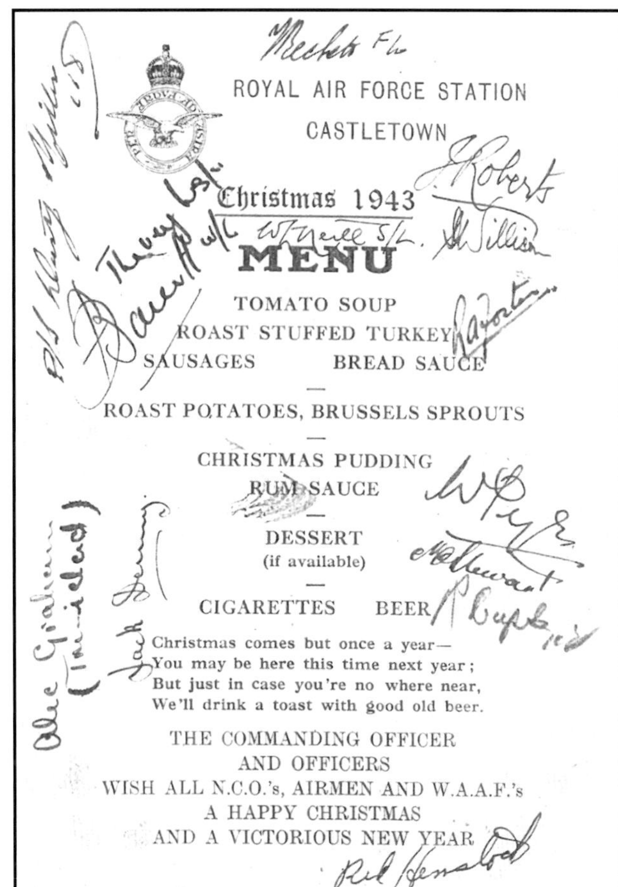

ROYAL AIR FORCE STATION
CASTLETOWN

Christmas 1943

MENU

TOMATO SOUP
ROAST STUFFED TURKEY
SAUSAGES BREAD SAUCE
—
ROAST POTATOES, BRUSSELS SPROUTS
—
CHRISTMAS PUDDING
RUM SAUCE
—
DESSERT
(if available)
—
CIGARETTES BEER

Christmas comes but once a year—
You may be here this time next year;
But just in case you're no where near,
We'll drink a toast with good old beer.

THE COMMANDING OFFICER
AND OFFICERS
WISH ALL N.C.O.'s, AIRMEN AND W.A.A.F.'s
A HAPPY CHRISTMAS
AND A VICTORIOUS NEW YEAR

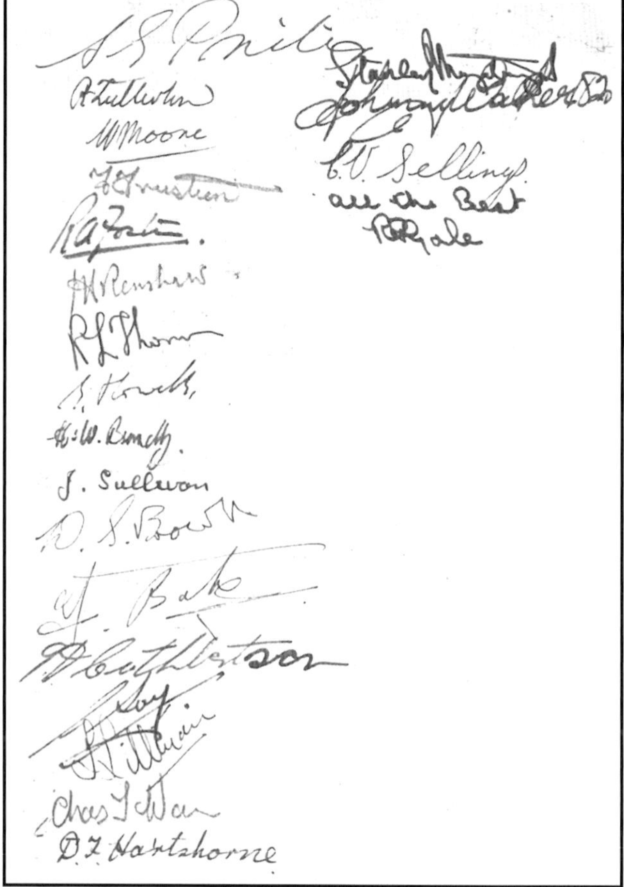

Winter was very bleak at Castletown with snow and high winds, this Christmas menu bringing some cheer to the aircrews in December 1943. Stephen Whines of Caledonia, Ontario, found this menu in his late father's papers and kindly sent it to us. His Dad served with the City of Glasgow Squadron, No. 602, although they were never based at Castletown. However, they were posted to Skeabrae (page 348) in the Orkney Islands in January 1944, so possibly LAC Robert Whines arrived early and broke his journey to partake in the fine Christmas fayre.

PETERHEAD

It is 1945 and the war is nearing its end. These pilots of No. 19 Squadron have come through unscathed and their former aerodrome in Scotland is now stilled from the roar of piston-engined fighters.

Four miles west of Peterhead alongside the A950 in Aberdeenshire, the aerodrome was originally called Longside. Frequently subject to fog and with the grass landing area constantly out of use due to wet conditions, three tarmac runways had been laid by the time war was declared. Measuring 1,500 x 50 yards, 1,470 x 50 yards and 1,272 x 50 yards, a 50-foot perimeter track led to five Teeside hangars and eight Extra Over Blisters. There were 77,000 gallons of aviation fuel and 5,000 gallons of MT petrol available, dispensed by bowser or tractor-drawn containers. Airfield control was from a Type 2 watch office controlling Drem runway lighting and VHF radio. Peterhead was classified as a sector station in No. 14 Group with satellites at Fraserburgh, Dyce and Fordoun.

Facilities were still uncompleted when No. 416 Squadron reformed there on November 22, 1941. A week later it received its Spitfire Is and began working-up. An enemy attack on November 30 gave the squadron its first taste of war when several Spitfires were damaged and one officer killed. When it was declared operational in February 1942, the squadron began convoy patrols but had little success in finding the enemy. Leaving a detachment at Peterhead, they moved to Dyce on March 14 but returned on April 3. The squadron transferred to Westhampnett on June 25 but came back to Peterhead on July 7. Sending a detachment to Dyce, the rest of the squadron finally moved to Martlesham Heath on July 16.

Seventy years separate these two views, a section of the north-east runway now used for refuelling North Sea helicopters.

No. 164 (Argentine/British) Squadron was established at the airfield on April 6, 1942 with many Polish and Czech personnel. Receiving Spitfire VAs, the squadron began its working-up period before moving to Skeabrae on May 5. They returned to Peterhead to convert to the Spitfire VB on September 10. With a detachment sent south to Tangmere, the squadron managed to damage a Ju 88 before they left for Fairwood Common on January 29, 1943, leaving a detachment behind at Peterhead. Shortly after this the squadron was declared non-operational to allow it time to get used to 40mm cannons. When competent, they exchanged their VBs for the Hurricane IIB and IV.

Peterhead now became home to several Fleet Air Arm squadrons beginning with No. 802 whose Sea Hurricanes arrived on May 21, 1942. They moved to Donibristle on July 6 to be replaced by the Fulmars of No. 884 Squadron on the same day, but five days later they were transferred to Turnhouse. Next to arrive were the Fulmars of No. 886; they flew in on August 13 and flew out to Stretton on October 7.

Two separate postings for No. 602 (City of Glasgow) Auxiliary Squadron saw their Spitfire VBs first arrive on July 17, 1942 for just a month. Moving to Biggin Hill, they returned to Peterhead on August 20 for three weeks before leaving for Skeabrae.

No. 245 (Northern Rhodesia) Squadron with Typhoon IBs flew north on January 29, 1943 from Charmy Down where they had converted to the type from Hurricane IICs. Declared operational by February, they took their Typhoons south to Gravesend on March 30. Spitfire VBs had returned the previous day when No. 165 (Ceylon) Squadron came up from Tangmere. They sent a detachment to Dyce, before moving to Ibsley on June 30 to begin operations over the Continent. In their place came No. 313 (Czech) Squadron with Spitfire VCs from Church Stanton on June 28. Leaving a detachment at Sumburgh, they departed to Hawkinge on August 21.

Air-sea rescue was in the hands of a detachment of No. 282 Squadron with Walrus and Ansons. Also during 1942 there was a period when Peterhead was used for flying training when No. 2 Flying Instructors School moved in during September. Staying for a year, they returned to the satellite whilst Spitfires of No. 556 OTU moved in for training and convoy escort duties.

There was a possibility that Peterhead might be used by the USAAF but this came to nothing with Spitfires returning on September 20, 1943 when the Mk VBs of No. 118 Squadron arrived. Changing to the Mk VI,

From Spitfires at Duxford in 1940 . . . to Mustangs at Peterhead in 1945! As we have seen earlier in the chapter on Duxford (and Fowlmere), No. 19 had the unique privilege of being the first RAF squadron to be equipped with the Spitfire, and at Peterhead it was one of the last with the North American Mustang.

It was the longer range of the Mustang — over 2,000 miles with drop tanks — that enabled the squadron to carry out deep penetration escort duties and dive-bombing. At first they were based in the south — at Gravesend, Ford, Rochford, etc — before crossing to airstrips on the Continent.

With the control tower a pile of rubble and the remaining buildings crumbling away, it was the members of the British Legion branch at Longside, seven miles west of the airfield, who decided that something had to be done to mark Peterhead's wartime history.

they sent a detachment to Skeabrae before moving to Castletown on October 19 leaving a detachment behind at Peterhead. A further move to Detling on January 20, 1944, saw them back at Peterhead three days later for conversion to the Mk IXC.

No. 504 (County of Nottingham) brought their Spitfire VIs in on October 18, 1943, leaving to join the Hornchurch wing on January 19, 1944. They had exchanged places with No. 129 (Mysore) Squadron that had arrived eight days earlier. When they moved out to Heston on March 16, the Belgian No. 350 Squadron had moved in with Spitfire IXBs on March 14. Converting to Spitfire VBs and VCs, they left for Friston on April 25, 1944.

The new sound of the Mustang III came to Peterhead on November 1 when No. 315 (Deblin) Polish Squadron arrived. Then began a succession of postings by Polish squadrons: No. 309 (Ziema Czerwienska) came in on November 14 and moved to Andrewsfield on December 14, 1944, while No. 315 Squadron remained a little longer, not moving to Andrewsfield until January 16, 1945. As they left, the Mustang IIIs of No. 65 (East India) Squadron arrived from Andrewsfield on January 16, 1945.

The Mustang IIIs of No. 19 Squadron followed on February 13, 1945. They converted to the Mk IV before leaving for Acklington on May 23. With No. 65 Squadron departing for Banff on January 28, they returned on February 1 for conversion to the Mk IV Mustang before leaving for Andrewsfield on May 6.

The last squadrons to serve at Peterhead, all Mustang-equipped, were No. 122 (Bombay); No. 234 (Madras Presidency), and No. 611 (West Lancashire) Auxiliary Squadron which disbanded there on May 7. It fell to the forming of No. 598 Squadron to close Peterhead's wartime service when a few Hurricane IICs arrived later in 1945.

With no further military use, the site was auctioned off in September 1959. A small area of the airfield has since re-opened for helicopter operations connected with the oil industry but most of the wartime buildings have been demolished.

The late Terry Wilson explained that they set up what they called the 'Cairn Committee' to raise the necessary funds, receiving huge support for the project. 'However, when I first viewed the site it was virtually a rubbish dump at the end of one of the old runways which included over 80 motor tyres. We set the date for the unveiling as September 14, 2003 and were promised a Guard of Honour from RAF Buchan and the participation of the Deputy Commander of No. 416 Squadron, RCAF, which was formed at Peterhead in 1941. We had a lone piper playing the Lament on a wee hill behind the Cairn and a Nimrod from No. 42 (R) Squadron based at RAF Kinloss flew four low, slow overhead passes which brought a day full of memories to a very touching and poignant end.'

SKEABRAE

Chris Cooper, who visited Orkney for us, was thrilled to be able to take this perfect comparison. The Spitfire is MD114 of No. 312 Squadron, part of the Station Flight, pictured in 1943 when engaged on defensive patrols over the naval base at Scapa Flow.

Skeabrae on the Orkney Islands was originally built for the Royal Navy but it was handed over to the Air Ministry to allow fighter squadrons to be based there for the protection of the Shetlands and north of Scotland. Situated 12 miles south-east of Kirkwall and 60 feet above sea level, the grass surface was classed as useless after rain so four runways were laid, two of 1,000 x 30 yards, one of 1,000 x 25 yards and the other 1,000 x 24 yards. Noted obstructions were wireless masts 80 feet high one and a quarter miles from the airfield. Sea mist and low cloud were frequent hazards yet night landing facilities only consisted of Glim lamps and Chance lights with meteorological facilities provided by Wick. VHF radio was installed, initially controlled from Kirkwall via a land-line with HF and RT until a watch office was built later. Hangar accommodation was 12 Teeside Type 'S' and one Bellman. Deemed a sector station in No. 14 Group with satellites at Grimsetter, Castletown, Dounreay and Skitten, Skeabrae was ready for occupation by August 15, 1940.

It was the Fleet Air Arm that first occupied the aerodrome when No. 804 Squadron brought their Sea Gladiators from HMS *Furious* on October 10, 1940. Beginning a slow conversion to the Martlet I, they moved to Hatston two weeks later returning on October 28. For just under three months this squadron was the sole unit defending the Orkneys, but having no contact with the enemy, they left for Skitten on January 7, 1941.

They were replaced by the Hurricane Is of No. 3 Squadron which arrived from Castletown. Sending a detachment to Sumburgh, they returned to Castletown on February 10. Civilian aircraft of Scottish Airways also used the airfield when bad weather closed Kirkwall, sharing the facilities with the military. Passengers were no doubt pleased to observe that the defence of the region was safe in the hands of No. 253 (Hyderabad State) Hurricane Is which were based there from February 10 to September 21. In between they converted to the Mk IIBs before departing to Hibaldstow.

Replaced by Hurricane IIBs of No. 331 (Norwegian) Squadron, they exchanged their Hurricanes for Spitfire IIAs in November and the Mk VB in April 1942. Mainly flying

With a detachment of Spitfire VCs already at the airfield, the rest of No. 118 Squadron joined them on March 10 having converted to the Mk IXC. They exchanged those for the Spitfire LF VB before returning to Detling on July 12, 1944. No. 602 Squadron returned on January 17 and converted from the Spitfire IXB to the LF VB variant. They returned to Detling on March 12, 1944. No. 313 (Czech) Squadron flew up from Lympne on July 11. They also converted from the Spitfire VB to the VC variant in August. Leaving a detachment at Sumburgh, they returned south to North Weald on October 4.

No. 611 (West Lancashire) Auxiliary Squadron Spitfire IXs arrived on October 3. After conversion to the Mk VII, a detachment was sent to Sumburgh whilst the rest of the squadron moved to Hawkinge on December 31. A Canadian squadron, No. 441 (Silver Fox) with Spitfire IXBs, took over the patrols of Scapa Flow on December 30, 1944 to April 3, 1945 when they were moved to Hawkinge having converted to the Mk IX.

The final two squadrons to fly from Skeabrae were No. 451 (Australian) with Spitfire XVIs (May 17-June 12, 1945) and No. 603 (City of Edinburgh) Auxiliary with Spitfire LF XVIEs (June 14-July 28, 1945). Skeabrae was relegated to care and maintenance shortly thereafter with the navy finally relinquishing control in 1957. Further plans for NATO to use the base did not come to fruition.

Skeabrae was the most northerly of Fighter Command's aerodromes, and it lay very close to the Royal Navy air station at Twatt which the Luftwaffe referred to as Skeabrae-Nord. Chris reported that the aerodrome has reverted to farmland and the only original building left standing is the camp cinema. However, the course of the runways and perimeter tracks are still very visible in the grass.

shipping and convoy patrols, they transferred south to North Weald on May 4, 1942.

The navy returned for a short spell on November 8, 1941 when No. 801 arrived with Sea Hurricanes for the defence of Scapa Flow but they left without seeing any action on February 15, 1942.

Spitfire IIBs came in on February 16 when No. 132 (City of Bombay) Squadron arrived from Peterhead. Sending a detachment to Sumburgh, they converted to the Mk VB and left for the satellite at Grimsetter on June 11. On May 5 they had been joined by the Spitfire VAs of No. 164 (Argentine-British) Squadron. With a detachment at Sumburgh, the squadron had several encounters with the Luftwaffe before they left for Peterhead on September 10.

There now began a period of frequent changes beginning on September 10, 1942 with the arrival of No. 602 (City of Glasgow) Auxiliary Squadron with Spitfire VBs. Converting to the VC, they left for Perranporth on January 20, 1943. Other movements were No. 129 (Mysore) with Spitfire VIs (January 19-February 13, 1943); No. 66 with Spitfire VB, VC and VIs (February 9-June 28, 1943); No. 234 (Madras Presidency) with Spitfire VIs (April 24-June 26, 1943); No. 312 (Czech) with Spitfire VCs (June 24-September 21, 1943), and No. 453 (Australian) with Spitfire VCs (October 15, 1943-January 19, 1944).

The return of the No. 801 Squadron on September 16, 1943 saw Seafires operating from Skeabrae. Leaving for Machrihanish, they were to alternate between HMS *Furious* and Skeabrae on 12 occasions, the last being on December 9, 1944 when they moved to Grimsetter before embarking on HMS *Implacable*.

SKITTEN

Lying four and a half miles north-west of Wick in the county of Caithness, Skitten was a Coastal Command operational satellite to the parent station of Wick and was also a night fighter satellite to Skeabrae. A large grass area surrounded by a 50-foot perimeter track had been built on a plateau 100 feet above sea level. At first facilities comprised a single Bellman hangar, a Beacon light, flarepath with floodlights, and an angle of glide indicator. Six hardstandings and seven double pens were provided for dispersals with four Blister hangars alongside. Other facilities were few as Skitten was initially to be used for emergency landings only.

Tarmac runways were under construction by 1940 when No. 232 Squadron Hurricane Is flew in from Castletown on October 13. Moving to Drem on the 24th, they came back on November 11 staying until December 4 when they reached full strength. Next to visit was No. 260 Squadron which had reformed at Castletown on November 22, 1940. Moving to Skitten in December, they were issued with Hurricane Is and left to return to Castletown on January 7, 1941, for working up. Before they departed No. 804 Fleet Air Arm Squadron arrived with Martlet Is, leaving for Yeovilton on February 10, 1941.

No. 607 (County of Durham) Auxiliary Squadron arrived a few months later on April 16, 1941. They converted from Hurricane Is to the Mk IIAs and IIBs and, in addition to convoy patrols, carried out training for Polish pilots. They left for Castletown on July 27.

The Canadian No. 404 (Buffalo) Squadron brought the first Blenheim IVFs to Skitten the same day. Carrying out coastal patrols they moved on to Dyce on October 9 to be replaced by the Hudson IIIs of No. 48 Squadron on October 20. They commenced shipping patrols and attacks on enemy craft as far away as the Norwegian coast before

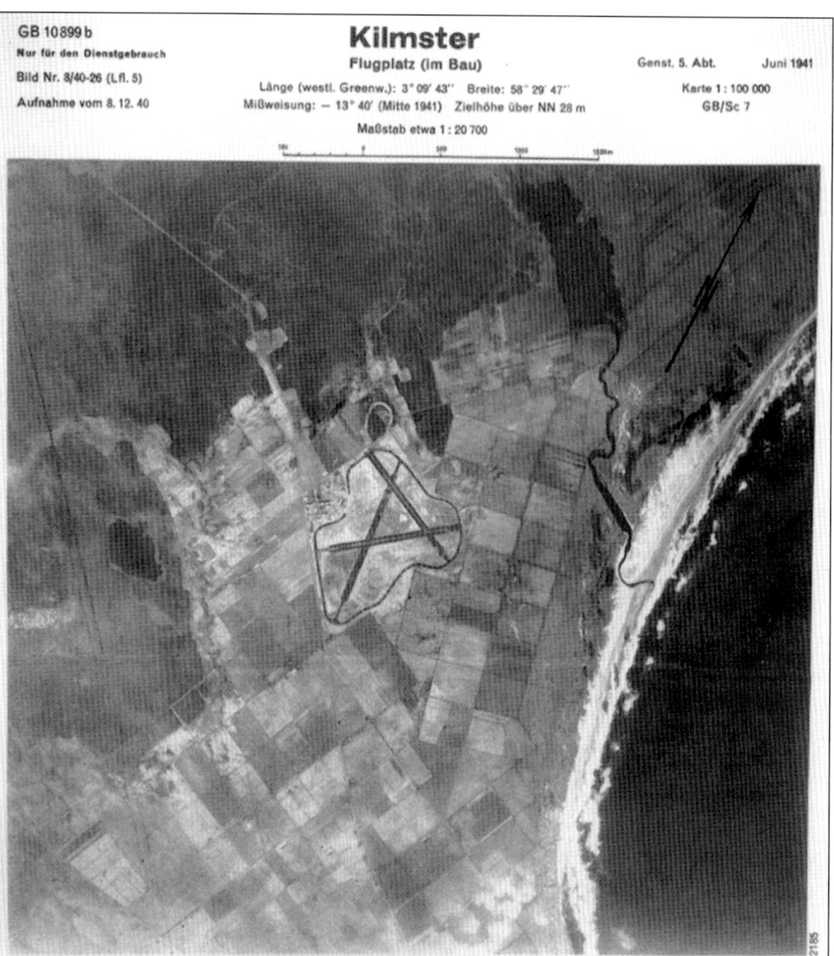

The Luftwaffe pictured Skitten in June 1941 when it was still under construction, calling it by the name of the hamlet on the western perimeter although mis-spelling Killimster.

Even though not completed, No. 260 Squadron were there in December 1940, also rotating through Castletown and Drem.

moving to Wick on January 6, 1942. The Beaufort IIs of No. 217 Squadron came in next from St Eval on February 16 but they only carried out a few escort operations before they moved to Leuchars on March 1 prior to embarking for Malta. Further Beaufort IIs came in on March 5, 1942, from No. 86 Squadron. Sending a detachment to Sumburgh, they also embarked for Malta on July 13.

An increase in the length of the main runway was indicative of the increased importance of Skitten which was then able to handle most bomber aircraft safely, an asset when carrying out raids to Norway. With this larger runway, a detachment of Wellington VIIIs from No. 172 Squadron arrived during August 1942. Equipped with a Leigh light — a powerful searchlight used for locating shipping at night — several aircraft were taken from the complement to form the nucleus of No. 179 Squadron which was formed at the airfield on September 1. Taking over the Wellington VIIIs from No. 172 Squadron, they moved to Gibraltar whilst No. 172 were re-equipped with Wellington XIIs. They too moved to Gibraltar during August 1943.

A force of Hampden Is from No. 489 Squadron moved in on August 5, 1942. They were tasked with carrying out armed reconnaissance sorties against shipping codenamed 'Rovers'. Flying just a few sorties, they moved to Wick on September 14, 1942.

With Skitten now designated a reserve base for Bomber Command, the main runway was lengthened once again to 1,400 yards. This work was carried out whilst No. 618 Squadron was established at Skitten for the sole purpose of attacking the *Tirpitz* in its Norwegian lair. Flying Mosquito IVs, they also acquired the Mk XVIII variant but, after enduring a long working-up period, they failed to carry out any attacks due to equipment and training problems. The squadron was moved to Wick on July 9, 1944.

The last squadron to be based at Skitten was No. 519 equipped with Venturas, Hudsons, Hampdens and Spitfires. They roamed over the North Atlantic until leaving for Wick on November 28, 1944. Shortly thereafter the airfield was put on care and maintenance before being abandoned.

Now John Gunn & Sons Ltd operate Skitten quarry on the airfield.

STAND-DOWN

RAF Fighter Command had been brought into being in 1936 for a specific purpose: to counter the perceived threat from Germany but by 1943 things had changed. Air attacks on Britain had largely reduced to a level of intruder sorties, often by single aircraft, and planners were looking ahead to take the ground war to the Continent.

The initial plans for the invasion were presented at the 'Quadrant' conference held in Quebec in August 1943 between President Roosevelt, Prime Minister Churchill, and the Canadian Premier, MacKenzie King. Argument over the person who would be the Supreme Commander were resolved when it was pointed out that two-thirds of the forces in the enterprise would be from the United States – hence he should be American. General George C. Marshall, Chief-of Staff of the US Army, was proposed but Roosevelt felt he was too valuable to lose so General Eisenhower was appointed instead.

On November 15 it was announced that the role of the Air Commander-in-Chief of the Allied Expeditionary Air Force was to be given to Air Marshal Sir Trafford Leigh-Mallory, the AOC-in-C of Fighter Command since November 1942. On the same day, RAF Fighter Command was split into two. Air Defence of Great Britain (ADGB) would, as its title suggested, be responsible for defending the home soil while the Second Tactical Air Force under Air Marshal Sir Arthur Coningham was to take the battle to Europe.

In October, Leigh-Mallory was appointed to command the Allied Air Forces in South-East Asia and it was decided not to replace him. Instead ADGB was dissolved and on October 15 became once again RAF Fighter Command under Air Marshal Sir James Robb who served in the post until May 14, 1945.

The Royal Air Force continued after the war with four separate commands — Fighter, Bomber, Coastal and Training — but by the 1960s it was seen that this structure, created in 1936 under the threat of war, had become outdated, and in 1968 Fighter Command and Bomber Command were merged to form Strike Command with a new headquarters at High Wycombe (see *After the Battle* No. 87). Then in 2007 the name was changed to Air Command.

During the war, the Royal Air Force had a total strength of around 240 'fighter' squadrons of which around 75 served in the United Kingdom under the auspices of Fighter Command. They were manned by airmen of many nations including those who had escaped from the occupied countries of Europe and the British Empire and Commonwealth. It is therefore very difficult to put an accurate total to the casualties suffered by RAF Fighter Command during the Second World War, but one estimate is that upwards of 3,500 were killed, 1,200 wounded and another 600-plus taken prisoner. If one singles out one aerodrome as an example, at North Weald —which had pilots of seven different nationalities based there — an exhaustive investigation in the records of Britain, Canada, Czechoslovakia, New Zealand, Norway, Poland and the United States gives a total of just over 200 killed between September 3, 1939 and May 8, 1945.

While some aerodromes were built or provided wholly for use by Fighter Command, there were others whose allegiance changed at various times during the war. All those airfields that have established connections with the Command have been included but those with only fleeting use are not. Of the 93 described in these pages, only nine remain in RAF hands while another four have been transferred to the Army. Seventeen have become airports — both major and minor — and even on the vast majority that have reverted to agriculture, one can find civilian airstrips retaining their aviation link with the past. And then there are the sad cases — Gravesend, Hawkinge *(above)*, Hendon, Hornchurch, Tangmere and West Malling — where pressure for building land in the South-East has led to their history being buried beneath streets and houses, while Ibsley, Scorton and Warmwell have had their faces lost in a different way: through quarrying. Although the men and women of RAF Fighter Command who made these aerodromes their home may now have flown into history, it was gratifying to find that devoted organisations and even philanthropic individuals have taken the trouble to erect memorials, remembering past service, and past deeds.

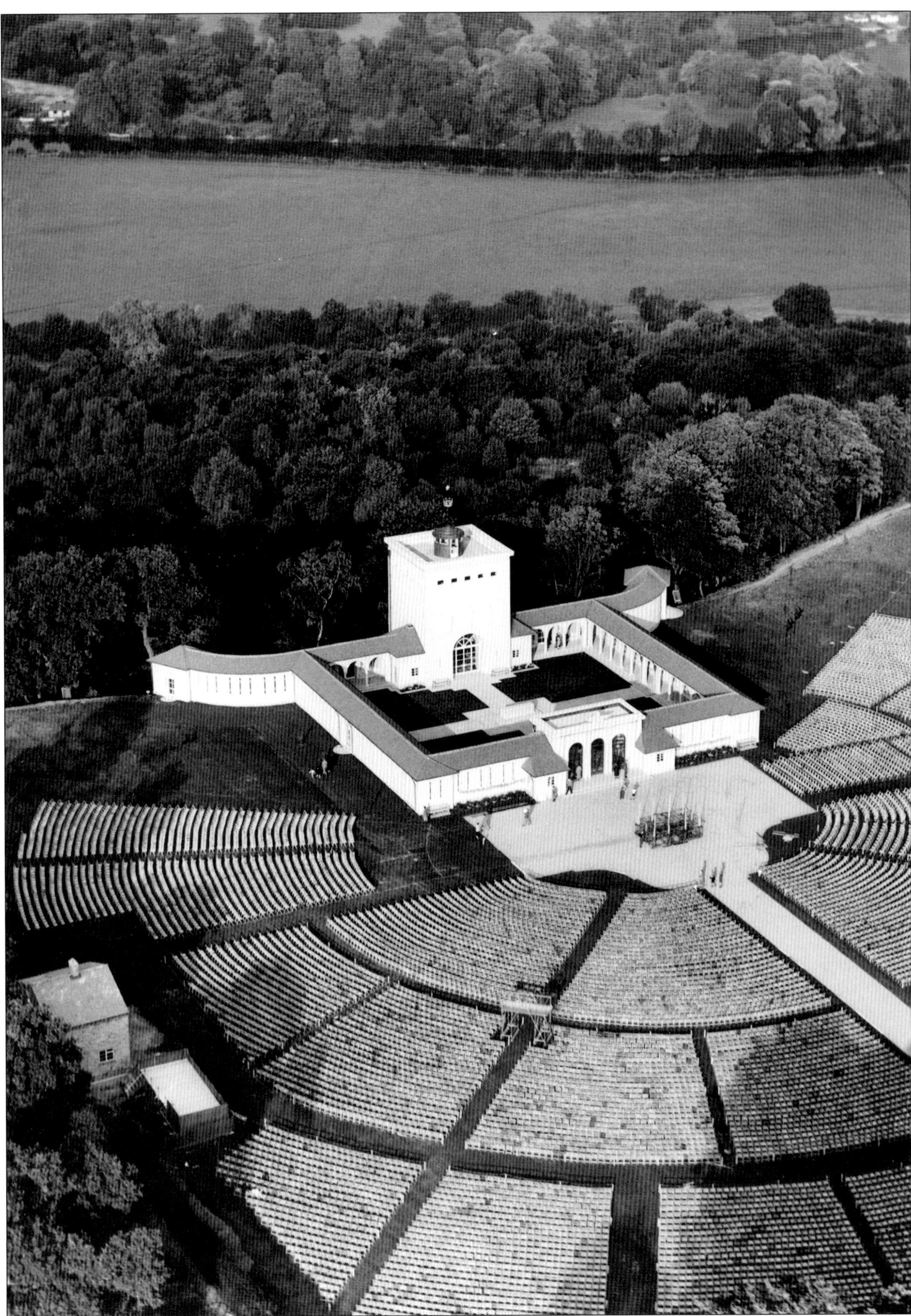

The serried ranks of empty seats prepared for the inauguration on October 17, 1953 of the memorial at Runnymede by HM Queen Elizabeth II stand almost as symbols for the 20,000 men of the Royal Air Force missing in action in north-west Europe during the Second World War. Among them will be those airmen from Fighter Command who failed to return.

INDEX

COMPILED BY PETER GUNN

Note: Page numbers in *italics* refer to illustrations. There may also be textual references on these pages.

SIMON CHAMBERLAIN 1984 — 2014

This book is dedicated to Simon Chamberlain who was tragically killed in an air crash shortly after take-off from North Weald on March 29, 2014. One of Simon's photographs appears on page 196.